1 MONTH OF
FREE
READING

at
www.ForgottenBooks.com

By purchasing this book you are eligible for one month membership to ForgottenBooks.com, giving you unlimited access to our entire collection of over 1,000,000 titles via our web site and mobile apps.

To claim your free month visit:
www.forgottenbooks.com/free1115071

ISBN 978-0-331-38118-4
PIBN 11115071

This book is a reproduction of an important historical work. Forgotten Books uses
state-of-the-art technology to digitally reconstruct the work, preserving the original format
whilst repairing imperfections present in the aged copy. In rare cases, an imperfection in
the original, such as a blemish or missing page, may be replicated in our edition. We do,
however, repair the vast majority of imperfections successfully; any imperfections that
remain are intentionally left to preserve the state of such historical works.

ATER COMMISSIONERS

TO THE

ouncils of the City of Erie,

FOR THE

Fiscal Year Ending April 30, 1879.

--- ----------

ACCOMPANIED BY THE REPORT OF THE

IEF ENGINEER OF THE PUMPING WORKS,

TO THE BOARD.

ERIE, PAY CLERK
A. P. DURLIN & SON, PRINTERS.
1879.

ANNUAL REPORT

OF THE

BOARD OF

WATER COMMISSIONERS

TO THE

Councils of the City of Erie,

FOR THE

Fiscal Year Ending April 30, 1879.

ACCOMPANIED BY THE REPORT OF THE

CHIEF ENGINEER OF THE PUMPING WORKS,

TO THE BOARD.

WATER COMMISSIONERS.

BOARD 1878-79,	BOARD 1879-80.
WM. W. REED, *Pres't,*	MICHAEL LIEBEL, *Pres't,*
MICHAEL LIEBEL,	J. M. BRYANT,
J. M. BRYANT.	G. W. F. SHERWIN.

Secretary—B. F. SLOAN,   *Clerk*—GEO. C. GENSHEIMER,

Superintendent—WM. E. HILTON,   *Inspector*—A. F. CRANE.

Chief Engineer at Pumping Works—N. W. DUNLAP.

First Assistant—GEO. R. MILLER.

Second Assistant—WM. O'LONE.

Superintendent of Reservoir and Grounds—J. M. REED.

OFFICE—No. 18, East Seventh Street, between French and State Streets.

OFFICE HOURS—From 7:30, A. M., to 5:45, P. M.

MEETINGS OF THE BOARD—Every Saturday, at 2 P. M., when all bills against the Works will be considered and, if correct, approved.

ANNUAL REPORT.

To the Honorable, the Select and Common Councils of the City of Erie.

Gentlemen:—

We herewith present to your honorable bodies the Annual Report of the Receipts and Expenditures of the ERIE WATER WORKS for the year ending April 30th, 1879, and also a statement of the number and location of Fire Hydrants put in during the year—the number and location of new Service connections made—the number and location of Stop Valves put in, and the length, size, and location of Distributing Mains laid in the same time; and also the report of the Chief Engineer of the Pumping works under his charge.

It will be seen by the Report that the Receipts from Water Rents was $32,340 16, and for Plumbing, and other sources, $469 83; of which there was expended,

For ordinary repairs,..................................	$21,846 84
" Laying Dis. Mains and Branches,.....	4,262 87
" Street Connections and Plumber's Stock,...........	1,683 39
" Alterations and Repairs of Engine and Boilers,.....	1,032 89
" Reservoir Land, and Legal Expenses,.............	694 59
" Engineering, (Mapping the City,).................	250 38
Total Expenses,........................	$29,770 96

The receipts for Water Rents were $1,085.82 in excess of the previous year, and the Commissioners confidently expect that from the increased prosperity of the City, and extension of distributing Mains, there will be a steady increase in the receipts from Water Rents from year to year; and as there will be little additional expense from increased consumption of water, except the cost of the fuel consumed in pumping the water, there is every reason to expect a constant yearly increase in the net receipts from the Water Works.

In this connection we beg to again call your attention to the injustice done the Water Works in no allowance being made to them for Fire Hydrants and other City uses. When the City commenced the construction of her Water Works she was under a contract with a Water Company to pay them $9,000 per year for the use of fifty fire hydrants, (or $180 per year for each hydrant,) if she did not commence the construction of Water Works within one year from the date of the contract; and had the Water Works not been constructed by the City she would now be paying about $24,000 per year from the general fund for water use, and this sum we think should be credited to the Water works for the last year, thus making the total receipts $56,809 99.

We are aware that practically it makes no difference, and that so far as the City is concerned it is taking money out of one pocket and putting it into another, but is it just to assess yearly a large sum for interest on Water bonds that is justly chargeable to general expenses? We think not; and we again renew our request that in the assessment of taxes an amount equal to the City use of water, be assessed for general purposes and deducted from the assessment for interest on Water bonds.

We have heard some complaint of a short supply of water for fire purposes on pipes extending to the outskirts of the City. This is unavoidable and can only be remedied by the completion of the plan of distribution. This plan contemplates two 12-inch feeders extending East and West from the pumping main on Chestnut Street, to the boundary line of the City, connecting at each street with pipes running North and South. The only part of these important works that the Commissioners have had funds to complete is on Seventh, from Chestnut to French; but the work will be continued as fast as money can be obtained for the extension, subject to the more important point of supplying water to those who need it for family use. When the Commissioners are able to extend these feeders, as planned, there will be a full supply of water in all parts of the City.

There was considerable complaint this spring of a fishy taste and smell to the water. The cause of this we are unable to determine. If it came from fish in the pipes, it would be permanent, but its short duration appears to preclude the possibility of its arising from that source. We were inclined to think that it resulted from fish that had died during the winter and were floating around the Bay, and from large swarms of fish entering the Bay to spawn; but we are informed that the same state of the water existed out in the lake. This would indicate that the causes are beyond our control. We are also informed that the same trouble existed at Dunkirk, N. Y., and probably at other points along the lake. If this condition of the water again occurs pumping will, if practicable, be suspended and the City supplied from the Reservoir until the trouble ceases.

The Commissioners have for some years contemplated drawing the water out of the pipes and flushing them out; but this involves shutting the water off from the city for a day or two, and the risk from fire and the inconvenience to water takers would be so great that only the most urgent necessity would justify its being done

It has been proposed to build a filter at the end of the pier and thus filter the water before it is pumped. This would undoubtedly be an improvement; but the Commissioners cannot forget that more than half the citizens of the City are not supplied with water, while they are taxed to pay the interest on the cost of the works;. and as the water we furnish is superior to that furnished by nine-tenths of the cities in the country, we think simple justice requires that the net receipts of the works should be expended in extending pipe to those who are without water, rather than improving the quality to those who have it.

There was considerable discussion last winter as to the advisability of changing the boilers at the works for others of a later and more improved plan. This is a question upon which there is a diversity of opinion among mechanical engineers—some contending that ours are the cheapest in a long run, and others that the difference in fuel will more than compensate for the increased cost of repairs of tubular boilers, and effect a considerable saving. We think there can be no question about our boilers being more reliable and less likely to get out of repair than tubular boilers; and if we were pumping supply direct we would, after the long test of our boilers, hesitate to make a change; but with the reservoir there is very little danger from stoppages to repair; and if your honorable bodies will appropriate $8,000 to be applied to the work, we will at once proceed with the construction of a new Engine House on a level with the Railway track, and put in new tubular boilers; but we deem it our duty to apply the net receipts from Water Rents to the extension of pipe on streets not supplied with water, rather than to use the money in improved boilers, and disregard the just claims of those who, being taxed to pay the interest on the cost of the works, are entitled to receive their benefits.

We have examined the bills for repairs and find the amount *expended on our* boilers for nearly eleven and a half years is only $110.69. There is a large sum for "Alteration and Re pairs of Engine and Boilers," about one-half of which is for repairs from breakages from dropping of the Engines, and the remainder includes changing fire fronts, grates, and all the other expenses and repairs; but on the boilers themselves only the above sum has been expended, being less than $10 a year. But the boilers having been in use eleven and a half years, we .may reasonably expect the repairs to be much larger in the future. It is proper to state, in this connection, that when the boilers were put in by Mr. Birkinbine they had combustion chambers, and on the recommendation of Mr. Kincaid these were taken out and return flues made on top of the boilers, which flues Mr. Dunlap claims were of insufficient size, and have therefore caused an imperfect combustion of and waste of fuel. It is due to Mr. Birkinbine to state that he always claimed the change to have been an error, and refers to tests made in which one battery of boilers was run with return flues and the other with combustion chambers, and the latter proved most economical

Our Engines are gravity engines, in which the steam is used to hoist a weight, which, in descending, pumps the water.— Their danger consists in their liability to drop if they fail to take suction, or the suction valve becomes clogged allowing the water to return to the pump-pit, in which event, from the dropping of seventeen tons a distance of ten feet, great damage is likely to occur. Nearly half of the entire expense of repairs at the pumping works has been from this cause

Since Mr. Dunlap took charge of the pumping works he has invented and applied a "Safety Check" by which the pressure of the pump piston on the water opens the equilibrium valve and allows the weight to descend as the steam condenses ·This appliance appears to be a perfect protection against the dropping of the engines, and removes a source of great anxiety to the Commissioners, and of expense to the works.

The audit of our accounts has been spasmodical, your predecessors neglecting to notice our requests for yearly audits, and making only three audits in eleven years. We sincerely hope you will be more prompt, and will cause the accounts to be at once audited to the close of the last fiscal year. We also request that the committee be authorized to · investigate all matters connected with the Water Works from the commencement to the close of the fiscal year, ending April 30th, 1879.

Respectfully yours,

WM. W. REED,
M. LIEBEL,
J. M. BRYANT,
Commissioners.

Erie, June 28th, 1879.

RECEIPTS AND EXPENDITURES

OF THE

ERIE WATER COMMISSIONERS,

FOR THE YEAR ENDING APRIL 30, 1879.

CASH ASSETS.

Cash on hand May 1st, 1878,.................	$ 750 18	
Bills Receivable, and other Cash Assets,.	1,176 10	$1,926 28

RECEIPTS.

From Water Rents,.......................	$32,340 16	
" Plumbing,.........................	359 76	
" Interest,.........................	31 02	
" Material Sold,.....................	79 05	$32,809 99
		$34,736 27

EXPENDITURES.

Paid on Reservoir Grounds,	$ 574 59	
" for Plumbing,	105 70	
" " Court Costs and Counsel fees,	120 00	
" " Service Pipe,	215 65	
" " Interest, Ex. and Disc't,	56 65	
" " Rep. and Alt'n of Eng. and Boilers,	1,032 89	
" " Care and Main. of Res.,	531 57	
" " Salaries,	6,453 33	
" " Stationery and Books,	126 56	
" " Engineers and Firemen,	4,001 17	
" " Fuel at Works,	7,771 42	
" " Laying Dis. Mains,	986 86	
" " Making St. Connections,	202 29	
" " Shop and Mis. Work of Sup't,	677 28	
" " Repairs of Dis. Mains,	1,105 39	
" " Waste and Packing	30 41	
" " Engineer's Small Stores,	90 43	
" " Repairs of R. R. Switch,	9 00	
" " Cartage,	34 33	
" " Tools and Repair of same,	78 07	
" " Distributing Mains and Branches,	2.252 13	
" " Postage,	233 15	
" " Fire Plugs,	244 81	
" " Hauling and Distributing Pipe,	26 89	
" " Printing and Advertising.	76 05	
" " Expense of Horse and Wagon,	101 39	
" " Office Rent and other Expenses,	603 37	
" " Oils and Tallow,	298 87	
" " Taxes,	82 75	
" " G. W. F. Sherwin, for Engineering	250 38	
" " Boxes and Covers,	154 05	
" " Stop Valves,	233 19	
" " Paving and Street Repairs,	15 87	
" " Lead,	271 07	
" " Expense of Gas Wells,	38 17	
" " Wooden Plugs,	3 00	
" " Service Fittings,	142 26	
" " Engine Room Furniture,	16 32	
" " Plumber's Stock,	346 02	
" " Repairs	126 86	
" " Old Rope for Packing	10 59	
" " Superintendent's Small Stores	40 18	
Balance of Cash in Office and in Bank, $1.094 01		
" in hands of City Treasurer, 3,600 20		
Bills Receivable, Unpaid, 271 10	4,965 31	$34.736 27

STATEMENT,

Showing the number of feet of Distributing Mains and Branches, of the size of 4 inches, and over, laid by the Erie Water Commissioners in the year, from May 1st, 1878, to April 30th, 1879.

LOCATION.	SIZE.	F'T, IN.
East 18th, from Peach to Holland,.........	6 in.	1,524 4
West Seventeenth,.......................	4 in.	1,012
Third,...................................	4 in.	703 4
Twenty-First,............................	4 in.	1,114 8
Holland,....	4 in.	1,270 6
Myrtle, bet. Seventeenth and Eighteenth,..	4 in.	191 6
Huron, from Chestnut to Cherry,..........	4 n.	1,436 10
Holland, from Second to Front,...........	4 in.	554
French, North of Eighteenth,.............	4 in.	29
West Sixth, bet. Myrtle and Chestnut,.....	4 in.	328 4
Seventeenth, Branch to Hydrant,..........	4 in.	13 4
East Eleventh, to replace pipe carried away by flood,.............................		192
Total,		8,459 10

STATEMENT,

Showing the number of Fire Hydrants, of the size of four inches, put in by the Erie Water Commissioners in the year from May 1st, 1878, to April 30th, 1879.

LOCATION.	NUMBER
On Seventeenth Street, bet. Sassafras and Myrtle,............	1
" Front Street, 275 feet East of French,...................	1
" Peach Street, 45 feet 4 inches South of Thirteenth,........	1
" Eighteenth, 15 feet 8 inches East of State...............	1
" Sassafras, North line of Twentieth,.....................	1
" Holland, 11 feet 2 inches South of Twenty-second,........	1
Total,	6

561

STATEMENT,

Showing the number and location of Stop Valves of the size of 4 inches and over, put in by the Erie Water Commissioners in the year from May 1st, 1878, to April 30th 1879.

LOCATION.	SIZE	NUMBER.
On Eighteenth Street, West line of Holland,......	6 in.	1
" " " East " " Peach,........	6 in.	1
" West Seventeenth, West " " Sassafras......	4 in.	1
" Twenty-First, " " " Holland,......	4 in.	-
" East Eleventh, bet. French and Holland,......	4 in.	1
" Huron Street, West line of Chestnut,..........	4 in.	1
" Holland, North line of Second,...............	4 in.	1
" French, North line of Eighteenth,,...........	4 in.	1
" Front, near Sassafras,........................	4 in.	1
" Twenty-Fifth, for Koehler Brothers,........,...	4 in.	1
Total,		10

STATEMENT,

Showing the number of Street, or Service connections, from main pipe to curb-stone, put in by the Erie Water Commissioners in the year ending April 30th, 1879.

STREETS.	NO.	STREETS.	NO.
Second,......................	1	Twenty-First,.................	2
Third,.	8	Twenty-Sixth,................	1
Fourth,......................	3	Wallace,.....................	1
Fifth,.......................	7	Holland,.....................	1
Sixth,.......................	5	State,.......................	2
Seventh,....................	1	Peach.......................	4
Eighth,.............	4	Sassafras,...................	2
Ninth,......................	2	Chestnut,....................	2
Tenth,......................	1	Walnut,.....................	1
Eleventh,....................	3	Cherry,.....................	1
Thirteenth,..................	1	Cascade,....................	1
Sixteenth, ...	1	Huron, ...	15
Seventeenth,.................	6	Myrtle,.....................	5
Eighteenth,..................	11	Front,......................	1
Nineteenth,.................	1	Short, ...	2
Total,			96

STATEMENT

Of the Amount the City would have to pay from the General Fund, and raise by taxation, for water for Fire and other City purposes, in the year ending April 30, 1879, provided the Water Works were owned by a private corporation.

121 Fire Hydrants, a: $180 per year..................		$21,780 00
2 Fountains in the Parks,.........................		1,500 00
2 Public Watering Troughs,.....................		100 00
For First Ward Engine House,.....................		19 50
" Second " " "		25 00
" Third " " "		20 00
" Fourth " " "		11 00
" Fifth " " "		9 00
" Police Station,..............................		10 00
Total,		$23,475 50

REPORT

OF THE CHIEF ENGINEER OF STEAM POWER.

TO THE BOARD OF WATER COMMISSIONERS OF THE CITY
OF ERIE:

In compliance with your directions I have the honor to submit the following report:

Upon taking charge of the Water Works Engines I found them in a condition not very well calculated to render the most efficient service. The condition of the pistons was such that nearly a barrel of lubricating oil was used monthly for the cylinders alone. The piston of Engine 88 was repaired in the month of May, of last year, and since the repairs were made the amount of oil used in that cylinder has been reduced to about one-third of the former amount. Repairs have also been made on the piston of Engine 89, resulting in a similar reduction in the use of lubricating oil. Under the present improved condition of the cylinders, one quart of oil is sufficient for twenty-four hours.

I also discovered that the practice of producing friction on the valve stems to regulate steam, equilibrium, and exhaust valves, had been resorted to, causing the stems to wear irregularly, or unevenly, and thus necessitating the use of weights to overcome the movement caused by that irregularity. This is now remedied by binders on the rockers, at hand on the working platform.

The feed pump of Engine 89 was out of repair, and it was necessary to resort to the Stand-Pipe for feed water. The water in the Stand-Pipe being much lower in temperature re-

quired a greater consumption of coal to do the same work.— ·
This is now overcome by re-fitting the pump with new
valves, giving a sufficient supply of feed water from the hot
well, and thus curtailing the consumption of fuel. When I
took charge the feed water ranged from seventy to eighty degrees; it now averages 115 degrees. Upon examination of
condenser I found there was no device whatever for producing rapid condensation, and afterwards introduced perforated
plates, bringing about the desired effect. Engine 88 has also
been supplied with new steam valve seat; and these, together
with some minor changes in valve gear, cover all the important repairs made upon the Engines while under my supervision.

These Engines, as you are aware, are of the improved Cornish design, and I will here state that engines of the Cornish
pattern have been almost exclusively used for heavy pumping
in the coal mines of England and Wales, and are also largely
in use in the Anthracite regions of Pennsylvania. They have,
until within ten years, been classed with the most efficient and
reliable, where heavy pumping machinery was required, and
they are still considered quite as desirable as many of the engines now in use for that purpose, notwithstanding the prepon-
derance of weight, moments of rest at the end of stroke, and
liability of plunger to drop at any time, should the receiving
valve become gagged. From this last mentioned cause alone,
your engines, previous to my taking charge of them, had sustained damage to the amount of seven thousand dollars, or
more, and this damage might have been obviated to some extent by a proper knowledge of, and adjustment of the pump
valves. Any further damage, however, from this source may
be considered quite impossible, as my patent safety device for
steam pumps, has been applied to both engines, and has been
in successful operation for about three months. I may here

say that either one of these engines is now sufficient to supply the City with water.

The furnaces were also in a condition poorly calculated to render the most economical service. This was owing to the fact that the side walls of the furnaces were carried up to and against the boilers at a point excluding the heat from contact with the same where it was most valuable. The furnaces have since been re-built, and this objection removed, causing some saving of fuel. The door frames were burnt out, and were found in such a condition that it was necessary to put in new ones, and this was done about the first of the year.

Although the chimney is about one hundred feet high, there was not sufficient draft for the proper combustion of fuel.— This difficulty has been met by the introduction of additional return flues, giving a much better draft in both banks of boilers and causing a further and important economy in the use of fuel and in the saving of grates.

The Boilers are of the cylindrical, double-flue pattern, like those recently adopted in the Pittsburgh Water Works, and the same as those in use on Southern and Western rivers, where the greatest elastic force is required. I find by the volume of cylinder, the relative volume and density of steam used, that these boilers have an evaporative power of about 6 5-10 pounds of water to one pound of coal. Of course I can only approximate to this in the absence of a daily record.

The engines have run 332 days and 18 hours during the year, have raised 766,138,130 gallons 234 feet and a daily supply (for 365 days), of 2,098,734 gallons—the largest yearly duty they have ever performed since they were in operation. During the years 1874,-75,-76,-77, when the supply of gas was quite large, the average amount of coal required to raise 1,000,000 gallons 234 feet, was 6,472 pounds—deducting ten per cent. for short *stroke* and adding coal consumed for firing up · and banking fires during the year. The gas being now sufficient for illuminating purposes only, it requires 5,600 pounds of coal to raise 1,000,000 gallons 238 5-10 feet, making the same deductions for short stroke, and adding same amount of coal for firing up and banking fires; thus producing an economy in the use of fuel amounting to about one ton daily. This economy is the result of improvements completed during the latter part of the year. I should here state that three firemen have been employed at the works until the last of March, at which time the number was reduced to two; making an annual reduction in regular salaries of four hundred and eighty dollars.

During the year considerable coal has been stolen from the cars while standing on the side switch, and I am at a loss to know how to prevent this in the future, as the pay of a watchman would probably exceed the value of the coal clandestinely removed. The importance of this matter should elicit the early attention of the Board.

The gas at the wells is slowly diminishing, and the quantity has become so small that I would suggest that an effort be made to increase the supply. This might be accomplished by sinking the East well deeper, and by a thorough cleaning of both. The Engine and Boiler House should be painted, in order to preserve the wood work, and the water tower should also be painted, or slushed with mineral oils.

With these suggestions I respectfully submit my report.

N. W. DUNLAP,

Chief Engineer of Water Works.

SCALE OF ANNUAL RATES.

Private dwellings. occupied by one family, $5.00; two families,....		$ 8 00
Bath Tubs in private houses,..............................		3 00
Each Additional,....................................		1 50
Public Bath Tubs, each,.................................		5 00
Hopper Water Closets, in private houses,.................		6 00
"　　"　　" 　 each additional,...................		3 00
Pan Water Closets, in private houses,....................		3 00
"　　"　　" 　 each additional,...............		1 50
Public Water Closet Pan, each,..........................		5 00
"　　"　　" 　 Hopper, each,......................		6 00
Urinals, each,...		2 00
Permanent Hand Basins, each,....:......................		50
Permanent Wash Tubs with Waste, each,...:..............		2 00
"　　"　　"　　"　　" in private houses.......		2 00
Each Additional,....................　　"·　　"　　.. .		1 00
Private Street Sprinklers, each, from....................:	3 00 to	10 00
Private Stables, for one or two horses,....................	·.	2 00
For each additional horse, over two,.....................		1 00
Livery Stables. each horse, including washing of Carriages.		2 00
Cows, each..		75
Fountains, average use four hours per day, from $5 to $30, according to size of jet.		
Dry Goods, Book and Hardware Stores, from.............	2 00 to	5 00
Saloons, Groceries and Provision Stores, from.............	3 00 to	50 00
Offices. from...........................	2 00 to	20 00
Hotels, Taverns and Boarding Houses, in addition to rates for private dwellings, for each room,...................		1 00
Public Schools, from.......................................	5 00 to	25 00
Building Purposes, for each bushel of lime,...............		02
Printing Offices, not including Steam Engine. from........	5 00 to	25 00
"　　"　　each Power Press,......................		4 00
"　　"　　each Balance Press......................		2 00
"　　"　　each Hand Press,.......................		1 00
Blacksmith Shops, one fire,...............................		5 00
Each additional fire.....................................		2 50
Barber Shops, one chair,.................................		4 00
Each additional chair,..................................∴.		2 00
Steam Engines, non-condensing, ten hours per day, each horse power...		2 50
Butchers' Stalls, each,...................................		3 00
Work Shops. from..	3 00 to	5 00

Water for all Manufacturing and other purposes. requiring large quantities thereof, 10 cents per 1,000 gallons.

REPORT

OF THE

D OF WATER COMMISSIONE

TO THE

COUNCILS OF THE CITY OF ERIE,

FOR THE

'ar and 2-3ds ending Dec. 31st, 1880.

ERIE, PA.

# REPORT

OF THE

RD OF WATER COMMISSIONERS,

TO THE

COUNCILS OF THE CITY OF ERIE,

FOR THE

'ear and 2-3ds ending Dec. 31st, 1880.

ERIE, PA.:
M. P. ATKINSON'S STEAM PRINTING HOUSE, 320 STATE STREET.
1881.

WATER COMMISSIONERS.

——— — - ••◆•• ———

MICHAEL LIEBEL, *President.*

J. M. BRYANT,

G. W. F. SHERWIN.

———

Secretary—B. F. SLOAN,   *Clerk*—GEO. C. GENSHEIMER,
   Superintendent of Pipe Laying and Repairs—WM. E. HILTON.
   Inspector—A. F. CRANE,
   Chief Engineer at Pumping Works—N. W. DUNLAP,
   First Assistant—GEO. R. MILLER,
   Second Assistant—WM. O'LONE,
   Superintendent of Reservoir and Grounds—J. M. REED.

———

OFFICE—No. 18 East Seventh Street, between French and State Streets.
OFFICE HOURS—From 7.30 A. M. to 5.45 P. M.
MEETINGS OF THE BOARD—Every Saturday at 2 P. M., when all bills against the Works will be considered, and, if correct, approved.

REPORT

OF THE

BOARD of WATER COMMISSIONERS,

OF THE

CITY OF ERIE, PA.

To THE HONORABLE, THE MAYOR AND THE SELECT AND COMMON COUNCILS OF THE CITY OF ERIE:

Gentlemen—Herewith is submitted a report of the condition of the Water Department of the city covering one year and eight months. Also, statement of the Secretary of the Receipts and Expenditures of the Department for the year 1880. (See Exhibit A). A report of the receipts and expenditures for the eight months not covered by the Secretary's present report was filed with the Clerk of the Select Council March 8, 1880, and to it—in connection with the present statement—we refer your honorable bodies for full details of the manner the revenues of the Department have been expended during the time embraced in this report.

The fiscal year of the Department has heretofore closed on the 30th of April, but at the suggestion of Councils, and for other obvious reasons, this has been changed to conform to that of other departments of the city government and to the general usages of business.

The publication of the last general report of the Board was delayed till October, 1879, and for this reason it was thought unnecessary to follow it so soon with one on the 1st of January, 1880.

During the time covered by this report the city has been constantly supplied with an abundance of good water, and the number of water-takers has been steadily on the increase. Wells are being abandoned, and often in the most favored localities, and the use of city water is becoming general.

It is gratifying to know that while few, if any, cities have any
better water than that furnished the people of Erie, no city furnishes it to consumers more cheaply. The enviable reputation
which Erie has already obtained for manufactures is only made possible by its large and ample supply of cheap water. In this connection we call attention to tables (see Exhibit B, C and D) comparing the cost of water to consumers in different cities. From this
compilation it will be seen that Erie ranks No. 1 in this respect
both to the manufacturer and to the householder.

AMOUNT OF WATER PUMPED AND WASTED.

During the last eight months of 1879 the amount of water pumped was 531,109,735 gallons. (See Exhibit E). In the year 1880
the amount pumped was 761,993,795 gallons. Total, 1,293,103,530
gallons. This gives for the twenty months a daily supply of about
77 gallons to every inhabitant in the city. But as only about two-
thirds of the city use city water the supply for each person entitled
to use it is fully 100 gallons per day. This enormous consumption
shows conclusively that there is a reckless—not to say criminal—
waste of water that can alone be prevented by the hearty co-operation of each tax-payer with the Board of Commissioners to prevent
it. This waste was so large that it was thought for a time that
there might be an underground leak leading into some sewer, or that
the Reservoir itself might leak; but a careful examination of the
Reservoir and inspection of the mains shows that this impression
was erroneous.

In the early history of the Department the supply could be kept
up by working one engine, and when the demand was not in excess
of the capacity of one engine, it made little difference whether
water-takers used little or much. The engines and boilers were
constructed duplex—one half the full capacity to be used, and the
other half held in reserve so as to meet the contingency of accidents, and thus never fail to have power to furnish a supply. This
provision was wise, and it is nearly indispensible where so large a
population and so extensive manufacturing interests are wholly dependent on the city water supply.

As stated above, the average daily consumption is over 2,000,000
gallons. The capacity of one engine is 2,500,000 per day, but there
are many days when the consumption amounts to nearly 3,000,000.

When this occurs, or it is not desirable to pump, as it is sometimes on account of the turbid state of the water in the bay, both engines have to be put in operation to keep up the supply. Now, should an acci-dent happen to one, the reserve engine, with the present wasteful use of water, could not keep up the supply, and the result would be a water famine, the direct product of extravagance and abuse.

PROSPECTIVE NECESSITY FOR ENLARGING THE WORKS.

Looking to such a contingency in the near future, the attention of the Commissioners has been directed to the best way of increasing the capacity of the Pumping Works. The 20-inch main will not take the water from the engines as fast as both can pump. For this reason, when both are worked to their full capacity, the water is forced over the top of the Stand Pipe. By using both engines, and accommodating their speed to the capacity of the main, the amount pumped is not double that by one engine when run to its full capacity. But, as shown, one cannot keep up the supply, and to run two is not economical, because to do so not only increases the working force in the boiler house, but requires the consumption of double the amount of fuel. During the year eight feet have been added to the height of the Stand Pipe to give a greater force to the current through the 20-inch main, and thus increase its working capacity, and by this means postpone as long as possible the necessity for laying an additional main to the Reservoir. The limit, however, of a safe pressure in the Stand Pipe has probably been reached, and if the ratio of increased consumption continues, the time has arrived for the Board to initiate measures to furnish increased capacity to the Works to supply the city with water.

A new pumping main, without lateral connections with the distributing mains, would, no doubt, give us temporary relief. With it both pumps could be worked to their full capacity with a good degree of economy. It would have the additional advantage of supplying the city almost wholly from the Reservoir, and thus provide for the deposit there of all substances held in suspension in the water before distribution to consumers.

The plain duty of the Commissioners is: First, to guard against as much waste as possible. In doing this it is fair to assume they will have the hearty co-operation of the city authorities and of the tax-payers generally. Second, when this waste is reduced to a minimum, to increase the capacity of the Works as rapidly as is consistent with a prudent regard to the financial ability of the Department to do so.

THE COST OF ENLARGEMENT.

The cost of a new 20-inch main to the Reservoir, at the present price of iron, would be from $30,000 to $35,000. It will take several years to save this amount from Water Rents, and at the same time meet the demands which increased population and business are constantly making for the extension of distributing mains. During the time covered by this report about five miles of distributing mains have been laid. (See Exhibit F.) This is one-sixth of the entire amount laid from the commencement of the Works to the date of the last report of the Board, and makes the entire length of such mains in the city thirty-five miles, a larger amount than is laid in any city of the population of Erie in the country. In the same time 346 new service connections with dwellings, stores and manufactories have been added, and five new fire plugs set. (See Exhibits G and H.) It is not doubted that the next five years will require an even larger expenditure for the extension of distributing mains than the past five, and if it does, then the laying of an additional pumping main to the Reservoir is an inevitable necessity. With this new main completed we could, and probably would be compelled to use all our present power in keeping up the supply. This might not be objectionable if we had a larger storage capacity. Without any pumping the Reservoir will supply the present proper use of water (not waste, however,) about fifteen days. This is hardly a sufficient time now, and each year will make it less. The Reservoir is valuable as a safeguard against any temporary interruption of the pumps, but the large and daily increasing consumption shows conclusively that even now we are in reality dependent on the continuous motion of the pumps for a continuous supply. This being so, the necessary sequence is that the reserve power contemplated in the original plan of the Works as being always available in case of emergency, is exhausted by the demands of increased consumption.

And here we are confronted with another fact. It was no more necessary to make the pumping power in duplicate in the first place than it is to keep it in duplicate now. If the safety and well-being of the city called for auxiliary power in the beginning—always ready to be used and sufficient to maintain the supply—it requires no further evidence to show that measures must soon be adopted to provide such auxillary power. Whether the desired object can be obtained best by directing the efforts of the Department to laying a new main to the Reservoir, or adding additional power to the Works, or both, is a problem for careful consideration. To do either will require the appropriation of the whole available financial resources at our command for at least three years, or six to finish both. By commencing at once and completing a portion each year, the capacity of the Works, in both mains and power, to meet the requirements of a population double that now supplied, can be accomplished in six years with the resources derived from Water Rents.

NEW BOILERS.

Early in the past year it became apparent that the boilers, eight in number, and in use since the Works were built. were not in good condition, and after mature consideration it was decided to replace them with four new ones of a much greater aggregate capacity. This has been done, and the new boilers are now in place doing duty. The change was accomplished without accident, and the pumps were idle on account of the change but two and one-half days. These four boilers have more than one-fifth greater capacity for producing steam than the eight old ones.

EXPERIMENTS WITH COAL.

Economy in consumption of fuel has received very close attention. Experiments were made with many kinds and grades of coal with very satisfactory results. From these experiments it became evident a cheaper grade might be used, and following what seems to be the line of economy we are now using coal at a greatly reduced price per ton, and with only a small increase in the amount consumed, still leaving a margin in favor of the cheaper coal. A further saving in the cost of fuel was hoped for by replacing the old boilers with new of an improved pattern. This hope has been realized, as a careful comparison of the first four months of 1880, using the old boilers, with the last four of 1880, using the new, shows a saving of fully 12½ per cent. (See Exhibit I). A still greater saving is looked for in the future when the coverings to the domes, steam pipes, &c., are completed, and the radiation from the fixtures, which greatly effects the production of steam, is reduced to its minimum.

RAILROAD TRACK THROUGH THE BOILER HOUSE.

In the arrangement of the new boilers it was found practicable to leave sufficient space north of them to admit laying a track through the boiler house for the convenience of receiving supplies of coal. This has been done and it is now in use. The action of Councils, granting the use of a portion of Front street, enables us to utilize this switch to its full capacity. There is room for one car on the scales in the house and for six east of it, while west of there is ample accommodation for the seven when unloaded. As the grade is sufficient to move them by their own gravity, it would seem that little more in the way of handling coal could be added to our facilities. To provide against the contingency of accidents which might delay the receipt of fuel by rail, we still maintain our facilities for receiving all that may be required to keep the Works in operation by wagon, as formerly.

NEW TRACK SCALES.

The propriety of weighing all the coal consumed at the Works has induced us to obtain a set of Track Scales which are now in complete working order, and hereafter all fuel will be accurately weighed as received. These scales are of standard quality, and guaranteed to weigh forty tons or five pounds with equal accuracy.

IMPROVED STREET STOP BOXES.

During the year, at the requests of Councils, we have adopted a plan of Street Stop Boxes and Covers for paved streets, made entirely of iron, which will, no doubt, meet the desired want and not prove much more expensive than the old ones.

MILL CREEK SEWERAGE.

We wish to repeat and emphasize the recommendation made during the past year that no time should be lost in carrying into effect the plan for carrying the waters of Mill Creek, with their abundance of sewerage, outside the Bay, as a means of preserving the purity of our water supply.

WATER USED AND WASTED.

By reference to the tables found in this report it will be seen that the water used by the city or wasted by consumers, is more than equal to the amount paid for. Assuming that this in great part is the result of waste, we shall, at the proper time, ask your honorable bodies to unite with us in adopting some measure calculated to prevent this waste; or, in the event of failure, to place the burden of expense thus incurred where it rightfully belongs.

WATER GAUGES.

We have now in use at the Pumping Works and at the Reservoir Water-Gauges to show each day the difference in height between the water in the Bay and the Reservoir, showing the actual lift of the pumps for each day, of which a daily record is made.

SEWERAGE AT THE WORKS.

The sewerage of the Pumping Works has been entirely reconstructed during the past year, and is now, we believe, in perfect order.

USE OF METERS.

The ingenuity of man has not yet devised a perfect arrangement for measuring water automatically, but there are meters now capable of doing their work regularly—that is with a certain per centage of loss or gain, and this loss or gain is regular until the wear of the meter is sufficient to change its capacity. This wear is always in proportion to the water measured. To obviate this objection to meters because they become inaccurate by use, we have constructed a METER TESTER which shows conclusively how the meter runs, whether it indicates more or less water than it should, and how much. The result is recorded in a book in the office against each meter. The per centage of loss or gain is added or substracted as the case may be, to or from the readings. To provide against the possibility of error the meter is tested before using, and again when its use is discontinued, and the average per centage of loss or gain is added to or substracted from the amount of water registered as having passed through the meter. By this means the exact amount is ascertained, and the consumer pays for what he gets, be it more or less.

CHANGE IN THE MANNER OF COLLECTING RENTS.

On the 18th of October, 1879, the rule assessing tenants instead of landlords for water rent was changed to take effect April 1, 1880. Due notice of this was given in all the papers. Since that time all assessments have been made accordingly, and the collections made from the owners or their authorized agents. The reasons for this change were briefly: First—Some of the largest owners of tenement houses in the city had already adopted the system of including water rent in their rental when leasing; and, second, because there was constant complaint by others that tenants would move at the expiration of their lease, leaving one or more quarters of water rent unpaid, no notice of which default had been given the landlord by the Department before ordering the water shut off for non-payment. By the new system this complaint is removed, and every owner is now notified on the first of each quarter in advance of the amount of rent due on each and every tenement leased. With this notice before him, if he allows his tenant to vacate the premises in arrears for water rent, the fault does not rest at the door of the Water office, and he has no ground for complaint if the Department shuts off the water and keeps it off until all arrearages are paid. A somewhat extensive correspondence with the officials of Water Works in other cities shows that in a majority of cases the system of collecting from landlords instead of tenants prevails. And in cities where it does not, the universal verdict of experience is that not to do so is a mistake.

THE WATER DEPARTMENT A CO-ORDINATE BRANCH.

The Water Department of the city is an independent branch of the city government, with limited powers and jurisdiction. There are some duties devolving equally on the Board of Commissioners and the City Councils. One of these duties is the adoption of rates, terms and conditions governing the use of water. The two bodies —the Councils elected by the people, and the Board of Commissioners appointed by the Court—must unite, and their united action in establishing rates, terms and conditions is alone legal. But in the enactment of By-Laws, Rules and Regulations for the management of the Department, the Board of Commissioners are made by the law alone competent to act. For the information of the public, the Commissioners are required to make a yearly report to Councils,

showing the condition of the trust confided to them by the law.
Through this provision the business of the Department—the condition of the engines and mains—its financial management, and all
matters pertaining to the efficiency and present and future government of the Works—comes under revision each year; and by this
wise provision of the law the people may know, officially, if the
trust reposed in the Board has been faithfully administered. The
exhibit should show—and this report does show—what work has
been done and what it has cost—what money has been received and
what has been done with it.

THE CITY SHOULD CREDIT THE DEPARTMENT WITH SERVICES.

Heretofore one element of this yearly exhibit has been conspicu-
ously absent, viz: a credit to the Water Department for services
rendered the city. The cost of the Works has been very great, and
our citizens have raised the money or increased their indebtedness
to pay for them cheerfully. The protection of property from loss by
fire was one of the objects in view in the construction of the Works.
To accomplish this, and furnish a full supply in case of emergency,
mains were laid of far greater size than would be required for ordinary use. Thus, where a four inch main would supply all demand
for house or manufacturing purposes, mains have been laid six and
twelve inches, in order to afford more volume for fire purposes.
This nearly doubles the cost of pipe laying. And so the whole
water pumping structure is more expensive in its first cost and in
its maintenance than it would be if it was not for fire purposes.
Again, a large proportion of the vigilance required to be exercised
by the Department is due to the fire protection side of the Water
Works—keeping hydrants in order at all times—keeping a full
supply in the Reservoir for emergencies, and the great drain upon
the supply by the use of water at fires. These things all conspire
to make running expenses greater. And this must be done, or we
have no use for the Fire Department. That branch of the city government could do nothing without water; and the Water Department never fails to co-operate to the fullest extent and render their
labors effective. But the co-operation is expensive.

The money which pays the expense is collected from the people,
but it is not collected for this service rendered. It is collected from
the householder and the manufacturer. And when the accounts of
the Water Department are balanced at the end of the year, there is

no credit to stand against the service performed and the expenses incurred in behalf of the Fire Department. Therefore it is claimed there should be an equitable charge against the city each year for this service. The credit should be commensurate with the service. No money need be paid to the Water Department for water for fire purposes, fountains, police stations, and flushing sewers, care and repair of fire hydrants, &c., but it should appear in the account charged to general expenses, and credited to the interest on Water Works bonds.

WHAT THE CREDIT SHOULD BE.

To show what this credit should be the following statistics are given: The number of gallons pumped in 1880 was 775,805,200. The number of gallons paid for by consumers was 373,750,000. Number of gallons used by the city or wasted was 402,055,200. If this amount was one-half used for city purposes, there should be a credit given of $20,097.50. This added to the sum collected from consumers would amount to $57,482.50.

From the financial statement of the Secretary, (see Exhibit A), it will be seen that the receipts of the current year from all sources were $38,413.47. Of this sum $19,397.45 was expended to pay current expenses, leaving a balance of net earnings to the credit of the Department of $19,016.02. If is added to this the above sum of $20,097.50 which, in all fairness should be allowed, and credited by the city to the account of interest on Water Works bonds, and charged to general expenses on account of services rendered by the Water Department, it will be seen that the Works have earned enough this year to pay $5\frac{xxx}{000}$ per cent. interest on the $675,000 bonds issued by the city for the construction of the Works. It is true $18,413.47 of the net earnings this year have been spent on account of construction; but this fact does not invalidate the statement that the Works are now paying within a small fraction of six per cent. on their cost to the city, because if that amount had been paid on interest on the bonds, a like amount would have been required from the general fund to pay for necessary improvements and extension of the Works.

WHAT IS ALLOWED FOR SIMILAR SERVICE IN OTHER CITIES.

That the sum named above is a low estimate for the services rendered is shown by the following facts: · Previous to the construction of the Works the city authorities were under a contract with a private corporation to pay $180 per year for a given number of hydrants. It has the use of 126 for which alone it would have to pay under that contract $22,680. The city of St Paul, Minn., pays the Water Works of that city—a private corporation—$600 per mile per annum for all mains laid; $75 per year for one hundred hydrants, and $50 per year for every one set above that number. Under such a contract Erie would pay $29,800. The city of Oswego, N. Y., pays to a private corporation $24,500 for water for city use. The company has twenty miles of mains—fifteen less than Erie—and 168 hydrants—42 more than Erie. Our sister city of Meadville pays $6,000 per year for water for city purposes to a private corporation. Based on number of miles of mains, hydrants and population supplied, this amount is about equal to $21,000 in Erie. In nearly all New England cities the rule is to credit the Water Department with a given sum for the use of water, and charge the amount to general expenses. Thus Lawrence, Mass., credits $10,000 in this way, while Fall River credits $65,000. These two sums are the extreme—the amount varying according to cost of works, length of mains, number of hydrants, and the character and extent of the use of water.

IN CONCLUSION.

As said in a former report, the Commissioners are aware that practically it makes no difference to the tax-payer whether the amount claimed is charged to general expenses, or to account of interest on Water Works bonds—it is but going through the form of taking money out of one pocket and putting it in another—but until the proper credit is given by the city to the Water Department for services rendered, and this credit appears in the annual statement of the financial condition of the city, many tax-payers will continue to think and say, as too many do now, that the debt contracted for the construction of the Works is a burthen from which the city derives no benefit. For this reason we again renew the request made in former reports, that in future, in the assessment of taxes, an amount equal to that the city would have to pay a private corporation for similar services, be assessed for general purposes and deducted from the assessment for interest on Water Works bonds.

All of which is respectfully submitted,

M. LEIBEL,
J. M. BRYANT,
G. W. F. SHERWIN,

ERIE, January 15, 1881.   Commissioners.

EXHIBIT A.

RECEIPTS

From Water Rent from Jan. 1st to Dec. 31st, 1880......$37,385	00	
" Plumbing and pipe laying......................	288	92
" Laying private mains.........................	490	40
" Old material sold............................	68	91
" Fire plugs sold..............................	39	83
" Engine sold..................................	125	00
" Stop valve sold..............................	15	05
" Discount on gas bill.........................		36
" Bal. in office and bank Dec. 31, 1879...........	314	83
		$38,728 30

CR.

By deposits in City Treasury in January.............$ 4,542	82	
" " " " " " February............	3,000	00
" " " " " " March...............	1,526	48
" " " " " " April...............	3,573	27
" " " " " " May.................	3,600	00
" " " " " " June................	1,678	46
" " " " " " July................	4,743	83
" " " " " " August..............	3,100	00
" " " " " " September...........	2,050	00
" " " " " " October.............	3,742	35
" " " " " " November...........	3,500	00
" " " " " " December...........	2,775	23
		$38,332 44
Balance in office Jan. 1, 1881........................	$ 395	86

CITY TREASURY TO WATER DEPARTMENT

DR.

To balance on hand Jan. 1, 1880, per Auditor's report... $ 1,187 62
To deposits from Jan. 1, 1880, to Dec. 31, 1880......... 38,332 44
                                                      ————$39,520 06

CR.

Warrants drawn in January............., ...$ 3,805 89
"	"	" February.........................	1,928 63
"	"	" March.....	2,107 17
"	"	" April..........................	2,441 53
"	"	" May........	1,925 89
"	"	" June....	2,765 97
"	"	" July............................	5,694 24
"	"	" August..........	3,690 97
"	"	" September......................	3,982 53
"	"	" October.........................	2,669 50
"	"	" November......................	4,085 39
"	"	" December......................	2,720 17
————$37,817 88

Balance..................... ... . $ 1,702 18

DR.

To warrant issued, not called for and still in office.....$ 6 96 $ 6 96

Actual bal. in Treasury, Dec. 31, 1880.... .... $ 1,709 14

I, P. Arbuckle, Comptroller of the City of Erie, do certify that the vouchers above reported were examined by me and do find them correct as stated, and find in the hands of John Boyle, City Treasurer, seventeen hundred and nine dollars and fourteen cents ($1,709 14) due the Water Department.

                                        P. ARBUCKLE,
                                                Comptroller.
ERIE, February 4, 1881.

EXPENDITURES.

FUEL.

Jan. 3	P'd R J Saltsman	415,900	lbs.	slack coal	at	$2	05	$ 426	30
Feb. 2	"	522,300	"	"	at	2	05	535	36
Mch. 1	"	521,900	"	"	at	2	05	534	95
Apr. 3	"	518,800	"	"	at	2	05	531	77
May 1	"	504,300	"	"	at	2	05	516	90
June 4	"	489,900	"	"	at	1	99	487	45
July 3	"	493,600	"	"	at	1	99	491	13
Aug. 2	"	164,700	"	"	at	1	99	163	88
Aug. 2	"	45,450	"	lump	at	4	00	90	90
Aug. 2	"	26,900	"	"	at	3	75	387	94
Sept. 4	"	424,800	"	"	at	3	75	796	50
Oct. 9	"	266,700	"	"	at	3	75	500	06
Oct. 9	"	166,900	" slack coal	at	1	99	166	07
Nov. 2	"	375,700	" slack "	at	1	99	373	81
Dec. 4	"	620,850	" slack "	at	1	99	617	75

————$6,620 77

CONSTRUCTION OF RAILROAD SWITCH.

Aug.	2	Paid Robert Cook for labor....................	$	19 50
Aug.	21	" " "		3 25
Aug.	21	Labor as per Supt's pay roll..............		85 27
Aug.	28	Harrison Foster for labor.................		9 39
Sept.	1	Labor as per Supt's pay roll..............		88 79
Sept.	18	" " " "		21 14
Oct.	2	" " " "		29 30
Oct.	9	" " " "		44 00
Oct.	9	Wm Himrod for ties....................		120 00
Nov.	20	Mt Hickory Iron Works for iron...........		316 00
Nov.	20	For labor as per Supt's pay roll...........		11 69
Nov.	20	Patrick Doyle.........................		4 50
Nov.	27	Labor as per Supt's pay roll..............		6 64
Dec.	11	" " " "		4 94
Dec.	18	Penn Company..........................		188 33
Dec.	24	Labor as per Supt's pay roll..............		2 51

————$ 955 2

SALARIES.

May	22	Paid M Liebel. Com. bal salary to May 1, '80...	443 00
May	22	G W F Sherwin. bal salary to May 1, '80...	338 00
May	22	J M Bryant. bal salary to May 1, '80.......	241 00
Dec.	31	B F Sloan, Sec, sal from Jan 1 to Dec 31, '80	1,000 00
Dec.	31	W E Hilton, Supt. sal fr Jan 1 to Dec 31, '80	960 00
Dec	31	A F Crane, Ins, salary fr Jan 1 to Dec 31, '80	840 00
Dec	31	G C Gensheimer, clk. sal fr Jan 1 to Dec 31 '80	480 00
Dec	31	M Liebel. Com, on act salary for '80 and '81	400 00
Dec	31	G W F Sherwin. Com, on act sal for '80 and '81	450 00
Dec	31	J M Bryant. Com. on act sal for '80 and '81	564 00

————$ 5,716 0

EXPENSE OF HORSE AND WAGON.

May	1	Paid J Fogerty bill for shoeing.................		80
May	6	C Klang for repairing wagon.............	26	63
May	13	William E Hilton for hay.................	8	98
July	13	J Fogarty bill for shoeing..............	1	80
Aug	7	Wm E Hilton for hay...................	10	42
Aug	28	J Fogarty bill for shoeing................	1	70
Oct	2	" " " " ".................	1	30
Nov	6	J B Crouch&Co oats fr Jan 21 to Oct 5......	40	60
Nov	27	J Fogarty bill for shoeing...............	1	80
Dec	31	W E Hilton for hay....................	15	87

$ 110 90

EXTENSION OF STAND PIPE.

Aug	28	Paid Stearns Manf Co..................$	147	10
Dec	18	Constable Bros............	47	72

$ 194 82

DISTRIBUTING MAINS AND BRANCHES.

Jan	3	Paid Cleveland & Co bill of castings............$	16	48
Jan	11	Drullard & Hayes invoice of pipe..........	1,858	12
Feb	3	H G Fink bill of sundries.................	1	34
Feb	3	Cornell Lead Co, Buffalo, invoice of lead...	96	75
Feb	3	Labor as per Supt's pay roll..............	12	10
Feb	3	Freight Transfer Co distributing pipe......	7	15
Feb	21	Cleveland & Co bill of castings...........	9	52
Mch	6	L S & M S R R fgt on car of pipe..........	13	87
Mch	13	Transfer Co for distributing pipe..........	3	37
Mch	13	Wm E Hilton ex to Buffalo to inspect pipe.	7	25
Mch	20	Labor as per Supt's pay roll..............	30	48
Apr	3	" " " "	37	76
Apr	10	Drullard & Hayes for invoice of pipe.......	599	60
Apr	10	Labor laying as per Supt's pay roll........	39	41
Apr	17	" " " " "	7	28
June	19	" " " " "	79	80
June	26	" " " " "	69	14
June	26	Cornell Lead Co invoice of lead..........	90	45
July	3	Labor as per Supt's pay roll..............	69	98
July	3	Freight and cartage on lead..............	2	11
July	3	E W Reed bill for wood...................	2	25
July	10	Empire Line fgt on pipe from Philadelphia.	87	36
July	17	Labor as per Supt's pay roll..............	60	70
July	17	L S & M S R R Co freight on pipe........	11	48
July	17	Wm E Hilton ex to Buffalo to inspect pipe.	6	00
July	24	R D Wood & Co, Phila, invoice of pipe....	470	80
July	24	Labor as per Supt's pay roll..............	59	93
Aug	2	" " " "	107	43
Aug	7	" " " "	73	90
Aug	14	Drullard & Hayes, Buffalo, invoice of pipe.	396	72
Aug	14	Labor as per Supt's pay roll..............	58	64
Aug	21	" " " "	7	76
Sept	1	" " " "	12	09

Carried Forward,......................$4,407 02

	Brought Forward,......................$4,407 02	
Sept 1	Freight and cartage on lead...............	2 02
Sept 11	Labor as per Supt's pay roll...............	67 27
Sept 18	" " " "	46 50
Sept 25	" " " "	35 11
Sept 25	Transfer Co for distributing pipe...........	3 58
Oct 2	L S & M S R R Co freight on pipe..........	12 66
Oct 2	Wm E Hilton ex to Buffalo to ins pipe.....	8 00
Oct 2	Labor as per Supt's pay roll...............	30 26
Oct 9	" " " "	32 59
Oct 9	Cornell Lead Co invoice of lead............	111 00
Oct 9	Transfer Co for distributing pipe...........	6 51
Oct 16	Labor as per Supt's pay roll...............	28 34
Oct 23	" " " "	17 50
Nov 1	" " " "	15 27
Nov 13	Drullard & Hayes invoice pipe.............	492 93
Dec 11	H P M Birkenbine inspecting pipe.........	24 03

————$ 5,340 59

REBUILDING INLET PIERS.

Aug 2	Paid W W Loomis estimate on contract........$ 426 66	
Aug 21	" " "	521 75
Sept 1	David Schlosser bill of lumber.............	15 51
Sept 11	Heilman & Brown est on contract for stone.	25 00
Sept 18	" final estimate	34 10
Sept 18	W W Loomis balance due on contract......	120 00
Dec 11	Labor as per Supt's pay roll...............	2 47

————$ 1,145 49

FIRE HYDRANTS.

Jan 3	Paid J M Moorhead bill for straw...............$	16 00
Jan 10	R D Wood & Co for two hydrants..........	76 00
July 17	" one hydrant and freight....	42 81
July 24	" one hydrant and cartage...	42 50
Aug 21	Labor as per Supt's pay roll...............	9 31
Oct 9	Stearns Manf Co for castings.............	4 64
Nov 27	W E Hilton for straw....................	15 14

———— 206 40

POSTAGE.

Dec 31 Paid U S P O for cards, stamps, etc............$ 127 80

————$ 127 80

EXCHANGE AND INTEREST.

Dec 31 Paid exchange on drafts and interest.......... 19 10

————$ 19 10

PAY OF ENGINEERS AND FIREMEN.

Dec	31	Paid sal of N W Dunlap C E, Jan to Dec 31 '80.			$1,000	00
Dec	31	" G R Miller A E " " ".			773	50
Dec	31	" Wm O'Lone A E " " ".			720	00
Dec	31	" J Kelley jr fireman " " ".			515	00
Dec	31	" R W Simons fireman" " ".			515	00
Dec	31	" J Kelley sr fireman " July 1, '80.			180	00
Dec	31	" Nelson Crouch June, Dec 13, '80·			319	50
Jan	1	Edward Ryon services as fireman 12¼ days..			16	63
Jan	10	" " " 4 " ..			5	32
Jan	14	George Hoffman " " 5 " ..			6	65
Apr	24	E J Platt " 6 ..			7	98
June	1	Edward Ryon " " 14 " ..			21	00
June	12	" " 10 " ..			15	00
June	19	John Kelley sr " " 15 " ..			15	00
July	1	Edward Ryon " " 20 " ..			30	00
July	17	" " 13½ " ..			20	25
July	17	John Kelley sr " 3¾ ' ..			5	25
Aug	2	Edward Ryon " 5 ' ..			7	50
Aug	21	" " 15 " ..			22	50
July	17	Wm Brady " 2½ ' ..			3	75
July	24	" 5 ' ..			7	50
Sept	1	Edward Ryon " " 10½ " ..			15	75
Nov	13	George Leushen " 2 " ..			3	00
Dec	4	Geo Baker et al..........................			50	25
Dec	4	Patrick Kelley...........................			9	00

$ 4,285 33

BOXES AND COVERS.

Jan	1	Paid D Schlosser bill of lumber................$		16 84
Feb	14	" " "		5 95
May	22	" " "		6 65
June	5	Jarecki, Hays & Co bill sundries..........		102 20
July	10	D Schlosser bill of lumber................		7 85
Aug	28	Cleveland & Co bill of castings............		24 30
Aug	28	D Schlosser " lumber............		7 30
Oct	16	Stearns Manf Co " castings............		29 98
Oct	23	D Schlosser " lumber............		8 50
Nov	27	Cleveland & Co "		19 66
Nov	27	D Schlosser " "		7 46
Dec	11	"		8 70

$ 245 39

OFFICE EXPENSES.

Jan	1	Paid for telegrams, &c, as per vouchers on file..$		9 43
Jan	10	Constable Bros bill for repairs..............		4 20
Jan	24	Erie Gas Co bill rendered...................		2 79
Feb	7	" " " " "		4 86
Mar	1	Cash for various items as per vouchers on file		2 30
Apr	3	J C Mack et al bills rendered..............		2 30
Apr	24	R M Johnson bill for livery..............		9 00
May	8	E W Reed bill rendered for coal..........		18 75
May	8	Cash for telegraphing....................		45

Carried Forward,.......................$ 54 08

		Brought Forward	$ 54 08
May	15	Erie Gas Co bill rendered	2 00
June	1	For thermometer et al	1 70
June	12	Am Dis Tel Co rent of telephone	24 80
June	12	Wm P Atkinson directory	3 00
July	3	Keystone Laundry for washing towels	65
July	17	James Hunter bill rendered	4 00
July	24	J C Mack bill sundries	50
Aug	2	J C Mackintosh et al sundries	2 02
Aug	14	H M Reed & Co sundries	1 75
Sept	1	Keystone Laundry	30
Oct	2	" "	45
Oct	9	E W Reed for coal	12 30
Oct	9	Erie Gas Co	2 75
Oct	9	W W Pierce & Co	25
Dec	31	O L Elliott office rent one year	250 00
Nov	1	Keystone Laundry	45
Dec	11	J C Mackintosh	25
Dec	24	Erie Dispatch sub six months	4 00
Dec	31	Am Dis Tel for use of tel six months	36 00

$ 401 16

PLUMBING AND PIPE LAYING.

Dec 31 Paid labor as per Supt's pay rolls from Jan 1 to December 31...........$ 47 41

$ 47 41

CARE OF GAS WELL.

July 3 Paid W E Bell for labor.....................$ 11 25

$ 11 25

REMODELING AND REPAIRS OF WATER WORKS BUILDINGS.

Jan	1	Paid Geo Carroll & Bro lumber	$ 5 86
Jan	10	Constable & Bro sundries	4 74
Jan	17	Labor as per Supt's pay roll	13 64
Mar	6	Geo Hoffman labor	15 30
Apr	10	Erie Lime and Cement Co lime	2 75
Apr	1	Wm & James Hoskinson brick	7 00
Apr	5	Erie Car Works lumber	18 59
Apr	12	John O Baker labor	30 00
July	3	" "	2 42
July	17	Labor as per Supt's pay roll	4 46
July	24	Geo Carroll & Bro lumber	26 05
Aug	2	T J Foglebach labor	14 00
Aug	2	Nick & Bros sundries	28 45
Aug	2	T J Foglebach	10 00
Aug	14	H M Reed & Co sundries	1 10
Aug	28	Stearns Manf Co	11 88
Sept	25	Labor as per Supt's pay roll	47 99
Sept	25	J D Tuohy labor	2 50
Oct	9	Erie Hardware Co	1 97
Oct	16	Chas S Spencer labor	5 37
Nov	6	Labor as per Supt's pay roll	116 06

Carried Forward.....................$ 370 13

	Brought Forward........................$	370	13
Nov 6	Erie Car Works lumber....................	16	68
Nov 6	August Mehler labor.......................	3	00
Nov 13	Labor as per Supt's pay roll..............	76	96
Nov 20	" " " "	72	31
Nov 20	Robert Dill painting......................	6	87
Nov 27	Labor as per Supt's pay roll..............	60	08
Nov 27	Erie Lime and Cement Co lime &c.........	21	35
Nov 27	Harrison Foster spikes....................	1	62
Dec 4	Labor as per Supt's pay roll..............	21	74
Dec 4	" " " "	14	02
Dec 4	August Mehler labor......................	11	25
Dec 18	Labor per Supt's pay roll.................	29	14
Dec 18	F J Senger labor..........................	2	25
Dec 18	Constable & Bros labor and material.......	190	91
Dec 18	Saltsman & Austin sewer pipe.............	114	49
Dec 24	John Mayerhoffer sundries................	1	50
Dec 31	Labor as per Supt's pay roll..............	23	91
		$ 1,038	21

ENGINEERS' SMALL STORES.

Jan 1	Paid James Gaffney sundries....................$	1	22
Jan 3	J W Swalley.............................	2	50
Jan 10	Hall & Warfel...........................	4	35
Jan 17	Henry Beckman..........................	16	89
Mar 1	T M Austin.............................		75
Mar 1	Erie Ice Co..............................	10	00
Mar 5	Ashby & Vincent et al....................	2	65
Apr 10	J W Swalley.............................	6	75
Apr 10	Hall & Warfel...........................	1	80
May 15	Ashby & Vincent.........................	11	67
June 19	J W Swalley.............................	2	50
July 3	James Gaffney...........................	11	44
July 10	Henry Beckman..........................	4	90
Aug 14	H M Reed & Co..........................		75
Oct 2	French & McKnight et al..................	1	63
Oct 9	W W Pierce & Co.........................	1	65
Nov 20	J W Swalley soap........................	5	00
Dec 24	Samuel Cummins bill sundries.............	15	03
		$ 102	08

FOR THE CONSTRUCTION OF NEW BOILERS.

	Paid Noble & Hall on contract................$5,100		00
June 1	Stearns Manf Co sundries.................	30	25
June 19	Erie City Iron Works.....................	7	50
July 24	Labor as per Supt's pay roll..............	23	39
Aug 2	Joshua Follansbee........................	15	00
Aug 14	H M Reed & Co bill......................	6	00
Sept 11	" "	14	63
Sept 25	Edward Ryon............................	10	50
Oct 2	Express charges..........................		25
Oct 2	Supt's pay roll..........................	20	00
Oct 16	" "	29	10
Oct 16	Chas S Spencer..........................	55	00
Oct 23	Edward Ryon labor.......................	3	00
Nov 9	Pennsylvania Co.........................	5	43
		$ 5,320	05

WOODEN PLUGS.

May   8 Paid P J Roth for turning Plugs................$ 3 25   3 25

STATIONERY AND BOOKS.

Feb	3	Paid S P Ensign & Co..........................$	50
Mar	1	Ashby & Vincent..........................	2 25
April	3	W J Sell bill.............................	6 25
May	15	Ashby & Vincent..........................	18 55
Aug	28	"	12 75
Oct	2	F B Brewer...............................	1 00
Nov	27	Mehl, Wallace & Co.......................	10 00
Dec	11	Economy Printing Co....................	1 00

                                                              ————$ 52 30

SUPERINTENDENT'S SMALL STORES.

Jan	1	Paid C E Gunnison bill of leather...............$	6 00
Jan	10	W W Pierce & Co sundries.................	64
Mch	1	Freight on block tin.......................	25
Apr	3	J C Mack bill sundries....................	1 83
Apr	10	Hall & Warfel "	30
May	8	E W Reed "	1 25
May	15	Erie Gas Co for coke.....................	15 03
July	17	Hall & Warfel sundries..................	4 80
July	24	J C Mack "	1 90
Oct	9	W W Pierce & Co "	66
Oct	9	Erie Gas Co coke.........................	3 54
Nov	1	A Mining et al..........................	65
Dec	11	Eclipse Oil Co oil.......................	5 50

                                                              ————$ 42 29

WASTE AND PACKING.

Jan	17	Paid Henry Beckman.........................$	6 00
Feb	7	M E Flannigan............................	4 80
Feb	21	Parsons & Faber..........................	8 10
Mch	1	W W Pierce & Co.........................	9 45
Mch	6	M E Flannigan...........................	28 85
Apr	17	"	4 00
June	12	S Dickinson & Son........................	1 00
June	19	L G Tillotson & Co.......................	43 21
July	3	Freight and cartage......................	1 54
July	24	M E Flannigan...........................	28 80
Aug	14	H M Reed & Co...........................	16 55
Sept	25	M E Flannigan...........................	12 00
Oct	3	H M Reed & Co...........................	17 19

                                                              ————$ 181 49

CARE AND MAINTENANCE OF RESERVOIR.

Jan	24	Paid labor as per Supt's pay roll...............$	1 05
Feb	7	" " " "	1 59
May	15	" " " "	12 95
May	15	Adam Gilcher labor.......................	7 50
May	15	Gorr & Baas.............................	25 93

Carried Forward........................$ 49 02

		Brought Forward...........................$	49 02
May	22	Labor as per Supt's pay roll...............	1 75
June	1	" " "	1 75
June	1	Geo Carroll & Bro.......................	50 00
June	1	George Lacer............................	1 25
June	1	L M Lytle................................	3 20
June	5	Labor as per pay roll.....................	1 29
June	5	Geo Lacer................................	1 25
June	5	Erie Cemetery labor......................	1 00
June	26	Labor as per Supt's pay roll...............	85
July	3	Henry Stender...........................	9 00
July	17	Labor as per Supt's pay roll...............	2 41
July	24	" " " "	37
Aug	21	John D Lackie...........................	9 15
Oct	16	Labor as per pay roll.....................	75
Oct	16	Miss Mary Reed services..................	2 00
Nov	27	Geo Neff.................................	17 50
Dec	31	J M Reed, Supt. salary from Jan 1 to Dec 31	360 00
Nov	20	Robert Dill..............................	1 25
Nov	27	Labor as per Supt's pay roll...............	2 11
Dec	18	" " " "	1 84
Dec	31	" " " "	2 16
			——$ 519 90

ENGINE ROOM FURNITURE, &C.

May	15	Paid H S Manning & Co flue brush..............	13 50
May	15	Erie Hardware Co wheelbarrow............	4 00
June	1	J Fogarty et al repairing.................	4 70
Aug	14	H M Reed & Co sundries..................	8 50
Oct	23	Jarecki Manf Co sundries................	4 80
Dec	11	Thos Shaw water thermometer.............	2 75
			——$ 38 25

SERVICE FITTINGS

June	5	Paid Jarecki, Hays & Co.....................$ 351 52	
			——$ 351 52

OIL AND TALLOW.

Jan	1	Paid James Gaffney bill for 50 pounds tallow....$	4 50
Jan	17	Henry Beckman bill for 23 pounds tallow...	2 30
Feb	7	Eichenlaub & Co one barrel tallow.........	13 20
Feb	7	Republic Refining Co barrel oil............	22 73
Apr	17	F H Penfield one barrel lubricating oil.....	29 95
Apr	17	C F Noyes 993 pounds tallow.............	55 85
May	22	F R Simmons 403 " "	23 16
July	1	French & McKnight bill rendered for oil...	2 50
July	3	Freight and cartage on oil...............	1 58
July	10	F H Penfield barrel lard oil...............	59 58
July	10	Henry Beckman bill rendered.............	8 50
Oct	2	Freight and cartage......................	1 04
Oct	16	F H Penfield one barrel lubricating oil.....	30 55
Dec	11	Eclipse Lubricating Oil Co...............	12 75
			——$ 268 19

SHOP TOOLS AND REPAIR OF TOOLS.

Jan 10	Paid W W Pierce & Co sundries................$	2	50
Jan 17	Humboldt Iron works repairs..............	7	94
Feb 3	M Shores filing saws......................		60
Feb 14	Humboldt Iron Works....................	13	20
Mar 1	F Armstrong sundries.....................	4	73
Mar 6	Humboldt Iron Works repairs............	1	92
Apr 11	" " " "	2	40
May 8	C Dinsmore et al..........................	12	09
June 5	Jarecki, Hayes & Co......................	6	79
July 3	Humboldt Iron Works repairs..............	11	33
Aug 2	M Shores filing saws.....................		30
Aug 7	Humboldt Iron Works repairs............	36	85
Aug 28	Cleveland & Co sundries..................	9	40
Oct 2	M Shores filing saws.....................		40
Oct 2	J Fogarty repairing tools.................	4	00
Oct 9	Stearns Manf Co repairing................	4	21
Oct 9	W W Pierce & Co.........................	1	00
Oct 9	Erie Hardware Co.........................	1	00
Oct 16	Stearns Manf Co.........................	7	12
Nov 27	J Fogarty repairing.......................	6	60
Dec 11	M Shores et al filing saws................		55
Dec 31	Jacob Simmons pump suckers.............	5	40

————$ 140 33

REPAIR OF DISTRIBUTING MAINS.

Mch 6	Paid John McConnell for labor.............$	1	13
Oct 30	M W Crawford sundries...................	1	00
Nov 27	Cleveland & Co castings..................	90	44
Dec 11	D R Beck sundries.......................	2	00
Dec 31	Labor as per Supt's pay rolls from Jan 1, '80 to Dec 31, 1880........................	421	46

————$ 516 03

PAVING AND STREET REPAIRS.

Feb 14	Paid J L Cosper............................$	21	60
Apr 24	Jacob Rastatter...........................	1	00
July 17	" "	5	50
Aug 7	" "	15	00
Aug 21	St. Peter's Cathedral.....................	3	25
Aug 21	Labor as per Supt's pay roll..............	1	39
Sept 18	Jacob Rastatter...........................	5	85
Nov 1	" "	1	62
Nov 20	" "	1	32

————$ 56 53

SHOP AND MISCELLANEOUS WORK.

Dec 21 Paid labor as per Supt's pay rolls et al...........$ 628 52

————$ 628 52

MAKING STREET CONNECTIONS.

Dec 31 Paid labor as per Supt's pay rolls..............$ 389 52

————$ 389 52

CARTAGE.

Jan		Paid Henry Burger et al......................	$	1 00
Jan		W H Messick.............................		50
Feb	3	Hugh Shields et al......................		2 39
Feb	3	Wm Little et al.........................		3 25
Mar	1	Wm Terry...............................		75
Apr	3	W H Messick et al.......................		2 29
May	8	Hugh Sheilds............................		1 00
July	3	E W Reed et al..........................		4 21
Aug	2	Wm Little et al.........................		1 50
Aug	2	I W Burke..............................		50
Nov	1	Hugh Shields............................		3 50
Nov	20	Patrick Doyle...........................		5 00
Dec	11	N P Wadsworth et al....................		2 75

$ 28 64

REPAIRS AND ALTERATIONS OF ENGINES AND BOILERS.

Jan	1	Paid John O Baker labor......................	$	5 00
Jan	10	W W Pierce & Co bill rendered...........		19 27
Jan	10	Constable Bros...........................		1 00
Jan	17	South Erie Iron Works grates..............		43 08
Jan	17	Noble & Hall sundries....................		400 03
Feb	2	R J Saltsman fire brick..................		6 30
Mar	1	Robert Henry labor......................		2 50
Mar	6	H P R Birkenbine services................		138 25
Mar	6	Joshua Follensbee inspection..............		10 00
Mar	20	Noble & Hall sundries....................		366 30
May	22	South Erie Iron Works grates.............		19 77
June	1	Pennsylvania Co..........................		1 93
June	1	Stearns Manf Co..........................		167 33
June	19	" " "		61 01
Aug	28	" " "		47 95
Oct	9	" " "		13 95
Oct	16	" " "		1 98
Dec	18	Saltsman & Austin.......................		11 50
Dec	24	Labor as per Supt's pay roll..............		22 54

$ 1,339 69

PLUMBER'S STOCK.

Feb	21	Paid Gibson & Price lead pipe..................		60 94
Mar	1	" " bal on pipe................		2 91
Mar	20	David Schlosser...........................		5 95
Apr	3	Lake Shore R R freight...................		2 16
Apr	24	National Tube Co pipe....................		111 70
May	8	Express charges on valves................		1 50
May	22	C E Gunnison & Co......................		5 59
June	1	Jarecki Manf Co..........................		6 64
June	5	Jarecki, Hays & Co.......................		65 01
July	3	Lake Shore Road freight..................		2 00
July	10	National Tube Co pipe....................		57 74
Oct	2	Freight and cartage......................		3 30
Oct	9	National Tube Co pipe....................		69 56
Oct	23	Jarecki Manf Co..........................		2 01
Nov	1	Freight et al on lead pipe................		1 04
Nov	13	Gibson & Price for lead pipe..............		41 50

$ 439 55

PRINTING AND ADVERTISING.

Jan	1	Paid F G Gorenflo	2	00
Jan	24	R B Brown	9	75
Feb	3	J M Glazier	4	00
Feb	7	A P Durlin & Son	31	00
Mar	27	R B Brown	8	25
Apr	10	F G Gorenflo	2	00
Apr	17	J R Willard	20	60
Apr	24	R B Brown	4	50
May	22	Daily Leuchtthrum	11	25
May	22	Erie Gazette	13	00
June	19	J R Willard	15	90
July	3	Evening Herald	43	50
July	10	A P Durlin & Son	6	75
Aug	2	R B Brown	3	00
Aug	2	J R Willard	6	75
Nov	13	" "	1	75
Nov	13	R B Brown	5	00
Dec	24	J R Willard	3	75

$ 192 75

WATER METERS

Dec	31	Paid Freight and cartage	2	07

$ 2 07

STOP VALVES.

May	22	Paid R D Wood & Co	11	03
July	10	Empire Line Freight	4	12
July	17	R D Wood & Co	161	85

$ 177 00

RAILROAD TRACK SCALES.

Nov	1	Paid Lake Shore R R for freight	7	05
Nov	6	John Mayerhoffer	15	00
Nov	27	Erie Lime & Cement Co	10	00
Dec	4	Buffalo Scale Co for scales	342	45
Dec	31	Labor as per Supt's pay rolls	190	77

$ 565 27

Total $37,817 88

RECAPITULATION.

Total receipts for the year 1880...................$38,413 47
Cash in Treasury January 1, 1880................... 1,187 62
Cash in Office January 1, 1880.....................   314 83
                                                   ————————$39,915 92

Paid on account of construction...................$18,413 47
Paid on account of general expenses................ 19,397 45
Cash in the Treasury January 1, 1881............... 1,709 14
Cash in the office January 1, 1881.................   395 86
                                                   ————————$39,915 92

EXHIBIT B.

TABLE showing the cost of Water to the Householder in twenty-six cities as compared with the cost in Erie, compiled from the official reports.

CITIES.	Family	P. Closet.	B. Tub.	W. Stand.	W. Tub.	Horse	Cow	Sprinkler.	Amount.
Erie.....................	$5 00	$3 00	$3 00	$ 50	$2 00	$2 00	$ 75	$3 00	$18 75
Lawrence, Mass.........	5 00	4 00	3 00	....	1 00	3 00	1 50	2 50	20 00
Lynn, Mass.............	6 00	5 00	5 00	2 00	2 00	5 00	1 50	3 00	29 50
Fitchburg, Mass.........	6 00	5 00	5 00	2 00	2 00	8 00	2 00	5 00	35 00
Newton, Mass...........	6 00	5 00	6 00	2 00	1 00	10 00	1 50	5 00	35 00
Cambridge, Mass........	7 00	6 00	6 00	2 50	2 50	5 00	2 00	10 00	41 00
Providence, R. I........	6 00	5 00	5 00	2 00	3 00	4 00	1 00	5 00	31 00
Taunton, Mass..........	5 00	5 00	3 00	2 00	2 00	4 00	1 50	5 00	27 50
Lowell, Mass...........	6 00	4 00	3 00	....	1 00	4 00	2 00	3 00	.23 00
Fall River, Mass........	5 00	5 00	5 00	2 50	2 50	4 00	1 00	6 00	31 00
Brooklyn, N. Y	16 00	2 00	....	....	?...	5 00	75	5 50	29 25
Albany, N. Y...........	18 00	2 00	....	....	....	3 00	....	8 00	31 00
Buffalo, N. Y...........	20 00	8 00	5 00	....	....	4 00	1 50	5 00	43 50
Niagara Falls	9 00	3 00	3 00	....	....	3 00	1 50	6 00	25 50
Detroit, Mich...........	7 00	3 00	2 00	1 25	2 00	4 00	1 00	3 00	23 25
Cincinnati, O...........	14 00	3 00	6 00	1 00	....	5 00	....	4 80	33 80
Cleveland, O............	10 00	5 00	2 50	....	....	2 50	....	1 50	21 50
Toledo, O..............	10 25	2 50	3 50	2 00	....	5 00	....	5 00	28 25
Chicago, Ill.............	19 00	5 00	3 00	....	....	4 00	....	3 00	34 00
Alton, Ill..............	7 00	5 00	8 00	....	....	8 00	2 00	9 00	39 00
Philadelphia, Pa........	8 75	2 00	3 00	1 00	1 00	3 00	....	9 00	27 75
Pittsburgh, Pa.........	27 77	17 55	10 85	8 25	....	8 25	2 05	6 87	71 50
Milwaukee, Wis........	11 50	5 00	3 00	2 00	....	4 00	1 00	8 00	34 50
Salem, Mass............	3 50	5 00	5 00	1 50	....	6 00	1 00	3 00	24 00
Louisville, Ky..........	10 00	3 00	4 00	....	1 00	5 00	1 00	7 50	31 50
Grand Rapids, Mich.....	8 00	4 50	3 75	2 00	3 00	2 50	1 00	2 00	26 75
Springfield, Mass........	8 00	4 00	4 00	....	....	4 00	2 00	5 00	27 00

EXHIBIT C.

TABLE comparing the cost of water in Erie to manufacturers with the cost in twenty-five other cities.

Stearns Manf. Co., Erie, use 3,746,500 gallons and annually pay. $	374 65
They would pay for same amount in Philadelphia................	621 91
They would pay for same amount in Boston, Mass..............	749 30
They would pay for same amount in Lawrence, Mass............	749 30
They would pay for same amount in Bangor, Me................	740 30
They would pay for same amount in St. Paul, Minn.............	936 75
They would pay for same amount in Lynn, Mass................	936 62
They would pay for same amount in Newark, N. J..............	449 21
They would pay for same amount in Schenectady, N. Y.........	1,123 95
They would pay for same amount in Hartford, Conn............	599 40
They would pay for same amount in Evansville, Ind............	532 27
They would pay for same amount in Cincinnati, O.............	561 97
They would pay for same amount in Louisville, Ky.............	1,086 48
They would pay for same amount in New Albany, Ind..........	561 67
They would pay for same amount in Milwaukee, Wis...........	561 67
They would pay for same amount in Worcester, Mass...........	561 67
They would pay for same amount in Fall River, Mass...........	1,086 48
They would pay for same amount in Syracuse, N. Y............	749 30
They would pay for same amount in Burlington, Iowa..........	749 30
They would pay for same amount in Titusville, Pa.............	468 31
They would pay for same amount in Grand Rapids, Mich........	749 30
They would pay for same amount in Portland, Me..............	1,086 48
They would pay for same amount in Binghamton, N. Y.........	936 75
They would pay for same amount in Toronto, Ont..............	674 37
They would pay for same amount in Burlington, Vt............	749 30
They would pay for same amount in Providence. R. I...........	949 29

NOTE.—The above is not the only advantage Erie's water supply offers to the manufacturer and the householder. Here the street connections, from the curb to the mains, are put in at the expense of the Department, whereas in most other cities the property has to pay for the whole expense. even to the tapping of mains.

EXHIBIT D.

TABLE showing the cost of coal, amount consumed, water pumped, and cost per million of gallons, etc., from the construction of the works to date.

Years	Tons coal consumed	Gallons of water pumped	Cost of coal	Cost per million raised to reservoir	Cost per million raised 1 foot	Gallons raised 1 foot by 1 lb of coal	Gallons raised to the reservoir by 1 lb of coal
1868	59,120	....	$ 309 61	$	$ cts.	....	......
1869	544,475	....	4,818 48	......	......	....	......
1870	1,064,500	246,648.960	5,159 10	......	......	....	......
1871	1,422,749	279,368,495	7,117 00	18,760	00.0801	39,417.3	168.45
1872	1,308,581	395,076,000	6,528 50	16,525	00.0760	35,324.6	150.96
1873	1,672,537	384,062,415	8,412 65	21,904	00.0940	26,865.5	114.81
1874	1,759,000	444,817,395	7,709 54	17,332	00.0715	29,585.9	126.44
1875	1,836,400	531,005,475	8,657 61	16,304	00.0696	23,829.4	145.57
1876	1,856,030	670,726,650	8,925 22	13,307	00.0568	41,279.1	180.68
1877	2,456,670	660,981,810	8,509 33	12,758	00.0545	31,763.2	135.74
1878	2,463,360	682,392,315	7,945 37	11,643	00.0498	31,938.6	136.49
1879	2,628,175	807,800,400	7,428 92	9,196	00.0393	35,961.1	153.68
1880	3,076,180	775,805.250	6,978 41	8,995	00.0384	29,507.4	126.01

EXHIBIT E.

STATEMENT, showing the Amount and Location of Distributing Mains laid by the Erie Water Department from May 1st. 1879, to Dec. 31st, 1880:

	1879.			1880.		
	Size	Feet	In.	Size	Feet	In.
State street	2	1085	9	4	475	
French street				4	209	
Holland street	4	385	5			
German street (to Fire Plug)	4	529		4	13	10
Parade street	6	668	9			
Division street	4	385	6			
Ash Lane	4	165	6			
Sassafras street (to Fire Plug)	4	17	4			
Myrtle street	4	889	5	4	308	5
Walnut street		489	5			
Cherry street	4	106	7	4	227	5
Front street	2	391	11			
East Third street				4	169	8
West Fourth street				6	255	
West Seventh street	4	641	7			
East Eighth street	4	2195				
East Ninth street (to Fire Plug. 1880)	4	1053	2	4	24	4
West Ninth street					102	9
West Tenth street				6	396	8
West Eleventh street	4	917				
East Twelfth street	6	745	6			
West Twelfth street (to Fire Plug)	4	2	2			
East Thirteenth street	4	362	2	4	1082	2
East Fourteenth street	4	467				
East Seventeenth street				4	692	
West Seventeenth street	4	946	9	4	728	
East Eighteenth street				6	104	9
East Twenty-first street (to Fire Plug)					9	10
West Twenty-first street	4	722	6			
East Twenty-second street	4	718	10			
West Twenty-second street	4	403	9			
East Twenty-third street,	4	736	6			
West Twenty-third street,	4	1064	5			
East Twenty-fifth street	4	1408	6			
West Twenty-fifth street	4	587	10			
P & E R R Co, private pipe bet. 15th & 16th sts.				4	705	
		18087	3		5504	2
		5504	2			
		23591	5			
Total		4$\frac{3471}{5280}$ Miles.				

EXHIBIT F.

STATEMENT, of the location, size, and number of Service Connections put in by the Erie Water Department from May 1st, 1879, to December 31st, 1880:

	1879.			1880.		
	Size	No.	Feet	Size	No.	Feet
State street	¾ in.	11	171- 1	¾ in.	15	460
State street	2	2	118- 7	3	1	53- 3
French street	¾	1	9- 5	¾	3	37-10
Holland street	¾	4	67	¾	2	33- 4
German street	¾	2	116	¾	6	77- 4
Parade street	¾	5	185	¾	7	84-10
Wallace street	¾	1	8- 2			
East Avenue	¾	1	7- 3			
Division street	¾	5	62- 7			
East Park	¾	1	3- 6			
West Park	¾	1	10- 8			
Peach street	¾	1	25- 1	¾	4	82- 4
Sassafras street	¾	8	114	¾	6	118
Myrtle street	¾	11	232- 6	¾	4	59- 4
Chestnut street	¾	7	124	¾	4	78- 4
Walnut Street	¾	6	154- 5	¾	1	25-10
Cherry street				1¼	1	8- 1
Cherry street	¾	1	6- 8	¾	3	25
Cherry street				2	1	8
Huron street	¾	7	152- 2			
Cascade street				¾	1	8- 7
Short street	¾	1	9- 6	¾	1	84
Plum street				¾	1	9- 3
West Second street				¾	1	13
West Third street	¾	1	24- 7			
East Third street	¾	2	28			
East Second street				¾	2	52- 8
East Fourth street	¾	1	5- 6	¾	1	9- 3
West Fourth street	¾	2	35- 7	¾	3	28
East Fifth street				¾	2	68- 9
West Fifth street	¾	2	31- 4	¾	1	26- 3
East Sixth street	¾	1	51	¾	1	24- 3
East Seventh street	¾	2	27- 7	¾	1	27- 4
West Seventh street	¾	7	118- 3	¾	1	28
East Eighth street	¾	17	271- 4	¾	2	18- 9
West Eighth street	¾	4	69- 8	¾	1	8- 3
East Ninth street	¾	11	187	¾	2	34- 4
West Ninth street				¾	1	7- 9
East Tenth street	¾	1	26	¾	2	99
West Tenth street	¾	2	97			
West Tenth street				1	1	39- 1
East Eleventh street	¾	1	25- 7			
West Eleventh street	¾	8	179	¾	5	108
East Twelfth street	¾	9	312	¾	1	7- 3
West Twelfth street				2	1	2-10
East Thirteenth street	¾	2	34-10	¾	2	18- 3

EXHIBIT F--Continued.

STATEMENT, of the location, size, and number of Service Connections put in by the Erie Water Department from May 1st. 1879, to December 31st, 1880 :

	1879.			1880.		
	Size	No.	Feet	Size	No.	Feet
East Fourteenth street	$\frac{3}{4}$ in.	4	33	$\frac{3}{4}$ in.	12	194- 2
West Fourteenth street					1	36-10
East Fifteenth street	$\frac{3}{4}$	1	43- 6	$\frac{3}{4}$	1	24- 3
West Sixteenth street					1	24- 6
East Seventeenth street	$\frac{3}{4}$	1	25-10	$\frac{3}{4}$	8	175- 7
West Seventeenth street	$\frac{3}{4}$	11	146	$\frac{3}{4}$	7	87- 7
East Eighteenth street	$\frac{3}{4}$	2	32- 8	$\frac{3}{4}$	6	93
West Eighteenth street	$\frac{3}{4}$	4	65- 5	$\frac{3}{4}$	8	155- 5
East Twenty-first street	$\frac{3}{4}$	2	153- 7			
West Twenty-first street	$\frac{3}{4}$	2	20	$\frac{3}{4}$	2	19- 3
East Twenty-second street	$\frac{3}{4}$	3	80			
West Twenty-second street	$\frac{3}{4}$	4	109- 5			
West Twenty-third street	$\frac{3}{4}$	4	110- 8	$\frac{3}{4}$	1	27
East Twenty-fifth street	$\frac{1}{2}$	1	8- 3	$\frac{3}{4}$	1	10- 7
West Twenty-fifth street	$\frac{3}{4}$	5	134	$\frac{3}{4}$	2	17- 7
West Twenty-sixth street				$\frac{3}{4}$	2	18- 8
West Turnpike street				$\frac{3}{4}$	1	44- 5
Total		200	4120		146	2892- 9
		146	2892- 9			

Total from May 1, 1879, to Dec. 31, 1880 ..... 346 7012- 9 ..... $11\frac{332}{339}$ miles

EXHIBIT G & H.

STATEMENT of the number and location of Fire Hydrants and Stop Valves put in by Erie Water Department from May 1, 1879, to December 31, 1880.

STOP VALVES—LOCATION.

	Size.	No.
On East 12th street, west line of Parade	6 in	1
On West 4th street, east line of Sassafras	6 in	1
On West 10th street, west of Chestnut	6 in	1
On Myrtle street, north line of 10th	4 in	1
On East 8th street, east line of Parade	4 in	1
On West 17th, west line of Peach	4 in	1
On Sassafras street, north line of 21st	4 in	1
On West 23d street, west line of Peach	4 in	1
On East 13th street, west line of German	4 in	1
On East 9th street, east line of Parade	4 in	1
On East 22d street, east line of Holland	4 in	1
On East 23d street, east line of Parade	4 in	1
On East 25th street, east line of Parade	4 in	1
On Holland street, south line of 2d	4 in	1
On Cherry street, south line of 12th	4 in	1
On Myrtle street, south line of 18th	4 in	1
On State street, south line of 21st	4 in	1
On East 17th street, south line of Holland	4 in	1
On West 17th street, east line of Cherry	4 in	1
On East 14th street, east line of Parade	4 in	1
		20

FIRE HYDRANTS.

	Size.	No.
On East 8th street, corner of Reed	4 in	1
On East 8th street, near corner of Wallace	4 in	1
On East 25th street, near corner of Wallace	4 in	1
On East 9th street, 312 feet west of German	4 in	1
On East 21st street near corner of French	4 in	1
		5

EXHIBIT I.

TABLE showing the comparative working capacity of the old and new boilers, cost of fuel, and amount of water pumped and cost per million gallons.

MONTH.	Engine 88 Revolutions	Engine 89 Revolutions	Totl Gallons.	Cost of Fuel.
January	188,335	98,840	46,723,875	$535 36
February...............	70,135	244,320	51,885,075	534 95
March	367,940	......	67,010,700	531 77
April.................,	160,650	147,930	50,915,700	516 99
Total 1st 4 months 1880.	787,060	487,090	210,235,350	$2,118 98
May	163,480	234,100	65,600,700	$487 45
June..................	64,420	328,245	64,789,725	491 13
July	201,600	245,010	73,690,650	642 72
August................	374,650	73,225	73,899,375	796 50
Total 2d 4 months 1880.	804,150	980,580	277,980,450	$2,417 80
September	294,176	101,240	65,243,640	$6,661 30
October...............	186,789	199,700	63,764,085	373 81
November.............	135,985	291,540	70,541,625	617 75
December.............,	248,290	221,470	77,510,400	783 94
Total 3d 4 months 1880.	865,240	833,950	277,059,750	$2,441 63
Total, 1880.........	2,456,450	2,301,620	765,275,550	$6,778 41

First four months—Old boilers—using bituminous slack, 210,235,350 gallons were pumped at a cost of $2,118.98, or $10⁰⁷⁹ per million gallons.

Last four months—New boilers—same kind of fuel, 277,059,750 gallons were pumped at a cost of 2,441.63, or $8⁵¹² per million. Per centage in favor of new boilers, 12½.

EXHIBIT K.

TABLE showing the relative cost of water in the city of Erie and the city of Oswego, N. Y., the latter being supplied by a private company.

FRONTAGE.	CITY OF OSWEGO. STORIES IN HEIGHT.					CITY OF ERIE
Family Use..............	1	1½	2	2½	3	
Under 25 feet...........	$ 7 50	$ 9 00	$12 00	$13 50	$15 00	
25 to 30 feet.............	10 50	13 00	15 00	16 50	18 00	
30 to 35 feet.............	13 50	16 00	18 00	19 50	21 00	$ 5 00
35 to 40 feet.............	16 50	19 00	21 00	22 50	24 00	
40 to 45 feet.............	21 00	24 00	25 50	27 00	28 50	
45 to 50 feet.............	25 50	28 00	30 00	31 50	33 00	
Bath Tubs...................................				$ 5 00		$ 3 00
Each Additional...........................				3 00		1 50
Water closets...............................				5 00		3 00
Each Additional				5 00		1 50
Barber Shops, 1st chair....................				8 00		4 00
Each Additional...........................				4 00		2 00
Blacksmith shops, 1st fire				10 00		5 00
Each Additional...........................				4 00		2 50
Machine Shops, 10 hands or less.............				10 00		3 00
Each Additional Hand......................				1 00		....
Offices....................................		$ 8 00		10 00		2 00
Printing Offices............................				10 00		5 00
Grocery Stores.............................				10 00		3 00 to 5 00
Drug Stores				15 00		3 00 to 5 00

METER RATES.

2,500 gallons 40 cts. per 1,000........	
2,500 gallons 5,000 35 cts. per 1,000 ..	A uniform rate of 10 cts per 1,000 gallons.
5,000 gallons 7,500 30 cts. per 1,000 ..	
7,500 gallons 10,000 22½ cts. per 1,000	
Over gallons 10,000 20 cts. per 1,000 .	

NOTE.—The rates in Oswego, running from $7.50 on a oone-story 25-foot front house to $33 for a three-story 50-foot front house, are for family use, except that the Oswego householder has the right to have permanent hand-basins, which in Erie are charged 50 cents each per year in addition to the $5.00.

Alumni, etc. Nos 15-16, 1881-82

مرکزی

OF THE BOARD OF

WATER COMMISSIONERS,

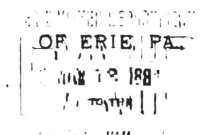

OF ERIE, PA.

MAY 12 1884

TO THE

MAYOR AND CITY COUNCILS,

FOR THE

YEAR ENDING DEC 31, 1883.

ERIE, PA.:
ERIE MORNING DISPATCH STEAM PRINTING HOUSE,
1884.

ANNUAL REPORT

OF THE BOARD OF

WATER COMMISSIONERS,

OF ERIE, PA., Water Commission

TO THE

MAYOR AND CITY COUNCILS,

FOR THE

YEAR ENDING DEC. 31, 1883.

––––––––

ERIE, PA.:
ERIE MORNING DISPATCH STEAM PRINTING HOUSE,
1884.

WATER COMMISSIONERS

The Water Commissioners are appointed by the Court of Common Pleas of Erie county for a term of three years, one member being named annually, in May.

EX-MEMBERS OF THE BOARD.

*WM. W. REED, 1867 to 1879.   *WM. L. SCOTT, 1867 to 1868.
*HENRY RAWLE, 1867 to 1872.   †JOHN C. SELDEN, 1868 to 1872.
JOHN GENSHEIMER, 1872 to 1878.   MATTHEW R. BARR, 1872 to 1877.
J. M. BRYANT, 1878 to 1881.

*Messrs. Scott, Rawle and Reed, the first Commissioners, were appointed respectively for terms of one, two and three years.

†Mr. Selden resigned before the expiration of his second term. Mr. Barr was substituted by the Board and afterward appointed by the Court.

PRESENT BOARD.

M. LIEBEL, 1877 to 1886.   G. W. F. SHERWIN, 1879 to 1885.
BENJAMIN WHITMAN, 1881 to 1884.

OFFICERS OF THE DEPARTMENT, JAN. 1st, 1884.

President of the Board—G. W. F. SHERWIN.
Secretary and Treasurer—B. F. SLOAN.
Assistant Secretary—GEO. C. GENSHEIMER.
Superintendent of Pipe Laying, &c.—WM. E. HILTON.
Inspectors—A. F. CRANE, F. W. KOEHLER.
Mechanical Engineer—F. A. ROTH.
Assistant Mechanical Engineers—GEO. R. MILLER, WM. O'LONE.
Firemen—JOHN KELLY, R. W. SIMONS, JOSEPH BURNS.
Keeper of Reservoir and Grounds—SAMUEL PFISTER.

OFFICE—No. 18 East Seventh street, bet. French and State streets.

OFFICE HOURS—From 7:30 A. M. to 5:45 P. M.

REGULAR MEETINGS OF THE BOARD—Every Saturday from 2 P. M. to 5 P. M.

ANNUAL REPORT.

To the Mayor and City Councils :—

GENTLEMEN :—In presenting their annual report the Board of Water Commissioners feel that they may properly call your attention and that of the citizens to the gratifying success that has attended the operations of the department during the past year, alike in the amount of revenue collected, the spirit of economy that has been infused into the expenses, and the progress that has been made in extending and improving the system. At a time when the tendency in many quarters seems to be too much in the direction of public extravagance and increased taxes, they have not only been able to effect a notable reduction in the cost of fuel for running the pumping works, but have lessened the general expense of maintenance and established systematic methods for carrying on the department, which cannot fail to bear good fruit for years to come. In bringing about these pleasing results, the Board have kept the theory steadily in mind that public affairs should be conducted on the same sound principles as private business. In the application of this maxim they have had, as a rule, the hearty co-operation of the employes of the department.

RECEIPTS FOR 1883.

The receipts of the department during the year 1883 have been $49,584.40, of which $48,269.89 have been from water rents and $1,314.51 from plumbing for hire and other sources. This is an increase over 1882, in the amount of water rents, of $4,451.16, being the largest gain for any one year since the second in which the works were operated.

ACTUAL EARNINGS.

As argued in previous reports, the rents collected (leaving the question of waste out of consideration) do not show the full earnings for the supply of water. The fire hydrants now number 196, all of which have been set, kept in working order, and supplied with water free of expense to the city treasury. In almost every other city in the Union an appropriation is made, or a credit allowed on this score, which enables the water departments to place their operations in the true light before the public. Throughout the state of Ohio, where the departments act under a general law, this sum is never less than $50 nor more than $100 per hydrant, while in the country at large the figures range from $25 to $150. After a comparison of the amounts allowed in some seventy-five cities, the Board, in 1881, adopted $45 as a fair rate for Erie, which will surely not be deemed excessive in view of the unusual height to which the water is pumped, the extraordinary pressure and the con-

sequent expense in maintaining the pipes and hydrants in efficient condition. Besides the fire protection service, the department furnishes
water, for which it receives no pay nor proper credit, to two large orna-
mental fountains in the parks, two public drinking fountains, six fire
engine houses, two public watering troughs, one police headquarters,
and for every occasion when the city tests its hose or steamers, flushes
its sewers or employs the public supply for other purposes. Estimating the value of the water used for these objects on the basis of former
reports, the actual earnings of the department during the past year
have been as follows :

Water rents received	$48,269.89
Plumbing and other sources	1,314.51
196 fire hydrants at $45 each	8,820.00
Fountains in the parks	2,000.00
Other public uses	2,000.00
Total	$62,404.40

RECEIPTS AND EXPENSES FROM THE BEGINNING.

The total receipts of the department from the commencement of its
operations to Dec. 31, 1883, including $675,955.10 of city bonds and ap-
propriations originally invested, have been $1,125,128.10, of which $812,-
666,65 have been expended for construction and $297,852.06 for mainten-
ance. It should be stated that these figures vary somewhat from the
last two reports, an unintentional error having been made in 1881 in
copying and arranging the items as they appeared upon the ledger.
The sum of $148,711.56, being the difference between the appropriations
voted by the city and the cost of construction, represents the surplus
earnings of the works from the date they were first operated to the close
of 1883.* This amount, which has been applied to the laying down of
mains, the putting in of connections, valves and hydrants, and the general features of extension, would have had to be furnished by taxation or otherwise, had it not been supplied from the earnings of
the department. The average annual cost of maintenance for the fifteen years the works have been in operation has been a little over
$19,850, or more than $2,300 in excess of the sum expended for that purpose during the year 1883.

EXPENSES FOR THE PAST YEAR.

The expense for construction for the past year has been $27,233.34,
and that for maintenance $17,308.52, exclusive of an item of extraordi-
nary expense of $230.59, leaving $7,545.87 as the amount of cash on hand.
This is a reduction over 1882 in the current expense of $204.59, and in
the current and extraordinary expense of $4,596.01, with nearly four
hundred more consumers and large additional demands in the line
of vigilance and efficiency. The cost of maintenance has apparently
been reduced to the lowest possible sum, and the probabilities are
that with "   'most economy in future, the tendency will be to add

*The   ȥ are exclusive of $7,545.87 cash in the treasury.

to the figures of 1883. Accepting the above table as a just statement of the actual earnings, the department has earned a profit during the year of $44,875.29, being over 6½ per cent. upon the original cost of the works.

STOCK LEFT OVER.

The construction account embraces $3,507.52 expended for pipe, hydrants, valves, &c., which the annual inventory shows to be still in stock in excess of the inventory taken at the close of 1882. This is ex plained by the fact that the Board availed themselves of an opportunity, early in the year, to buy pipe and other material at an unusually low price, by taking a large quantity at one time.

PUMPING ENGINE STATISTICS.

Your special attention is asked to the table giving the results of the pumping engine service, which shows that 815,939,685 gallons of water were raised during the year, to an average height of nearly 235 feet, at a cost for coal of $3,908.59. This is a decrease in the pumpage, as compared with the preceding year, of nearly 14,000,000 gallons, and in the coal bill of $1,447.34, though there has been a steady increase in the population of the city. The cost for coal in 1883, with more than 5,000 water takers, was less than one-half what it was in 1876, when the consumers numbered only a few over 2,700. These results have been brought about, firstly, by the changes in the boilers, rendering it practicable to burn a lower grade of coal ; secondly, by the shutting off of waste, through the measures elsewhere described ; and, thirdly, by the care and skill of the present employes at the pumping works.

INTERESTING FACTS.

The pumping engine records prove that each million of gallons of water has been raised one foot high for the incredibly small sum of nineteen mills for coal, and that the cost of coal for raising each million of gallons from the surface of the bay to the reservoir, a distance of about two miles and an average height of nearly 235 feet, has been but $4.66. Though the pumps are of an old and almost obsolete pattern, as regards their use for water works, it is doubtful whether any of the improved engines of the day can show better results, taking a whole year's duty, than are here given. The coal used was Mercer county bituminous slack and for the last four months it was not of the best grade. The highest daily pumpage of the year was in August, when a sudden hot spell came on, which led to such reckless sprinkling, that both pumps had to be run for eight days to keep up the supply. The two gas wells, which were resuscitated in 1882, have yielded, according to the experiments, about 2½ per cent. of the fuel used under the boilers, besides lighting the buildings and grounds. On the 12th of March the mechanical engineer added an improvement to the west pump which raised the temperature of the feed water from an average of 110 to 180 and the vacuum from 20 to 26 inches. A similar attachment was made to the east pump a month later, with equally satisfactory results.

THE FISHY TASTE AND SMELL.

Ever since the works started a disagreeably fishy taste and smell have been noticed each year, in May or June, according to the character of the weather. Investigation satisfied the Board that this is a peculiarity of the water of the lakes, which cannot be remedied. It appears regularly at the beginning of summer at every point on the lakes, and has long been observed and discussed by sailors. To avert its unpleasant features, as far as practicable, the mechanical engineer was instructed to stop pumping as soon as the fishy odor was detected, and let the city supply be drawn from the reservoir. By pursuing this course there was no complaint about the water, for the first time since the works went into operation. The fishy smell was first noticed on the 11th of June and the pumps were stopped until the 18th of the same month, when it disappeared. During the eight idle days the water in the reservoir dropped from 234 feet to 226 feet above the surface of the bay, or exactly a foot a day. To prevent misapprehension about the capacity of the reservoir, it needs to be added that the month of June is one in which the consumption of city water is the lightest.

DISTRIBUTING MAINS.

The amount of distributing pipe laid was the largest since the first year or two of the works, being 17,377 feet and 8 inches, or more than 3¼ miles. The city now contains a little over 44 miles of distributing mains, all of which, except about 20 miles which were put down from the proceeds of the city appropriations, has been paid for out of the surplus earnings of the department. As there are over 130 miles of streets within the corporation, it will be seen that only about one-third of its territorial limits has the advantage of the public water supply. The statement is suggestive of the future demands upon the resources of the department, if the city continues to grow and spread as it has in the last twenty years.

RULE RESPECTING EXTENSIONS.

The practice of the department has been, in laying down new distributing pipe of a less size than twelve inches, to require a petition from the property owners who want the water, and a written guarantee from them that the annual revenue from the extension shall equal one-tenth of the cost of a four inch pipe. The soundness of this plan having been questioned, the Board corresponded with the departments of Chicago, Buffalo, Detroit, Cleveland and Pittsburgh, to learn the custom there, and the replies received show conclusively that the rule in Erie is almost identical with that in the enterprising cities named. If anything, it is more liberal than usual, as the guarantee required in most cities is larger than here, while the expense of making the street connections is nearly invariably charged in other places to the property owner. With this knowledge, the Board have adopted a fixed rule on the subject, which will be strictly adhered to in future.

STREET CONNECTIONS.

The number of street connections put in during 1883 was 213, and the length of pipe used was 5,120 feet, or nearly a mile. There are now 3,387 street connections in the city, the total length of which is about 15 miles. One of the most unpleasant matters that the department has to deal with is the putting in of connections on paved streets. After the paving has been disturbed it is next to impossible to get it replaced in as good shape as before, and the street, in consequence, presents a rough and unsightly surface. The recently enacted city ordinance, which prohibits any street from being paved until the water, gas and sewer connections have been put in at suitable distances, will do much towards obviating the difficulties heretofore experienced.

STOP VALVES.

Forty-one stop valves—all four and six inch—have been added, being more than twice as many as in any former year. The total number is now 273, which is scarcely more than half of what are required. The system of distribution cannot be considered perfect until there is a sufficient number of stops to enable any square to be shut off without affecting the supply of the neighborhood. With the limited number of stop valves at present, there are portions of the city where fully one-fourth of a mile square of territory has to be deprived of the water while a hydrant is being set, a branch put in or a leak in the main repaired.

NUMBER OF WATER TAKERS.

The number of water takers has increased within the year from 4,687 to 5,079. The gain is not equal to that of 1882, but is quite up to the average before that. Estimating five persons to each family or establishment, about 25,000 are using the city water.

FIRE HYDRANTS.

Twenty-five new fire hydrants were set, of which 21 were public and 4 private, making 196 in all. Of the entire number, 169 are public and 27 private. All of the fire hydrants set for several years have been of the latest and best approved pattern. Though the new hydrants are twice the number of any previous year, the department, owing to the press of other work, did not succeed in getting in one-half as many as were desired and intended. There should be a hydrant, as early as possible, at every street intersection in the built up portions of the city. Most of the old hydrants, which are not only unsightly and unreliable, but cost a good deal to keep in order, should be replaced by new ones of an improved pattern. Each fire hydrant is examined and tested three times a year by a trained employee of the department, and it gives the Board much pleasure to know that during the present severe winter not one has failed to work when needed.

RAILROAD TRACK.

The railroad track on the east side of the pumping works has been

an almost constant source of expense, on account of the quicksand
formation of the high bluff at the foot of which it was built. After
every thaw or rain great bodies of mud would be deposited on the
track, rendering the employment of one or more laborers necessary, a
good share of the time for months, to keep it in condition for use.
The annual cost for that purpose has been from $150 to $200, with no
permanent advantage. As a remedy for the trouble, the Board decided
to grade and sod the bluff south of the track, which was done during
the closing months of the summer. The work was more difficult than
was anticipated, but if it accomplishes its aim, the annual saving will,
in a few years, make up for the expense, not to speak of the better appearance that has been given to the locality.

THE ROADWAY.

The roadway to the works, being cut through clay and quicksand,
containing numerous springs, has been almost impassable during a
good portion of each year, though large sums have been expended to
keep it in repair. As it has to be frequently used in hauling coal, heavy
castings, and the various supplies for the pumping department, and as it
is desirable that visitors should have easy access to the works, the importance of having the road in a condition to effectually answer its purpose must be apparent to all. This has been done by improving the
grade, putting in the necessary tiling and sewer pipe, and macadamiz-
ing the surface, making a solid, safe, and durable roadway. The cost
was considerable, but the results effected fully justify the expenditure.

IMPROVEMENT OF THE GROUNDS.

About the time the grading of the bluff was agreed upon, a communication was received, signed by a number of leading citizens and large
property owners, urging the general improvement of the grounds
around the pumping works. The press took the question up, and
every journal in the city warmly advocated the proposition. Sim-
ultaneously with this movement, Mr. Charles H. Strong offered to
donate to the department a lot at the foot of Chestnut street, adjoining the grounds under its control, upon the condition that it should
be included in any plan of improvement that might be adopted. With
such strong influences in behalf of the proposed measure and with an
apparently unanimous public sentiment, the Board could not well refuse
to take favorable action on the subject. The tract offered by Mr.
Strong was formally accepted, a comprehensive system of improvement was planned, and an effort has been made to combine good taste
with convenience and permanency. Some idea of the number of persons who visit the pumping works will be had when it is stated that
from the 1st of October, 1882, to the same date in 1883, two thousand
persons went up the stand-pipe alone, of whom three-fifths were
strangers from every part of the Union. The city owes it to itself that
a point of such extensive resort should be made and kept as attractive
as the means at command will allow.

THE RESERVOIR.

While such gratifying progress has been made in improving the works and their surroundings, the reservoir, which shares equally with the other in popular interest, has not been neglected. The gravel walks to the summit, which washed into gulleys whenever it rained have been replaced with brick, the flowers have been maintained in finer style than before, the magnificent vine has been carefully trained and the whole aspect of the premises has been changed for the better, much to the credit of the keeper and the delight of visitors.

MAINS AND CONNECTIONS LOWERED.

Great trouble has been caused in years past by the action of the city authorities in altering the grades of streets containing water mains and connections without notice to the department. In most cases the first knowledge of a change in the grades has reached the department through the complaints of citizens that their water connections were frozen, and that they had been put to much expense and inconvenience thereby. This annoyance to the people and the department will be cured by a faithful enforcement of the city ordinance lately enacted on the subject. The department has performed its part in the matter by lowering all mains and connections known to have been affected by the cutting down of the streets, to a uniform depth of five feet below the established surface. So far as its officers have any information, there is not now a public water pipe in the city that is not out of danger of frost.

EXCESSIVE SPRINKLING.

One of the most perplexing matters the department has to deal with is that of reckless and wasteful street sprinkling. The summer just past was cooler and more rainy than usual, but the few extremely hot days in August, referred to under the head of "Pumping Engine Statistics," furnished ample proof of the importance of checking the use of water for this purpose. Although the sprinkling rules are more liberal in Erie than in almost any other city in the Union, it has been found next to impossible, by mild means, to secure their enforcement. The emergency required an example to be made, and one of the most defiant law-breakers was arrested and fined. This had the desired effect during the balance of the season and gave evidence that it is only necessary to act firmly in order to carry out any law that is for the public advantage. If the department could have the co-operation of the police, as is the case nearly everywhere else, much good could be effected in this direction.

WASTE AND ITS PREVENTION.

The question of waste and the best means for its prevention have received much attention during the last two years. At the close of 1881

the Board were confronted with the startling fact that the pumping
record of the year showed the enormous quantity of 975,000,000 gallons to have been raised from the bay, an increase over 1880 of 200,000,-
000 gallons. This was at the rate of nearly 2,700,000 gallons per diem,
or about 90 gallons to each man, woman and child in the city, more
than the capacity of one pump, running incessantly day and night. A
proportionate increase for another year, or two at the most, meant an
absolute and immediate necessity for a new pump, an enlarged engine
room, additional boilers and a thirty-inch main from the works to the
reservoir, at a cost of not less than $150,000. To make the situation
worse, the city was up to its constitutional limit of debt, taxes were as
high as the property could well stand, and the revenues of the department were not more than sufficient to meet its current expenses and
the pressing demands for ordinary extension. After giving the subject
the most thorough study, the Board concluded that they would take
determined measures to reduce the wasteful use of water, which it was
palpable must be very great, before asking the tax-paying citizens to
impose extra burdens upon themselves for increasing the capacity of
the works. This effort has been persevered in with unceasing vigilance, and the results speak for themselves.

DEFECTIVE FIXTURES.

The first step was to find out the condition of the plumbing and fixtures in the city, and the manner, as nearly as could be, in which the people were in the habit of using the water. To this end two inspectors
were employed, who were instructed to visit every building into which
the city water had been introduced and make a record of the fixtures
and the general character of the plumbing. On their first round, from
October 1st to December 31st, 359 defective and leaky fixtures were reported. After seeing that they had been corrected, the inspectors
started on their second round. On this occasion, which was during
and after the coldest part of the winter of 1882-3, the number of leaky
fixtures was found to be 418, an increase of 59, showing, undoubtedly,
the effects of frost. The larger part of these would have been allowed
to run the year through, and the waste, which was quite extensive in
some cases, it is estimated, would have equalled one-tenth of the pumpage. All have been compelled to be put in order, and the Board are
waiting, with some curiosity, the result of the third inspection now in
progress. Besides looking after the defective fixtures, the inspectors
are required to give careful instruction in the use of the stops, see that
they are in easy working order, and show the people how to protect
their pipes against cold weather and use the water with the least annoyance and waste. It is a striking circumstance that they have
found the most negligence in the buildings of, and received the least
encouragement from, some of those who, by reason of their property
interests, should be most interested in keeping down the rate of taxation.

IMPERFECT PLUMBING.

The inspections developed the fact that much of the plumbing was so imperfect that it was not possible for the occupants of the premises to avoid letting their water run in winter to prevent freezing. It became essential, as a part of the scheme to check waste, that all plumbing of this nature should be corrected. No argument is needed to satisfy any thinking person that a party who lets his water run steadily two or three months in the year uses more than one in the same class whose plumbing does not require such a resort. Where the latter, who is not likely, from the circumstances of the case, to commit any gross violation of the rules, pays five dollars, a charge of ten to twenty dollars or more, according to the character of the use, should be made against the former. The Board found the remedy for the evil of faulty plumbing in the scale of annual rates, which allows a varying charge in numerous cases. All plumbing was ordered to be divided into first and second class, the latter to include premises where it was certain, from the lack of protection and the way in which the plumbing was done, that the water must either freeze or be allowed to run in winter. The charge for first-class plumbing was allowed to remain as before, while that for plumbing of the second class was doubled. The inspectors reported 328 premises as subject to the second class rate, and their owners were given abundant time to have the plumbing adjusted. This most of them did with considerable promptness and all but 33 places have been put back in the grade of first-class. Besides the regular inspections, the plumbers are obliged to report all frozen pipes that come to their notice during the winter, so that by the close of 1884, it is hoped there will be no plumbing in the city but what is either in good condition or properly rated.

In this connection it may be stated that the rule adopted in 1882, requiring all new plumbing to be inspected and approved before a supply of water is allowed to the premises, has worked fully up to the expectation of the Board. The effect has been to make the plumbers more careful, and not a single complaint has reached the Board of the work done in 1883, after it has received the approval of the inspectors.

METERS AND COUNTERS.

As a part of the same policy, the Board have continued to attach meters and counters to places using, or supposed to be using, large quantities of water, as fast as the means at their disposal would permit. Thirty-seven meters and four counters are now in use, and, in almost every instance, they have shown a far greater consumption of water than the premises had been previously charged for. In a number of cases the enormous flow that was developed was as much of a surprise to the officers of the department as to the consumers. A few parties have been inclined to complain of the increased charges to which they have been subjected on account of the meters, but it will not be seriously argued that if they use the quantity of water indicated they should not pay for it. In business dealings every man is expected to pay in proportion to the amount of any article he purchases. The only fair way in assessing water charges is to adhere to the common sense rules of business. In addition to the enlarged revenue the use of meters has tended materially to the diminution of waste.

SUMMARY OF RESULTS.

The net results of the measures adopted by the Department are as follows. They need no comment :

YEARS.	NUMBER OF WATER TAKERS.	NUMBER OF FIRE HYDRANTS.	PUMPAGE IN GALLONS.	WATER RENTS COLLECTED.	COAL BILL AT THE PUMP-ING WORKS.
1881	4,110	161	975,640,934	$40,385	$6,517
1882	4,687	171	829,759,260	43,818	5,355
1883	5,077	196	815,939,685	48,269	3,908

NEEDS OF THE FUTURE.

It must not be thought, however, from the success that has attended the efforts of the department to postpone the day for enlargement that the question is one that can be dismissed from further consideration. The city is growing rapidly, and, with the utmost care on the part of the department, in a few years the demand will exceed the limit at which it is safe to depend upon the present system. The Board renew their recommendations on this topic in the last three annual reports and trust they will not be lost sight of by the city authorities and the public. It will be much wiser to provide adequate facilities in advance of the actual need than to delay until a serious accident to one or both of the pumps or some other alarming emergency calls for hasty action.

In order that there may be no misunderstanding on this subject, the following recapitulation is given of the measures that are crowding more or less closely upon the attention of the department:

1st. The rebuilding of the east side of the main pier at the works, and the making of the necessary repairs and improvements to the inlet.

2d. The extension of the twelve-inch mains on Seventh and Twenty-first streets to Parade street, embracing a length of about one mile, in order to furnish a steady and ample supply to the east side of the city.

3d. The building of a coal house at the pumping works, so that from 500 to 1,000 tons of coal may be stored as a precaution against strikes and delays in transportation.

4th. A thirty-inch pumping main alongside the present twenty-inch main from the standpipe to Seventh street, to be eventually continued to the reservoir.

5th. The duplicating of the present power by the purchase of a
pump capable of raising 5,000,000 gallons per day. This must be accompanied by increased boiler capacity and will compel the erection
of a wing to the engine house.

These items, it must be remembered, are exclusive of the additiona
hydrants, stop valves, meters, &c., that are needed, as before suggested
and of the ordinary work of construction. Their cost is estimated at
not less than $150,000, and may even exceed that sum. The purpose
of the Board is to use the balance in the treasury to lay the twelve-
inch pipe on Seventh and Twenty-first streets during the ensuing summer, and, if the means will allow, to do such work as may be needed on
the piers and inlet. It must be clear to all who study the matter that there
will be abundant use for the surplus earnings of the department for years
to come, and it will only be by the strictest economy and the most fortunate chain of circumstances that an appeal to the Councils will be
averted for an appropriation to meet a portion of the expense. At
the utmost, it is not probable that the extra pump and larger pumping
main can be dispensed with more than a few years.

MAPS AND REPORTS.

The large map showing the location of the distributing mains, stop
valves and fire hydrants was completed early in the season, and with
the atlases of the street connections, has been posted to the end of the
year. To ascertain the location of any public pipe, valve or hydrant
is now only a matter of a moment. Daily, weekly or monthly re
ports, as the case may require, are made by the chiefs of the various
divisions, and every feature of the department's operations has been so
systematized that the Board may be said to have everything directly
under their own eyes.

PURITY OF THE WATER.

Your attention is called to the delay in turning the city sewage outside
of the harbor, the best methods of effecting which have been discussed
in previous reports. As the purity of the water they drink is essential
both to the health and comfort of the people, and there are grave
reasons for thinking that the bay is much polluted by the sewage,
no more time should be lost than is positively necessary in removing
the objectionable features that exist at present.

CONCLUSION.

The Board are aware that this report is unusually lengthy, but, as
the year has been a very important one, both in the measures adopted
and the results effected, it has seemed to be their duty to enter into a
fuller statement of the operations of the department than would otherwise be the case.

In concluding, they return thanks to the Mayor and Councils for their

co-operative action, to the newspapers for their readiness to print facts
of value to the taxpayers, and to the people for the alacrity with which
they have generally responded to the efforts in behalf of economy and
efficiency.

Respectfully submitted,

G. W. F. SHERWIN,
M. LIEBEL,
BENJAMIN WHITMAN,
Water Commissioners.

EXHIBIT A.

Receipts of the Erie Water Department for the Year Ending December 31st, 1883.

WATER RENTS.

First quarter—water rent—January....	$5,392 90		
" " " " February..	3,025 99		
" " " " March	2,290 39		
		$10,709 28	
Second quarter—water rent—April. ...	5,389 44		
" " " " May	3,783 94		
" " " " June............	2,857 54		
		12,030 92	
Third quarter—water rent—July............	5,271 40		
" " " " August.....	4,663 67		
" " " " September	2,512 65		
		12,447 72	
Fourth quarter—water rent—October.............	5,565 36		
" " " " November.............	4,154 08		
" " " " December..........	3,362 53	13,081 97	
Total from water rents.............			$48,269 89

OTHER SOURCES.

From plumbing and pipe laying.............	$1,169 99		
" material sold..............	115 33		
" fines and penalties.............	5 00		
" rebate on freight.............	24 19		
		1,314 51	1,314 51
Total from all sources.............			49,584 40
Add cash in office and bank Dec. 31, 1882.......			780 64
Total.............			$50,365 04

—CR.—

Deposited in city treasury, first quarter, January ...	$5,500 00		
" " " " " February..	2,500 00		
" " " " " March.......	2,500 00		
		$10,500 00	
Deposited in city treasury, second quarter, April....	5,000 00		
" " " " " May	3,500 00		
" " " " " June.....	3,500 00		
		12,000 00	
Deposited in city treasury, third quarter, July.........	5,000 00		
" " " " " August	5,000 00		
" " " " " Septem'er	3,200 00		
		13,200 00	
Deposited in city treasury, fourth quarter, October.	5,000 00		
" " " " " Nov'ber.	4,500 00		
" " " " " Decem'r	3,800 00	13,300 00	49,000 00
Balance in office and bank Dec. 31, 1883........			$1,365 04

EXHIBIT B.

Account of the Water Department with the City Treasury for the Year 1883.

1883.   —DR.—

Jan. 1	To balance as per last report	$ 1,993 86		
	To deposits from Jan. 1, to Dec. 31, 1883	49,000 00		
			$50,993 86	$50,993 86

—CR.—

Warrants drawn—first quarter—January	2,272 81		
" " " " February.	2,102 99		
" " " " March.	1,884 02		
		$6,209 82	
Warrants drawn—second quarter—April	2,252 42		
" " " " May	2,568 53		
" " " " June	3,968 66		
		8,789 61	
Warrants drawn—third quarter—July	7,111 55		
" " " " August	5,222 14		
" " " " September	6,278 23		
		18,611 92	
Warrants drawn—fourth quarter—October	4,969 72		
" " " " November	2,147 25		
" " " " December	4,034 18	11,151 15	44,762 50
Balance in treasury Dec. 31, 1883			$6,231 36

EXHIBIT C.

Expenditures for the Year 1883; also, from the Commencement of the Works to January 1st, 1883.

		FUEL AT WORKS.	FROM JAN. 1, 1883, TO DEC. 31, 1883.	1867 TO 1883.
Jan.	1	From commencement of works to Dec. 31, 1882.....		$99,639 40
	6	Paid E. W. Reed for 465,700 lbs. slack @ $1.75........	$407 49	
Feb.	10	" " 315,500 " " "	276 06	
Mar.	10	" " 274,350 " " "	240 06	
April	7	" " 644,500 " " "	563 94	
May	26	" " 208,050 " " "	177 67	
June	9	" " 360,650 " " $1.55........	279 50	
July	7	" " 306,600 " " "	237 62	
Aug.	4	" " 553,200 " " "	498 73	
Sept.	8	" " 419,550 " " "	325 15	
Oct.	13	" " 372,800 " " "	288 92	
Nov.	10	" " 457,770 " " "	354 77	
Dec.	8	" " 424,100 " " "	328 68	
		Total 4,797,770		$3,908 59

ON ACOUNT OF SALARIES.

Jan.	1	From commencement of works to Dec. 31, 1882.....		75,700 67
Dec.	31	Paid B. F. Sloan, secretary..........	$1,200 00	
		" Wm. E. Hilton, superintendent of pipe laying.	960 00	
		" A. F. Crane, inspector...............................	820 00	
		" Geo. C. Gensheimer, clerk	680 00	
		" John Holland, inspector.............................	581 00	
		" J. W. F. Sherwin, commissioner.......	875 00	
		" Michael Liebel, "	461 00	
		" Benjamin Whitman, "	653 00	
				6,230 00

POSTAGE.

Jan.	1	From commencement of works to Dec. 31, 1882.....		2,298 89
Dec.	31	Paid for envelopes and postal cards.......................	$152 11	
			152 11	

FIRE HYDRANTS.

Jan.	1	From commencement of works to Dec. 31, 1882		8,000 61
	20	Paid freight and cartage.................................	$ 4 53	
Aug.	11	" Empire Line, freight...............................	8 97	
Oct.	13	" Penn'a Co., "	10 00	
	27	" Empire Line, "	23 58	
Dec.	1	" B. F. Sloan, secretary, cash for cartage..	3 00	
	31	" labor, as per superintendent's pay roll...........	99 86	
	31	" D. R. Wood & Co. for 50 hydrants.................	1,996 00	
				2,145 94

CARE AND REPAIR OF HYDRANTS.

May	14	Paid Stearns Manufacturing Co., sundries........	$ 1 38	
Oct.	13	" Humboldt Iron Works, sundries	11 65	
Dec.	31	" John Meyerhoffer, rent, labor, &c...............	21 00	
	31	" labor, as per superintendent's pay roll...........	33 75	
				67 78

ENGINEERS AND FIREMEN.

Jan.	1	From commencement of works to Dec. 31, 1882.....		53,834 50
Dec.	31	Paid F. A. Roth, mechanical engineer........	$996 67	
	31	" Geo. R. Miller, assistant mechanical engineer,	808 40	
	31	" Wm. O'Lone, " " "	820 00	
	31	" John Kelley, fireman.................................	602 50	
	31	" R. W. Simons, "	552 75	
	31	" Jos. Burns, "	550 50	
	31	" extra firemen.................................	92 30	
			4,433 12	

DISTRIBUTING MAINS.

Jan.	1	From commencement of works to Dec. 31, 1882		295,056 51
	20	Paid L. Little, distributing pipe.............................	$3 41	
		Carried forward.......................................	$3 41	$16,937 54	$534,530 58

Date		Description	Amount	From Jan. 1, 1888, to Dec. 31, 1888	1867 to 1888
		Brought forward....................................	$ 3 41	$16,937 54	$534,580 58
Jan.	27	Paid labor, distributing pipe, supt's pay roll..........	2 35		
Feb.	3	" B. F. Sloan, secretary, for sundries..............	1 50		
	10	" Erie Gas Co., for coke.............................	1 12		
Mar.	10	" Penn'a Co., switching cars	6 00		
May	5	" I. H. Burke, distributing pipe...................	4 49		
June	16	" labor, distributing pipe, supt's pay roll........	2 60		
	16	" Lake Shore R. R. Co., freight.................	24 21		
	16	" I. H. Burke, distributing pipe	6 10		
	16	" Lake Shore R. R. Co., freight.................	25 02		
	16	" I. H. Burke, distributing pipe.................	11 22		
	23	" labor, distributing pipe, supt's pay roll.........	3 06		
	23	" W. E. Hilton, expenses to Buffalo, inspecting pipe....................................	18 00		
	30	" labor, distributing pipe, supt's pay roll..........	5 90		
	30	" I. H. Burke, distributing pipe..................	21 00		
July	7	" I. H. Burke, et. al., distributing pipe............	13 74		
	14	" H. P. M. Birkenbine, inspecting pipe	212 25		
	21	" labor, distributing pipe, supt's pay roll........	13 45		
	28	" " " " "	2 14		
	28	" Arthur Conway, for old rope..................	2 60		
	28	" labor, distributing pipe, supt's pay roll........	9 45		
	28	" L. S. & M. S. Railway, for freight..............	97 49		
	28	" I. H. Burke, distributing pipe.................	3 00		
Aug.	4	" labor, distributing pipe, supt's pay roll.........	4 57		
	11	" W. E. Hilton, expenses, inspecting pipe in Buffalo...............................	22 50		
	11	" Erie Gas Co., for coke..........................	8 24		
	25	" Jas. P. Daily, labor	10 00		
Sept.	1	" L. S. & M. S. Railway, freight..................	3 24		
	8	" I. H. Burke, distributing pipe..................	4 83		
	8	" B. F. Sloan, sec'y, cash expended for sundries,	3 00		
	15	" Althof & Sons, lumber	6 63		
	22	" L. S. & M. S. Railway Co., freight.............	6 18		
	29	" labor, distributing pipe, supt's pay roll.....	2 65		
	29	" Martin Quigley, for old rope	13 84		
	29	" I. H. Burke, distributing pipe..................	2 73		
Oct.	6	" B. F. Sloan, sec'y, cash expended for sundries,	1 20		
	6	" I. H. Burke, distributing pipe..................	9 07		
	6	" labor, distributing pipe, supt's pay roll	2 63		
	20	" I. H. Burke, distributing pipe.................	5 00		
	27	" labor, distributing pipe, supt's pay roll........	3 16		
Nov.	3	" " " " "	3 63		
	10	" H. Burke, distributing pipe....................	1 87		
	17	" labor, distributing pipe, supt's pay roll........	1 39		
Dec.	13	" " " " "	2 44		
	13	" B. F. Sloan, sec'y, cash expended for sundries,	2 75		
	15	" Mrs. P. Hays, damages......................	4 00		
	15	" Lake Shore Foundry, for special castings.....	26 42		
	15	" L. S. & M. S. Railway Co., freight.............	3 93		
	15	" labor, distributing pipe, supt's pay roll........	1 40		
	15	" Adolph Brugger, for wooden plugs...........	9 25		
	31	" Geo. B. Hays, Buffalo, contract for pipe........	4,711 00		
	31	" Mellert Manufacturing Co., Reading, contract for pipe	4,939 97		
	31	" labor, superintendent's pay roll, laying pipe...	2,709 82		
	31	" lead	753 09		
				$18,771 15	

STOP VALVES AND BOXES AND COVERS.

Date		Description	Amount	From Jan. 1, 1888, to Dec. 31, 1888	1867 to 1888
Jan.	1				13,296 84
	6		....	$ 38 70		
Feb.	10	" R. D. Wood & Co., for valves.................	230 10		
	10	" Empire Line, freight........................	5 24		
	10	" Schlosser & Feelheim, for lumber..............	6 85		
May	12	" Stearns Manufacturing Co., for castings	51 09		
June	9	" Schlosser & Feelheim, for lumber..............	9 44		
July	14	" R. D. Wood & Co., for valves..................	216 08		
	21	" Penn'a Co., freight.	4 64		
Aug.	4	" Humboldt Iron Works, castings	30 04		
	11	" Schlosser & Feelheim, for lumber............	12 44		
Sept.	15	" Humboldt Iron Works, castings	109 95		
	15	" Penn'a Co., freight..........................	6 24		
	22	" R. D. Wood & Co., valves...................	311 33		
Oct.	13	" Humboldt Iron Works, castings.............	42 39		
		Carried forward...................................	$1,074 53	$30,708 69	$547,827 42

			FROM JAN. 1, 1883, TO DEC. 31, 1883.		1867 TO 1883.
		Brought forward...................................	$1,074 53	$30,708 69	$547,827 42
Oct.	13	Paid Schlosser & Feelheim, lumber........	4 88		
	13	" Penn'a Co., freight....................	5 31		
	20	" R. D. Wood & Co., valves.............	288 27		
	27	" Empire Line, freight.	7 50		
Nov.	3	" Humboldt Iron Works, castings..	36 75		
Dec.	15	" " " "	41 31		
	15	" Schlosser & Feelheim, lumber	8 35		
				1,466 85	

REPAIRS OF ENGINES AND BOILERS.

Jan.	1	From commencement of works to Dec. 31, 1882......	....	....	22,916 28
	6	Paid Saltsman & Austin, for fire-clay..............	$ 2 25		
	6	" South Erie Iron Works, for grates, fire fronts,	108 60		
	20	" Roger McDonough, for labor	7 50		
Feb.	3	" Stearns Manufacturing Co., sundries.............	62 17		
	3	" Larry Cummins, et. al., labor.................	18 75		
	24	" Stearns Manufacturing Co., sundries	7 35		
	24	" Alfred Keenem, et. al., labor................	9 00		
Mar.	10	" Stearns Manufacturing Co., sundries	56 95		
	10	" D. C. Weller, sundries	1 48		
	17	" D. Murphy, mason work	28 00		
	31	" Saltsman & Austin, fire-brick, &c	19 25		
April	7	" Roger McDonough, labor................	6 75		
	14	" E. A. Steubgen, insurance	2 80		
	14	" Stearns Manufacturing Co., sundries	8 59		
	21	" D. Murphy, mason work.................	17 50		
	28	" Saltsman & Austin, fire-brick, &c.............	19 25		
May	12	" Stearns Manufacturing Co., sundries.............	48 96		
June	2	" D. Murphy, et. al., mason work, &c...........	22 13		
	30	" labor, L. H. Couse's pay roll	1 50		
July	14	" Humboldt Iron Works, sundries	71 67		
	14	" Saltsman & Austin, fire-clay	3 55		
	28	" Jarecki, Hayes & Co., sundries.............	20 31		
Aug.	4	" Humboldt Iron Works, sundries.............	66 24		
Sept.	1	" Riblet Bros., sundries.................	8 05		
	7	" B. F. Sloan, secretary cash expended as per voucher.........	1 50		
	8	" Humboldt Iron Works, sundries...............	57 15		
Oct.	3	" " " "	9 21		
Nov.	3	" " " "	13 13		
	17	" W. W. Reed, bill for stone.............	16 00		
Dec.	15	" Stearns Manufacturing Co., et. al.............	4 01		
	15	" Humboldt Iron Works, sundries.................	73 45		
				793 05	

FOR NEW VALVES.

Dec.	15	Paid Humboldt Iron Works.................	$220 54		
				220 54	

BUILDINGS, GROUNDS AND STAND PIPE.

Jan.	1	From commencement of works to Dec. 31, 1882......	....	....	62,628 00
	20	" Beckman & Williams, for grass seed..	$ 75		
Feb.	3	" B. F. Sloan, secretary, cash expended as per voucher.........	75		
	24				
Mar.	17	" Roger McDonough, et. al., labor....................	9 75		
April	7	" " " "	15 75		
	7	" " " "	10 50		
	7	" Constable Bros., et. al., sundries............	6 30		
	7	" Schlaudecker Bros., drain pipe	3 00		
	28	" E. A. Steubgen, insurance................	40 00		
May	5	" John O. Baker, et. al., labor...............	69 22		
	12	" James Kelley and M. Carroll, labor.	56 63		
	19	" Thos. Gooley, et. al., labor............	25 50		
June	2	" N. Murphy, contract price for new roof..........	136 92		
	9	" John Kelly, painting	50 00		
	16	" Martin Carroll, labor................	17 25		
July	7	" C. Kessler, sundries	2 00		
	14	" B. F. Sloan, secretary, cash expended	1 40		
	28	" Constable Bros., bill rendered............	9 83		
Aug.	4	" labor, L. H. Couse's pay roll............	8 83		
	4	" "	7 50		
	11	" J. C. Hilton, recording deed................	2 35		
Sept.	1	" labor, L. H. Couse's pay roll............	16 81		
	1	" J. O. Baker, labor................	6 62		
	8	" B. F. Sloan, secretary, paid pay roll, Aug. 25..	140 03		
	8	" labor, as per superintendent's pay roll..........	1 18		
		Carried forward...................................	$618 82	$33,189 13	$633,371 70

			FROM JAN. 1, 1883, TO DEC. 31, 1883.		1867 TO 1883.
		Brought forward...............................	$538 82	$33,189 13	$633,371 70
Sept.	8	Paid Parsons & Boyer, sundries...........................	5 00		
	8	" Constable Bros., sundries...................	3 11		
	8	" B. F. Sloan, secretary, pay roll, Sept. 1........	202 33		
	15	" W. F. Nick, for paints and oils...................	62 58		
	15	" South Erie Iron Works, gas posts............	22 00		
	22	" B. F. Sloan, secretary, pay roll, Sept. 15........	25 80		
	22	" labor, superintendent's pay roll...............	2 00		
	29	" B. F. Sloan, secretary, pay roll, Sept. 22.........	18 04		
	29	" C. H. Walbridge, et. al., lumber, labor, &c......	146 44		
Oct.	6	" Wm. Reifle, bill for posts........................	7 87		
	6	" Selden & Goodrich, brick..................	31 50		
	6	" Carroll Bros., et. al., lumber, &c.............	21 30		
	13	" Larry Cummins, et. al., labor...................	15 75		
	27	" Roger McDonough, et. al., labor..............	12 75		
Nov.	3	" Constable Bros., bill for labor and material.....	13 59		
	3	" Erie Car Works, lumber	4 05		
	17	" Roger McDonough, labor......................	6 00		
	24	" H. G. Fink, Carroll Bros., et. al	16 70		
Dec.	1	" B. F. Sloan, secretary, cash expended for sundries..................................	5 00		
	1	" Phillip Osborne, for trees and setting	25 29		
	1	" Roger McDonough, et. al., labor.............	16 05	1,302 02	
		STAND PIPE.			
Jan.	6	Paid J. W. Stewart, for sand........................	$ 1 75		
	20	" Beckman & Williams, sundries......................	13 12		
	27	" Wm. F. Nick, paints, oils, &c.................	3 68		
Feb.	10	" C. Kessler, sundries...............................	4 43		
	17	" Constable Bros., sundries......................	1 55		
Mar.	20	" D. C. Weller, sundries..........................	8 25		
May	12	" Erie Lime and Cement Co.....................	1 75	24 53	
		CARE AND MAINTENANCE OF RESERVOIR AND KEEPER'S HOUSE.			
Jan.	1	From commencement of works to Dec. 31, 1882.....			6,118 92
	6	Paid R. J. Saltsman, for fuel........................	$ 6 00		
April	14	" E. A. Steubgen, insurance......................	11 20		
May	12	" Geo. Carroll & Bro., lumber..................	2 70		
	12	" Erie Hardware Co., sundries	1 20		
	26	" Schneider Bros., et. al., sundries......	2 04		
June	9	" Wm. Brewster, for plants	10 00		
Aug.	4	" W. W. Pierce & Co., bill......................	75		
	11	" H. C. Dunn, for brick.......................	188 60		
	11	" F. P. Keller, for laying pavement.	36 80		
	11	" Erie Cemetery Co., for use of roller..	1 57		
Dec.	29	" R. J. Saltsman, for fuel.......................	6 10		
	29	" Titus Berst, care of plants	4 00		
	31	" B. F. Sloan, secretary, cash expended as per vouchers..............................	12 38		
	31	" labor, as per superintendent's pay roll	39 18		
	31	" Samuel Phister salary for the year ..	300 00	572 44	
		ENGINEER'S SMALL STORES.			
Jan.	1	From commencement of works to Dec. 31, 1882.....			946 88
Feb.	10	Paid C. Kessler, sundries........................	$ 6 74		
Mar.	3	" W. W. Pierce & Co., sundries.....................	40		
	10	" D. C. Weller, "	2 48		
	17	" Erie Ice Co., bill for 1882......................	36 00		
May	5	" J. W Swalley, soap........................	5 00		
	5	" James Gaffney, sundries.....................	12 30		
June	9	" Parsons & Boyer, "	1 56		
	16	" C. Kessler, "	3 26		
Sept.	22	" " "	2 25		
Oct.	6	" D. C. Weller, "	4 62		
	13	" W. W. Pierce & Co., "	5 40		
	27	" Swalley & Warfel, soap..	2 50		
Dec.	1	" Samuel Merrett, for sundries.	1 50		
	15	" Erie Ice Co., bill for 1883...	22 00		
	31	" B. F Sloan, secretary cash expended......... .	2 74	108 75	
		PRINTING AND ADVERTISING.			
Jan.	1	From commencement of works to Dec. 1, 1882			2,718 72
Dec.	31	Paid Erie Herald Printing Co. annual report &c...	$133 40		
		Carried forward	$133 40	$35,206 87	$643,156 22

			FROM JAN. 1, 1883, TO DEC. 31, 1883.		1867 TO 1883.
		Brought forward	$153 40	$25,206 87	$648,156 22
Dec.	31	Paid Erie Leuchtthurm, sundry bills................	21 50		
	31	" Erie Observer, "	31 90		
	31	" Erie Dispatch, "	24 05		
	31	" A. P. Durlin & Son, bill rendered	18 00		
				228 85	
		SUPERINTENDENT'S SMALL STORES.			
					336 96
	27	Paid H. C. Liddell, for wood......	$ 2 10		
Mar.	3	" W. W. Pierce & Co., sundries......	2 50		
Dec.	31	" G. W. Goodrich, sundry bills for oil.	11 75		
	31	" B. F. Sloan, secretary, cash expended as per vouchers	10 01		
				26 36	
		ENGINE ROOM FURNITURE.			
Jan.	1	From commencement of works to Dec. 31, 1882.....	....	....	543 51
	13	Paid W. W. Pierce & Co., sundries	$ 4 00		
Mar.	17	" Parsons & Boyer, et. al., sundries...........	4 95		
May	26	" Erie Rubber Works, for hose.................	12 95		
	26	" J. Fogerty, sundries....................	4 00		
June	9	" Parsons & Boyer, "	11 15		
July	14	" L. Koster, "	14 16		
	28	" Jarecki, Hayes & Co., sundries	7 90		
Aug.	4	" W. W. Pierce & Co., ...	3 70		
Sept.	1	" B. F. Sloan, secretary, cash expended	1 40		
	8	" J. Fogerty, et. al., sundries............	6 44		
	29	" Martin Quigley, et. al., sundries.................	9 00		
Oct.	6	" D. C. Weller, bill	11 95		
	13	" Humboldt Iron Works	1 48		
				93 08	
		OFFICE FURNITURE, RENT AND EXPENSES.			
Jan.	1	From commencement of works to Dec. 31, 1882.....	....	....	9,278 31
	20	Paid Baas & Althof, for railing...................	$ 13 50		
	27	" Wm. Dinkey, altering counter	11 61		
Feb.	10	" Jarecki Manufacturing Co	26 00		
	10	" Erie Gas Co	7 88		
Mar.	3	" W W. Pierce & Co., sundries	75		
	17	" Erie Ice Co., bill rendered	9 00		
	17	" Wm. Baumgartner, et. al., stamp, &c.	6 95		
April	7	" Dr. P. Hall, bill for glass................	8 00		
	14	" E. A. Steubgen, insurance	8 00		
	14	" T. J. Sevin & Son, sundries	3 00		
May	12	" Jarecki Manufacturing Co., sundries .	2 50		
June	9	" W. J. Butler, sundries	2 60		
July	21	" T. J. Sevin & Son, et. al., sundries	4 90		
Aug.	4	" Erie Dispatch, bill rendered	5 65		
	11	" Erie Gas Co	11 08		
	25	" Baas & Althof, railing for counters.. .	14 68		
Sept.	15	" Wm. Dinkey, new desk	51 38		
	22	" Ross & Williams, painting..................	2 96		
Oct.	27	" Wm. H. Luce, for chair, ...	3 50		
Dec.	1	" Roger McDonough, et. al., labor	6 50		
	29	" Titus Berst, sundries................	3 00		
	29	" Wm. Ensworth, labor..........	4 50		
	31	" American District Telegraph Co	78 00		
	31	" E. W. Reed, fuel	80 75		
	31	" B. F. Sloan, secretary, cash expended as per vouchers	70 31		
	31	" O. L. Elliott, rent........	250 00		
				686 95	
		BOOKS AND STATIONERY			
Jan.	1	From commencement of works to Dec. 31, 1882.....	....	....	1,073 16
Dec.	31	Paid Ashby & Vincent, bills rendered...	$ 52 90		
	31	" Erie Herald Printing Co., bills rendered...	10 75		
	31	" W. J. Sell, bills rendered..............	2 75		
	31	" B. F. Sloan, secretary, cash expended	2 75		
				69 15	
		WASTE AND PACKING.			
Jan.	1	From commencement of works to Dec. 31, 1882	....	....	1,541 76
Mar.	10	Paid M. E. Flannigan, packing	$ 25 2		
Dec.	31	" Parsons & Faber, "	140 58	....	
		Carried forward...	$163 80	$26,311 26	$655,929 92

			FROM JAN. 1, 1883, TO DEC 31, 1883.		1867 TO 1883.
		Brought forward...	$165 80	$36,311 26	$655,929 92
Dec	31	Paid D. C. Weller, packing..............................	28 90		
	31	" C. Kessler, for waste...................................	57 85		
				252 53	
		CARTAGE.			
Jan	1	From commencement of works to Dec 31, 1882	....	....	348 31
Oct.	13	Paid Lafayette Little......	$ 3 50		
Dec.	31	" B. F. Sloan, secretary, as per vouchers.............	18 35		
				21 85	
		SHOP TOOLS AND REPAIRS.			
Jan	1	From commencement of works to Dec. 31, 1882.....	....	....	2,177 58
Feb.	12	Paid Stearns Manufacturing Co	$11 84		
Mar.	10	" " "	6 96		
April	21	" E. A. Steubgen, insurance.................	18 40		
May	12	" Erie Hardware Co., sundries.........	4 49		
	12	" Stearns Manufacturing Co.. repairs...............	5 99		
	26	" Schneider Bros., et. al., "	5 97		
Sept.	15	" Henry Mayer, for pump, &c	12 18		
Oct.	27	" Union Water Meter Co	6 25		
Dec.	29	" C. E. Junnison & Co., leather...............	5 47		
	31	" Humboldt Iron Works	80 42		
	31	" B. F. Sloan, secretary, cash expended as per vouchers......	6 34		
				164 31	
		WATER METERS.			
Jan.	1	From commencement of works to Dec. 31, 1882 ..	....	....	5,443 34
Feb.	3	Paid Stearns Manufacturing Co. sundries..............	$ 3 24		
	10	" Schlosser & Feelheim, lumber...........	16 12		
June	16	" " "	13 90		
Sept.	29	" National Meter Co...... ...	201 25		
Oct.	13	" Schlosser & Feelheim, lumber......................	3 23		
	20	" H. H. Thorp Manufacturing Co	32 40		
Dec.	29	" National Meter Co	76 00		
	31	" B. F. Sloan, secretary, cash expended as per vouchers......	3 93		
	31	" labor, as per superintendent's pay roll	118 43		
				468 50	
		INTEREST AND EXCHANGE.			
Jan.	1	From commencement of works to Dec. 31, 1882.....	....	....	11,019 80
Dec.	31	Paid Second National Bank, for exchange..............	$11 67		
				11 67	
		PLUMBING FOR HIRE.			
Jan.	1	From commencement of works to Dec. 31, 1882.....	....	....	2,533 66
Dec.	31	Paid labor, as per superintendent's pay rolls..........	$165 58		
				165 58	
		SHOP AND MISCELLANEOUS WORK.			
Jan.	1	From commencement of works to Dec. 31, 1882......	....	....	7,176 08
Dec.	31	Paid labor, as per superintendent's pay rolls..........	$393 10		
				393 10	
		WATER RENTS RETURNED.			
April	28	Paid M. Hartleb, for over charges	$52 50		
				52 50	
		INLET PIERS.			
Jan.	1	From commencement of works to Dec. 31, 1882......	....	....	31,569 69
	3	Paid Larry Cummins, for labor	$ 6 75		
	13	" W. W. Pierce & Co., sundries.........	23 70		
	20	" Wm. Ensworth labor.............................	6 00		
April	15	" A. Conway, for iron............................	13 12		
Oct	13	" Humboldt Iron Works	14 00		
Dec.	31	" John O. Baker, several bills for labor	93 27		
	31	" C. H. Walbridge for lumber	92 42		
	31	" B.F. Sloan, secretary, cash expended as per voucher....................................	1 50		
				250 31	
		REPAIRS OF DISTRIBUTING MAINS.			
Jan.	1	From commencement of works to Dec. 32, 1882......	....	....	9,470 55
Dec.	31	Paid labor, as per superintendent's pay rolls	$387 33	387 33	
		Carried forward..	....	$38,478 94	$725,668 93

			FROM JAN. 1, 1883, TO DEC. 31, 1883.	1867 TO 1883.
		Brought forward.............	.... $38,478 94	$725,668 93

STREET CONNECTIONS.

Jan.	1	From commencement of works to Dec. 31, 1882.....			33,214 72
Dec.	31	Paid labor, as per superintendent's pay rolls..........	697 44		
	31	" Jarecki Manufacturing Co., sundries...............	423 28		
	31	" Jarecki, Hayes & Co.. "	304 40		
	31	" Gibson & Price, et. al., lead pipe, &c..............	127 57		
				1,552 69	

ON ACCOUNT OF SERVICE PIPE.

Jan.	1	From commencement of works to Dec. 31, 1882.....			10,979 35
Dec.	31	Paid National Tube Works, et. al...........................	$423 42		
				423 42	

ON ACCOUNT OF PAVING AND STREET REPAIRS.

Jan.	1	From commencement of works to Dec. 31, 1882.....			1,296 31
Sept.	8	Paid Saltsman & Austin, sundries......	$157 15		
	29	" F. P. Keller, laying pavement	12 50		
Oct.	6	" J. C. Selden, for brick	45 00		
	13	" Humboldt Iron Works, castings	6 36		
Dec.	1	" Roger McDonough, et. al., labor.....................	4 25		
	15	" Schlosser & Feelheim, lumber.....................	1 00		
	29	" St. Peter's Cathedral, for stone	25 06		
Dec.	31	" Jacob Rastatter, sundry bills for repairs.........	145 36		
	31	" B. F. Sloan, secretary, labor, as per pay rolls..	44 50		
				441 12	

GAS WELLS AND CARE.

Jan.	1	From commencement of works to Dec. 31 1882.....			7,996 15
	6	Paid Fred. Diehl, seed bag...........................	$ 4 50		
	20	" Beckman & Williams, rope, &c....................	50 02		
	27	" Patterson & Hayes, et al., sundries............. .	5 78		
Feb	10	" Jarecki Manufacturing Co., "	4 40		
May	12	" Carroll Bros., lumber	29 32		
	26	" N. Murphy, sundries..........	75		
Dec.	31	" L. Cummins, et. al., labor................	57 67		
				152 44	

LEGAL COSTS AND COUNSEL FEES.

Jan.	2	From commencement of works to Dec. 31, 1882			1,222 38
Dec.	31	Paid J. P. Vincent, professional services.................	$65 00		
	31	" M. E. Dunlap, in settlement....................	80 00		
				145 00	

HORSE AND WAGON.

Jan.	1	From commencement of works to Dec. 31, 1882.....			2,083 87
Sept.	15	Paid Geo. L. Siegel, for hay...................................	$ 3 5		
Oct.	6	" Henry Mayo, sundries................................	4 00		
Dec.	31	" Jere. Fogarty, various bills for shoeing	9 60		
	31	" S. Erhart & Son, sundries........	10 15		
	31	" W. E. Hilton, cash expended for hay, &c........	18 16		
	31	" J. B. Crouch & Co., bills for oats, &c..............	96 19		
				141 60	

OIL AND TALLOW.

Jan.	1	From commencement of works to Dec. 31, 1882.....			4,048 04
Mar.	24	Paid Eclipse Oil Co	$ 6 00		
Dec.	31	" C. Kessler, sundry bills...............................	356 45		
				362 45	

PROTECTION OF R. R. TRACK.

May	19	Paid Geo. Carroll & Bro., lumber	$ 9 72		
	26	" W. W. Pierce & Co., for tools.......................	12 15		
June	30	" Jere. Fogarty, dressing tools..................	2 98		
	30	" Geo. Carroll & Bro., lumber........................	3 36		
July	14	" Saltsman & Austin drain tile....................	12 03		
Aug.	4	" B. F. Sloan, secretary, cash expended for sundries	68		
	11	" John Donovan, et. al., labor......................	7 67		
Sept.	8	" Saltsman & Austin, for tile......	3 60		
Dec.	1	" B. F. Sloan, secretary, cash expended for sundries	1 00		
	15	" American District Telegraph Co., for wire......	3 00		
	31	" Anthony Mullane, paid contract sodding.........	259 90		
	31	" labor, as per superintendent's pay rolls...........	1,395 97	1,712 04	

		Carried forward...	.... $43,409 73	$786,509 75

			FROM JAN. 1, 1883, TO DEC. 31, 1883.		1867 TO 1883.
	Brought forward...			$43,409 73	$786,509 75

IMPROVEMENT OF GROUNDS.

May	19	Paid Geo. Carroll & Bro., lumber		4 86	
	26	" W. W. Pierce & Co., for tools.........................		6 07	
June	30	" Jere Fogarty, dressing tools.........		1 46	
	30	" Geo. Carroll & Bro., lumber.		1 67	
July	14	" Saltsman & Austin, drain tile.........................		6 02	
Aug.	4	" B F Sloan sec'y, cash expended for sundries.		33	
	11	" John Donovan, et. al , for labor......................		3 83	
Sept.	8	" Saltsman & Austin, for tile.		1 80	
Dec	1	" B. F. Sloan, secretary, cash expended for sundries		50	
	15	" Ameriban District Telegraph Co., for wire		1 50	
	31	" Anthony Mullane, contract.............................		129 94	
	31	" labor, as per superintendent's pay roll		697 99	
			855 97		

LOWERING DISTRIBUTING MAINS.

Jan.	1	From commencement of works to Dec. 31, 1882	....		1,250 03
Dec.	31	Paid labor, as per superintendent's pay rolls........	$175 58		
			175 58		

LOWERING STREET CONNECTIONS

Dec.	31	Paid labor, as per superintendent's pay roll............	$262 81	
			262 81	

THAWING OUT PIPE.

Dec.	31	Paid labor, as per superintendent's pay rolls...........	$58 41	
			58 41	

RESERVOIR GROUNDS.

Jan.	1	From commencement of works to Dec. 31, 1882......	5,337 16

NEW BOILERS.

Jan.	1	Paid contract price for boilers and additions.........	8,518 90

ENGINEERING.

Jan.	1	From commencement of works to Dec. 31, 1883................	7,122 85

RAILROAD SWITCH AND SCALES.

Jan.	1	From commencement of works to Dec. 31, 1883............	1,128 64

CONSTRUCTION OF RESERVOIR.

Jan.	1	From commencement of works to Dec. 31, 1883......	116,586 84

ENGINES.

Jan.	1	From commencement of works to Dec. 31, 1883............	57,798 05

PARK FOUNTAINS.

Jan.	1	From commencement of works to Dec. 31, 1883......	3,244 68

DISCOUNT ON CITY BONDS.

Jan.	1	Discount on sale of city loan, as shown by ledger...	88,033 94
		.... $44,762 50	$1,075,580 84

INVENTORY (STOCK.)

Summary of Annual Inventory of Tools, Material, &c., on hand.

DIVSION.	JAN. 1, 1883.	JAN. 1, 1884.
Superintendent of pipe laying..............	$5,301 38	$8,849 51
Mechanical engineer..........	646 90	593 75
Keeper at reservoir..	51 25	63 79
	$5,999 53	$9,507 05
Increase	....	3,507 52

EXHIBIT D.

Amount of Water Rents Collected each year, with the Increase and Decrease, since the Commencement of the Works.

	Am't Rec'd.	Increase.	Decrease.
From Jan. 1, 1869, to Dec. 31, 1869............	$ 4,264 47	$	$
" " 1870 " 1870..........	9,237 30	4,972 83	
" " 1871 " 1871............	18,138 08	8,900 78	
' 1872 ' 1872............	21,652 68	3,514 60	
' 1873 ' 1873............	25,560 40	3,907 72	
' 1874 ' 1874............	27,938 90	2,378 50	
' 1875 ' 1875............	29,639 38	1,700 48	
' 1876 ' 1876............	31,048 76	1,409 38	
' 1877 ' 1877............	32,276 57	1,227 81	
' 1878 ' 1878............	29,636 01		2,640 56
' 1879 ' 1879............	33,343 20	3,707 19	
' 1880 ' 1880............	37,385 00	4,041 80	
" " 1881 ' 1881............	40,385 87	3,000 87	
' 1882 ' 1882	43,818 73	3,432 86	
" " 1883 " 1883	48,269 89	4,451 16	

Total water rents received................ $432,650 24

EXHIBIT E.

Location, Size and Length of Distributing Mains, Hydrant Branches, and Large Private Pipe laid during the year 1883.

LOCATION.	SIZE.	FEET.	IN.
DISTRIBUTING MAINS.			
East Sixth street	6 in.	2721	6
West Twelfth "	6 in.	710	9
East Twelfth "	6 in.	662	8
East Sixteenth "	6 in.	1463	9
State "	6 in.	747	6
Cascade "	6 in.	579	6
		6885	9
West Second street	4 in.	1628	4
West Fifth "	4 in.	96	
West Ninth "	4 in.	261	8
West Eleventh "	4 in.	672	6
East Thirteenth "	4 in.	370	11
West Fourteenth "	4 in.	697	
West Nineteenth "	4 in.	253	
West Twentieth "	4 in.	288	
West Twenty-second "	4 in.	287	
Myrtle street	4 in.	730	
Holland "	4 in.	677	
Liberty "	4 in.	689	
Chestnut "	4 in.	386	
Sassafras "	4 in.	878	
Wallace "	4 in.	336	
German "	4 in.	386	0
Walnut "	4 in.	489	1
		9078	8
East Second street, (temporary)	1 in.	60	7
Wallace " (temporary)	1 in.	181	0
Alley east of Wallace, between Fourth and Fifth, (temporary)	1 in.	210	1
		452	6
BRANCHES TO FIRE HYDRANTS.			
East Sixth street	4 in.	39	10
East Seventh "	4 in.	21	11
West Eighth "	4 in.	10	
East Ninth "	4 in.	8	8
West Eleventh "	4 in.	8	10
West Twelfth "	4 in.	26	8
East Twelfth "	4 in.	12	
West Fourteenth street	4 in.	11	4
Liberty "	4 in.	16	
State "	4 in.	25	6
Sassafras "	4 in.	21	6
East Sixteenth "	4 in.	8	11
Parade "	4 in.	14	4
German "	4 in	9	4
		234	10
LAID FOR PRIVATE PARTIES.			
Erie City Boiler Works. (East Avenue)	4 in.	415	6
Lovell Manufacturing Co., (East Thirteenth)	4 in.	96	9
T. M. Nagle, (East Sixteenth)	4 in.	60	2
Black & Jermer, (East Sixteenth)	4 in.	153	6
		725	11

RECAPITULATION.

Laid in 1883.. 17,377 feet, 8 inches.

Previously laid.. 215,280 " 7 "

232 658 feet, 3 inches.

MILES OF DISTRIBUTING MAINS.

Laid previous to 1883... 40

Laid during 1883... 3

Total... 44

Altogether, the city embraces about 150 miles of streets, leaving more than two-thirds of territory still to be supplied with water pipe.

EXHIBIT F.

Location, Number and Length of Street Connections put in during the year ending Dec. 31, 1883.

LOCATION.	NO.	FEET.	IN.
Wallace street	2	33	10
Myrtle street	3	27	2
Chestnut street	6	57	1
Poplar street	1	10	11
Huron street	8	59	5
Walnut street	3	42	3
Sassafras street	8	157	—
German street	5	140	10
French street	1	7	4
Holland street	8	150	11
Parade street	4	170	5
Division street	1	7	3
Turnpike street	1	6	10
State street	4	161	10
South Park Row	1	42	1
East Avenue	1	44	1
Peach street	3	109	4
Liberty street	10	329	3
Short street	1	8	9
Cherry street	2	52	—
Ash street	1	41	6
Waterford turnpike	2	44	—
Front street	1	8	—
Cascade street	1	9	8
Hickory street	1	6	6
North Park Row	1	7	3
Second street	15	298	8
Third street	4	101	11
Fourth street	7	89	6
Fifth street	4	68	3
Sixth street	28	1184	8
Seventh street	5	69	11
Eighth street	6	83	8
Ninth street	3	89	11
Tenth street	2	52	10
Eleventh street	8	149	8
Twelfth street	12	349	8
Thirteenth street	4	35	6
Fourteenth street	4	53	1
Fifteenth street	5	80	1
Seventeenth street	4	80	6
Eighteenth street	6	109	4
Nineteenth street	3	43	2
Twentieth street	4	53	11
Twenty-First street	1	10	11
Twenty-Second street	4	72	10
Twenty-Third street	4	107	10
Twenty-Fifth street	2	66	9
Twenty-Sixth street	3	130	4
Total for 1883	213	5,120	0
Previously put in	3,174	72,955	6
Total	3,387	78,075	6
Total in Miles			14¹⁴⁷⁄₅₂₈₀

EXHIBIT G.

Location, Size, Number and Style of Fire Hydrants put in during the year 1883.

LOCATION.	NO.	SIZE.	STYLE.
PUBLIC HYDRANTS.			
Corner of Twelfth and Raspberry streets..	1	4 inch	Matthews.
" Fourteenth and Sassafras streets..	1	"	"
" Sixth and Reed streets	1	"	"
East Sixth street, 116½ feet east of Wayne street...........................	1	"	"
Corner of Sixth street and East Avenue...	1	"	"
" Twelfth and French streets..	1	"	"
" Eleventh and State streets.........	1	"	"
East Seventh street, 228½ feet east of Holland street...........	1	"	"
Corner of Sixth and German streets......	1	"	"
" Sixteenth and State streets.................................	1	"	"
" Fifteenth and Liberty streets............................	1	"	"
" Eighth and State streets....................................	1	"	"
" Third and State streets..............................	1	"	"
" Sixteenth and German..........................	1	"	"
" Twelfth and Cascade streets................	1	"	"
" Seventh and Parade streets................	1	"	"
" Ninth and Parade streets...	1	"	"
" Eleventh and Parade streets.............................	1	"	"
" Twenty-fourth and Sassafras streets..................	1	"	"
" Twenty-fifth and Sassafras streets..................	1	"	"
" Third and German streets........................	1	"	"
	21		
PRIVATE HYDRANTS.			
Erie City Boiler Works, East Avenue...........................	1	4 inch	Matthews
Lovell Manufacturing Co.'s Works, East Thirteenth street........................	1	"	"
Nagle Machine Shops, East Sixteenth street........................	1	"	"
Black & Germer's new works, East Sixteenth street.............................	1	"	"
	4		
Total......	25		

Defective Hydrants Replaced with New.

LOCATION.	NO.	SIZE.	STYLE.
North Park Row, front of Park Church............................	1	4 inch	Matthews
Corner of Twenty-first and Peach............................	1	"	"
" Fifteenth and Myrtle............................	1	"	"

RECAPITULATION.

Public Fire Hydrants put in previous to Jan 1, 1883.. 148
"   "   "   "   during the year 1883......................... 21
        (Exclusive of old ones replaced.)   — 169

Private Fire Hydrants put in previous to Jan. 1, 1883.............................. 23
"   "   "   "   during the year 1883.................. 4
                                          — 27

Total number of Fire Hydrants... 196

Make of Hydrants in Use.

Old style Matthews.......................................	10	Ludlow.......................................	4
New style "	63	Morris, Tasker & Co............................	6
Bay State.......................................	45	Atlas...	2
West Jersey......................	33	Union..	1
Home-made.......................................	7	Brown	2
Pittsburgh	23		

All are steamer hydrants except one.   Five of the number are two-way hydrants; all the rest are one-way.

EXHIBIT H.

Location, Number and Size of Stop-Valves set during the year 1883.

LOCATION.	NO.	SIZE.
PUBLIC STOP-VALVES.		
West Twelfth street, west line of Cascade.	1	6 inch.
State street, north line of Eighteenth	1	6 "
East Sixth street, east line of Ash	1	6 "
" " " " Reed	1	6 "
" " " " Wayne	1	6 "
" " " west line of Perry	1	6 "
East Twelfth street, east line of State	1	6 "
" " " " French	1	6 "
East Sixteenth " " Holland	1	6 "
" " " west line of Parade	1	6 "
Cascade street, north line of Twelfth	1	6 "
West Twentieth street, west line of Sassafras	1	4 "
Myrtle street, north line of Seventh	1	4 "
" " south " "	1	4 "
Liberty street, north line of Seventeenth	1	4 "
Sassafras street, south line of Fourteenth	1	4 "
Fourteenth street, west line of Peach	1	4 "
" " east line of Sassafras	1	4 "
West Second street, west line of Sassafras	1	4 "
" " " east	1	4 "
" Eleventh street, west line of State	1	4 "
" " " east line of Sassafras	1	4 "
Myrtle street, north line of Eighteenth	1	4 "
Nineteenth street, west line of Myrtle	1	4 "
East Eleventh street, east line of French	1	4 "
Chestnut street, south line of Fourth	1	4 "
Holland street, south line of Sixth	1	4 "
Walnut street, north " "	1	4 "
Myrtle street, south " "	1	4 "
Sassafras street, north " "	1	4 "
Myrtle street, north " "	1	4 "
Walnut street, " " Tenth	1	4 "
East Thirteenth street, west line of Holland	1	4 "
Wallace street, south line of Twenty-fifth	1	4 "
Sassafras street, " " Twenty-third	1	4 "
West Fifth street, west line of Peach	1	4 "
Sassafras street, north line of Twenty-sixth	1	4 "
German street, " " Fourth	1	4 "
	38	
PRIVATE STOP-VALVES.		
Lovell Manufacturing Co., East Thirteenth street	1	4 "
T. M. Nagle, East Sixteenth street	1	4 "
Block & Germer, East Sixteenth street	1	4 "
	3	
OLD VALVES REPLACED.		
Corner of Parade and Eighth streets	1	4 "
" Peach and Ninth streets	1	4 "
" Peach and Eighth streets	1	4 "
" Sassafras and Seventh streets	1	4 "
" French and Seventh streets	1	4 "
" German and Ninth streets	1	4 "
	6	
Total	47	

RECAPITULATION.

Stop-Valves set previous to 1883 232
"   "   during 1863 41

(Not including old ones replaced.)

Total 273

All of the valves in use were made by R. D. Wood & Co., with, perhaps, a few exceptions during the first years the works were operated.

EXHIBIT I.

Number of Families, Stores, Offices, Manufactories, &c., Supplied with City Water in the year ending Dec. 31. 1883.

Butcher Shops	40	Mineral Water and Beer Bot-	
Barber Shops	27	ling Works	6
Billiard Rooms	5	Malt Houses	9
Breweries	4	Malleable Iron Works	2
Brass Foundries	2	Match Factories	1
Bakeries	8	Nickel Plating Works	2
Brush Factories	1	Orphan Asylums	2
Board of Trade	1	Offices	155
Boat Houses	5	Oil Works	2
Banks	9	Opera House	1
Butterine Factory	1	Organ Factories	1
Boot and Shoe Factories	1	Rubber Works	1
Boiler Works	1	Photograph Rooms	7
Chemical Works	1	Pulley Works	1
Carriage Factories	3	Potteries	1
Cigar Factories	4	Planing Mills	7
Churn Factories	1	Pump Factories	4
Candy Factories	2	Printing Offices	8
Coffee and Spice Mills	1	Police Stations	1
Cemeteries	1	Post Offices	1
Churches	12	Public Halls	27
Custom House	1	Paper Mills	1
Car Works	1	Stores	302
Convents	1	Saloons and Eating Houses	145
Coal and Iron Dock	1	Soap Factories	1
Club Houses	2	Steam Furniture Works	8
Dying Works	2	Steam Bending Works	1
Driving Parks	1	Stove Works	3
Engine Houses	6	Schools	16
Express Companies	2	Slaughter Houses	11
Fountains—Private	11	Show Case Factories	1
" Public	4	Street Railway Stables	1
Families	3798	Spring Bed Factories	1
" by Special Permits	148	Sewing Machine Factories	1
Flouring Mills	3	Railroad Depots	7
Fish Markets	6	Railroad Machine Shops	2
Forge Works	1	Railroads	4
Gas Works	1	Round Houses	5
Elevators	3	Transfer Companies	1
Green Houses	3	Work Shops	71
Hotels and Boarding Houses	69	Wooden Ware Works	5
Hospitals	2	Wringer Factories	1
Iron Foundries and Machine		Watering Troughs	17
Shops	13	Tanneries	2
Jails	1	U. S. Signal Stations	1
Livery Stables	13	Internal Revenue Offices	1
Lime Kilns	1		
Laundries	9	Total	5079
Lumber Yards	3	Last Enumeration, Jan. 1, '83	4687
		Increase in one year	392

EXHIBIT J.

PUMPING ENGINE STATISTICS.

The Pumps are two in number, of the kind known as the Cornish Bull Engine. The diameter of each plunger is 30½ inches, and each pump has a stroke of 10 feet. Allowing for loss, the capacity of each pump is calculated in this report at 165 gallons to every stroke. The reservoir is nearly two miles from the pumping works, and the water is pumped through a 20 inch pipe, with which all the east and west mains are connected. The bottom of the reservoir is 210 feet above the surface of the bay, and the water is kept at an average depth of nearly 25 feet, the exact lift being obtained by a daily comparison of the gauges at the works and at the reservoir.

MONTHS.	NO. OF DAYS BOTH PUMPS WERE IDLE.	NO. OF DAYS SINGLE PUMP WAS RUN.	NO. OF DAYS BOTH PUMPS WERE RUN.	NO. OF STROKES OF THE PUMP.	NO. OF GALLONS PUMPED.	DAILY AVERAGE OF GALLONS PUMPED.	EDGE LIFT IN FEET.	NO. OF LBS. OF BITUMENOUS SLACK COAL PURCHASED.	COAL BILL FOR THE MONTH.
January	3	25	3	419,524	69,221,460	2,232,941	236.00	465,700	$407 49
February	4	24	—	361,265	59,508,725	2,128,883	235 80	315,500	276 06
March	3	28	—	407,410	67,222,650	2,168,472	235.80	274,350	240 06
April	4	26	—	335,856	55,416,240	1,847,208	235 85	644,500	563 44
May	4	27	—	381,524	62,918,460	2,247,087	235.56	203,050	177 67
June	9	11	10	382,750	63,153,750	2,105,125	233.10	360,650	279 50
July	2	23	6	432,976	71,441,040	2,304,549	233.52	306,600	237 62
August	1	22	8	493,964	81,504,060	2,029,163	233.98	553,200	428 73
September	—	25	5	471,342	77,771,430	2,592,381	234.13	419 550	325 18
October	1	19	11	441,199	72,797,835	2,348,317	234 50	572,800	288 92
November	2	28	—	405,639	66,930,435	2,231,014	234 16	457,770	354 77
December	3	26	2	411,640	67,920,600	2,190,987	234.15	424,100	328 68
Totals and Averages	36	284	45	4,945,089	815,939,685	2,252,177	234.71	4,797,770	3,908 59

*Pumping was stopped from the 11th to the 18th of June inclusive, while the fishy smell and taste were in the water of the bay. During this period the water in the reservoir ran down 8 feet or from a height of 234 feet to one of 226.

The feed water improvement, elsewhere referred to, was added to engine 88 on March 12th; to engine 89 on April 12th. Its effect was to raise the temperature of the feed water from an average of 110 to an average of 130 A vacuum of 26 inches has also been maintained as compared with 20 inches before.

Experiments show that the supply of natural gas, from both wells furnishes about 2½ per cent of the heat used under the boilers, in addition to what is required for lighting the buildings and grounds.

The regular employees at the pumping works are 1 mechanical engineer, 2 assistant engineers and 3 firemen. The mechanical engineer stands a watch of 5 hours, from 7 to 12 every forenoon; the assistants divide the remainder of each day equally between them; each one of the firemen stands a watch of 8 hours. Besides firing, the firemen unload the coal from the cars, except when both pumps are run, in which case a laborer is usually hired specially for that purpose The mechanical engineer gives ten hours daily to the service of the department the hours when he is not on watch being employed in repairs, supervision, &c In addition to standing their regular watch, the assistant engineers aid their superior officer in keeping the machinery in order.

The pumps are run at an average of about 10½ strokes per minute, when operated singly, but when both are used the number of strokes is reduced to about 9 for each pump in the daytime and 7½ at night, the capacity of the delivery main being too small to admit of more rapid pumping.

EXHIBIT K.

Amount and kind of Coal Consumed, Cost of Coal, Water Pumped, Average Height Pumped, &c., from the First Year the Works were operated to January 1, 1884.

Year.	Tons of Coal Consumed, 2000 lbs. to a Ton.	Contract Price of Coal per Ton from May 1st of each year.	Cost of Coal delivered in Pumping House.	Kind of Coal.	Gallons of Water Pumped.	Increase or Decrease.	No. of Families and Establishments supplied.	No. of Fire Hydrants supplied.	Average height of water in Reservoir above bay surface.	Cost of Coal per Million Gallons raised to Reservoir.	Cost of Coal per Million Gallons raised one foot.	Gallons raised one foot by one pound of Coal.	Gallons raised to Reservoir by one lb. of Coal.
1868	59.1	$5.05	$309.61	Lump	246,648,960		1218	97					
1869	544.4	5.05	4,818.48	"	279,368,495	132,719,535 I	1727	99	232.00	18.76	00.080	22.656	98.52
1870	1,064.5	5.05	5,159.10	"	395,076,000	115,8005 I	2140	103	232.00	16.52	00.076	35.092	150.96
1871	1,422.7	5.05	7,117.00	"	384,062,415	11,013,585 D	2475	107	232.00	21.90	00.094	26.636	114.81
1872	1,308.5	5.05	6,528.50	"	444,817,395	60,754,980 I	2663	107	232.00	17.33	00.071	26.636	126.44
1873	1,672.5	5.05	8,412.65	"	531,005,475	86,188,080 I	2700	110	232.00	16.30	00.069	33.772	145.57
1874	1,759.0	4.85	7,709.54	"	670,726,650	139,7215 I	2763	112	232.00	13.30	00.056	33.950	159.31
1875	1,836.4	4.85	8,657.61	"	660,981,810	9,744,840 D	2854	114	232.00	13.30	00.054	36.950	135.74
1876	2,105.1	4.00	8,925.22	"	682,392,315	21,390,505 I	2915	115	232.00	12.75	00.049	31.491	136.49
1877	2,456.6	3.70	8,509.33	"	807,800,400	125,408,085 I	3011	121	232.00	11.64	00.039	31.665	153.68
1878	2,463.3	3.35	7,945.37	"	775,805,250	31,995,150 I	3568	126	232.00	9.19	00.038	35.653	126.01
1879	2,628.1	3.09	7,428.92	"	975,640,634	00,235,084 I	4110	*161	232.00	8.99	00.028	29.234	142.20
1880	3,076.1	1.99	6,978.41	Slack.	829,759,260	145,881,674 D	4687	*171	234.00	6.68	00.027	32.990	139.77
1881	3,430.3	1.90	6,517.58	"	815...	13,819,575 D	5077	*196	234.71	6.45	00.019	32.706	170.00
1882	2,968.2	1.75	5,355.93	"						4.66		39.900	
1883	2,398.2	1.55	3,908.59	"									

All coal used from the commencement of the works has been Mercer county bituminous. The coal contract is awarded annually to the lowest bidder, the coal being delivered in the works, and paid for according to the weight shown by the department scales.

Two gas wells were put down at the pumping works in the spring of 1871, yielding a large supply. The gas was applied to the boilers the same year and furnished about one-fourth of the fuel at the works for a year or two. The gas steadily decreased until about 1875, when it failed almost entirely. The wells were resuscitated in the summer of 1881, and the gas was soon after applied again to the boilers, since which time, besides all the light used at the works and grounds, it has furnished an average of about two and one-half per cent. of the fuel employed in pumping.

*The fire hydrant column includes both public and private for the years 1881, 1882 and 1883.

EXHIBIT L.

HOW CITY WATER MAY BE WASTED.

Gallons and hundredths of gallons of water that will be discharged per minute through various sized orifices at the heads stated.

Head in Feet.	Pressure per Square Inch.	Diameters of Orifices in inches and fractions of an inch.													
		$\frac{1}{64}$	$\frac{1}{32}$	$\frac{1}{16}$	$\frac{1}{8}$	$\frac{1}{4}$	$\frac{3}{8}$	$\frac{1}{2}$	$\frac{5}{8}$	$\frac{3}{4}$	1	$1\frac{1}{4}$	$1\frac{1}{2}$	$1\frac{3}{4}$	2
20	8.66	0.02	0.07	0.30	1.20	5.10	11.70	20.60	32.20	46.20	82.30	128.40	184.80	252.00	328.80
40	17.32	0.02	0.11	0.45	1.80	7.40	16.30	29.60	45.50	65.50	116.50	182.40	261.60	356.40	465.00
60	25.99	0.03	0.14	0.55	2.20	8.90	20.00	35.60	57.70	80.30	142.80	223.20	320.40	436.80	571.20
80	34.65	0.04	0.16	0.65	2.60	10.30	23.20	41.20	64.30	92.60	164.40	258.00	370.80	505.20	658.80
100	43.31	0.04	0.18	0.75	2.90	11.50	25.90	46.10	72.00	103.70	183.60	288.00	415.20	565.20	788.00
120	51.98	0.05	0.19	0.78	3.10	12.60	28.30	50.40	78.80	113.50	201.60	315.00	453.60	624.40	807.60
140	60.64	0.05	0.21	0.85	3.40	13.60	30.60	54.50	85.20	122.40	217.20	340.80	490.80	668.40	872.40
150	64.97	0.05	0.22	0.88	3.50	14.10	31.70	56.40	88.20	127.20	225.60	352.80	507.60	691.20	902.40
175	75.80	0.06	0.24	0.95	3.80	15.20	34.20	61.00	95.80	136.80	243.60	380.40	548.40	748.80	975.60
200	86.63	0.06	0.26	1.02	4.10	16.30	36.60	65.20	101.80	146.40	260.40	406.80	588.00	798.00	1042.80
235	101.08	0.07	0.28	1.12	4.50	17.90	41.30	71.50	137.70	185.80	285.20	445.80	642.20	871.30	1140.80

The bottom of the Erie Reservoir is 210 feet above the surface of Presque Isle Bay, from which the water is pumped, and the water in the reservoir is kept at an average height of nearly 25 feet, or 235 feet above the bay. The pressure at the points named below will give an idea of the average throughout the city: Twenty-fourth and Sassafras streets, 20 lbs.: Twenty-third and Myrtle, 30 lbs.; Twentieth and Chestnut, 40 lbs.: Eighteenth and Peach, 50 lbs.: Fourteenth and State, 60 lbs.; Eighth and State, 70 lbs.; Third and State, 80 lbs.; Front and State, 100 lbs.

The wire of which pins are made is $\frac{3}{32}$ of an inch in diameter— No. 21, wire gauge. The finest cambric needle, made of wire $\frac{1}{64}$th of an inch in diameter—No. 27, wire gauge. A stream the size of a pin, running one year with head of 235 feet, will flow 147,168 gallons, equaling 4,600 barrels, at a loss—counting at the rate of 10 cents per 000 gallons—of $14.71. A stream the size of a cambric needle, running at the same pressure, and for the same time, will waste 36,792 gallons, a loss of $3.68.

EXHIBIT M.

Advantages offered in Erie to Manufacturers.

The following are the highest and lowest charges per 1,000 gallons for water by meter measurement, up to a daily average of 50,000 gallons, in the cities named. The rates are taken from the official reports:

	HIGH-EST	LOW-EST.		HIGH-EST	LOW-EST.
Erie	10	6	New York City, (uniform		
Albany, N. Y	40	10	charge	—	10
Boston (uniform charge)	—	20	Oil City, Pa., (uniform		
Binghampton, N.Y.	25	6	charge)	—	13
Bangor, Maine	30	10	Oswego, N. Y	40	20
Baltimore (uniform ch'g)	—	8	Portland, Maine	50	30
Brooklyn, N. Y. "	—	15	Philadelphia, Pa., (uni-		
Chicago, Ill.	10	8	form charge)	—	16¾
Cleveland, O	16	8	Rochester, N. Y.	30	10
Cincinnati, O., (uniform			St. Paul, Minn	50	25
charge)	—	12	Springfield, Mass.	30	15
Columbus, O	20	7	San Francisco, (uniform		
Dayton, O	50	15	charge)	—	33
Detroit	20	10	Syracuse, N. Y	40	20
Elmira, N. Y	50	40	St. Louis	20	15
East Saginaw, Mich	60	15	Sandusky, (uniform		
Hartford, Conn	30	16	charge)	—	20
Louisville, Ky	15	6	Toronto.	27	18
Lawrence, Mass	30	15	Toledo	20	8
Milwaukee	20	10	Troy, N. Y	20	10
Meadville	15	8	Titusville	30	12½
Montreal	30	12	Utica, N. Y	50	25

The above list might be extended indefinitely. Only two cities in the country furnish water in large quantities at a less rate per gallon than Erie; in a very few the rates are about the same; all the rest charge from 10 to 100, and in some cases 400 per cent. higher than Erie. In addition to the low rates, meters are set here and kept in order by the department, while in most cities the consumers are charged with the same.

Steam Engine Charges per Horse Power, (10 hours per day.)

Erie	$2.50	New York City	$5.00 to 6.00
Chicago	4.00	Newark	5.00
Boston	6.00 to 10.00	Omaha	2.50
Kansas City	5.00	Cleveland	2.50
Minneapolis	2.00 to 4.00	Columbus	3.00
St. Paul	4.00 to 5.00	Philadelphia	3.00
Buffalo	3.00	Pittsburgh	2.50
Toledo	2.50	Rochester	3.00

EXHIBIT N.

Cost of Water to the Householder in Twenty-five Cities, as compared with the Cost in Erie, (compiled from the Official Reports.)

CITIES.	Family.	P. Closet.	B. Tub.	W. Stand.	W. Tub.	Horse.	Cow.	Sprinkler	Amount.
Erie	$5 00	$3 00	$3 00	$ 50	$2 00	$2 00	$ 75	$3 00	$18 75
Lawrence, Mass	5 00	4 00	3 00	......	1 00	3 00	1 50	2 50	20 00
Lynn, Mass	6 00	5 00	5 00	2 00	2 00	5 00	1 50	3 00	29 50
Fitchburg, Mass	6 00	5 00	5 00	2 00	2 00	8 00	2 00	5 00	35 00
Newton, Mass	6 00	5 00	6 00	2 00	1 00	10 00	1 50	5 00	35 00
Cambridge, Mass	7 00	6 00	6 00	2 50	2 50	5 00	2 00	10 00	41 00
Providence, R. I	6 00	5 00	5 00	2 00	3 00	4 00	1 00	5 00	31 00
Taunton, Mass	5 00	5 00	3 00	2 00	2 00	4 00	1 50	5 00	27 50
Lowell, Mass	6 00	4 00	3 00	......	1 00	4 00	2 00	3 00	23 00
Fall River, Mass	5 00	5 00	5 00	2 50	2 50	4 00	1 00	6 00	31 00
Brooklyn, N. Y	16 00	2 00	......	......	......	5 00	75	5 50	29 25
Albany, N. Y	18 00	2 00	......	......	......	3 00	......	8 00	31 00
Buffalo, N. Y	20 00	8 00	5 00	......	......	4 00	1 50	5 00	43 50
Niagara Falls	9 00	3 00	3 00	......	......	3 00	1 50	6 00	25 50
Detroit, Mich	7 00	3 00	2 00	1 25	2 00	4 00	1 00	3 00	23 25
Cincinnati, O	14 00	3 00	6 00	1 00	......	5 00	......	4 80	33 80
Toledo, O	10 25	2 50	3 50	2 00	......	5 00	......	5 00	28 25
Chicago, Ill	19 00	5 00	3 00	......	......	4 00	......	3 00	34 00
Alton, Ill	7 00	5 00	8 00	......	......	8 00	2 00	9 00	39 00
Philadelphia, Pa	8 75	2 00	3 00	1 00	1 00	3 00	......	9 00	27 75
Pittsburgh, Pa	27 77	17 55	10 85	8 25	......	8 25	2 05	6 87	71 50
Milwaukee, Wis	11 50	5 00	3 00	2 00	......	4 00	1 00	8 00	34 50
Salem, Mass	3 50	5 00	5 00	1 50	......	6 00	1 00	3 00	24 00
Louisville, Ky	10 00	3 00	4 00	......	1 00	5 00	1 00	7 50	31 50
Grand Rapids, Mich	8 00	4 50	3 75	2 00	3 00	2 50	1 00	2 00	26 75
Springfield, Mass	8 00	4 00	4 00	......	......	4 00	2 00	5 00	27 00

The low rate at which water is supplied is not the only advantage offered in Erie. Here the department lays down the street main, puts in the connections from the main to the curb, and sets the stops and stop boxes, free of expense to the consumer, while in most cities these items are a charge against the property benefited.

ANNUAL RATES.

Water rents are payable quarterly in advance — except where the water is furnished by meter measurement or special contract — as follows:

FIRST QUARTER—January, February, March—JANUARY 1ST.
SECOND QUARTER—April, May, June—APRIL 1ST.
THIRD QUARTER—July, August, September—JULY 1ST.
FOURTH QUARTER—October, November, December—OCTOBER 1ST.

If the rents are not paid for any quarter within the FIRST MONTH thereof, FIVE PER CENT. may be added to the amount. If payment is not made by the first day of February, May, August and November of each quarter, the delinquent shall be notified that the water will be turned off from the premises on the fifteenth day after date of notice, and not turned on again until all back rents and penalties are paid and the further sum of two dollars for turning off and on the water.

When water is furnished by meter measurement or special contract, payment is due at the end of each current quarter. If the rents are not paid within ONE MONTH after they are due, the same penalties and conditions will apply as above.

	PER ANNUM.
Private dwellings, occupied by one family, from	$3 00 to $10 00
" " " by more than one family, $1.00 less than the above rates for each family using the water	
Bath tub in private house	3 00
" " each additional	1 50
Public bath tubs, each	5 00
Hopper water closet, in private house	6 00
" " " each additional	3 00
Pan water closet, in private house	3 00
" " " each additional	1 50
Public water closet, pan, each	5 00
" " " hopper, each	6 00
Urinals, each	2 00
Permanent hand basins, each	50
Permanent wash tub with waste	2 00
" " each additional	1 00
Private street sprinklers, each, per season	3 00 to 10 00
Private stables, for one or two horses	2 00
" " each additional horse over two	1 00
Livery stables, for each horse, including washing of carriages	2 00
Cows, each	75
Fountains, average use four hours per day:	
One 1-16 inch jet	5 00
One 1-8 inch jet	10 00
One 1-4 inch jet	15 00
One 3-8 inch jet	20 00
One 1-2 inch jet	30 00
Larger jets at special rates	
Dry goods, book and hardware stores, from	2 00 to 5 00
Saloons, groceries and provision stores, from	3 00 to 50 00
Offices, from	2 00 to 20 00
Hotels, taverns and boarding houses, in addition to rates for private dwellings, for each room	1 00
Public schools, per scholar	10
Building purposes, for each bushel of lime	02
Printing offices, not including steam engine, from	5 00 to 25 00
" " each power press	4 00
" " each balance press	2 00
" " each hand press	1 00
Blacksmith shops, one fire	5 00
" " each additional fire	2 50
Barber shops, one chair	4 00
" " each additional chair	2 00
Steam engines, non-condensing, ten hours per day, each horse power	2 50
Butchers' stalls, each	3 00
Work shops, from	3 00 to 5 00

METER RATES.

The rate for each current quarter, per each thousand gallons, by meter measurement, is as follows:

For a daily average of 15,000 gallons or less	10 cents
" " " more than 15,000 gallons and not in excess of 20,000 gallons	9½ "
" " " " 20,000 " " " " 25,000 "	9 "
" " " " 25,000 " " " " 30,000 "	8½ "
" " " " 30,000 " " " " 35,000 "	8 "
" " " " 35,000 " " " " 40,000 "	7½ "
" " " " 40,000 " " " " 45,000 "	7 "
" " " " 45,000 " " " " 50,000 "	6½ "
" " " " 50,000 "	6 "

IN THE

COUN(

FOR THE

R ENDING DEC. 31, 1884.

ERIE, PA:
ALKER & GALLAGHER, PRINTERS.
1885.

ANNUAL REPORT

OF THE BOARD OF

WATER COMMISSIONERS,

OF ERIE, PA.,

TO THE

MAYOR AND CITY COUNCILS,

FOR THE

YEAR ENDING DEC. 31, 1884.

ERIE, PA.:
WALKER & GALLAGHER, PRINTERS.
1885.

WATER COMMISSIONERS.

The Water Commissioners are appointed by the Court of Common Pleas of Erie County, Penn'a, for a term of three years, one member being named annually, in May.

EX-MEMBERS OF THE BOARD.

*WM. W. REED, 1867 to 1879.   *WM. L. SCOTT, 1867 to 1868.
*HENRY RAWLE, 1867 to 1872.   †JOHN C. SELDEN, 1868 to 1872.
JOHN GENSHEIMER, 1872 to 1878.   MATTHEW R. BARR, 1872 to 1877.
                    J. M. BRYANT, 1878 to 1881.

*Messrs. Scott, Rawle and Reed, the first Commissioners, were appointed respectively for terms of one, two and three years.

†Mr. Selden resigned before the expiration of his second term. Mr. Barr was substituted by the Board and afterward appointed by the Court.

PRESENT BOARD.

M. LIEBEL, 1877 to 1886.   G. W. F. SHERWIN, 1879 to 1885.
                    BENJAMIN WHITMAN, 1881 to 1887.

OFFICERS OF THE DEPARTMENT, JAN. 1st, 1885.

President of the Board—BENJAMIN WHITMAN.
Secretary and Treasurer—B. F. SLOAN.
Assistant Secretary—GEO. C. GENSHEIMER.
Acting Foreman of Street Work—WM. O'LONE.
Inspectors—A. F. CRANE, F. W. KOEHLER.
Mechanical Engineer—F. A. ROTH.
Assistant Mechanical Engineers—GEO. R. MILLER, JOHN KELLY.
Firemen—R. W. SIMONS, JOSEPH BURNS, JACOB MULLEN.
Keeper of Reservoir and Grounds—SAMUEL PFISTER.
Watchman at Pumping Works—ROGER MCDONOUGH.

OFFICE—No. 18 East Seventh Street, between French and State.
OFFICE HOURS—From 7:30 A. M. to 5:45 P. M.
REGULAR MEETINGS OF THE BOARD—Every Saturday at 2 P. M.

ANNUAL REPORT.

To the Mayor and City Councils:

GENTLEMEN:—It affords us no little satisfaction to report that more progress has been made during the last twelve months in extending and perfecting the public system of water supply than in any year since the works went into operation. These improvements, it is also gratifying to state, have been paid for out of the surplus earnings of the Department, after deducting the cost of maintenance, without calling for a dollar of appropriation from the City Councils, or, in any other respect, adding to the burdens of the people. It is safe to say, that the instances are very rare, in places of the population of Erie, and with like conditions of low rates, sparsely settled territory, extraordinary pressure and the unusual expenses incident to the two latter features, where the revenues of the Water Department, seventeen years after their organization, are not only sufficient for their maintenance and all ordinary work of extension, but even assure a surplus that will easily provide, within a few years, for doubling the capacity of the system. That the situation here is so different from what exists in most of the smaller cities of the Union must be a source of as much enjoyment to our people as it is to the officers immediately concerned.

LEADING IMPROVEMENTS.

The most important steps taken during the year, aside from the regular work of construction, detailed in another place, have been as follows :

1st. The laying down of more than a mile of 12-inch mains on Seventh and Twenty-First streets, in extension of the mains of the same size previously laid on those streets from Chestnut street eastward.

2d. The repairing, cementing and painting of the Standpipe.

3d. The repairing and repainting of the outside of the Engine and Boiler Houses.

4th. The sinking of an Inlet Tube in the centre of the main pier to secure a more nearly pure supply of water.

5th. The rebuilding of the main pier and the filling of the pier to the top of the timbers.

THE TWELVE-INCH MAINS.

The 12-inch mains were laid on Seventh street from a point nearly midway between State and French, and on Twenty-first street from the east side of Peach, to Parade street in both cases: 1st, as a preliminary step to

the contemplated enlargement of the system; and, 2d, in order to furnish
an adequate supply to the Eastern part of the city.   This thrifty section,
which includes some of the largest manufactories, was dependent on slender
lines of pipe that barely afforded enough water to meet the demand.
With two 12-inch mains, each three-fourths of a mile long, located at the
most advantageous points, directly connected with the pumping main on
Chestnut street, and giving a practically unrestricted supply to the laterals
on both sides of them, the wants, in the direction intended, of that portion
of the city which lies east of State street, have been provided for for many
years to come.

THE STANDPIPE AND PUMPING WORKS.

The action of the elements had removed much of the mortar and
crumbled many of the bricks of the outer surface of the Standpipe, giving an unsightly appearance to the structure and suggesting doubts whether
it might not become unsafe in course of time.   These faults have been remedied by carefully cementing the brickwork on the outside, rejointing the
stonework, and covering the whole column except the foundation with
three good coats of paint.

The exterior of the Engine and Boiler Houses had not been overhauled
for some years, and badly needed attention.   The wood, stone and brick
work have all been thoroughly repaired and painted to correspond with the
Standpipe.   In both cases the effort has been more to preserve than to
beautify, though both objects have been kept in view.

THE OLD INLET.

In the early history of the pumping works, two cribs, each twelve feet
wide, were sunk parallel with each other, and at a slight distance apart,
commencing at a point near the buildings and extending six hundred and
forty-three feet into the bay.   These were filled with stone to the surface of
the water and with earth to the top of the cribs, the narrow passage between
them being designed as an inlet for the supply of water to the pumps.   The
inlet was covered with heavy timbers and earth, which served the double
purpose of a roof and to bind the cribs together.   After a time it was
noticed that the tendency of the pier thus formed was to drive the muddy
water carried into the bay by the streams west of the works to the mouth
of the inlet.   Three small piers, 30x30 feet in size, and eighty feet apart,
were therefore built on the same line as the main pier and upon a similar
plan (that is, with an open space in the centre to serve as an inlet), the
purpose being to allow the dirty water to pass between the several parts of
the pier system, on its way down the bay.   The minor piers were connected
with the main pier and with each other by three iron pipes of four feet inside diameter, sunk from two to six feet below the surface of the bay,
through which it was thought the water would be drawn from the further
end of the piers.   Briefly stated, the plan was this: A channel 648 feet
long in the main pier, an iron pipe of eighty feet, another channel in the

first of the small piers, a second pipe, and so on, to the terminus of the pier work, a distance from the pumping house of about 973 feet.

THE NEW INLET.

· Having observed that muddy water was forced into the delivery pipes under circumstances which indicated that it could not have been drawn from the mouth of the pumping channel, an examination was set on foot last spring which led to some startling developments. It was made clear, beyond question, that the whole supply to the pumps came through the sides of the main pier at and near to the shore line, being sucked into the channel through the interstices between the timbers and stone. In the belief that the purity of the water furnished to the people was the object of first consequence, the Board promptly decided to adopt measures which should render it absolutely certain that the supply would come from the source intended. After submitting the plan to an eminent hydraulic engineer, and securing his full approval, it was agreed to sink a wooden tube in the channel of the main pier at a sufficient depth below the surface of the water to prevent decay. The original design was to build the tube of five feet inside diameter, but, on opening the passage, and learning that one of that dimension could not be sunk in it without great risk and expense, on account of the limited and irregular space, the Board reluctantly changed the size to four feet three inches. The work occupied some four months, commencing about the 1st of July, and was carried on to completion at much inconvenience and with unexpected delays. For want of funds, the tube could not be extended to the extreme end of the pier system, but a contract has been entered into which assures that result by the 1st of May next. The purpose is to join the wooden tube to the old iron four-feet pipe, which has been taken up and cleaned, and make the latter continuous, by adding new sections, from the end of the main pier to the further side 'of the last of the small piers, where the water is thirteen feet deep. Measuring from its exterior, the pipe, at its mouth, will rest five feet below the surface and four feet above the bed of the bay, which insures almost perfect freedom from objectionable matter.

REBUILDING OF THE MAIN PIER.

The east side of the main pier, which had decayed to the water's edge, has been rebuilt, and the whole pier has been filled with stone, earth and gravel—the latter having been used around and above the inlet tube. It is the purpose, by next spring, to add a railing and walk, after the pattern that has proved so effective elsewhere on the grounds, to the west side of the pier, as a protection against the waves which often beat against it with terrific force from that quarter. When this is done, the surface of the pier will be planted to grass, trees will be set out and seats will be suitably placed, making one of the most attractive points about the city.

CONTRACT WORK.

The work above described, with the exception of the laying of the 12-inch pipe, was done by contract, after due publication and awarded to the lowest responsible bidder. The policy of the Department, for several years past, has been to make as many of its purchases, and do as much of its work as practicable upon this system. All supplies of pipe, coal, brass, lead, iron, &c., and all repairs of engines, boilers, tools, &c., are let to the parties offering the best terms, after receiving bids from those who choose to compete for the contracts.

MAIN PIPES.

Including the 12-inch pipe, 17,423 feet, or nearly 3¼ miles, of distributing mains have been laid during the year, which is about the same in length as in 1883. This is hardly a fair statement, however, of the actual work done in the line of pipe laying. The capacity of a 12-inch pipe is equal to nine of 4, and four of 6-inch. Reducing the amount of 12-inch pipe laid to the average of both, it gives the equivalent of 6½ miles of 4 and 6-inch, or altogether, some 8¾ miles, being more than twice the amount put down in a single season since the first years of the system. About half-a-mile of the 6-inch pipe was laid to secure better distribution in sections where the supply was deficient or irregular. The total amount of main pipe now laid in the city is about 44⅓ miles; more, probably, than in any place of equal population in the country, a fact due to the unusual number of sparsely settled streets within the corporate limits, and to the desire of the Board to accommodate every important manufacturing and commercial interest. In buying pipe, the Department has, for a long time past, required it to be hammer tested at a pressure of 300 ℔s. to the square inch, with the result that not a piece laid during the last five years has broken. Our stock of 4 and 6-inch pipe on hand, bought at low prices, is thought to be sufficient to meet the calls for extension during the ensuing year. Some idea may be had of the future demands upon the Department, when it is stated that about a hundred miles of streets are still without the city water.

STOP VALVES.

The number of stop valves set was 63, being much in excess of any previous season. The total number now in the city is 300, which is very far from being the proportion due to the amount of pipage. To avoid inconvenience and be prepared for emergencies, there should be a stop valve at every street intersection, at least within the closely built portions of the city. Provision has been made in the rules governing the Foreman of Street Work that, in laying new mains, a stop valve shall be set for every long block or two short blocks.

STREET CONNECTIONS.

Much to our surprise, considering the business depression, the number of street connections put in has exceeded that of 1883, being 281 against 213 in the latter year. The total number now in is 3,668, representing almost 16 miles of pipe. We renew the suggestion. in last year's report that, whenever the city authorities change the grades of streets or sidewalks, or paving is done on any street, notice should be given this Department in time to lower main pipes or connections that may require it to be out of danger of frost. Often the first information we have of a change in grade comes through a frozen pipe, which may cause much expense to the Department and a great deal of trouble to the persons affected. The Department is doing all in its power to relieve the public of annoyance in this respect by lowering shallow mains and connnections put in during the early years of the works, as soon as can be after they are discovered, to the standard depth of five feet above the top of the pipe.

NUMBER OF WATER TAKERS.

The number of parties against whom separate accounts are kept for the use of city water, is 5,395, an increase over the previous year of 316. Of these 4,084 represent families, and 82 large manufacturing establishments. Counting five persons to a family, and making due allowance for other uses, it is believed that about 25,000 of the 35,000 persons in the corporate limits depend on the city water. The collection of the water rents has grown to be a matter of immense labor, necessitating extra clerical force in the office. A ledger account has to be kept with each one of the 5,395 patrons, bills have to be mailed and collected four times a year, and many parties have to be twice notified, making some 25,000 separate transactions in this branch of the Department alone. Of late the delinquent list has increased to such an extent that it is a question whether the penalties imposed by law in such cases will not have to be strictly enforced in future.

FIRE HYDRANTS.

To such taxpayers as are unable to obtain the use of the water on their premises, the matter of fire protection, when a hydrant can be placed with- in convenient reach of them, is the chief, and, in fact, the sole benefit de- rived from the public system. Bearing in mind that they have paid interest on the water bonds for many years, and wishing to deal, as nearly as can be, justly by every citizen, the Board have made strenuous efforts to pro- mote the efficiency of the Fire Department (which largely depends on the vigilance and good management of the Water Department), by adding new hydrants as fast as the revenues would permit. The number of hydrants in new locations put in during the year—most of them being of the latest and best patterns—was 57, giving a total of 254, or more than twice that of 1880. In addition to those named, 18 of the old kind have been replaced with hydrants of modern style, making about three times as much progress in this direction as was ever effected before in a single year. Great pains have also been taken to put the fire hydrants in complete re- pair, to perfect their drainage, and to protect them against frost, so that they may always be in working order.   In the belief that each branch of the government owes it to the city to do what it properly can towards keeping up a neat appearance, the Board have adopted a rule that the hydrants shall be painted every spring as soon as the weather will allow.   Each hydrant is carefully inspected three times a year—during the first weeks of April, July and November—by trained employees of the Department, who keep a record of their condition which is always open to reference.   Where a hydrant is in good working order in November, it is not thought to be a good plan to test it during the ensuing winter, unless compelled by a fire or other emergency.

DEFECTIVE PLUMBING.

The measures inaugurated two years ago to cure defective plumbing have been steadily persevered in on the plan indicated in our last report. Two Inspectors continue to be employed, who make the same number of house to house visitations of the entire city each year, and oblige every leaky fixture they find to be promptly repaired.   Besides this work, they inspect and assess new plumbing, grade old work as First or Second Class, report matters generally which need the attention of the Department, and aim to educate the people how to use the water with the least waste and inconvenience.   These reports show that the Second Class premises have been reduced to half a dozen, where 328 were found in 1882, while the number of leaky fixtures is kept within quite moderate limits.   The plumbers are also obliged to report frozen fixtures requiring their services during the winter, which enables the Department to look after them in proper season.   To those who may still be inclined to complain of our measures to improve the plumbing and reduce the waste, we answer as before that the necessities of the case have literally forced them upon us.   But for the efforts put forth in this respect, the supply could not have been kept up at certain periods during the past year, and the citizens would long before this have been called upon for increased taxes to enlarge the system.   The aim of the Board has been to postpone enlargement until it could be done with the surplus revenues of the Department, without levying more taxes upon the people, and, if those who have the interest of the city at stake will lend them a reasonable co-operation, they feel quite sure, as will be shown hereafter, of accomplishing their purpose.

METERS AND COUNTERS.

Forty-three meters and five counters have been in use during the year, being six more of the former and one of the latter in excess of the number in 1883.   The Board adhere to the belief that the plan of measuring water is the only true one of disposing of it, where large quantities are consumed, but have been thwarted in their purpose to introduce meters more generally by pressing demands for extension and otherwise.   In every city where the meter system has been adopted on an extensive scale the income of the *Water Department* has been much increased in proportion to the consumption.

GOOD TASTE AND SYSTEM.

The encouragement given by the people and press has warranted us in continuing to improve the grounds at the pumping works and reservoir. The aim has been to put everything in such shape as will make, as nearly as possible, a permanent job of it, while giving an appearance to the property that will accord with its public character. In nearly all the cities of America, the Water Works are among the most attractive features, and it is believed our people have sufficient pride in Erie not to want it to be an exception to the rule.

The systematic methods introduced into the various branches of the Department are producing excellent fruits. Every employee knows what is expected of him, and performs his part with an alacrity that is much to be commended. The books and maps are now so complete that there is scarcely a matter of value connected with the operations of the Department, that cannot be readily found when wanted.

PUMPING STATISTICS.

With all of the care exercised during the year, the pumpage shows a sudden and alarming increase, amounting as it does to 917,781,850 gallons, or more than 101,000,000 in excess of 1883. How to account for this, in the face of the vigilance taken to avoid waste, is a problem which the Board confess themselves unable to solve. The increase began in January and continued nearly uniformly throughout the year, compelling the use of both pumps 66 days, not counting their duty during the construction of the inlet, an amount of extra service far in advance of any of the last three years. This unexpectedly large demand has been a source of much anxious thought to the Board and the employees, and it has only been met by untiring watchfulness on the part of both.

The extra pumpage has not only increased the cost of fuel, but has developed the fact more plainly than ever that both pumps cannot be run together with the same economy, proportionately, as when a single one is operated. With the same employees and methods at the works as in 1883, the average duty of the pumps, compared with last year, is very much reduced. This is doubtless, due, in large part, to the small size of the pumping main, which will not allow of two pumps being run at the same time, with advantage.

During the construction of the inlet tube there were 15 days in July, 9 in August and 20 in September when neither of the pumps were run in the daytime, the supply being kept up by using both at night, usually commencing about nine o'clock and continuing till seven or eight in the morning.

COAL SUPPLY, ETC.

Difficulty having been found during the winters of 1882 and 1883 in procuring a regular supply of slack coal, an additional bunker to the one in the boiler room was built during the last spring, which will enable 300 tons to be kept in store. The purpose is to use from these only when the usual supply by rail fails, and to fill them up again as soon as enough is on hand to warrant the same.

The water in the bay has been remarkably low during the last five months of the year, compelling a lift on the part of the pumps of from one to two feet more than is the case when it is at its ordinary level.

THE FISHY TASTE.

The plan adopted two years ago of shutting down the pumping works while the fishy taste and smell were noticeable in the water was continued. The pumps stopped working on this account at 7 a. m., on June 5th, and resumed at 10 a. m., on June 9th, when the water had thrown off its disagreeable qualities, with the result that they were scarcely apparent in the city after the first day. While the pumps were idle, the water in the reservoir, which is kept at an average depth of 25 feet, fell seven feet and a-half, indicating a supply of about two weeks in one of the most favorable months, which would be greatly diminished during the extremes of summer and winter.

RECEIPTS AND EXPENSES.

The receipts of the Department from Dec. 31, 1883, to the same date in 1884 were $51,852.78 from water rents, $717.80 from plumbing for hire, and $68.39 for material sold, a total of $52,638.97 and a gain over the previous year in the amount of water rents of $3,582.89. Including the balance of $7,594.76 from 1883, the sum in the treasury during the year was $60,233.73. Within ten years the revenues have nearly doubled, and, if the same rate of increase continues, in another ten years they will reach $85,000, enough, above the probable expenses for construction and maintenance, to enable fully $40,000 to be turned into the city treasury.

The expenses during the same period were $57,658.37, divided as follows: Construction $36,635.35; Extraordinary Repairs (standpipe, pier, building, etc.) $2,516.68; Maintenance $18,506.34. Although much more than usual has been done in the line of repairs to hydrants, valves, etc., and in lowering pipes and connections, it is satisfactory to know that the maintenance account is below the average of the years past. It will be noticed by the inventory that the expense account embraces $868.24 worth of pipe and other material on hand in excess of the amount at the beginning of the year. The item of extraordinary repairs will probably be small for some years to come, as nearly every costly feature of the Department's property is now thought to be in good condition.

TOTAL COST.

The total cost of the system has been $1,182,786.47, of which $856,302.83 have been charged to construction and $326,583.64 to maintenance. Of this sum, the city advanced $675,955.10, from the commencement of the works to the close of 1873, at which date the Department became self-sustaining. In considering the original cost, it should be remembered that a discount of $88,033.94 was made in the sale of the bonds issued for the establishment of the system. It is hardly to be doubted that the same amount of work could be done at the prices of to-day for two-thirds of the sum expended in the early history of the Department.

ACTUAL EARNINGS.

It is no more than just to remind the public again that the receipts shown above are very far from representing the entire sum of earnings during the year with which the Department should be credited. This subject was discussed at length in our reports for 1882 and 1883, to which we refer those who may desire further information. Adding to the $52,638.97 of income the sum earned for keeping up the fire hydrants (254 at $45 each), for the supply of the public fountains, for flushing sewers and for the various other city uses, estimated in all to be worth $15,400, the actual earnings have been slightly over $88,000. On this basis, which none who study the question will deny to be within moderate bounds, the surplus earnings of 1884, after deducting the cost of maintainance and extraordinary repairs, have been in round numbers $47,000, which is just about seven per cent. on the amount appropriated by the city towards the construction of the works.

"WHY DON'T THE WATER WORKS PAY?"

The question is often asked, "Why don't the Department pay the interest on the water bonds issued to the city?" The above figures show that it does *earn* an amount above maintenance equal to the interest account and a good deal more. The only reason why it does not appear to be doing so, to those who are not familiar with the facts, is, that, instead of applying the surplus proceeds to the payment of the interest and then levying a tax for the extension of the system, the tax is now applied to the interest and the surplus to construction. It is simply a different way of reaching the same object, and, if there is any valid objection to it, the fault cannot be laid at the doors of the present Board, who have acted under the law and the custom precisely as they found them. Aside, from the question of direct revenue, there is another view of the matter that seems to be lost sight of by those who talk of the water works as an unprofitable investment. At the lowest estimate, $100,000 are collected annually in this city as the premium on fire insurance policies in force within its limits. No well informed person will question that without the water system the fire insurance rates would be one-fourth higher than they are, which would be $25,000 additional, a saving in itself more than enough to maintain the Department, not to speak of the protection to property afforded by the public supply. It should not be forgotten, either, that the water rates are less and the system more liberal to patrons in Erie, than those of almost any other city in the country. With the rates for both public and private use in proportion to those of the vast majority of cities, and properly equalized, so that each consumer could be made to pay his just share, the Department would not only meet all expenses of ordinary construction and maintenance, but have enough revenue left to pay *the interest on the* bonds and something to spare.

PUMPAGE VS. REVENUE.

These remarks lead us to consider the surprising contrast between the quantity of water pumped and the amount of revenue collected. A pumpage of 917,000,000 gallons should have produced, at ten cents per thousand gallons, the price to manufacturers, upwards of $91,000, whereas the real amount of water rents taken in was but $51,852,78. These figures give a very fair idea of the extent to which the water is wasted, and show how the careful taxpayers are made to pay for the negligence or worse of those who are less conscientious. If every water taker used no more than he is fairly entitled to, even making the most liberal allowance, there would be no need for enlargement for the next ten years, and the large sum that will soon have to be expended for that purpose could be applied to the reduction of taxes.

The plain truth is, that while most people clamor for honesty and efficiency in public office, too few are ready to assist those who seek to enforce them, especially in municipal affairs. A pumpage of 917,000,000 gallons per year represents 100 gallons daily to each man, woman and child of the 25,-000 who are supposed to be using the city water. No person will seriously argue that one-half of that quantity is needed, either for the requirements of health, comfort or business. The greater portion of the water must be wasted —not wilfully and deliberately, it is conceded, but through sheer thoughtlessness or mistaken ideas on the subject. Those who are in fault—and they include too many of the largest taxpayers—fail to reflect that no article of public use can be had that does not have to be paid for in some way, sooner or later. The sum saved by neglecting. leaky fixtures will have to be made up eventually in providing the means for enlarging the water system ; the water wasted by one man or establishment is certain, in the long run, to add to the expense of some other person, who should not, in justice, be asked to bear it. When John Doe gets more from the public than he is entitled to, it means that Richard Roe, his more prudent or scrupulous neighbor, must pay an additional tax, in time, to make up the difference.

EQUALIZATION OF RATES.

However, we frankly confess, that appeals and arguments on the subject of waste are of slight avail. In every report for years the Board have discussed the matter from the standpoint of justice and economy, and endeavored to explain the certain consequences. Those who should be foremost in seconding our efforts, from their interest as taxpayers, are too often the ones who give us the least support. The only way left is to prepare for enlargement and provide the means that will be necessary for the purpose. The latter end can be much hastened by making such changes in the rates as will compel those whose use mainly renders enlargement necessary to pay their just share of the revenue In many cases the present rates fall much below what an equitable adjustment would seem to require. The income from *sprinkling*, for example, was but $2,436 in 1884, while it is absolutely sure that one-sixth of the pumpage, a quantity equal in value to $8,000, during the six months from May 1st to November 1st, was used in that manner. A careful investigation should be made of the various uses to which the water is applied, and the rates should be so fixed as to make each patron pay, as nearly as practicable, for the quantity he consumes.

NEED FOR ENLARGEMENT.

Those who have read the annual reports of this Department for the last four years will bear witness to the statement that the present Board have strained every nerve to avoid the necessity for enlarging the public water system. We had hoped that our measures to improve the plumbing and decrease the waste, seemingly effective as they were for two years, would save the expense of enlargement for some years to come, though continually reminding the citizens that the day was not far distant when provision must be made for a new pump and pumping main, with their accompanying fixtures. The enormous increase of more than a hundred millions shown by the pumpage of the year just past compels us to face the problem sooner than we expected; in short, it makes the matter of enlargement one of immediate and paramount importance.

When the water system was planned, Erie was a city of about 17,500 inhabitants, and it was hardly expected that its capacity would be equal to the wants of twice that number of people, which is the smallest estimate of population to-day. The two pumps were built to furnish 2,500,000 gallons each per day, when running at their extreme speed, the full twenty-four hours. It was never intended, however, that the regular duty of either pump should be more than eighty per cent. of its capacity, nor that both should be operated at the same time, except on extraordinary occasions, the idea of having them in duplicate being that one should always be ready in case of accident to the other. From the nature of their construction, they are liable to sudden and serious breakages, which may take a long while to repair. The pumps have broken down on three separate occasions, and each time it has taken from two weeks to a month to get the injured one in working order.

During the last year there has never been a day, unless the works were stopped for cause, when either pump, running alone, has done a duty of less than 2,500,000 gallons, and. much of the time it has been forced to render a still greater service in order to keep up the supply. In addition to this extraordinary and unsafe use of a single pump, the two pumps, as shown in another part of this report, have been run together 66 days, or nearly one-fifth of the year, exclusive of the duty rendered while the sinking of the inlet tube was in progress. The demand for water has, at periods, amounted to upwards of 8,000,000 gallons per diem for weeks at a time, and it is evident, that had one of the pumps broken down, the capacity of the other would have been severely strained, if indeed, it would have been equal to the emergency. It is true that we have the reservoir to rely upon in case of accident to the pumps, but, in seasons of prolonged drouth or cold, that might not hold out till the broken pump could be repaired. The only safe-

ty lies in providing duplicate power, on the original plan, each part of which
shall equal in capacity the greatest possible consumption of the city and
leave a good working margin besides.   -

To add to the difficulty, the 20-inch pumping main, which extends from
the works to the reservoir, a distance of nearly two miles, is no longer adequate to its purpose. As long as a single pump is used, the pipe answers
well enough, but its size is too small to allow the use of both pumps, without slowing them down, so that just about fifty per cent. of increase
results. To make this statement more plain: When a single pump is running, at the utmost speed that is considered safe, it will average say 10½
strokes per minute, or about 2,494,800 gallons a day, while the number of
strokes when two pumps are used can only be increased to an average of
16, equal to about 3,811,600 gallons, but a little more than half-a-million
in excess of the quantity required per diem on several occasions during the
last year. Experience also shows that when the two pumps are operated
together the cost for fuel is much more, proportionately, than that of
of running a single pump. (See Note.)

NOTE.—The months of January, February and March, 1885, have furnished a still more forcible argument on the necessity for enlargement. This
period will long be remembered, as the most extended term of bitter cold
weather known in this section for many years. The frost penetrated the ground
to a depth of four to five feet. While none of the mains or hydrants and
but twenty-five or thirty of the old street connections were affected, the
number of frozen service pipes and inside fixtures was unprecedentedly
large. This led to an enormous use of water, caused, no doubt, by letting it flow continuously to prevent freezing. The pumpage during January was 86,464,950 gallons (against 69,221,400 in 1884) a daily average of
2,789,191. During February, it was 94,073,100 gallons (against 59,608,725
in 1884) a daily average of 3,359,793, being the greatest consumption in any
one month in the history of the works. Had one of the pumps broken
down in February, it would have been simply impossible to keep up the
supply, and had both given out the reservoir would not have lasted ten
days.

PLAN FOR ENLARGEMENT.

Thoroughly impressed as we are with the importance of an early enlargement, the Board have perfected plans for that object, which have received
the close study and full approval of some of the best hydraulic engineers in
the country. These contemplate—

1st. The laying down, during the ensuing year, of a thirty-inch pumping
main on the west side of Chestnut street, from the works to Seventh street,
with the purpose of ultimately extending it to the reservoir. This will be
connected by a thirty-inch branch at Seventh street with the present twenty-inch main, directly opposite the point of intersection with the 12-
inch pipe which extends to Parade street. With the advantage
there of a twelve and twenty-inch outlet, it is believed that the length of
thirty-inch main indicated will meet the wants of the city until the means
are on hand for its extension either to Twenty-first street, where connection
can be made with another twelve-inch pipe, or to the reservoir. Arrange-

ments have been made by which the thirty-inch pipe to be laid in 1885 will be purchased at $24.90 per ton delivered, a lower price than ever before known. After the thirty-inch pipe reaches the reservoir, it is designed to use it solely as a pumping main, drawing the supply to the city through the old twenty-inch pipe as long as it will answer the purpose, and then adding another distributing main from the reservoir out Twenty-sixth street east and west, to the opposite sides of the city. This will give the water an opportunity to settle before reaching the consumer, instead of being drawn into the laterals on its way from the pumping works, as is the case now, and leave it free from nearly every objectionable feature when it is distributed in the city. The connections between the twenty and thirty-inch mains on Chestnut street will be of such a character that if a break occurs either can be used as a pumping or a delivery main.

2d. The erection of a wing on the east side of the present pumping room with such foundation work, well space, etc., as may be needed to fit it for a new engine. This will probably be done during the year 1886, including the setting up of such additional boilers as may be required.

8d. The purchase in 1887 or 1888, as the means of the Department may allow, of an engine of the most approved kind, capable of pumping 5,000,000 gallons per day, or more than both the present pumps working together at a safe speed, as soon thereafter as the money to pay for the same can be provided. This will give the duplicate power contemplated in the original plan of the works, with the advantage that the improved pump will be less liable to accidents than the present ones and can be more quickly repaired when one occurs. After the new pump is in place, it is probable that it will be used most of the time, holding the old ones mainly for reserve power, which will effect a great saving in fuel and labor.

COST AND TIME.

It is believed that the above plan, when carried out, will double the capacity of the system, at an expense of less than one-fourth of its original cost, and provide power sufficient for the wants of the city for the next twenty-five years. The thirty-inch pumping main can easily carry off nine millions of gallons daily, and, if another pump should be needed a place has been provided in the plan, so that it can be set up at comparatively small expense. Unless something unforseen occurs, there does not appear to be any good cause why the new pump should not be in operation within four years. The extension of the pumping main from Seventh street to the reservoir may be delayed two or three years longer, according to the amount of other work which may be forced upon the Department

NO EXTRA TAX UPON THE PEOPLE.

The most gratifying feature of this plan is, that it can be carried out entirely by means of the surplus revenues of the Department, from year to year, so that not a dollar of extra tax will be laid upon the general public. We are aware that such a consummation as the doubling of their capacity out of their own earnings, while at the same time meeting the cost of maintenance and ordinary extension, is something almost unknown in the history of public water works in this country, but believe that we are not the least deceived in our estimates nor over sanguine in our expectations. To succeed in our purpose, however, we must have the co-operation of the citizens in keeping down the use of the water to a safe limit until the enlargement is effected, and of the Mayor and Councils in equalizing the rates so that each consumer can be made to pay what is fairly and justly his due. After the plans are consummated—say in from six to eight years — we see no reason why the Water Department, if properly managed, may not turn into the city treasury annually, of its surplus revenues, an amount sufficient at least to pay the interest on the bonds issued for the original construction of the works.

TURNING THE SEWAGE OUT OF THE BAY.

Attention is again called to the fact that no progress has been made in turning the sewage of the city outside of the bay, though it has been strongly and repeatedly urged by the Health Officer, in addition to the recommendations of the Water Department. When this is done, and the water is taken from a depth of thirteen feet and all impurities are allowed to settle in the reservoir, Erie will have a water supply equaled in quality by few other cities in the Union.

Respectfully submitted,

M. LIEBEL,

G. W. F. SHERWIN,

BENJAMIN WHITMAN,

Water Commissioners.

EXHIBIT A.

Receipts of the Erie Water Department for the Year Ending December 31st, 1884.

WATER RENTS.			
First quarter — January	$4,446 00		
February	3,154 69		
March	3,189 09		
		$10,789 78	
Second quarter—April	5,879 48		
May	4,812 51		
June	3,034 09		
		13,726 47	
Third quarter — July	6,082 92		
August	4,712 02		
September	2,574 41		
		13,369 35	
Fourth quarter—October	5,578 44		
November	5,872 76		
December	2,514 98		
		13,966 18	
Total from water rents			$51,852 78
OTHER SOURCES.			
Plumbing and pipe laying	717 80		
Material sold	68 39		
			786 19
Balance last report			1,365 04
Total			$54,004 01
—CR.—			
Deposited in City Treasury—First quarter	$10,400 00		
Second	14,200 00		
Third	14,500 00		
Fourth	14,467 61		
			$53,567 61
Balance			$436 40

EXHIBIT B.

Account of the Water Department with the City Treasurer for the Year Ending December 31st, 1884.

1884 Jan. 1,	—DR.—			
	To balance in Treasury December 31, 1883..............	$ 6,229 33		
	To deposits from January 1 to December 31, 1884...	53,567 61	$59,796 94	$59,796 94
	—CR.—			
	By Warrants Drawn—first quarter—January........	2,386 16		
	" " " " February......	2,249 53		
	" " " " March............	2,006 96		
			6,642 65	
	By Warrants Drawn—second quarter—April.........	2,755 73		
	" " " " May...........	4,344 42		
	" " " " June..........	7,299 37		
			14,399 52	
	By Warrants Drawn—third quarter—July,............	7,886 83		
	" " " " August........	7,029 67		
	" " " " September...	4,028 45		
			18,944 95	
	By Warrants Drawn—fourth quarter—October......	6,376 43		
	" " " " November..	6,687 20		
	" " " " December...	4,607 62	17,671 25	57,658 37
	Balance...			$2,138 57
	DR.			
	To Warrants Issued, but not Redeemed, Jan. 1, '85,			232 09
	Actual Balance in Treasury Jan. 1, 1885,.........			$2,370 66

CITY CONTROLLER'S STATEMENT.

Balance to Cr. of Water Department in City Treasury Jan. 1, 1884.......	$ 7,909 87	
Total Receipts by Treasurer during year 1884......................................	53,567 61	
		$ 61,477 48
Warrants paid during the year 1884..		59,106 82
Balance...		$ 2,370 66

OFFICE OF CITY CONTROLLER. }
ERIE, PA., Jan. 16, 1885. }

I hereby certify that the foregoing has been carefully compared with the records of this of-fice and those of the office of the City Treasurer and Water Commissioners and found correct, and the balance $2,370.66 is due the Water Commissioners, and also that the cash on hand veri-fies therewith. EUGENE METZ,
City Controller.

EXHIBIT C.

Expenditures for the Year 1884; also, from the Commencement of the Works to January 1, 1884.

1884	SALARIES.	FROM JAN. 1, 1884, TO DEC. 31, 1884.	1867 TO 1884.
Jan. 1	From commencement of works to Dec. 31, 1883.....		81,930 67
Dec. 31	Paid B. F. Sloan, secretary.....	1,200 00	
"	Wm. E. Hilton, sup't of pipe laying, &c........	495 79	
"	Wm. O'Lone, ass't and acting sup't.............	563 32	
"	A. F. Crane, inspector...................	826 01	
"	F. W. Koehler, inspector.................	498 34	
"	John Holland, inspector..............	104 60	
"	Geo. G. Gensheimer, ass't secretary.........	720 00	
"	Eugene Liebel, clerk................	141 66	
"	Benj. Whitman, commissioner...............	698 00	
"	G. W. F. Sherwin, "	779 00	
"	Michael Liebel, "	444 00	
		6,470 72	
	MECHANICAL ENGINEERS AND FIREMEN.		
Jan. 1	From commencement of Works to Dec. 31, 1883.....		58,267 62
Dec. 31	Paid Fred. A Roth, mechanical engineer.............	1,000 00	
"	George R. Miller, ass't mechanical engineer..	840 00	
"	Wm. O'Lone, ass't mechanical engineer	233 33	
"	John Kelly, ass't mechanical engineer	643 32	
"	R. W. Simons, fireman	540 00	
"	Jos. Burns "	540 00	
"	Jacob Mullen "	390 00	
"	Extra firemen	286 13	
		4,472 78	
	FUEL AT WORKS.		
Jan. 1	From commencement of works to Dec. 31, 1883.....		103,547 99
5	Paid E. W. Reed for 616.500 lbs. coal @ $1.55..	477 79	
Feb. 9	" " " 483,650 " " " "	374 83	
Mar. 8	" " " 462,600 " " " "	358 52	
April 5	" " " 613,000 " " " "	475 08	
May 3	" " " 377,500 " " " "	280 56	
3	" " " 31,000 " " " 2.50.*.....	38 75	
June 7	" R. J. Saltzman, 563,200 " " " 1.45*.....	408 32	
July 12	" " " 890,400 " " " " *.....	650 49	
Aug. 9	" " " 448,600 " " " "	325 23	
Sept. 13	" " " 324,600 " " " "	235 33	
Oct. 4	" " " 587,500 " " " "	425 94	
Nov. 8	" " " 521,800 " " " "	378 30	
Dec. 6	" " " 537,000 " " " "	389 32	
		4,818 46	
	Total,.......... 6,457,350		
	POSTAGE.		
Jan. 1	From commencement of works to Dec. 31, 1883.....		2,451 00
Dec. 31	Paid for envelopes and postal cards...........	176 90	
		176 90	
	FIRE HYDRANTS.		
Jan. 1	From commencement of works to Dec. 31, 1883.....		10,214 33
May 3	Paid Empire Line, freight.............	5 00	
24	" D. C. Weller, sundries.............	6 90	
31	" Empire Line, freight.............	8 97	
June 21	" " "	8 71	
July 12	" R. P. Burke, et. al., cartage.............	4 56	
12	" Empire Line, freight.............	5 38	
Sept. 27	" " "	3 09	
Dec. 13	" " "	4 68	
31	" Labor, as per superintendent's pay roll.....	298 79	
"	" R D Wood & Co., hydrants.............	1,242 00	
		1,588 02	
	Carried forward.......	$17,527 88	$256,411 61

NOTE.—76½ tons of the coal paid for in June and 141⅛ tons paid for in July were stored in the bunker and remain on hand.

		FROM JAN. 1, 1884, TO DEC. 31, 1884.	1867 TO 1884.
	Brought forward	$17,527 88	$256,411 61
1884.	**CARE AND REPAIR OF HYDRANTS.**		
Dec. 31	Paid Humboldt Iron Works, sundries	$ 18 87	
	" Erie Rubber Works, sundries	2 25	
	" D. C. Weller, sundries	5 50	
	" Jarecki, Hayes & Co., sundries	4 50	
	" John Meyerhoffer, rent	16 50	
	" Dr. P. Hall, paints, &c	20 83	
	" Noble & Hall, sundries	98 37	
	" For sundries	1 04	
	" Frank Hoffman, et. al. gravel, &c	36 50	
	" Erie Hardware Co., sundries	3 83	
	" Schlosser & Felheim, lumber	50	
	" Labor, as per superintendent's pay rolls	341 89	
			550 58
1884.	**DISTRIBUTING MAINS.**		
Jan. 1	From commencement of works to Dec. 31, 1883		308,827 66
May 24	Paid D. C. Weller, sundries	2 25	
24	" G. L. Siegel & Co. sundries	2 25	
24	" Labor, superintendent's pay roll	18 80	
31	" Erie Gas Co., coke	5 68	
July 31	" Patrick Pearl, labor	1 50	
31	" G. L. Siegel & Co., et al., sundries	6 75	
31	" Erie Gas Co., coke	8 00	
Aug. 2	" A. Brugger, wooden plugs	4 50	
2	" Jacob Haller, wood	2 25	
9	" Mich Manning, et al., damages	54 50	
16	" Noble & Hall, special castings	26 05	
Nov. 8	" D. C. Weller, wood	2 25	
Dec. 20	" Jarecki, Hayes & Co, pipe	43 18	
27	" Frank Hoffman	6 75	
31	" For sundries	4 42	
	" Martin Quigley, et al., old rope	38 64	
	" Lake Shore R. R., freight	465 08	
	" R. P. Burke, distributing pipe	158 99	
	" Schlosser & Felheim, lumber	32 34	
	" Geo. B. Hayes, special castings	283 80	
	" Expenses inspecting pipe in Cleveland	67 95	
	" Lake Shore Foundry, pipe	11,822 28	
	" Labor, Superintendent's pay roll, laying pipe	2,881 70	
	" For lead	1,222 21	
			17,172 12
	STOP VALVES, BOXES AND COVERS.		
Jan. 1	From commencement of works to Dec. 31, 1883		14,763 69
Dec. 31	Paid Humboldt Iron Works, sundries	152 26	
	" Noble & Hall, sundries	516 92	
	" Wm. Zimmerly, brick	42 00	
	" Schlosser & Felheim, lumber	24 08	
	" Empire Line, freight	33 66	
	" J. C. Selden, brick	49 50	
	" Donnelly Bros., brick work	93 00	
	" Labor, superintendent's pay rolls	151 40	
	" R. D. Wood & Co	1,301 14	
			2,363 96
	REPAIRS OF ENGINES AND BOILERS.		
Jan. 1	From commencement of works to Dec. 31, 1883		23,929 87
Dec. 31	Paid D. P. Murphy, et al., for brick work	$ 110 00	
	" Roger McDonough, labor	21 00	
	" C. Kessler, sundries	8 14	
	" Saltsman & Austin, lime, firebrick, etc	110 30	
	" Noble & Hall, sundries	361 47	
	" Humboldt Iron Works, sundries	285 91	
	" Jarecki, Hayes & Co. "	46 02	
	" Erie Rubber Works, et al.,	57 65	
			1,000 49
	Carried forward	$38,615 03	$603,982 88

		FROM JAN. 1, 1884, TO DEC. 31, 1884.	1867 TO 1884.
	Brought forward..	$38,615 03	$603,932 83
1884.	**REPAIRS OF DISTRIBUTING MAINS.**		
Jan. 1	From commencement of works to Dec. 31, 1883.......		9,857 88
Dec. 31	Paid labor as per superintendent's pay roll............	432 12	
		432 12	
	IMPROVEMENT OF GROUNDS.		
Jan. 1	From commencement of works to Dec. 31, 1883......		855 97
Dec. 31	Paid Roger McDonough, labor................................	214 11	
	" H. G. Fink, sundries....................	14 20	
	" G. W. Baxter, wire....................	3 00	
	" Larry Cummins, et al., labor.................	32 44	
	" Beckman & Williams, seeds, etc................	15 77	
	" W. W. Loomis, manure..........................	4 00	
	" Wm. Brewster, trees..........................	20 25	
	" Anthony Mullane, contract	78 85	
		382 62	
	BUILDINGS, GROUNDS AND STANDPIPE.		
Jan. 1	From commencement of works to Dec. 31, 1883......		63,964 55
Dec. 31	Paid Roger McDonough, watchman	214 12	
	" Wm. F. Nick, paint and oil.......................	94 66	
	" Erie Hardware Co., sundries....................	8 68	
	" Fred Genck, et al., brick for smoke stack, etc.	52 10	
	" J. O. Baker, for labor on " "	87 71	
	" Stearns Mfg. Co., sundries	28 50	
	" Art Novelty Co., "	3 45	
	" Constable Bros., et al , sundries...............	25 36	
	" Humboldt Iron Works, "	15 39	
	" D. P. Murphy, et al., mason work	92 50	
	" Saltsman & Austin, lime, etc................	17 55	
	" Schlosser & Felheim, lumber.................	74 34	
	" Jas. Burke, et al., labor.................	53 25	
	" Jos. Boyd, et al., painting buildings.............	182 98	
	" Noble & Hall, sundries..........................	5 39	
	" For sundries...................................	4 81	
	" Donnelly Bros., contract, standpipe............	1,147 00	
		2,107 79	
	CARE AND MAINTENANCE OF RESERVOIR AND KEEPER'S HOUSE.		
Jan. 1	From commencement of works to Dec. 31 1883.......		6,691 36
Dec. 31	Paid Samuel Phister, salary for year.....................	300 00	
	" E. Goodrich, clay..............................	9 00	
	" W. J Butler, sundries	5 55	
	" Saltsman & Austin, sundries	6 25	
	" Schlosser & Felheim, lumber....................	7 44	
	" For sundries......	12 77	
	" Labor as per superintendent's pay roll............	142 31	
		483 32	
	ENGINEER'S SMALL STORES.		
Jan. 1	From commencement of works to Dec. 31, 1883.......		1,055 63
Dec. 31	Paid R. J. Saltsman, et al., coal, etc....................	40 80	
	" James Gaffney, sundries........................	37 03	
	" C. W. Parsons, et al., sundries..................	10 38	
	" C. Kessler, "	16 68	
	" Swalley & Warfel, soap.	5 00	
	" D. C. Weller, et al., hardware................	8 12	
	" Erie Ice Co., ice bill.....................	18 45	
	" For sundries.....................	1 57	
	" W. W. Pierce & Co., sundries.................	1 52	
		139 55	
	SUPERINTENDENT'S SMALL STORES.		
Jan. 1	From commencement of works to Dec. 31, 1883.... ...		363 32
	Paid G. W. Goodrich, oil...............	12 25	
	" Schneider Bros., sundries..............	1 14	
	" C. Kessler, "	7 67	
	" For sundries	10 62	
		31 68	
	Carried forward...	$42,192 11	$686,721

	FROM JAN. 1, 1884, TO DEC. 31, 1884.		1867 TO 1884.
Brought forward........................	....	$42,192 11	$686,721 54

PRINTING AND ADVERTISING.

1884.
Jan. 1
Dec. 31

			2,947 57
"	......	20 75	
"	....	52 20	
"	......	139 15	
"	......	1 75	
"	......	4 63	
"		23 45	
"	" "	9 25	
"	....	6 50	
		257 68	

BOOKS AND STATIONERY.

Jan. 1	From commencement of works to Dec. 31, 1883......	....	....	1,142 31
Dec. 31	Paid Ashby & Vincent, et al., sundries...................	62 94		
	" For sundries.................	6 80		
			69 74	

ENGINE ROOM FURNITURE.

Jan. 1	F	1883	....	....	626 59
Dec. 31	Paid	....	8 60		
	"		10 40		
	"	......	2 20		
	"		26 95		
	"	......	3 00		
	"		10 53		
	"	......	5 25		
	"	... ...	4 26		
	"		10 60		
	"	......	3 58		
	"	......	9 75		
			95 12		

OFFICE FURNITURE, RENT & EXPENSES.

Jan. 1		31, 1883	....	....	9,965 26
Dec. 31	Paid		250 00		
	"	instruments	84 00		
	"	....	97 55		
	"	....	21 75		
	"	....	24 48		
	"		8 00		
	"	....	29 25		
	"	undries...................	2 00		
	"		7 11		
	"	lls rendered...........	14 00		
	"	....	60 23		
			598 57		

WASTE AND PACKING.

Jan. 1	From commencement of works to Dec. 31, 1883......	....	....	1,794 29
Dec. 31	Paid C. W. Parsons, sundry bills................	153 05		
	" D. C. Weller, et al "	35 48		
	" Erie Hardware Co "	14 57		
	" C. Kessler "	53 36		
		256 46		

OIL AND TALLOW.

Jan. 1	From commencement of works to Dec. 31, 1883......	....	....	4,410 49
Dec. 31	Paid C. Kessler, sundry bills................	631 79		
	" B. P. Bell, bill rendered...........	37 10		
		668 89		

CARTAGE.

Jan. 1	From commencement of works to Dec. 31, 1883......	....	....	370 16
Dec. 31	Paid R. P. Burke, et al., sundry bills...........	21 00		
	" Frank Hoffmann, et al.. "	38 25		
	" For sundries................. ..	27 10		
		86 35		

Carried forward........................	....	$44,224 72	$707,988 21

		FROM JAN. 1, 1884 TO DEC. 31, 1884.	1867 TO 1884.
	Brought forward...	................$44,224 72	$707,988 21

SHOP TOOLS AND REPAIRS.

1884				
Jan. 1	From commencement of works to Dec. 31, 1883.......		....	2,341 89
Dec. 31	Paid Humboldt Iron Works.................................	42 09		
"	Noble & Hall, sundry bills......................	117 69		
"	W. W. Pierce & Co. sundry bills	35 45		
"	C. Kessler, " "	9 53		
"	Mrs. Julia A. Teel, rent.......................	21 95		
"	Schneider Bros., et al., sundry bills.............	17 66		
"	Erie Hardware Co. " "	11 02		
"	E. W. Walker & Co., cart........................	11 25		
"	Union Meter Co., jack-screws....................	14 45		
"	Jarecki, Hayes & Co., sundry bills................	67 64		
"	Henry Mayer, " "	18 83		
"	For sundries.................................	6 04		
			373 60	

WATER METERS AND THEIR CARE.

Jan. 1	From commencement of works to Dec. 31, 1883......	....	....	5,911 84
Dec. 31	Paid labor as per superintendent's pay roll...........	71 74		
"	H. R. Worthington, et al., meters and freight	341 19		
"	Schlosser & Felheim, lumber.........................	12 48		
"	For sundries.................................	2 13		
			427 54	

GAS WELLS AND CARE.

Jan. 1	From commencement of works to Dec. 31, 1884.......	....	....	8,148 59

LEGAL COSTS AND COUNSEL FEES.

Jan. 1	From commencement of works to Dec. 31, 1883.......	....	....	1,367 38
Dec. 31	Paid Davenport & Griffith.................................	10 00		
"	E. Camphausen.............................	77 50		
"	J. P. Vincent, et al........................	55 00		
			142 50	

PUTTING IN INLET PIPE.

Dec. 31	Paid Bauschard & Son., making temporary gate....	32 33		
"	Beckman & Williams, canvas........................	4 05		
"	Noble & Hall, iron gate..........................	290 53		
"	Saltsman & Austin, cement......................	16 75		
"	James Burke, et al., labor.......................	13 25		
"	Commissioners, trip to Cleveland..................	18 55		
"	J. O. Baker, fitting castings.....................	10 44		
"	Baas & Althof, wire screens.......................	16 68		
"	Wm. Roward, laying brick........................	32 00		
"	W. W. Loomis, contract	466 52		
"	Constable Bros., sundries..........................	10 05		
"	J. P. Gifford, straw.............................	5 00		
"	J. C. Selden, brick.............................	24 00		
"	J. Louis Linn, contract for tube.................	3,521 05		
"	J. Louis Linn, dredging............................	292 50		
"	Jarecki Mfg. Co., sundries.....................	18 77		
"	D. P. Murphy, laying brick......................	3 00		
"	John Genck, et al., filling piers.................	26 60		
"	Joshua Follansbee, services.....................	25 00		
"	Schlosser & Felheim, lumber........................	3 78		
"	R. J. Saltsman, fuel............................	108 75		
"	Labor, per superintendent's pay roll...........	320 75		
"	John Dunlap, on contract......................	500 00		
			5,760 35	
	Carried forward	................$50,927 98	$725,757 91

		FROM JAN. 1, 1884 TO DEC. 31, 1884	1867 TO 1884.
	Brought forward...	.... $50,927 98	$725,757 91
1884.	**INLET PIERS AND REPAIRS.**		
Jan. 1	From commencement of works to Dec. 31, 1883.....	....	31,820 00
Dec. 31	Paid Jonas Bowers, contract...................................	1,382 19	
"	J. O. Baker, et al., labor, etc........................	5 85	
		1,388 04	
	EXPENSE OF HORSE AND WAGON.		
Jan. 1	From commencement of works to Dec. 31, 1883.......	....	2,225 47
Dec. 31	Paid Jere Fogarty, shoes..	9 30	
"	Wm. O'Lone, et al., hay	25 50	
"	J. B. Crouch & Co., oats, etc...........................	37 25	
"	J. L. Siegel & Co., hay, etc...........................	22 67	
"	Fred Gross, labor..	6 05	
"	L. Kester & Son, boarding horse.......	76 68	
"	Henry Mayo, et al., harness, etc	30 25	
"	John O. Baker, labor	5 98	
"	Geo. Carroll & Bro., et al., lumber................	13 45	
"	Andrew Garlow, labor	8 00	
"	Mrs. Julia A. Teel, rent...............................	5 00	
"	Dr. J. Bryce, services, etc.............................	8 00	
"	Erie Hardware Co., sundries..........................	3 00	
"	For sundries...	2 52	
		253 65	
	INTEREST AND EXCHANGE.		
Jan. 1	From commencement of works to Dec. 31, 1883.....	....	11,031 47
	WATER RENTS RETURNED.		
Jan. 1	From commencement of works to Dec. 31, 1883.....	....	52 50
	PROTECTION TO R. R. TRACK.		
Jan. 1	From commencement of works to Dec. 31, 1883......	....	1,712 04
	STREET CONNECTIONS.		
Jan. 1	From commencement of works to Dec. 31, 1883.....	....	34,767 41
Dec. 31	Paid labor as per superintendent's pay roll...	797 01	
"	Gibson & Price, lead pipe, tin, etc	90 44	
"	Jarecki & Hayes, sundries.............................	1,485 80	
"	Jarecki Mfg. Co., "	21 25	
"	For sundries	3 59	
		2,398 09	
	ON ACCOUNT OF SERVICE PIPE.		
Jan. 1	From commencement of works to Dec. 31, 1883.....	....	11,402 77
Dec. 31	Paid National Tube Works, bill rendered..............	233 75	
"	Jarecki, Hayes & Co., " "	171 16	
"	Penn'a Co., freight......................................	4 18	
		409 09	
	ON ACCOUNT OF PAVING AND STREET REPAIRS.		
Jan. 1	From commencement of works to Dec. 31, 1883......	....	1,737 43
Dec. 31	Paid Jacob Rastatter, labor	64 40	
"	Anthony Mullane, "	21 00	
"	Donnelly Bros. "	17 52	
"	Wm. Krueger "	13 75	
"	Labor, superintendent's pay roll...................	15 33	
"	For sundries...	94	
		132 94	
	PLUMBING FOR HIRE.		
Jan. 1	From commencement of works to Dec. 31, 1883.....	....	2,699 24
	Paid labor as per superintendent's pay roll.............	151 27	
		151 27	
	SHOP AND MISCELLANEOUS WORK.		
Jan. 1	From commencement of works to Dec. 31, 1883......	....	7,569 13
Dec. 31	Paid labor as per superintendent's pay roll............	659 14	
		·659 14	
	Carried forward...	.... $56,921 20	$830,775 57

		FROM JAN. 1, 1884, TO DEC. 31, 1884.	1867 TO 1884.
	Brought forward......................................	..............$56,320 20	$830,775 37
1884.	**LOWERING DISTRIBUTING MAINS.**		
Jan. 1	From commencement of works to Dec. 31, 1883......		1,425 61
Dec. 31	Paid Labor as per superintendent's pay roll..........	86 58	
		86 58	
	THAWING OUT PIPE.		
Jan. 1	From commencement of works to Dec. 31, 1883.......		58 41
Dec. 31	Paid labor, as per superintendent's pay roll..........	4 83	
		4 83	
	RESERVOIR GROUNDS.		
Jan. 1	From commencement of works to Dec. 31, 1883......		5,237 16
Dec. 31	Paid Mrs. Rebecca Thayer, balance on purchase...	1,223 33	
		1,223 33	
	LOWERING STREET CONNECTIONS.		
Jan. 1	From commencement of works to Dec. 31, 1883.......		262 81
Dec. 31	Paid labor as per superintendent's pay roll..........	23 43	
		23 43	
	ENGINES AND BOILERS.		
Jan. 1	From commencement of works to Dec. 31, 1883......		66,316 95
	CIVIL ENGINEERING.		
Jan. 1	From commencement of works to Dec. 31, 1883......		7,122 85
	RAILROAD SWITCH AND SCALES.		
Jan. 1	From commencement of works to Dec. 31, 1883.......		1,128 61
	CONSTRUCTION OF RESERVOIR.		
Jan. 1	From commencement of works to Dec. 31, 1883......		116,586 84
	PARK FOUNTAINS.		
Jan. 1	From commencement of works to Dec. 31, 1883......		3,244 68
	DISCOUNT ON CITY BONDS.		
Jan. 1	From commencement of works to Dec. 31, 1883......		88,033 94
	Total...	..............$57,658 37	$1,120,293 34

RECAPITULATION.

DR.

Balance in Treasury, Jan. 1, 1884.... ....$ 7,594 37
Receipts during the year 1884............................. ....52,638 97
————$60,233 34

CR.

Expended for construction....................... ....$36,635 35
"   " extraordinary repairs...).................... 2,516 88
"   " maintenance... .... 18,506 34
————$57,658 37

Balance.. $2,574 97

EXHIBIT D.

Amount of Water Rents Collected each year, with the Increase and Decrease, since the Commencement of the Works.

	A'm't Rec'd	Increase.	Decrease
From Jan 1, 1869, to Dec. 31, 1869	$ 4,264 47	$	$
" " 1870 " 1870	9,237 30	4,972 83	
" " 1871 " 1871	18,138 03	8,900 78	
" " 1872 " 1872	21,652 68	3,514 60	
" " 1873 " 1873	25,560 40	3,907 72	
" " 1874 " 1874	27,938 90	2,378 50	
" " 1875 " 1875	29,639 38	1,700 48	
" " 1876 " 1876	31,048 76	1,409 38	
" " 1877 " 1877	32,276 57	1,227 81	
" " 1878 " 1878	29,636 01		2,640 56
" " 1879 " 1879	33,343 20	3,707 19	
" " 1880 " 1880	37,385 00	4,041 80	
" " 1881 " 1881	40,385 87	3,000 87	
" " 1882 " 1882	43,818 73	3,432 86	
" " 1883 " 1883	48,269 89	4,451 16	
" " 1884 " 1884	51,852 78	3,582 89	
Total water rents received	$ 484,448 02		

INVENTORY

Of Stock, Tools, Material, etc., on hand.

DIVISION.	Jan. 1, 1883	Jan. 1, 1884	Jan. 1, 1885
Superintendent of pipe laying, etc. . . .	$ 5,301 38	$ 8,849 51	$ 7,724 79
Mechanical engineer	646 90	593 75	560 60
Keeper at reservoir	51 25	63 79	57 65
Secretary and Treasurer	. . . . .	. . . . .	1,832 25
	5,999 53	9,507 52	10,175 29
Increase each year		3,507 05	668 24

EXHIBIT E.

Location, Size and Length of Distributing Mains and Fire Hydrant Branches laid during the year 1884.

LOCATION.	FEET.	IN.
12-INCH MAINS.		
7th street, from 165 feet east of State to Parade................................	2,510	2
21st " " east side of Peach to Parade..................................	3,004	0
	5,514	2
6-INCH MAINS.		
12th street from Raspberry westward..	116	3
26th " " Peach to State...................................	446	6
East Avenue, from 15th to Buffalo road	1,692	0
Parade street from 18th to 21st...	1,007	0
	2,261	9
4-INCH MAINS.		
Front street, from French to State	385	0
3d street, from Chestnut to Walnut, and from Sassafras eastward.........	878	6
5th " between Cherry and Poplar	410	0
7th " from Ash to Reed................................	706	0
17th " " State to Peach............................	415	6
19th " " Sassafras to Myrtle......................	722	9
20th " " Peach westward...........................	335	0
22d " between French and State.....................	21	0
24th " from Holland westward......................	510	0
25th " between Sassafras and Myrtle...............	120	0
26th " from Stop House of Reservoir to Maple........	912	0
Ash " " from 7th to 8th.........................	389	9
Holland street " 19th to 21st...........................	658	0
French " between 22d and 23d	51	0
State " from 26th northward.....................	27	6
Walnut street, from 3d to 4th and from 8th to 9th...................	785	0
Plum " " 4th to West Public Square.............	620	7
	7,947	7
TEMPORARY 1-INCH MAINS.		
Holland street, between 25th and 26th...........................	405	0
26th " " Holland and German..................	161	0
	566	0
TEMPORARY THREE-FOURTHS-INCH MAINS.		
3d street, between Peach and Sassafras..........................	87	0
5th " " Plum and Liberty.....................	249	5
11th " " Wayne and East avenue...............	225	0
	561	5
BRANCHES TO FIRE HYDRANTS.		
6-INCH BRANCHES.		
7th street, at Peach and French	14	10
Peach street, at 9th and 11th	18	8
21st " at Peach	5	6
	39	0
4-INCH BRANCHES.		
2d street, at Peach..........................	4	8
3d " " Holland........................	4	8
5th " between Cherry and Poplar	26	0
7th " at Holland, Wallace and Reed...........	30	10
8th " at Chestnut, Sassafras, French and Ash ..	48	0
9th " at Wallace and Myrtle.................	10	7
12th " at Wallace, Reed and Holland..........	45	7
14th " at Wallace and Holland..............	12	2
16th " at Peach..........................	10	0
17th " at Chestnut and Holland.............	21	9
18th " at Peach, Perry, East, German, Walnut and Wallace.	39	9
19th " at Sassafras, Chestnut and Myrtle....	31	11
20th " at Chestnut...................	8	8
21st " at Sassafras, Holland and Parade.......	25	1
Carried forward................................	319	3

(MAINS AND FIRE HYDRANT BRANCHES, CONTINUED.)

LOCATION.	FEET	IN.
Brought forward	319	3
22d " at Chestnut, Peach, German and Sassafras	38	8
23d " at Myrtle	10	0
24th " at Peach, and between French and Holland	20	2
26th " at Chestnut, Sassafras, Myrtle, State and Cherry	43	10
Cascade, between 10th and 11th	6	4
Myrtle, at 21st	5	6
French, at 8th	5	8
Walnut and 3d	8	11
State, at Front	10	2
Parade, at 13th	20	4
Sassafras, at 19th	11	8
Plum, at West Public Square	10	6
Chestnut at 18th	2	3
German, at 7th and 12th	20	6
Total	533	9

Total Distributing Mains.

	MILES	FEET.
*Laid previous to 1884	41	3,926
Less 4 and 6-inch pipe taken up in 1884, and replaced with 12-inch, as follows; on Seventh st., 1,440 feet ; on Twenty-first st., 1,256 feet—total		2,696
Leaving	41	1,030
Laid in 1884 (Less 573 feet of Hydrant Branches)	3	1,010
Total Distributing Mains, Dec. 31, 1884	44	2,240
LENGTHS OF VARIOUS SIZES OF DISTRIBUTING MAINS.		
20-inch pipe	1	4,720
12 " "	2	1,680
6 " "	13	370
4 " "	26	670
†2 " "		1,080
†1 inch and ¾ inch pipe		4,280
Total	44	2,240

The total length of hydrant branches is about 3,048 feet, all 4-inch except 72 feet.

About 150 miles of streets are embraced within the city limits, leaving more than two-thirds of its area to be supplied with water pipe.

*Measurements show that the figures heretofore given were more than 2 miles in excess of the actual amount.
†The ¾, 1 and 2-inch pipe were laid for temporary use.

EXHIBIT F.

Location, Number and Length of Street Connections put in by the Department during the year 1884.

LOCATION	NO.	FEET.	IN.	LOCATION.	NO.	FEET.	IN.
Reed Dock	1	3	10	Ash street	6	101	9
Short street	5	119	10	Wallace street	4	119	2
2d "	4	58	2	Parade "	2	21	9
3d "	26	432	10	Division "	3	50	0
4th "	12	181	2	Holland "	5	80	9
5th	14	279	9	French "	3	56	2
6th	5	83	2	State "	10	269	5
7th	19	421	3	Peach "	6	138	1
8th "	8	154	3	Turnpike "	1	43	0
9th "	4	44	0	Sassafras "	7	78	4
10th	1	22	5	Myrtle "	5	113	0
11th "	7	130	5	Hickory "	1	8	0
12th "	13	337	10	Chestnut "	4	99	3
13th "	7	114	4	Huron "	1	25	4
14th "	8	140	7	Walnut "	12	195	6
16th	6	151	3	Cherry "	1	9	2
17th "	11	142	8	Poplar "	3	83	1
18th	12	265	9	Liberty "	1	45	11
19th	5	55	3	Plum "	2	32	8
20th	3	62	11	Cascade "	1	26	4
21st "	14	287	5	Buffalo road	1	25	4
22d	2	20	4				
23d	4	53	9	Total in 1884	281	5,457	11
24th	5	128	1	Previously put in	3,387	78,075	0
25th	4	74	8		3,668	83,532	11
26th	2	60	0				

Total in miles .... $15\frac{4332}{5280}$

EXHIBIT G.

Location, Size, Style, etc., of Fire Hydrants set during the year 1884.

LOCATION.	SIZE.	STYLE.
HYDRANTS IN NEW LOCATIONS.		
THREE WAY.		
Corner of 7th and Peach	6 inch	Matthews
" 7th " French	6 "	"
" 9th " Peach	6 "	"
" 11th " "	6 "	"
" 21st " "	6 "	"
Total ....5.		
ONE WAY.		
Corner of Front and State streets	4 "	
" 2d " Peach "	4 "	..
" 3d " Holland ".	4 "	
" 3d " Walnut "	4 "	West Jersey
5th street, between Cherry and Poplar	4 "	Morris, T., & Co.
Corner of 7th and German streets	4 "	
" 7th and Wallace "	4 "	Matthews
" 7th and Reed "	4 "	Morris, T., & Co.
" 8th and French "	4 "	Matthews
" 8th and Chestnut "	4 "	"
" 8th and Ash "	4 "	West Jersey
" 8th and Sassafras "	4 "	Matthews
" 9th and Wallace "	4 "	"
" 9th and Myrtle "	4 "	"
" 12th and Wallace "	4 "	..
" 12th and German "	4 "	..
" 12th and Reed "	4 "	::
" 12th and Holland "	4 "	::
" 14th and Holland "	4 "	
" 14th and Wallace "	4 "	
" 16th and Peach "	4 "	...
" 17th and Chestnut "	4 "	...
" 17th and Holland "	4 "	"
" 18th and Peach "	4 "	"
" 18th and Perry "	4 "	Pittsburg
" 18th and German "	4 "	Matthews
" 18th and Walnut "	4 "	"
" 18th and Wallace "	4 "	" .
" 19th and Sassafras "	4 "	::
" 19th and Chestnut "	4 "	...
" 19th and Myrtle "	4 "	
" 20th and Chestnut "	4 "	..
" 21st and Sassafras "	4 "	"
" 21st and Myrtle "	4 "	
" 21st and Holland "	4 "	West Jersey
" 21st and Parade "	4 "	Pittsburg
" 22d and Chestnut "	4 "	Matthews
" 22d and Peach "	4 "	"
" 22d and German "	4 "	"
" 22d and Sassafras "	4 "	"
" 23d and Myrtle "	4 "	Pittsburg
" 24th and Peach "	4 "	Matthews
24th street, between French and Holland	4 "	West Jersey
Corner of 26th and Chestnut streets	4 "	Matthews
" 26th and Sassafras "	4 "	"
" 26th and Myrtle "	4 "	
" 26th and State "	4 "	Bay State
" 26th and Cherry "	4 "	West Jersey
Peach street, between 27th and 28th	4 "	
Corner of Plum and West Public Square	4 "	Matthews
Cascade street, between 10th and 11th	4 "	West Jersey
Buffalo road and East Avenue	4 "	"
Total.....................52.		
Grand Total...... ....57.		

(SEE NEXT PAGE.)

(FIRE HYDRANTS CONTINUED.)

Old or Defective Hydrants replaced with New.

LOCATION.	SIZE.	STYLE.
ONE WAY.		
Corner of 2d and State streets..	4 inch	Matthews
" 5th and French "	4 "	"
6th street between Peach and Sassafras............................	4 "	"
Corner of 7th and State streets.......................................	4 "	"
" 9th and State "	4 "	"
" 9th and Sassafras"	4 "	"
" 10th and Peach "	4 "	"
" 10th and State "	4 "	"
" 12th and Peach "	4 "	"
" 12th and State "	4 "	"
" 13th and Parade "	4 "	"
" 14th and Peach "	4 "	"
" 15th and Peach "	4 "	"
" 18th and Chestnut street........................,.................	4 "	"
" 21st and Peach street..	4 "	"
North Park, front of Reed House.....................................	4 "	"
" " " Opera House..	4 "	"
Parade street, between 13th and 14th...............................	4 "	"
Total... 18		

• RECAPITULATION.

Public Fire Hydrants set previous to Jan. 1, 1884...171
"   "   " " during the year 1884, exclusive of old ones replaced 57
— 228
Private Fire Hydrants.. 26

Total number of Fire Hydrants... 254

Style of Fire Hydrants in Use.

Old Style Matthews............................ 12	Ludlow............................ 4
New style " 119	Morris. Tasker & Co.................................. 4
Bay State................................ 40	Union.................................... 1
West Jersey................................. 44	Brown......................:................... 2
Home-made....................................... 6	
Pittsburg.................... 22	Total..............................254

All are steamer and hose hydrants except one. Five of the number are three way hydrants; seven are two-way; the remainder are one way.

Besides the above there are 6 hydrants for the use of street sprinkling wagons, as follows :

NO.	LOCATION.	SIZE.
1	State, South east corner of east Park..	1½
1	" between 10th and 11th streets..	1½
1	" " 12th " 13th "	1½
1	9th " State " French"	1½
1	Turnpike bet. 14th " 15th "	1½
1	18th between Peach and Sassafras streets......	1½

EXHIBIT H.

Location and Size of Stop Valves set during the year 1884.

STOP VALVES IN NEW LOCATIONS.

12 INCH.

7th street, West line of Peach......................	21st street, East line of State........................
" " French...................	" " Holland........................
" " East "	" " West " Parade.........................
" " West " Holland..................	Peach street, South line of 9th..................
" " West " Parade..................	Total.. 9

6 INCH.

4th street, East line of State......................	26th street, East line of Peach....................
" " French...................	" " Sassafras................
7th " branch to fire hydrant, corner of	East Avenue, North line of 15th..................
Peach......................	Parade street, " " 21st..................
7th street, branch to fire hydrant, corner of	" " South " 18th..................
French......................	French " North line of 7th..................
10th street. West line of Parade..................	Peach " " 24th..................
12th " " " Raspberry...............	" " branch to fire hydrant, corner of
18th " East " Cherry..................	9th..................
21st " branch to fire hydrant, corner of	Peach street, branch to fire hydrant, corner of
Peach......................	11th..................
21st street, North line of Myrtle..................	Total..18

4 INCH.

Front street. West line of French..................	25th street, West line of Sassafras.............
3d " East " Sassafras........	26th " East " Cherry..................
5th " " " French..................	" " 55 feet West of stop house.........
" " West " Cherry..................	Ash " North line of 8th..................
7th " South " Sassafras..................	Parade " South " 7th..................
" " East " Ash..................	" " North " 7th..................
" " " " Wallace..................	" " South " 10th..................
8th " West " Peach..........,..........	" " " " 13th..................
" " " " Sassafras..................	Holland " " " 7th..................
" " East " French..................	" " North " 7th..................
9th " " " Parade	" " South " 21st..................
" " " " Wallace..................	" " North " 21st..................
17th " West " State..................	French " South " 7th..................
" " East " Peach..................	State " North " 26th..................
20th " West " Peach..................	Walnut " South " 3d..................
22d " East " Sassafras..................	Plum " " " 4th..................
23d " " " Myrtle.	" " " " 5th..................
24th " West " Holland..................	Total..............................;..35

PRIVATE 4 INCH VALVE.

Watson Paper Mill, East 16th street................ | Total..............   1

Grand Total...63.

DEFECTIVE VALVES REPLACED.

6 INCH.

4th street, South line of Peach. .... | North Park Row and Peach..................

Total.. ....2.

4 INCH.

7th street, South line of Sassafras..................	German st., north line of 12th..................
10th " " " Parade..................	Peach, " " " 5th..................
12th " " " French..................	State, " " " 11th..................
16th " West " Peach.....................	Chestnut, " fire hydrant, bet. 15th and 16th.
23d " " " Peach..................	Total...10
Parade street, " " 11th..................	

Grand Total ....12.

RECAPITULATION.

	20 in.	12 in.	6 in.	4 in.	Total.
Stop valves set up to Dec. 31, 1883..	5	6	39	187	237
" " " in 1884 (exclusive of valves replaced).................	...	9	18	56	63
	5	15	57	237	300

NOTE.—The stop valves heretofore reported were 86 in excess of the actual number.

EXHIBIT I.

Number of Families, Stores, Offices, Manufactories, etc., Supplied with City Water for the year 1884.

Butcher shops	43	Laundries	9
Barber shops	32	Lumber yards	3
Billiard rooms	6	Mineral water and Bottling	
Breweries	4	works	6
Bakeries	8	Manufactories	91
Board of Trade	1	Orphan asylums	2
Boat Houses	4	Offices	163
Banks	8	Oil Works	2
Coffee & Spice Mills	1	Opera House	1
Cemeteries	1	Photograph rooms	7
Churches	16	Printing offices	10
Custom House	1	Police station	1
Convents	1	Post office	1
Coal and Iron Docks	1	Public halls	21
Club houses	2	Railroad Depots	5
Dyeing works	1	Railroad Machine shops	2
Driving Parks	1	Railroads	4
Engine houses	5	Rinks	3
Express offices	2	Stores	305
Fountains—private	6	Saloons and eating houses	148
public	4	Schools	20
Families	4085	Slaughter houses	11
" and others by special		Street Railways	1
permits*	230	Transfer Companies	1
Flouring Mills	3	Work shops	75
Fish Markets	6	Watering troughs	17
Gas Works	1	U. S. Signal station	1
Grain Elevators	3	Internal Revenue Office	1
Greenhouses	3		
Hotels and Boarding houses	88	Total	5395
Hospitals	2	Last enumeration	5079
Jail and Court House	1		
Livery stables	14	Increase in one year	316

*Special permits for families are generally issued for 1 month.

EXHIBIT J.

PUMPING ENGINE STATISTICS FOR 1884.

The Pumps are two in number, of the kind known as the Cornish Bull Engine. The diameter of each plunger is 20¾ inches, and each pump has a stroke of 10 feet. Allowing for loss, the capacity of each pump is calculated at 165 gallons to every stroke. The Standpipe is 247 feet high. The reservoir is nearly two miles from the pumping works, and the water is pumped through a 20-inch pipe, with which all the east and west main sare connected. The bottom of the reservoir is 210 feet above the surface of the bay, and the water is kept at an average depth of about 24 feet, the exact lift being obtained by a daily comparison of the gauges at the works and at the reservoir. The pumps are run at an average of about 10½ strokes per minute, when operated singly, but when both are used the number of strokes is reduced to about 8½ for each pump in the daytime and 7½ at night, the capacity of the delivery main being too small to admit of more rapid pumping.

Months.	No. of Days a single Pump was run.	No. of Days in which both pumps were run	No. of days both Pumps were idle.	No. of strokes of the pumps.	No. of gals. pumped.	Daily average of gals. pumped.	Average lift in feet.	No. of lbs. of bituminous slack coal used.	Cost of coal.	Price of coal per ton of 2,000 lbs.
January	27	4	...	493,048	81,352,920	2,624,287	234.00	616,500	$477 79	1 55
February	29	...	...	442,728	73,059,030	2,519,276	234.40	483,650	374 83	1 55
March	26	5	...	487,170	80,383,050	2,593,000	235.05	462,600	356 52	1 55
April	12	10	8	412,480	68,059,200	2,268,640	232.50	613,000	475 08	1 55
May	25	5	1	460,145	75,923,925	2,449,158	234.30	408,500	319 31	1 55
June	15	10	5	490,355	80,908,575	2,696,952	233.00	410,200	297 40	1 45
July	8	19	4	449,700	74,200,500	2,393,564	233.22	607,735	445 56	1 45
August	...	19	12	438,800	72,402,000	2,335,545	232.00	448,600	325 23	1 45
September	...	20	10	540,000	89,100,000	2,970,000	228.00	324,600	235 33	1 45
October	9	18	4	564,540	93,149,100	3,004,809	234.00	587,500	425 94	1 45
November	28	...	2	421,464	69,541,760	2,318,059	236.05	521,800	378 30	1 45
December	29	...	2	361,826	59,701,290	1,925,848	235.38	537,000	389 32	1 45
Totals and average	208	110	48	5,562,256	917,781,350	2,508,261	234.32	6,021,685	4,502 61	1 50

The bills paid in June, July and September are exclusive of $424.60 for coal used in pumping out the inlet and stored in the outside bunker. The coal stored in the bunker remains on hand.

During 15 days in July, 9 in August and 20 in September both pumps were run during the night time only, to avoid interference with the work on the inlet. They were generally started up at 8 p. m., in July, 11 p. m., in August, and 9:30 p. m., in September, shutting down as a rule at 8 o'clock each morning.

The pumps were idle 4 days in June, to allow the fishy taste and smell to pass away from the water. During this period the water in the reservoir fell 7.52 feet.

The average temperature of the feed water during the year has been 180, and the vacuum has been maintained at 25 inches.

Experiments show that the supply of natural gas, from both wells, furnishes about 2½ per cent. of the heat used under the boilers in addition to lighting the buildings.

The regular employees at the pumping works are 1 mechanical engineer, 2 assistant engineers, 3 firemen, and 1 watchman. The mechanical engineer stands a watch of 5 hours, from 7 to 12 every forenoon ; the assistants divide the remainder of each day equally between them; each one of the firemen stands a watch of 8 hours. Besides firing, the firemen unload the coal from the cars, except when both pumps are run, in which case they are assisted by the watchman or a laborer. The mechanical engineer gives ten hours daily to the service of the Department, the hours when he is not on watch being employed in repairs, supervision, &c. In addition to standing their regular watch, the assistant engineers aid their superior officer in keeping the machinery in order. The watchman takes care of the buildings and grounds, besides doing such other work as may be required of him.

EXHIBIT K.

Amount, Kind and Cost of Coal Consumed, Gallons of Water Pumped, Average Height Pumped, Cost per Million Gallons, &c., from the First Year the Works were operated to January 1, 1885.

Years	Tons of Coal Consumed, 2000 lbs to a Ton.	Contract Price of Coal per Ton from May 1st of each year.	Cost of Coal delivered in Pumping House.	Grades of Bituminous Coal.	Gallons of Water Pumped.	Increase or Decrease.	Families and No. of Establishments supplied.	No. of Fire Hydrants supplied.	Average height of water in reservoir above surface of bay.	Cost of Coal per Million Gallons raised to Reservoir.	Cost of Coal per Million Gallons raised one foot.	Gallons raised one foot by one pound of Coal.	Gallons raised to Reservoir by one lb of Coal.
1868	59.1	$5.05	$ 309.61	Lump									
1869	544.4	5.05	4,818.48	"									
1870	1,064.5	5.05	5,159.10	"	246,648,960		1218	97	232.00				
1871	1,422.7	5.05	7,117.00	"	279,368,495	132,719,535 I	1727	99	232.00	18.76	.080	22.656	98.52
1872	1,308.5	5.05	6,528.50	"	395,076,000	115,708,505 I	2140	103	232.00	16.52	.076	35.092	150.96
1873	1,672.5	5.05	8,412.65	"	384,062,415	11,013,585 D	2475	107	232.00	21.90	.094	26.636	114.81
1874	1,759.0	4.85	7,709.54	"	444,817,395	60,754,980 I	2663	107	232.00	17.83	.071	29.234	126.44
1875	1,836.4	4.85	8,657.61	"	531,005,475	86,188,080 I	2700	110	232.00	16.30	.069	33.772	145.57
1876	2,105.1	4.00	8,925.22	"	670,726,650	139,721,175 I	2763	112	232.00	13.30	.056	36.959	159.31
1877	2,456.6	3.70	8,509.33	"	660,981,810	9,744,840 D	2854	114	232.00	12.75	.054	31.491	135.74
1878	2,463.3	3.35	7,945.37	"	682,392,315	21,330,505 I	2915	115	232.00	11.64	.049	31.665	136.49
1879	2,628.1	3.09	7,428.92	Slack	807,800,400	125,408,085 I	3011	121	232.00	9.19	.039	35.653	153.68
1880	3,076.1	1.99	6,978.41	"	775,805,250	31,995,150 I	3568	126	232.00	8.99	.038	29.234	126.01
1881	3,430.3	1.90	6,517.58	"	975,640,634	200,235,684 I	4110	161	232.00	6.68	.028	32.990	142.20
1882	2,968.2	1.75	5,355.93	"	829,759,260	145,881,674 D	4687	171	234.00	6.45	.027	32.706	139.77
1883	2,398.2	1.55	3,908.59	"	815,939,685	13,819,575 D	5077	197	234.71	4.66	.019	39.900	170.00
1884	3,010.8	1.45	4,502.61	"	917,781,350	101,841,665 I	5395	254	234.32	4.90	.020	35.712	152.41

The reduced duty of the pumps for 1884 is mainly due to the necessity for running both together a large portion of the time and to their irregular and disadvantageous use during the construction of the inlet pipes.

All coal used from the commencement of the works has been Mercer county bituminous. The coal contract is awarded annually to the lowest bidder, the coal being delivered in the works at the contract price.

Two gas wells were put down at the pumping works in the spring of 1871, yielding a large supply. The gas was applied to the boilers the same year, for some two years furnished about one-fourth of the fuel at the works. The gas steadily decreased until about 1875, when it failed almost entirely, and wells were resuscitated in the summer of 1881, and the gas was soon after applied again to the boilers, since which time, besides all the light used at the works and grounds, it has furnished an average of about two and one-half per cent. of the fuel employed in pumping.

EXHIBIT L.

HOW CITY WATER MAY BE WASTED.

Gallons and hundredths of gallons of water that will be discharged per minute through various sized orifices at the heads stated, as ascertained by careful experiments.

Head in Feet.	Pressure per Square Inch.	Diameters of Orifices in inches and fractions of an inch.													
		1/64	1/32	1/16	1/8	1/4	3/8	1/2	5/8	3/4	1	1¼	1½	1¾	2
20	8.66	0.02	0.07	0.30	1.20	5.10	11.70	20.60	32.20	46.20	82.30	128.40	184.80	252.00	328.80
40	17.32	0.02	0.11	0.45	1.80	7.40	16.30	29.60	45.50	65.50	116.50	182.40	261.60	256.40	465.60
60	25.99	0.03	0.14	0.55	2.20	8.90	20.00	35.60	57.70	80.30	142.80	223.20	320.40	436.80	571.20
80	34.65	0.04	0.16	0.65	2.60	10.30	23.20	41.20	64.30	92.60	164.40	258.00	370.80	505.20	658.80
100	43.31	0.04	0.18	0.75	2.90	11.50	25.90	46.10	72.00	103.70	183.60	288.00	415.20	565.20	738.00
120	51.98	0.05	0.19	0.78	3.10	12.60	28.30	50.40	78.80	113.50	201.60	315.60	453.60	624.40	807.60
140	60.64	0.05	0.21	0.85	3.40	13.60	30.60	54.50	85.20	122.40	217.20	340.80	490.80	668.40	872.40
150	64.97	0.05	0.22	0.88	3.50	14.10	31.70	56.40	88.20	127.20	225.60	352.80	507.60	691.20	902.40
175	75.80	0.06	0.24	0.95	3.80	15.20	34.20	61.00	95.30	136.80	243.60	380.40	548.40	748.80	975.60
200	86.83	0.06	0.26	1.02	4.10	16.30	36.60	65.20	101.80	146.40	260.40	406.80	588.00	798.00	1042.80
235	101.08	0.07	0.28	1.12	4.50	17.90	41.30	71.50	137.70	185.80	285.20	445.90	642.20	871.30	1140.80

The bottom of the Erie Reservoir is 210 feet above the surface of Presque Isle Bay, from which the water is pumped, and the water in the reservoir is kept at an average height of nearly 25 feet, or 235 feet above the bay. The pressure at the points named below will give an idea of the average throughout the city: Twenty-fourth and Sassafras streets, 20 lbs.; Twenty-third and Myrtle, 30 lbs.; Twentieth and Chestnut, 40 lbs.; Eighteenth and Peach, 50 lbs.; Fourteenth and State, 60 lbs.; Eighth and State, 70 lbs.; Third and State, 80 lbs.; Front and State, 100 lbs.

The wire of which pins are made is 1/32d of an inch in diameter—No. 21, wire gauge. The finest cambric needle is made of wire 1/84th of an inch in diameter—No. 27, wire gauge. A stream the size of a pin, running one year with a head of 235 feet, will flow 147,168 gallons, equaling 4,600 barrels, at a loss—counting at the rate of 10 cents per 1,000 gallons—of $14.71. A stream the size of a cambric needle, running at the same pressure, and for the same time, will waste 36,792 gallons, a loss of $3.68.

EXHIBIT M.

Advantages offered in Erie to Manufacturers.

The following are the highest and lowest charges per 1,000 gallons for water by meter measurement, up to a daily average of 50,000 gallons, in the cities named. The rates are taken from the official reports:

	HIGH-EST	LOW-EST		HIGH-EST	LOW-EST
Erie	10	6	New York City, (uniform charge)	—	10
Albany, N. Y.	40	10	Oil City, Pa., (uniform charge)	—	13
Boston (uniform charge)	—	20	Oswego, N. Y.	40	20
Binghampton, N. Y.	25	6	Portland, Maine	50	30
Bangor, Maine	30	10	Philadelphia, Pa., (uniform charge)	—	16⅔
Baltimore (uniform ch'g)	—	8	Rochester, N. Y.	30	10
Brooklyn, N. Y	—	15	St. Paul, Minn.	50	25
Chicago, Ill	10	8	Springfield, Mass.	30	15
Cleveland, O.	16	8	San Francisco, (uniform charge)	---	33
Cincinnati, O. (uniform charge)	—	12	Syracuse, N. Y.	40	20
Columbus, O.	20	7	St. Louis.	20	15
Dayton, O.	50	15	Sandusky, (uniform charge)	---	21
Detroit.	20	10	Toronto.	27	28
Elmira, N. Y.	50	40	Toledo.	20	08
East Saginaw, Mich	60	15	Troy, N. Y,	20	10
Hartford, Conn	30	16	Titusville.	30	12½
Louisville, Ky.	15	6	Utica, N. Y.	50	25
Lawrence, Mass.	30	15			
Milwaukee.	20	10			
Meadville.	15	8			
Montreal	30	12			

The above list might be extended indefinitely. Only one of the cities named furnishes water by meter at a lower rate than Erie; in a very few the charge is about the same; all the rest charge from 10 to 100, and in some cases 400 per cent. higher than Erie. In addition to the low rates, meters are set here and kept in order by the Department, while in most cities the consumers are charged with the same.

Steam Engine charges per Horse Power, (10 hours per day.)

Erie	$2 50	New York City	$5.00 to 6.00
Chicago	4 00	Newark	5.00
Boston	6.00 to 10.00	Omaha	2 50
Kansas City	5.00	Cleveland	2.50
Minneapolis	2.00 to 4.00	Columbus	3.00
St. Paul	4.00 to 5 00	Philadelphia	3.00
Buffalo	3 00	Pittsburgh	4.12
Toledo	2.50	Rochester	3.00

EXHIBIT N.

Cost of Water to the average Householder in Twenty-five Cities, as compared with the Cost in Erie.

Cities.	Family av. charge.	Pan Water Closet.	Bath Tub.	Wash Stand.	Permanent W. Tub.	Horse.	Cow.	Street Sprinkler.	Total.
Erie	$5 00	$3 00	$3 00	$ 50	$2 00	$2 00	$ 75	$3 00	$18 75
Albany, N. Y.	18 00	2 00				3 00		8 00	31 00
Alton, Ill.	7 00	5 00	8 00			8 00	2 00	9 00	39 00
Brooklyn, N. Y.	16 00	2 00				5 00	75	5 50	29 25
Buffalo, N. Y.	20 00	8 00	5 00			4 00	1 50	5 00	43 50
Cambridge, Mass.	7 00	6 00	6 00	2 50	2 50	5 00	2 00	10 00	41 00
Cincinnati, O.	14 00	3 00	6 00	1 00		5 00		4 80	33 80
Chicago, Ill.	19 00	5 00	3 00			4 00		3 00	34 00
Detroit, Mich.	7 00	3 00	2 00	1 25	2 00	4 00	1 00	3 00	23 25
Fitchburg, Mass.	6 00	5 00	5 00	2 00	2 00	8 00	2 00	5 00	35 00
Fall River, Mass.	5 00	5 00	5 00	2 50	2 50	4 00	1 00	6 00	31 00
Grand Rapids, Mich.	8 00	4 50	3 75	2 00	3 00	2 50	1 00	2 00	28 75
Lynn, Mass.	6 00	5 00	5 00	2 00	2 00	5 00	1 50	3 00	29 50
Lawrence, Mass.	5 00	4 00	3 00		1 00	3 00	1 50	2 50	20 00
Lowell, Mass.	6 00	4 00	3 00		1 00	4 00	2 00	3 00	23 00
Louisville, Ky.	10 00	3 00	4 00		1 00	5 00	1 00	7 50	31 50
Milwaukee, Wis.	11 50	5 00	3 00	2 00		4 00	1 00	8 00	34 50
Newton, Mass.	6 00	5 00	6 00	2 00	1 00	10 00	1 50	5 00	35 00
Niagara Falls	9 00	3 00	3 00			3 00	1 50	6 00	25 50
Philadelphia, Pa.	8 75	2 00	3 00	1 00	1 00	3 00		9 00	27 75
Pittsburgh, Pa.	27 77	17 55	10 85	8 25		8 25	2 05	6 87	71 50
Providence, R. I.	6 00	5 00	5 00	2 00	3 00	4 00	1 00	5 00	31 00
Salem, Mass.	3 50	5 00	5 00	1 50		6 00	1 00	3 00	24 00
Springfield, Mass	8 00	4 00	4 00			4 00	2 00	5 00	27 00
Taunton, Mass	5 00	5 00	3 00	2 00	2 00	4 00	1 50	5 00	27 50
Toledo, O.	10 25	2 50	3 50	2 00		5 00		5 00	28 25

The low rate at which water is supplied is not the only advantage offered in Erie. Here the Department lays down the street mains, puts in the connections from the main to the curb, and sets the stops and stop boxes, free of expense to the consumer, while in most cities these items are a charge against the property benefited.

ANNUAL RATES.

Water rents are payable quarterly in advance—except where the water is furnished by meter measurement or special contract—as follows:

> FIRST QUARTER—January, February, March—JANUARY 1st.
> SECOND QUARTER—April, May, June—APRIL 1st.
> THIRD QUARTER—July, August, September—JULY 1st.
> FOURTH QUARTER—October, November, December—OCTOBER 1st.

If the rents are not paid for any quarter within the FIRST MONTH thereof, FIVE PER CENT. may be added to the amount. If payment is not made by the first day of February, May, August or November of each quarter, the delinquent shall be notified that the water will be turned off from the premises on the fifteenth day after date of notice, and not turned on again until all back rents and penalties are paid and the further sum of two dollars for turning off and on the water.

When water is furnished by meter measurement or special contract, payment is due at the end of each current quarter. If the rents are not paid within ONE MONTH after they are due the same penalties and conditions will apply as above.

PER ANNUM.

Private dwellings, occupied by one family, from	$5 00 to $10 00
" " " by more than one family, $1.00 less than the above rates for each family using the water	
Bath tub in private house	3 00
" " " each additional	1 50
Public bath tubs, each	5 00
Hopper water closet, in private house	6 00
" " " " each additional	3 00
Pan water closet, in private house	3 00
" " " " each additional	1 50
Public water closet, pan, each	5 00
" " " hopper, each	6 00
Urinals, each	2 00
Permanent hand basins, each	50
Permanent wash tub with waste	2 00
" " " each additional	1 00
Private street sprinklers each, per season	3 00 to 10 00
Private stables, for one or two horses	2 00
" " each additional horse over two	1 00
Livery stables, for each horse including washing of carriages	2 00
Cows, each	75
Fountains, average use four hours per day:	
One 1-16 inch jet	5 00
One 1-8 inch jet	10 00
One 1-4 inch jet	12 00
One 3-8 inch jet	20 00
One 1-2 inch jet	30 00
Larger jets at special rates	
Dry goods, book and hardware stores, from	2 00 to 5 00
Saloons, groceries and provision stores, from	3 00 to 50 00
Offices, from	2 00 to 20 00
Hotels, taverns and boarding houses, in addition to rates for private dwellings, for each room	1 00
Public schools, per scholar	10
Building purposes, for each bushel of lime	02
Printing offices, not including steam engine, from	5 00 to 25 00
" " each power press	4 00
" " " balance press	2 00
" " " hand press	1 00
Blacksmith shops, one fire	5 00
" " each additional fire	2 50
Barber shops, one chair	4 00
" " each additional chair	2 00
Steam engines, non-condensing, ten hours per day, each horse power	2 50
Butchers' stalls, each	3 00
Work shops, from	3 00 to 5 00

[FOR METER RATES, SEE NEXT PAGE.

METER RATES.

The rate for each current quarter, per each thousand gallons, by meter measurement, is as follows:

For a daily average of 15,000 gallons or less...10 cents.
"   "   "   more than 15,000 gallons and not in excess of 20,000 gallons.... 9½ "
"   "   "   "   " 20,000 "   "   "   "   25,000 "   ..... 9 "
"   "   "   "   " 25,000 "   "   "   "   30,000 "   .... 8½ "
"   "   "   "   " 30,000 "   "   "   "   35,000 "   .... 8 "
"   "   "   "   " 35,000 "   "   "   "   40,000 "   .... 7½ "
"   "   "   "   " 40,000 "   "   "   "   45,000 "   .... 7 "
"   "   "   "   " 45,000 "   "   "   "   50,000 "   .... 6½ "
"   "   "   "   " 50,000 "   .... 6 "

OF ERIE, PA.,

TO THE

AND CITY COUNCILS,

FOR THE

⅃ ENDING DEC. 31, 1885.

ERIE, PENN'A:

& GALLAGHER, Printers and Paper Dealers.

1886.

ANNUAL REPORT

OF THE BOARD OF

WATER COMMISSIONERS

OF ERIE, PA.,

TO THE

MAYOR AND CITY COUNCILS,

FOR THE

YEAR ENDING DEC. 31, 1885.

ERIE, PENN'A:
WALKER & GALLAGHER, Printers and Paper Dealers,
1886.

WATER COMMISSIONERS.

The Water Commissioners are appointed by the Court of Common Pleas of Erie County, Penn'a, for a term of three years, one member being named annually, in May.

EX-MEMBERS OF THE BOARD.

*WM. W. REED, 1867 to 1879.

*HENRY RAWLE, 1867 to 1872.

JOHN GENSHEIMER, 1872 to 1878.

J. M. BRYANT, 1878 to 1881.

*WM. L. SCOTT, 1867 to 1868.

†JOHN C. SELDEN, 1868 to 1872.

MATTHEW R. BARR, 1872 to 1877.

G. W. F. SHERWIN, 1879 to 1885.

*Messrs. Scott, Rawle and Reed, the first Commissioners, were appointed respectively for terms of one, two and three years.

†Mr. Selden resigned before the expiration of his second term. Mr. Barr was substituted by the Board and afterward appointed by the Court.

PRESENT BOARD.

M. LIEBEL, 1877 to 1886.   BENJAMIN WHITMAN, 1881 to 1887.

GEO. W. STARR, 1885 to 1888.

OFFICERS OF THE DEPARTMENT, JAN. 1st, 1886.

President of the Board—BENJAMIN WHITMAN.

Secretary and Treasurer—B. F. SLOAN.

Assistant Secretary—GEO. C. GENSHEIMER.

Clerk—ALLAN C. SWALLEY.

Superintendent of Street Work—WM. O'LONE.

Inspectors—A. F. CRANE, F. W. KOEHLER, FRANK J. ELLISON, (temp.)

Mechanical Engineer—F. A. ROTH.

Assistant Mechanical Engineers—GEO. R. MILLER, JOHN KELLY.

Firemen—R. W. SIMMONS, JOSEPH BURNS, JACOB MULLEN.

Watchman at Pumping Works—THOS. TIDMAN,

Keeper of Reservoir and Grounds—SAMUEL PFISTER.

OFFICE—No. 18 East Seventh Street, between French and State.

OFFICE HOURS—From 7:30 A. M. to 5:45 P. M.

REGULAR MEETINGS OF THE BOARD—Every Saturday at 2 P. M.

ANNUAL REPORT.

To the Mayor and City Councils:

GENTLEMEN:—Herewith find the usual exhibits showing the operations of this Department during the year 1885.

The receipts have been as follows :

Balance in office Dec. 31, 1884,	-	$ 436.40
" " City Treasury Dec. 31, 1884,		2,138.57
From Water Rents,	- - -	53,550.35
" Plumbing and other sources,		1,329.27
Total,	- - - -	$57,454.59

The income from water rents has exceeded that of 1884
by $1,697.57, being less of a gain than has been the case for
some years, due, undoubtedly, to the depressed condition of
business. The expenses during the same period were—

For Construction,	- - - -	$35,245.29
" Extraordinary Repairs,	- -	3,267.06
" Maintenance,	- - - -	17,386.01
Balance in Office and City Treasury,		1,556.23
Total	- - - -	$57,454.59

It is gratifying to be able to show that the business principles upon which it has been the aim to conduct the Department have resulted in a decrease of $1,100 in the current
expense over last year, and a reduction of much more than
that as compared with the average sum since the works went
into operation. Although there is a steady growth in the

demands upon the Department, the Board are hopeful that they can cut down the maintenance account to a still lower figure. It does not seem possible that the extraordinary repairs can cost much for some years to come, as every expensive feature of the system has been given attention during the last two or three seasons.

NET EARNINGS.

The sum of $35,245.29 expended for construction represents the profits of the Department during the year, as far as they are indicated by the cash receipts. It should be borne in mind, however, that the Department receives no pay nor proper credit from the city for the' care and supply of fire hydrants, for the water furnished to the municipal offices, public fountains and State Fish Hatchery, nor for flushing sewers and other duties of a like nature. Estimating the value of these services at $13,450, which is quite moderate, the actual net earnings have been $48,695.29, or more than seven per centum on the original cost of the system.*

NUMBER OF CONSUMERS.

The number of persons, firms and corporations against whom accounts are kept for water rents is 5,658, an increase of 203 since 1885. Statistics collected by the inspectors show that each name on the books represents about five consumers, making the number supplied 28,290, or about four-fifths the population of the city.

STREET CONNECTIONS.

The street connections of which a record can be found count up to 3,924, being 237 more than at the beginning of the year. These have required some sixteen and a half miles of pipe, ranging in size from three-fourths of an inch to two inches. The early records are quite deficient, and there is reason to believe that the number of connections here given is several hundreds too few. A systematic effort will be

---

*NOTE.—The city of Corry has recently made a contract with a company to pay $3,000 per year for the use of sixty fire hydrants, or at the rate of $50 each. In the above calculation the same service in Erie is figured at $35 per hydrant.

made during the ensuing season to secure a complete list of the connections, with precise measurements of the same, which will be kept in a convenient form for the information of consumers as well as of the Department. The undertaking will be long, tedious and costly, but the benefits that will be derived are expected to more than compensate for the expense.

MAIN PIPES.

Two miles and 1902 feet of distributing pipe have been laid during the year, of which nearly half a mile is embraced in the new thirty-inch force main from the pumping works to Seventh street. The latter, as was explained in the report for 1884, was decided upon after consultation with and upon the advice of John Whitelaw, Esq., for many years Superintendent of the Cleveland Water Department, chiefly for the purpose of giving relief to the pumps and enabling them to be used together, with greater advantage. The work of laying the pipe was attended with much difficulty, especially at Front, Short and Seventh streets, and the expense far exceeded the expectation of the Board. Bills have been paid on account of the new force main to the amount of $22,378.66, and other outstanding items will swell the figures to about $25,000. In order to resist the severe strain upon the above stated part of the distributing system, pipe of extra weight and quality and valves of the most approved make were purchased. The new main affords two channels for the water from the works into the heart of the city, either of which can be used in case of a break in the other.

TOTAL PIPEAGE.

The total amount of distributing pipe now in use, inclusive of some large private pipe, is upward of fifty miles, which is more than in any other place having the population of Erie from which reports are received at this office, though some three-fifths of the regularly laid out streets are still without the public water supply. Looking to the future growth of the city and the need of the most effective fire protection, the

Board have resolved to lay down no more four-inch pipe south of Second street, and to place all new fire hydrants, as far as practicable, on the six and twelve-inch mains.

LOWERED PIPES AND CONNECTIONS.

The extreme and long continued cold weather of January, February and March developed that many of the old connections were too shallow, and kept the street force busy a good share of the time in freeing them from frost. To prevent a repetition of the trouble, all connections known to have been frozen were lowered during the summer to the standard depth of five feet. Such distributing pipe as was thought to be too near the surface was also placed beyond danger.

STOP VALVES AND METERS.

Fifty new stop valves were set during the year, three of which were thirty and two twenty inches inside diameter. The total number in the city is 426, which is still below the requirements of convenience and economy. The distributing system will not be complete until sufficient stop valves have been set to enable any block to be shut off without interfering with the supply of its neighbors.

Fifty-two meters are in use, being nine more than last year. Except in one or two instances, every meter that has been set has shown a greater consumption of water than had been suspected. No consumer can justly complain when a meter is applied to his premises, as every failure in the operation of the same must, from the nature of their construction, be in his favor.

FIRE HYDRANTS.

The number of fire hydrants is 270, being nearly double that of six years ago. Twenty-four were set during the year in new locations; six old hydrants were replaced with those of modern style; and two, which had been temporarily placed at the ends of pipes, were taken out. The Board duly appreciate the importance of adequate fire protection, and have done all in their power, within the last four years, consistent with the pressing demands upon their resources for other purposes, to improve the facilities in this respect. Their effort during the ensuing year will be to complete the plan of furnishing each street intersection in the built up portions of the city with a fire hydrant, after which additional ones will be placed at the centres of the long blocks, as the needs in each case may seem to require.

It is a matter of regret that the means at the disposal of the Department will not admit of the old style hydrants being replaced at once with hydrants of modern make, as they are expensive to keep up and liable, with the best of care, to get out of order. All fire hydrants are specially inspected in the spring and fall of each year, and it speaks well for the efficiency of the officers who have them in direct charge that, during the unusually severe cold spell at the beginning of the year, but two or three, and those of the old pattern, were found to be frozen.

BOOKS AND MAPS.

Good progress has been made in perfecting the records of the office, so that such information as it is desirable to preserve, or as may be important in the every day work of the Department, can be readily found. By the close of the ensuing year it is hoped to have as practical and complete a set of books and maps as can be found anywhere.

PUMPAGE.

The quantity of water pumped during 1885 was 1,036,496,665 gallons, an increase of 118,000,000 gallons over the previous year, and of more than 220,000,000 gallons over 1883. These figures give an average of about 2,800,000 gallons daily, or 300,000 gallons more than the intended duty of either of the two pumps. Estimating the population at 35,000, eighty gallons per day were furnished for each man, woman and child in the city. The average daily pumpage of the year was much exceeded at several periods, that of February having been 3,359,703 gallons, of July 3,073,845, and of August 3,210,825. Indeed, there has scarcely been a day in the year

when the consumption has not been in excess of the limit of
safety with the present pumping capacity. The two pumps
were operated together 146 days, or more than a third of the
time, while the works were idle but 29 days, and then only
for repairs, or to enable connections to be made with the
force mains or the inlet. That the quantity of water pumped
is very much more than the actual need of the citizens will
not be disputed, but it is utterly impossible to stop the waste
by any device known to the Board, short of a general and
costly system of meterage.

AN ADDITIONAL PUMP NEEDED.

The danger of an inadequate supply to which the city is
liable under the present conditions, through the disabling of
one or both of the pumps, which experience proves is likely
to happen at any time, is the cause of ceaseless anxiety and
watchfulness on the part of both the Board and its employees.
Every day confirms the view expressed in last year's report,
that a new pump, equal in capacity to both of those now in
use, so that duplex power shall always be ready in case of a
contingency, is an imperative necessity. The Board intend
to strain every nerve to secure the attainment of this object
by or before the spring of 1887. It is sufficient explanation
of the delay to state that the Board have no other resource
than the revenue from water rents, and that the steady demand
for additional distributing pipe, connections, valves and fire
hydrants fixes a bound to the sum that can be applied to the
purpose. The purchase of a pump will compel the erection
of a wing to the east side of the engine house, and heavy
outlay for extending the well, preparing foundations, &c.,
involving altogether from $30,000 to $35,000. In making
choice of a new pump, the Board will endeavor to secure the
best light that can be obtained on the subject, and are determined that it shall be of the best approved pattern, capable
of doing its daily work with the utmost economy in fuel and
least liable to wear and accident.

DUTY OF THE PUMPS.

The cost of slack bituminous coal used under the boilers during the year was $4,575.79, a sum just about one-half what was expended for the purpose ten years ago. Based on the cost of coal burned per each million of gallons raised one foot high, which is the formula in all water works, this is the best result in the history of the Department, though greatly below the duty of the improved engines of the day. There is not the least question that after the new pump is in regular operation a material reduction will ensue in the expenses at the works.

SLACK COAL vs. RUN OF THE MINE.

Experiments were made in March with a view of testing the relative merits of No. 1 slack coal and run of the mine, which proved the advantage to be largely in favor of the cheaper grade. Raising the water to a height of 236 feet, the slack, costing $1.45 per ton, gave 182 gallons per pound, while the run of the mine, at a cost of $1.90 per ton, yielded but 192 gallons.

INLET PIPE AND PIERS.

The inlet pipe, which terminated at the end of the main pier, was extended, early in the year, through the "dummies" to the northern extreme of the pier system, where it takes its supply at a distance of 973 feet from the works, and at a depth of five feet below the surface of the bay and of four feet above the bed of the same. The pipe is of wood throughout the length of the main pier, and of stout boiler iron the balance of the way; the inside diameter of the wooden section being four feet three inches and of the iron part four feet. On the completion of the extension, the piers, most of the contents of which had been allowed to wash out soon after their construction, were filled with stone and earth, a heavy railing and a wide board walk, after the plan which had proven so effectual at another point of the water works

property, was built on the west side of the main pier, and the
remainder of the pier was sown to grass, which quickly grew
up, forming one of the most attractive features of the grounds.
Although the fall storms were very severe, the material in
the piers remains undisturbed.

THE JUNE FLOOD.

A terrible rain storm on the night of June 4th cut
three enormous gashes in the slope back of the works,
carried a portion of the earth against the south wall of the
boiler house, and broke it down, luckily doing no injury to the
boilers themselves. In repairing the damage an attempt has
been made, it is believed with success, to avert a second disaster of the kind.

BUILDINGS AND GROUNDS.

The improvement of the buildings and grounds, aside from
the work above referred to, has continued to receive the attention of the Board, in the belief that all public property should
be as tastefully kept up as the circumstances will admit.
With the foundation that has already been laid, there is no
reason why the water works and their surroundings should
not, at moderate yearly expense, soon become one of the
most creditable features of the city. The Board have no
doubt that the public will cordially sustain any measures in
this direction that are within proper limits.

PLUMBING AND INSPECTION.

The house to house system of inspection that was inaugurated three years ago has become one of the settled features
of the Department. Though it has been less effective in checking waste than the Board were led to believe from the experience of the first year, there is no question that its results
have fully warranted the small additional expense which it
has entailed. The plumbing of the city, as a whole, is far in
advance of what it was, the assessments are more prompt
and correct, and the water supply has been maintained
with less danger and more economy than would have been
the case had not some check been placed upon the waste.

NEW RULES AND RATES.

By the co-operation of the Mayor and Councils, an amended set of rules and a more equitable scale of rates were adopted in December, which are expected to promote the efficiency of the Department. Though the new rates went into effect immediately, it has been deemed best, in order that no unfair advantage might be taken of any consumer, to postpone their enforcement until the second quarter of the ensuing year, which begins on the first of April.

QUALITY OF THE WATER.

The well-known truth that people seldom appreciate the good things they are accustomed to is strongly confirmed by the occasional complaints of some of our citizens about the city water. This Department has scores of calls during the course of each year from gentlemen who are familiar with other works, and the instances are very rare in which they do not speak of the excellent water with which Erie is favored and wish that the whole country were blessed with the same advantage. The Board are firm in the belief that the public water supply of Erie is equal to any and better than that of nine-tenths of the cities in the land. In this they are substantiated by Mr. Page, of the State Fish Hatchery, who has experimented in various localities between Maine and Florida, and who authorizes the statement that he finds the water here, which he draws directly from the city pipes, the purest and best for his purpose that he has ever used. Instead of unreasonable criticisms, our citizens should make an effort to spread the facts before the outside public, and offer them as an inducement why people who are looking for a pleasant and healthy place to locate should make their homes among us.

If there is any undesirable trait about the water, it must come from the sewerage that flows into some parts of the bay, for the latter body, in its natural state, was as pure as the great lake. The remedy for this—as the Board have

pointed out in every report for several years—is to empty
the sewers outside of the bay; and this work can be done in
so simple a manner and at such moderate cost, that it is difficult to understand why the proper authorities delay action on
the subject.

CONCLUSION.

In conclusion, it is a source of gratification to the Board to
know that within two years, if no unforseen occurrence hap-
pens, the capacity of the original water system will be more
than doubled, without increasing the general taxes a dollar or
adding the slightest item to the city debt.   With the addition
of the proposed new pump, all actually necessary improvements, outside of the routine work of the Department, will
be made, and no valid reason would seem to exist why a
respectable sum should not be turned over to the city authorities each year to be applied on the payment of the funded
debt.

The thanks of the Board are due to the Mayor, the Councils and the city officers generally for their kind co-operation
during the year.

Respectfully submitted,

M. LIEBEL,
BENJAMIN WHITMAN,
GEO. W. STARR,
   Water Commissioners.

EXHIBIT A.

Receipts of Erie Water Department for the Year Ending December 31st, 1885.

WATER RENTS.

First quarter—January	$4,821 28			
" " February	4,463 80			
" " March	2,301 19			
		$11,586 27		
Second quarter—April	5,559 53			
" " May	5,128 01			
" " June	4,038 50			
		14,726 04		
Third quarter—July	4,788 48			
" " August	6,117 48			
" " September	1,682 70			
		12,588 66		
Fourth quarter—October	6,054 80			
" " November	6,261 60			
" " December	2,333 22			
		14,649 62		
Total from water rents			$53,550 59	

OTHER SOURCES.

Plumbing and pipe laying	1,013 58			
Water Meters sold	103 55			
Material sold	212 14			
		1,329 27		
Balance last report		436 40	1,765 67	
Total from all sources			$55,316 26	

CR.

Deposited in Treasury—First quarter	$11,400 00			
" " " Second "	14,850 00			
" " " Third "	13,300 00			
" " " Fourth "	15,450 00			
			$55,000 00	
Balance			$316 26	

EXHIBIT B.

Account of Water Department with City Treasurer for the Year Ending December 31st, 1885.

1885				
Jan. 1.	**DR.**			
	To balance in Treasury December 31, 1884..............	$ 2,138 57		
	To deposits from January 1 to December 31, 1885....	55,000 00		$57,138 57
	CR.			
	By Warrants Drawn—first quarter —January.....	3,496 31		
	" " " " February...	2,027 81		
	" " " " March........	3,247 81	$8,951 70	
	By Warrants Drawn—second quarter—April........	3,153 35		
	" " " " May	7,388 09		
	" " " " June........	4,239 80	15,781 24	
	By Warrants Drawn—third quarter—July..........	6,345 95		
	" " " " August	6,799 63		
	" " " " September	2,455 18	15,600 76	
	By Warrants Drawn—fourth quarter—October.....	5,525 58		
	" " " " November..	8,383 86		
	" " " " December..	3,656 22	15,564 66	$55,898 36
	Balance			$1,240 21
	DR.			
	To Warrants Issued, not Redeemed, ...			$287 10
	Actual Balance in Treasury, Dec. 31, 1885.....			$1,527 31

CONTROLLER'S AUDIT.

Water Commissioners' Cash and Warrant Accounts; also Account with City Treasurer for Year 1885.

Cash on hand January 1st, 1885...$ 426 40
Received from Water Rents.. 53,550 59
Received from other Sources 1,329 27

Total Receipts $55,316 26
Amount paid City Treasurer 55,000 00

Amount of Cash on hand and in Bank ....$ 316 26

Amount of Warrants outstanding January 1st, 1885.............................$ 232 09
Total Amounts of Warrants issued during 1885.............................. 55,898 38

Total.Warrants............ ....$56,130 47
Warrants paid during the Year 1885 .... 55,843 37

Amounts of Warrants outstanding January 1st, 1886 ....$ 287 10

Balance to the Credit of the Water Department, in the City Treasury,
January 1st, 1885......... ....$ 2,370 66
Total Receipts by City Treasurer during the Year 1885 .... 55,000 00

Total $57,370 66
Warrants paid by the Treasurer during 1885 ....$55,843 37

Balance to the Credit of the Water Commissioners in the City Treasury,
January 1st, 1886 ....$ 1,527 31

OFFICE OF CITY CONTROLLER,
ERIE, PA., Feb. 4, 1886.

I hereby certify that the above statement has been carefully compared with the records in the office of the City Treasurer and Water Commissioners, and found correct : and the balance $1,527.31 was due the Water Commissioners by the City Treasurer, January 1st, 1886.

CHAS. S. CLARKE,
City Controller.

EXHIBIT C.

Expenditures for the Year 1885; also, from the Commencement of the Works to January 1, 1885.

1885		FUEL AT WORKS.	FROM JAN. 1, 1885, TO DEC. 31, 1885.	1867 TO 1885.
Jan.	1	From commencement of works to Dec. 31, 1884......		$108,366 45
	3	Paid R. J. Saltsman 548,350 lbs., $1.45	$ 397 56	
Feb.	7	" " 385,600 " "	279 56	
Mar.	7	" " 364,700 " "	264 40	
"	7	" " 311,400 " 1.90	295 83	
April	4	" " 487,000 " 1.45	353 08	
"	4	" " 166,700 " 1.90	158 36	
May	2	" " 526,700 " 1.45	381 85	
"	2	" " 94,600 " 1.90	89 87	
June	6	" Wm. Himrod, 257,900 " 1.05	135 39	
"	6	" " 137,100 " 1.30 "	89 11	
July	3	" " 257,900 " "	286 90	
Aug.	1	" " 705,100 " "	458 32	
Sept.	5	" " 679,500 " "	441 68	
Oct.	1	" " 474,900 " "	277 07	
"	1	" R. J. Saltsman 81,100 " 1.65	66 90	
Nov.	21	" Wm. Himrod, 559,000 " 1.30	336 32	
Dec.	12	" " 450,100 " "	263 59	
		Total ....6,487,650 lbs.	$4,575 79	
		SALARIES.		
Jan.	1	From commencement of works to Dec. 31, 1884......		88,401 39
Dec.	31	Paid B. F. Sloan, Secretary and Treasurer............	1,200 00	
		" Geo. C. Gensheimer, Ass't Secretary.....	720 00	
		" Jacob Wiss, Temporary Clerk	97 95	
		" A. C. Swalley, et. al, Clerk...........................	137 00	
		" Wm. O'Lone, Sup't of Street Work	835 00	
		" A. F. Crane, Inspector.........	486 20	
		" F. W. Koehler, "	655 00	
		" Benjamin Whitman, Commissioner.............	696 00	
		" Michael Liebel, "	572 00	
		" G. W. F. Sherwin, "	454 00	
			5,853 15	
		MECHANICAL ENGINEERS AND FIREMEN		
Jan.	1	From commencement of works to Dec. 31, 1884......		62,740 40
Dec.	31	Paid Fred. A. Roth, Mechanical Engineer.............	1,000 00	
		" Geo. R. Miller, Ass't " " "	840 00	
		" John Kelley, " " "	715 00	
		" R. W. Simmons, Fireman..................■.......	540 00	
		" Jos. Burns, "	540 00	
		" Jacob Mullen, "	540 00	
		" Extra Firemen, ...	334 21	
			4,509 21	
		POSTAGE.		
Jan.	1	From commencement of works to Dec. 31, 1884.		2,627 90
Dec.	31	Paid for Envelopes, Stamps and Postal Cards......	172 30	
			172 30	
		FIRE HYDRANTS.		
Jan.	1	From commencement of works to Dec. 31, 1884......		12,352 93
Dec.	31	Paid R. D. Wood & Co., for Hydrants....................	684 00	
		" Labor per Pay Rolls	106 88	
		" Frank Hoffman, for Labor, &c.	9 00	
		" Cash for Sundries..............................	2 50	
		" Empire Line Freight	19 00	
			821 38	
		Carried forward	$15,931 83	$ 274,489 07

		FROM JAN. 1, 1885, TO DEC. 31, 1835.	1867 TO 1885
	Brought forward	$15,931 83	$ 474,489 07
1885	**CARE AND REPAIR OF HYDRANTS.**		
Dec. 31	Paid Noble & Hall, Sundries................................	$ 19 81	
"	Mehl & Liebel	2 71	
"	Cash for Sundries..................................	7 20	
"	Beckman & Williams.............	5 00	
"	Frank Hoffman, Labor	1 50	
"	P. Hall, Paints, &c..................................	9 75	
"	Labor, Pay Rolls..................................	273 04	
			319 15
	PLUMBING FOR HIRE.		
Jan. 1	From commencement of works to Dec. 31, 1884.....	....	2,850 51
Dec. 31	Paid Labor as per Pay Rolls	215 16	
			215 16
	DISTRIBUTING MAINS		
Jan. 1	From commencement of works to Dec. 31, 1884.....	....	325,999 78
Dec. 31	Paid Adolph Brugger, Sundries........................	9 70	
"	Erie Gas Co., Coke..................................	7 80	
"	W. W. Pierce & Co., Wood, &c	18 00	
"	I. H. Burke, Distributing Pipe....................	34 50	
"	O. C. Thayer, Fire Clay.......................	5 00	
"	Noble & Hall, Sundries........................	39 43	
"	Lake Shore R. R. Co., Freight...............	23 65	
"	Lake Shore Foundry, Specials.....	19 52	
"	Labor as per Pay Roll..............................	1,207 16	
"	Cornell Lead Co., Lead	450 00	
			$1,814 74
	ON ACCOUNT OF THIRTY-INCH MAIN.		
	Paid Lake Shore Foundry, Pipe, &c.....................	13,293 40	
"	Labor as per Pay Rolls	4,598 26	
"	A. F. Crane, Sup't of Laying	353 80	
"	Cornell Lead Co, Lead..............................	1,259 14	
"	Lake Shore R. R. Co., Freight....................	525 18	
"	I. H. Burke, Distributing Pipe.................	395 10	
"	Boston Machine Co., Valves........................	756 00	
"	Noble & Hall, Sundries............................	297 71	
"	G. W. F. Sherwin, Services..........................	149 85	
"	John Whitelaw, Services	28 25	
"	W. H. Dickson, Sundries	19 95	
"	J. W. Doyle, Inspecting Pipe	104 70	
"	Schlosser & Felheim, Lumber......................	39 77	
"	Cash for Sundries..................................	9 86	
"	Jas. M'Brier & Co., Lumber....................	62 03	
"	A. L. Barber, Paving	50 00	
"	Farmers' Brass Co., Sundries	7 00	
"	L. M. Rumsey Manufacturing Co., Sundries	131 97	
"	N. Murphy, Sundries	8 40	
"	C. Kessler, "	10 91	
"	Mehl & Liebel, "	43 89	
"	Wm. Zimmerly, Brick...............................	28 00	
"	Constable Bros., Sundries...........................	33 18	
"	D. P. Murphy, Labor, &c............................	61 75	
"	August Mehler, Stone, &c	51 18	
"	Thos. Watkins, Sundries	25 50	
"	Henry Mayer, "	12 25	
"	Jas. Gaffney "	15 31	
"	O. C. Thayer, Potter's Clay	7 47	
			22,378 66
	STOP VALVES, BOXES AND COVERS.		
Jan. 1	From commencement of works to Dec. 31, 1884.....	....	17,127 6:
Dec. 31	Paid R. D. Wood & Co. for Valves	457 76	
"	Noble & Hall, Castings, &c.....	276 22	
"	Labor as per Pay Rolls	85 44	
"	D. P. Murphy, Bricklaying....................	24 39	
"	Empire Line, Freight........................	13 57	
"	Erie City Foundry, Castings......................	6 90	
"	Schlosser & Felheim, Lumber......................	5 42	
			869 70
	Carried forward..................................	$41,529 24	$620,467 0:

		FROM JAN. 1, 1885, TO DEC. 31, 1885.	1867 TO 1885.
	Brought forward...................................	.... $41,529 24	$620,467 01
1885	**REPAIRS OF ENGINES AND BOILERS.**		
Jan. 1	From commencement of works to Dec. 31, 1884......	....	.... 24,930 36
Dec. 31	Paid Noble & Hall, Sundries	$ 374 73	
"	" D. P. Murphy, Bricklaying	62 80	
"	" Roger McDonough, et. al., Labor..................	17 00	
"	" Saltsman & Austin, et. al., ...	111 05	
"	" Erie Car Works, et. al., Sundries	40 89	
"	" Jarecki-Hayes Co., Sundries....................	27 29	
"	" J. C. Selden, Brick	27 00	
"	" Erie Rubber Co., Valves.	53 55	
"	" C. Kessler, Sundries............................	3 74	
		718 05	
	REPAIRS OF DISTRIBUTING MAINS.		
Jan. 1	From commencement of works to Dec. 31, 1884......	....	.... 10,290 00
Dec. 31	Paid Labor as per Pay Rolls	326 34	
"	" Noble & Hall, et. al., Sundries..................	49 48	
		375 82	
	CARE AND MAINTENANCE OF RESERVOIR AND KEEPER'S HOUSE.		
Jan. 1	From commencement of works to Dec. 31, 1884......	....	.... 7,174 68
Dec. 31	Paid Samuel Phister, Salary	300 00	
"	" Labor as per Pay Rolls	90 41	
"	" Cash for Sundries..........	9 19	
"	" Frank Hoffman, Labor...............	2 00	
"	" J. E. Baker, Repairs of Boat	3 92	
"	" Wm. Brewster, for Plants.......................	10 80	
		416 32	
	BUILDINGS, GROUNDS AND STANDPIPE.		
Jan. 1	From commencement of works to Dec. 31, 1884......	....	.... 67,301 31
Dec. 31	Paid Roger McDonough, Watchman	513 00	
"	" Donnelly & Bro., Labor	41 25	
"	" Noble & Hall, Sundries.........................	12 00	
"	" August Mehler, "	9 80	
"	" Constable Bros., "	9 97	
"	" Mehl & Liebel, "	15 01	
"	" P. Hall, bill of Paint, &c..............	24 20	
"	" Wm F. Nick, bill of Paint, &c	28 08	
"	" Labor as per Pay Rolls	25 51	
"	" J. O. Baker, Labor	19 57	
"	" Jas. Kelley, "	6 37	
"	" D. P. Murphy, Bricklaying.......................	2 00	
"	" Phil. Osborne, for Trees.......................	21 05	
"	" Frank Hoffman, Labor	2 25	
"	" Pennsylvania Co., Repairs of Switch	9 23	
"	" C. Flickinger, Repairs of Roof	20 00	
"	" H. G. Fink, Sundries............................	10 45	
		769 74	
	ON ACCOUNT OF SLIDE IN BANK.		
	Paid Labor as per Pay Rolls	973 42	
	" Anthony Mullane for Sodding.....................	182 90	
	" W. J. Callow, Contract and Material.............	205 15	
	" Schlosser & Felheim, Lumber....	14 80	
	" Adam Laux, Repair of Roller....................	8 00	
	" Constable Bros., Sundries........	22 34	
	" Saltsman & Austin, Sundries	82 80	
	" August Mehler, "	4 50	
	" Henry Mayer, Repairs	58 00	
		1,551 91	
	SUPERINTENDENT'S SMALL STORES.		
Jan. 1	From commencement of works to Dec. 31, 1884......	....	.... 395 00
Dec. 31	Paid Mehl & Liebel, Sundries	9 12	
"	" P. Hall, "	2 90	
"	" C. Kessler, "	12 51	
"	" W. W. Pierce & Co., Sundries	2 91	
"	" Cash, Sundries	2 50	
		29 94	
	Brought forward..................................	...............$45,391 02	$730,568 36

		FROM JAN. 1, 1885, TO DEC. 31, 1885.	1867 TO 1885.
	Brought forward	.... $45,391 02	$730,568 36
1885	**OFFICE FURNITURE, RENT & EXPENSES.**		
Jan. 1	From commencement of works to Dec. 31, 1884	....	$ 10,563 63
Dec. 31	Paid O. L. Elliot, Rent for Year	$ 250 00	
	" Telephone Co., Rent of Instruments............	90 41	
	" R. J. Saltsman, for Coal................................	56 75	
	" Janitor, et. al......................................	89 86	
	" Erie Gas Co..	38 20	
	" Wm. Dinkey, et. al., bills rendered............	28 16	
	" Constable Bros., " "	25 00	
	" Ashby & Vincent, " "	11 13	
	" Warner Bros., " "	7 10	
	" Mehl & Liebel, " "	5 25	
	" W. W. Pierce & Co., " "	7 00	
	" Erie & Chicago Stove Co...............	7 00	
		615 86	
	WASTE AND PACKING.		
Jan. 1	From commencement of works to Dec. 31, 1884......	....	2,050 75
Dec. 31	Paid C. W. Parsons, Sundry Bills.....................	136 90	
	" C. Kessler, " "	109 74	
	" Mehl & Liebel " "	47 25	
		293 89	
	OIL AND TALLOW.		
Jan. 1	From commencement of works to Dec 31, 1884......	....	5,079 38
Dec. 31	Paid C. Kessler, Sundry Bills..........................	403 67	
		403 67	
	CARTAGE.		
Jan. 1	From commencement of works to Dec. 31, 1884......	....	456 51
Dec. 31	Paid I. H. Burke, Sundry Bills.............................	9 53	
	" Cash for " "	14 25	
		23 78	
	WATER METERS AND CARE.		
Jan. 1	From commencement of works to Dec. 31, 1884.....	....	6,339 38
Dec. 31	Paid National Meter Co................................	171 80	
	" Union Meter Co. for Repairs	33 32	
	" Schlosser & Felheim, Lumber.....	3 50	
	" Labor as per Pay Rolls	61 68	
	" Cash for Freight, &c............................	7 55	
		277 85	
	SHOP TOOLS AND REPAIRS.		
Jan. 1	From commencement of works to Dec. 31, 1884......	... .	2,715 49
Dec. 31	Paid Noble & Hall, Sundry Bills.........................	145 99	
	" Mehl & Liebel, " "	59 95	
	" W. W. Pierce & Co., Sundry Bills	11 94	
	" Humboldt Iron Works................................	21 49	
	" Julia A. Teel, Rent	30 00	
	" Gilbert & Price, Bill Rendered...................	9 89	
	" Erie City Foundry, " "	19 08	
	" Jacob Simon " "	7 50	
	" Cash for Sundries	4 67	
	" C. Kessler, Sundries...........................	2 00	
		312 51	
	COURT COSTS AND COUNSEL FEES.		
Jan. 1	From commencement of works to Dec. 31, 1884......	....	1,509 88
Dec. 31	Paid D. A. Sawdey, Legal Services.......................	10 00	
		10 00	
	INLET PIPE.		
Jan. 1	Previously Expended..........................		5,760 35
Dec. 31	Paid John Dunlap, Balance Contract	2,532 00	
	" Noble & Hall, Repairs of Tube.......................	341 55	
		2,873 55	
	Carried forward	.... $50,202 13	$765,043 73

		FROM JAN. 1, 1885, TO DEC. 31, 1885.	1867 TO 1885.
	Brought forward	..............$50,202 13	$765,(43 73
	INLET PIERS AND REPAIRS.		
1885			
Jan. 1	From commencement of works to Dec. 31, 1884.....	....	33,208 04
Dec. 31	Paid L. Cummins, et. al., Labor	$ 191 63	
	" Labor as per Pay Rolls......................	222 74	
	" Schlosser & Felheim, Lumber......................	61 11	
	" W. W Loomis, Contract, &c..................	505 23	
	" Noble & Hall, Castings	10 60	
	" A. T. Loomis, Bill Rendered.....................	16 50	
	" D. P. Murphy, " "	4 00	
	" Frank Hoffman," "	5 25	
	" John Walsh, " "	3 50	
	" Cash for Sundries........	1 50	
	" J. C. Selden, for Brick.....................	15 00	
			1,037 06
	ENGINEERS' SMALL STORES.		
Jan. 1	From commencement of works to Dec. 31, 1884.....	....	1,195 18
Dec. 31	Paid C. Kessler, Sundries...........................	24 17	
	" W. W. Pierce & Co., Sundries............	10 50	
	" Swalley & Warfel, "	10 00	
	" J. R. Saltsman, "	5 50	
	" James Gaffney, "	32 57	
	" Mehl & Leibel, "	5 59	
	" C. W. Parsons, "	2 81	
	" Ashby & Vincent. "	1 20	
	" Jarecki-Hayes Co. "	6 42	
	" D. C. Weller, "	1 81	
			100 57
	PRINTING AND ADVERTISING.		
Jan. 1	From commencement of works to Dec. 31, 1884.....	....	3,205 25
Dec. 31	Paid Walker & Gallagher, Printing, An. Rep't &c.	94 45	
	" R. B. Brown, Sundry Bills	42 75	
	" Erie Herald Printing & Pub. Co. Sundry Bills	9 25	
	" Erie Dispatch, Sundry Bills.............	25 25	
	" Cash for " "	3 60	
			175 30
	BOOKS AND STATIONERY.		
Jan. 1	From commencement of works to Dec. 31, 1884.....	....	1,212 05
Dec. 31	Paid Ashby & Vincent, Sundry Bills..................	64 30	
	" Herald Printing Co., " "	32 00	
	" Cash for Sundry Bills	5 50	
			101 80
	ENGINE ROOM TOOLS AND FURNITURE.		
Jan. 1	From commencement of works to Dec. 31, 1884.....	....	731 71
Dec. 31	Paid D. C. Weller, Sundry Bills..................	15 12	
	" Mehl & Liebel, " "	50 97	
	" Wm. F. Nick, " "	11 30	
	" Erie Rubber Co., Bill Rendered.........	9 25	
	" C. Kessler, " "	4 50	
	" W. W. Pierce & Co. " "	2 50	
	" Noble & Hall, et.al. " "	5 85	
	" Cash for Sundries	3 80	
			103 29
	EXPENSE OF HORSE AND WAGON.		
Jan. 1	From commencement of works to Dec. 31, 1884.....	....	2,479 12
Dec. 31	Paid C. Klang for Wagon.....................	125 00	
	" J. B. Crouch & Co., et. al. for feed	61 16	
	" Wm. O'Lone, Hay, Oats, &c..................	43 96	
	" Julia A. Teel, et. al., rent.................	36 00	
	" Labor as per Pay Roll...................	102 00	
	" J. Fogarty, Sundry Bills	9 10	
	" W. W. Pierce & Co., Sundry Bills	3 56	
	" Schneider Bros..	14 25	
	" Schlosser & Felheim, Lumber..................	13 83	
	" Mehl & Leibel, Sundries.....................	4 05	
	" Cash for Sundries.................	8 72	
			421 63
	Carried forward	..........$52,141 77	$847,127 58

		FROM JAN. 1, 1885, TO DEC. 31, 1885.	1867 TO 1885.
	Brought forward	$52,141 77	$807,127 58
1885	**WATER RENTS RETURNED.**		
Jan. 1	From commencement of works to Dec. 31, 1884......		52 50
Dec. 31	Paid Heiss Bros.................................	10 00	
		10 00	
	STREET CONNECTIONS.		
Jan. 1	From commencement of works to Dec. 31, 1884......		37,165 50
Dec. 31	Paid Jarecki-Hays Co., Bills Rendered................	934 57	
	" Jarecki Manufacturing Co., Bills Rendered...	59 70	
	" Gibson & Price, " " ...	64 66	
	" F. R. Simmons, " " ...	5 00	
	" Labor as per Pay Rolls	686 54	
		1,750 47	
	ON ACCOUNT OF SERVICE PIPE.		
Jan. 1	From commencement of works to Dec. 31, 1884......		11,811 86
Dec. 31	Paid National Tube Co., Pipe.........	196 70	
	" Jarecki-Hays Co., Pipe	35 37	
	" Cash for Freight, etc.	14 19	
		246 26	
	ON ACCOUNT OF PAVING AND STREET REPAIRS.		
Jan. 1	From commencement of works to Dec. 31, 1884 ...		1,870 37
Dec. 31	Paid Wm. Krueger, Sundry Bills.........................	224 15	
	" Frank Hoffman, et. al................................ ...	24 15	
	" Labor as per Pay Rolls...	3 26	
		251 56	
	SHOP AND MISCELLANEOUS WORK.		
Jan. 1	From commencement of works to Dec. 31, 1884		8,228 27
Dec. 31	Paid Labor as per Pay Rolls........................	421 87	
		421 87	
	LOWERING STREET CONNECTIONS.		
Jan. 1	From commencement of works to Dec. 31, 1884......		296 24
Dec. 31	Paid Labor as per Pay Rolls..............	502 39	
		502 39	
	LOWERING DISTRIBUTING MAINS.		
Jan. 1	From commencement of works to Dec. 31, 1884.... .		1,512 19
Dec. 31	Paid Labor as per Pay Rolls.............................	289 84	
		289 84	
	THAWING OUT PIPE.		
Jan. 1	From commencement of works to Dec. 31, 1884......		63 24
Dec. 31	Paid Labor as per Pay Rolls...............................	117 26	
	" Miller Bros., Bill Rendered..................... ...	41 95	
	" R. T. & R. Williams, Bill Rendered...............	79 82	
	" Geo. E. Fry, et. al., " "	27 66	
		266 69	
	RESERVOIR GROUNDS.		
Jan. 1	From commencement of works to Dec. 31, 1884......		6,560 49
Dec. 31	Paid J. C. Hilton, Recording Deed.......................	3 50	
		3 50	
	DAMAGES.		
Dec. 1	Paid A. J. Louch, et. al.,.....................................	14 00	
		14 00	
	INTEREST AND EXCHANGE.		
Jan. 1	From commencement of works to Dec. 31, 1884......		11,031 47
	RAILROAD SWITCH AND SCALES.		
Jan. 1	From commencement of works to Dec. 31, 1884......		2,840 65
	ENGINES AND BOILERS.		
Jan. 1	From commencement of works to Dec. 31, 1884		66,316 95
	Carried forward	$55,898 36	$954,814 81

		FROM JAN. 1, 1885, TO DEC. 31, 1885.	1867 TO 1885.
	Brought forward	$55,898 36	$954,814 81
1885 Jan. 1	CIVIL ENGINEERING. From commencement of works to Dec. 31, 1884		7,122 85
Jan. 1	GAS WELLS AND CARE. From commencement of works to Dec. 31, 1884		8,148 59
Jan. 1	CONSTRUCTION OF RESERVOIR. From commencement of works to Dec. 31, 1884		116,586 84
Jan. 1	PARK FOUNTAINS. From commencement of works to Dec. 31, 1884		3,244 68
Jan. 1	DISCOUNT ON CITY BONDS. From commencement of works to Dec. 31, 1884		88,033 94
	Total	$55,898 36	$1,177,951 71

RECAPITULATION.

EXPENSES IN 1885.

For Construction $35,245 29
For Extraordinary Repairs 3,267 06
For Current Expenses... 17,386 01

Total $55,898 36

EXPENSES FROM JULY, 1867, TO DEC. 31, 1885.

For Construction...$891,548 12
For Maintenance... 342,301 95

Total..1,233,850 07

NET EARNINGS FROM JULY, 1867, TO DEC. 31, 1885.

Total Cost of Construction..$891,548 12
Advanced by City (Bonds)... 675,955 10

Net Earnings..$215,593 02

EXHIBIT D.

Amount of Water Rents Collected each year, with the Increase and Decrease, since the Commencement of the Works.

	A'm't Rec'd.	Increase.	Decrease.
From Jan. 1, 1869, to Dec. 31, 1869 . . .	$ 4,264 47	$	$
" " 1870 " 1870 . . .	9,237 30	4,972 83	
" " 1871 " 1871 . . .	18,138 08	8,900 78	
" " 1872 " 1872 . . .	21,652 68	3,514 60	
" " 1873 " 1873 . . .	25,560 40	3,907 72	
" " 1874 " 1874 . . .	27,938 90	2,378 50	
" " 1875 " 1875 . .	29,639 38	1,700 48	
" " 1876 " 1876 . . .	31,048 76	1,409 38	
" " 1877 " 1877 . . .	32,276 57	1,227 81	
" " 1878 " 1878 . . .	29,636 01		2,640 56
" " 1879 " 1879 . . .	33,343 20	3,707 19	
" " 1880 " 1880 . . .	37,385 00	4,041 80	
" " 1881 " 1881 . . .	40,385 87	3,000 87	
" " 1882 " 1882 . . .	43,818 78	3,432 86	
" " 1883 " 1883 . . .	48,269 89	4,451 16	
" " 1884 " 1884 . . .	51,852 78	3,582 89	
" " 1885 " 1885 . . .	53,550 35	1,697 57	
Total water rents received	$ 537,998 37		

INVENTORY

Of Stock, Tools, Material, etc., on hand Jan. 1st, 1886.

Superintendent street work . . . . $ 7,437 81
Mechanical engineer 941 20
Keeper at reservoir 50 85
Secretary and Treasurer 1,832 25

Total $10,261 60

EXHIBIT E.

Location, Size and Length of Main Pipe, Large Private Pipe and Fire Hydrant Branches laid in 1885.

LOCATION.	FEET.	IN.
30-INCH (New Pumping Main).		
From East of Pumping Works to 16 feet South of the North line of 7th street.....	2,711	8
20-INCH PIPE.		
On Front and Chestnut streets (branches. &c.)...............	46	3
12-INCH PIPE.		
At 7th and Chestnut streets...............	13	......
6-INCH PIPE.		
At 7th and Chestnut streets	16	2
11th street, between Chestnut and Walnut...............	218	5
11th " " Sassafras and Myrtle...............	257	8
12th " " Raspberry and Cranberry...............	624	......
Ash street, from 6th to 263 feet North of 3d...............	1,498	6
State street, from 7th to 9th, in place of 4-inch...............	775	2
	3,389	11
4-INCH PIPE.		
2d street, between German and Parade	681	......
North Park, (For Reed House)...............	92	4
13th street, East of Division...............	165	......
14th street. East of Wallace...............	216	......
14th street, West of Ash...............	141	9
15th street, West of Parade	137	4
15th street, between Walnut and Cherry, (For F. F. Adams & Co.)...............	728	......
16th street, West of German, (For T. M. Nagle.)	73	......
20th street, between Peach and Sassafras...............	394	......
24th street, West of Sassafras...............	166	......
25th street, East of Holland	342	......
Ash street, South of 25th	510	......
Ash street, (For Soldiers' Home)...............	105	......
Wallace street, South of 8th	176	4
Vine street, between 7th and 8th...............	399	8
German street, " " "...............	398	8
Holland street, North from 25th...............	42	......
Walnut street, South from 12th...............	402	8
Walnut street, North from Huron...............	176	8
Maple street, South from 26th...............	792	......
	6,139	5
Less 4-inch pipe taken up on State street...............	775	2
	5,364	3
2-INCH PIPE.		
15th and Peach streets, (For Street Sprinkling Wagons)	29	2
15th, East of Cherry, (For F. F. Adams & Co.)...............	329	......
	358	2
TEMPORARY ¾-INCH PIPE.		
Liberty street, from 4th to 5th (For Wm. Kues.)	320	2
Carried forward...............	12,503	6

LOCATION.	FEET.	IN.
Brought forward	12,203	6
FIRE HYDRANT BRANCHES, (All 4-inch.)		
3d and Cascade streets	25	8
4th and Chestnut streets	9	3
5th and Walnut streets	7	6
7th and Chestnut streets	7	6
8th and Poplar streets	9	11
11th and Chestnut streets, 11th and Cherrry " 11th and Walnut " 11th and Sassafras "	33	7
13th and Sassafras streets	7	1
15th, and Cherry streets	23	4
15th East of Cherry street, (For F. F. Adams & Co.)	14	.....
24th and Holland streets	6	4
Ash and 25th streets	6	3
Ash and 3d streets	9	1
Division and 14th streets	17	2
Turnpike and 14th streets	8	7
Myrtle and 7th streets	8	2
Chestnut and 7th streets	4	4
Walnut and 13th streets	10	5
Walnut and Huron streets	7	8
Walnut and 9th streets	11	1
Cherry and 7th streets	8	10
Maple and 26th streets	13	... ...
	258	9
Total in feet and inches	12,462	3

RECAPITULATION.

	MILES.	FEET.	INCHES.
Total Main Pipe Laid in 1885	2	1,902	3
Previously Laid	49	2,777	3
Total Length of Main Pipe, Jan. 1, 1886	51	4,679	6

EXHIBIT E–E.

Distributing Pipe, Large Private Pipe, and Hydrant Branches laid from beginning of Works to January 1, 1886.

STREETS.	Less than 4-inch.	4-inch.	6-inch.	12-inch.	20-inch.	30-inch.
EAST AND WEST STREETS.						
Railroad		1780.				
East	225.	718.3	2830.6			
Ash		6186.2	1498.6			
Wallace	181.10	1340.4				
Vine		399.8				
Parade		5529.11	2614.			
German		3385.4				
Division		317.2				
Holland	1008.4	8598.4				
French	259.	6526.5				
State	1105.9	2007.1	4695.2			
Turnpike	6.5	8.7	795.			
Peach		1087.	5974.4	1996.		
Waterford Pike		910.				
Sassafras	570.	9132.6				
Myrtle		3933.1				
Hickory		631.6				
Chestnut		4614.		24.	9222.3	2457.1
Walnut		3571.				
Cherry		2846.				
Maple		805.				
Poplar		819.6				
Liberty	320.2	1085.5				
Plum		631.1				
Cascade	2300.	474.10	2628.8			
NORTH AND SOUTH STREETS.						
Front and Docks	505.	1530.10			22.	254.7
Short		1458.				
Second	719.7	4419.6				
Third	237.	5892.1				
Fourth		2389.2	4625.6			
Fifth	428.5	6394.1				
North Park Row		176.4	820.			
Sixth		470.1	10030.1			
South Park Row	140.	20.7	424.			
Seventh		3316.	31.2	5362.2		
Eighth	293.11	9670.2				
Ninth	9.	7045.2				
Tenth	49.	595.5	9319.1			
Eleventh	275.	8491.3	476.1			
Twelfth		2084.7	13006.6			
Thirteenth		3141.11				
Fourteenth		2988.9				
Fifteenth	621.	3180.11				
Huron		1436.10				
Sixteenth	497.11	2156.	1463.9			
Seventeenth		7424.8				
Eighteenth	11.	2971.10	11720.7			
Buffalo Road		1168.				
Nineteenth		2134.				
Twentieth		1043.3				
Carried forward	9763.9	148917.7	73156.11	7382.2	9244.3	2711.8

STREETS.	Less than 4-inch.	4-inch.	6-inch.	12-inch.	20-inch.	30-inch.
Brought forward	9763.9	148917.7	73156.11	7382.2	9244.3	2711.8
Twenty-First		34.2	5.6	5178.11		
Twenty-Second...		3637.8				
Twenty-Third...		2917.2				
Twenty-Fourth..	1206.6	1624.10				
Twenty-Fifth		3098.11				
Twenty-Sixth..	461.	965.	2623.		1064.6	
	11,431.3	161195 4	75785.5	12561.1	10308.9	2711.8

RECAPITULATION.

	MILES	FEET.	IN.
Small Pipe...	2	871	3
Four-Inch Pipe	30	2,765	4
Six-inch Pipe	14	1,861	5
Twelve-Inch Pipe	2	2,001	1
Twenty-Inch Pipe	1	5,028	9
Thirty-Inch Pipe...	....	2,711	8
Total...	51	4,679	6

The early records of the Department are very imperfect. The above statement is as nearly correct as the information at hand will permit.

EXHIBIT F.

Location, Number and Length of Street Connections made in 1885; also Total Number in the City, Dec. 31, 1885.

STREETS.	Made in 1885. No.	Feet	In.	Total No. Dec.31,'85	STREETS.	Made in 1885. No.	Feet	In.	Total No. Dec.31,'85
EAST AND WEST STREETS.									
Front	1	2	.....	23	NORTH & SOUTH STREETS.				
Short	1	27	3	24					
Second	4	53	5	82	East Avenue	.....	.....	...	4
Third	6	100	8	103	Wayne				1
Fourth	9	109	7	163	Ash	2	18	2	11
Fifth	5	90	3	146	Wallace	3	63	1	19
Sixth	8	305	3	167	Parade	5	167	3	115
North and South Park Row				7	Vine	1	22	10	2
Seventh	13	223	4	166	Division	.....	.....		11
Eighth	10	190	9	213	German	5	138	4	64
Ninth	4	70	8	160	Holland	7	97	1	108
Tenth	7	202	4	155	French	1	9	9	114
Eleventh	8	71	1	190	State	6	209	9	199
Twelfth	9	316	5	169	Turnpike				14
Thirteenth	15	213	7	94	Peach	8	112	1	253
Fourteenth	9	118	2	52	Waterford Pike				16
Fifteenth	3	30	4	31	Sassafras	8	70	1	123
Huron	1	10	10	31	Hickory				16
Sixteenth	2	55	7	48	Myrtle	3	62	8	69
Seventeenth	16	241	11	102	Chestnut	4	73	3	108
Eighteenth	13	141	6	165	Walnut	4	87	7	48
Buffalo Road				2	Cherry	2	11	6	19
Nineteenth	3	47	8	28	Maple	11	241	6	10
Twentieth	4	31	6	11	Poplar	1	28	.....	13
Twenty-first	4	73	3	42	Liberty				15
Twenty-second	2	31	7	54	Plum				2
Twenty-third	2	36	3	36	Cascade	...	...	...	21
Twenty-fourth	2	36	3	23					
Twenty-fifth	4	83	4	31					
Twenty-sixth	3	28	8	31	Total	237	4292	7	3924

RECAPITULATION.

	No.	Feet.	In.
Connections made in 1885	237	4.292	7
Previously made	3,687	83,532	11
Total	3,924	87,825	6
Total in Miles	16$\frac{3}{2}\frac{1}{8}\frac{5}{0}$		

NOTE.—The above are all the Connections shown by the records, but it is believed that many more will be developed by the investigation to be made during the ensuing year.

EXHIBIT G.

Location and Style of Fire Hydrants set in 1885, all being 4 inch.

Hydrants, Set in New Locations.

South East corner 3d and Cascade streets				Matthews.
North East	"	4th "	Chestnut "	"
" "	"	5th "	Walnut "	"
" "	"	7th "	Chestnut "	"
" "	"	8th "	Poplar "	
" West	"	11th "	Chestnut "	"
" "	"	11th "	Walnut "	"
" East	"	11th "	Sassafras "	
" "	"	13th "	"	"
South "	"	15th "	"	"
In yard of F. F. Adams & Co., 15th street				"
In yard of T. M. Nagle, 14th street				"
North East corner Ash and 3d streets				"
Turnpike street, near 14th street				"
North East corner Myrtle and 7th streets				"
" " "	Chestnut and 9th streets			"
" " "	Walnut and 13th streets			"
" " "	Walnut and Huron streets			"
" " "	Walnut and 9th streets			"
South " "	Cherry and 7th streets.			
North " "	11th and Cherry streets			Bay State.
South " "	Ash and 25th streets			"
Maple, South of 26th street				"
North West corner 24th and Holland streets				West Jersey

Old or Defective Fire Hydrants Replaced with New.

North West corner 12th and Myrtle streets				Mathews.
" East "	Division and 14th streets			"
South " "	French and 4th streets			"
North " "	State and 5th streets			"
South " "	Sassafras and 2d streets			"
" " "	Walnut and 6th streets			

Hydrants Taken Out.

24th street, between French and Holland streets	Old Style.
Cascade street, between 10th and 11th streets	"

Recapitulation.

Hydrants in new locations	24
Old Hydrants, replaced with new	6
Hydrants taken out	2
Total number Hydrants, January 1, 1886	270

Style of Fire Hydrants in use.*

Old Style Mathews	11	Pittsburgh	20
New Style "	150	Ludlow	4
Bay State	41	Morris, Tasker & Co	4
West Jersey	32	Brown	1
Home Made	7		
		Total	270

*Besides the above, there are six 1½ inch hydrants for the supply of street sprinkling wagons. One of these was removed in 1885, from Turnpike street to 15th, near Peach.

EXHIBIT H.

Location, Size and Kind of Stop Valves Set in 1885.

LOCATION.	SIZE IN IN.	KIND.
Front street, East of Pumping Works	30	B. M'f'g Co.
" " Branch between 30 inch Main and Standpipe	20	"
Short and Sassafras streets	4	Eddy.
Second and German streets	4	"
" " Parade	4	"
Fourth and Peach streets, (to replace old one.)	6	"
North Park Row, (for Reed House.)	4	"
" " and State streets	6	"
Seventh and Chestnut streets	6	"
" " Sassafras "	12	"
" " Chestnut " (to replace old one.)	12	"
Eighth " German "	4	"
" " French " (to replace old one)	4	"
Ninth and State "	4	"
Eleventh and Myrtle "	6	"
Twelfth " "	6	"
Fourteenth and Wallace "	4	"
Fifteenth and Peach " (Street Sprinkling Hydrant)	2	J-H. Co.
" " German "	4	Eddy.
" " Cherry " (For F. F. Adams & Co.)	4	"
Fifteenth, between Cherry and Walnut sts. (For F. F. Adams & Co.)	2	J-H. Co.
" " " " " " "	2	"
" " " " " " "	2	"
" " " " " " "	2	"
" " " " " " "	2	"
Huron and Walnut streets	4	Eddy.
Sixteenth and German streets, (For T. M. Nagle.)	4	"
Twenty-Fourth and Sassafras streets	4	"
Ash and 25th streets	6	"
" " 6th "	6	"
" " 4th "	4	"
" North of 3d street, (For Soldiers' Home)	4	"
Wallace and 8th streets	4	"
Vine and 8th streets	4	"
German and 7th streets	4	"
Holland and 25th streets	4	"
State and 7th streets, (in place of 4-inch.)	6	"
" " 8th "	6	"
" " 8th "	6	"
" " 9th " (in place of 4-inch.)	6	"
Sassafras and 10th sts.(to replace old one.)	4	"
" " 16th streets	4	"
Chestnut and Short streets	20	B. M'f'g Co.
" " 7th " (to replace old one.)	20	Eddy.
" " 7th "	30	"
" " 7th "	30	"
Walnut " 12th "	4	"
" " 10th " (to replace old one)	4	"
" " Huron "	4	"
Cherry " 12th " (to replace old one.)	4	"

RECAPITULATION.

2-inch Valves	6	12-inch Valves	2
4 " "	25	20 " "	3
6 " "	11	30 " "	3

Total set in 1885 50
Previously set 376

426

SIZE OF VALVES.

Thirty-inch	3	Six-inch	95
Twenty "	16	Four-inch and less	294
Twelve "	18		

Total 426

EXHIBIT I.

Number of Families, Stores, Offices, Manufactories, etc., Supplied with City Water during the year 1885.

Breweries	4	Jail and Court House	1
Board of Trade	1	Lumber Yards	4
Boat Houses	4	Laundries	8
Bakeries	10	Livery Stables	9
Butcher Shops	46	Manufactories	75
Barber Shops	31	Malt Houses	5
Banks	6	Orphan Asylums	2
Billiard Rooms	4	Oil Works	3
Bottling Works	7	Opera House	1
Coffee and Spice Mill	1	Offices	152
Churches	16	Photograph Galleries	6
Cemetery	1	Police Station	1
Custom House	1	Post Office	1
Convent	1	Public Halls	25
Coal and Iron Dock	1	Printing Offices	7
Club House	1	Passenger Depots	2
Dyeing Works	2	Railroads	4
Driving Park	1	Railroad Machine Shops	2
Engine Houses	6	Rinks	2
Express Offices	2	Soldiers' and Sailors' Home	1
Electric Light Co	1	School Houses	21
Fish Hatchery	1	Stores	327
Families	4246	Saloons and Eating Houses	175
" by special permit	110	Slaughter Houses	16
Freight Houses	4	Street Railway	1
Fountains—Private	10	Transfer Company	1
" Public	2	U. S. Signal Station	1
" Drinking	2	Work Shops	79
Flouring Mills	4	Watering Troughs	16
Fish Markets	7	Internal Revenue Office	1
Gas Works	1		
Grain Elevators	4	Total	5658
Greenhouses	2	Last Enumeration	5395
Hospitals	2		
Hotels and Boarding Houses	65	Increase, 1885	263
Ice Houses	2		

EXHIBIT J.

PUMPING ENGINE STATISTICS FOR 1885.

The Pumps are two in number, of the kind known as the Cornish Bull Engine. The diameter of each plunger is 39¾ inches, and each pump has a stroke of 10 feet. Allowing for loss, the capacity of each pump is calculated at 165 gallons to every stroke. The Standpipe is 247 feet high. The reservoir is nearly two miles from the pumping works, and the water was pumped through a 20-inch pipe, with which all the east and west mains are connected. The bottom of the reservoir is 210 feet above the surface of the bay, and the water has been kept, during the year, at an average depth of about 23 feet. The pumps are run at an average of about 10¼ strokes per minute, when operated singly, but when both are used the number of strokes is reduced to about 9 for each pump in the daytime and 8 at night.

Months.	No. of Days a single Pump was run.	No. of Days both Pumps were run.	No. of Days both Pumps were idle.	No. of strokes of the Pumps.	No. of gals. pumped.	Daily average of gals. pumped.	Average lift in feet.	No. lbs. of Bituminous slack coal used.	Coal Bill for Month.
January	15	14	2	524,030	86,464,050	2,789,191	233.7	548,350	$ 397 56
February	14	14	.....	570,140	94,073,100	3,359,753	234.0	385,600	279 56
March	18	11	2	504,979	83,321,535	2,687,791	235.0	676,100	760 23
April	15	15	7	431,848	71,254,920	2,375,164	232.8	653,700	511 41
May	15	16	.....	556,472	91,810,455	2,961,227	234.6	621,300	471 72
June	12	12	6	479,189	79,066,185	2,635,539	230.2	395,000	224 50
July	14	13	4	577,571	95,289,215	3,073,845	232.2	257,900	286 80
August	18	13	.....	603,246	99,535,520	3,210,825	233.2	705,100	458 32
September	17	11	2	528,187	87,150,855	2,905,028	234.0	679,500	441 68
October	23	6	2	507,562	83,747,730	2,701,539	234.8	556,000	343 92
November	15	13	2	488,333	80,574,945	2,685,831	239.4	559,000	338 32
December	21	8	2	510,347	84,207,255	2,716,363	231.4	450,100	263 59
Totals and Averages	190	146	29	6,281,904	1,036,496,665	2,879,574	232.9	6,487,650	4,575 79

The weather from January 1st to May 1st was unusually cold, and especially so between the 10th and 14th of February; on the 12th of the latter month it was 14 degrees below zero.

Both pumps were shut down seven days in April while repairs were being made to the foundation of No. 88; also six days in June and four in July, while the connection was being made between the 30-inch main and the Standpipe.

On the 26th and 27th of December, pump 89 had to stop working on account of anchor ice choking the mouth of the inlet and stopping the flow of water. The ice gathered on the latter date to a thickness of six inches. It was easily removed by the use of a pole and hook.

The average temperature of the feed water during the year has been 180, and the vacuum has been maintained at 25 inches.

The regular employees at the pumping works are 1 mechanical engineer, 2 assistant engineers, 3 firemen, and 1 watchman. The mechanical engineer stands a watch of 5 hours, from 7 to 12 every forenoon; the assistants divide the remainder of each day equally between them; each one of the firemen stands a watch of 8 hours. Besides firing, the firemen unload the coal from the cars, except when both pumps are run, in which case they are assisted by the watchman or a laborer. The mechanical engineer gives ten hours daily to the service of the Department, the hours when he is not on watch being employed in repairs, supervision, &c. In addition to standing their regular watch, the assistant engineers aid their superior officer in keeping the machinery in order. The watchman takes care of the buildings and grounds, besides doing such other work as may be required of him.

EXHIBIT K.

Amount, Kind and Cost of Coal Consumed, Gallons of Water Pumped, Average Height Pumped, Cost per Million Gallons, Etc., from the First Year the Works were operated to January 1, 1886.

Years	Tons of Coal Consumed (2000 lbs. to a Ton)	Contract Price of Coal per ton from May 1st of each year	Cost of Coal delivered in Pumping House	Grades of Bituminous Coal	Gallons of Water Pumped	Increase or Decrease	Families and No. of Establishments supplied	No. of Fire Hydrants supplied	Average height of water in reservoir above surface of bay	Cost of Coal per Million Gallons raised to Reservoir	Cost of Coal per Million Gallons raised one foot	Gallons raised one foot by one pound of Coal	Gallons raised to Reservoir by one lb. of Coal
1868	59.1	$5.05	$309 61	Lump									
1869	544.4	5.05	4,818.48	"									
1870	1,064.5	5.05	5,159.10	"	246,648,960		1218	97	232.00				
1871	1,422.7	5.05	7,117.00	"	179,368,495	132,719,535 I	1727	99	232.00	$18.76	.080	22.656	98.52
1872	1,308.5	5.05	6,528.50	"	395,076,000	115,708,505 I	2140	108	232.00	16.52	.076	35.092	150.96
1873	1,672.5	5.05	8,412.65	"	384,062,415	11,013,585 D	2475	107	232.00	21.90	.094	26.636	114.81
1874	1,759.0	4.85	7,709.54	"	444,817,895	60,754,980 I	2663	107	232.00	17.33	.071	29.234	128.44
1875	1,836.4	4.85	8,657.61	"	531,005,475	86,181,080 I	2700	110	232.00	16.30	.069	33.772	145.57
1876	2,105.1	4.00	8,925.22	"	670,726,650	139,721,175 I	2763	112	232.00	13.30	.056	36.959	159.31
1877	2,456.6	3.70	8,509.33	"	680,981,810	9,744,840 D	2854	114	232.00	12.75	.054	31.491	135.74
1878	2,463.3	3.35	7,945.37	"	682,392,315	21,390,505 I	2915	115	232.00	11.64	.049	31.665	136.49
1879	2,628.1	3.09	7,428.92	Slack.	807,800,400	125,408,085 I	3011	121	232.00	9.19	.039	35.653	153.68
1880	3,076.1	1.99	6,978.41	"	775,805,250	31,995,150 D	3568	126	232.00	8.99	.038	29.234	128.01
1881	3,430.3	1.90	6,517.58	"	975,640,634	200,235,684 I	4110	161	232.00	6.68	.028	32.990	142.20
1882	2,968.2	1.75	5,355.93	"	829,759,260	145,881,674 D	4687	171	234.00	6.45	.027	32.706	139.77
1883	2,398.2	1.55	3,908.59	"	815,939,685	13,819,575 D	5077	197	234.71	4.66	.019	39.900	170.00
1884	3,010.8	1.45	4,502.61	"	917,781,350	101,841,665 I	5395	248	234.32	4.99	.020	35.712	152.41
1885	3,243.8	1.30	4,575.79	"	1,036,496,665	118,715,315 I	5658	270	232.90	4.40	.018	37.208	159.76

All coal used from the commencement of the works has been Western Pennsylvania bituminous. The coal contract is awarded annually to the lowest bidder, the coal being delivered in the works at the contract price.

Two gas wells were put down at the pumping works in the spring of 1871, yielding a large supply. The gas was applied to the boilers the same year, and, for some two years furnished about one-fourth of the fuel at the works. The gas steadily decreased until about 1875, when it failed almost entirely. The wells were pumped out in the summer of 1881, since which time they have supplied the light used at the works and grounds.

EXHIBIT L.

HOW CITY WATER MAY BE WASTED.

Gallons and hundredths of gallons of water that will be discharged per minute through various sized orifices at the heads stated.

Head in Feet.	Pressure per Square Inch.	Diameters of Orifices in inches and fractions of an inch.													
		1/64	1/32	1/16	1/8	1/4	3/8	1/2	5/8	3/4	1	1 1/4	1 1/2	1 3/4	2
20	8 66	0 02	0 07	0 30	1 20	5 10	11 70	20 20	32 20	46 20	82 30	128 40	184 80	252 00	328 80
40	17 32	0 02	0 11	0 45	1 80	7 40	16 30	29 60	45 50	65 50	116 50	182 40	261 60	356 40	465 60
60	25 99	0 03	0 14	0 55	2 20	8 90	20 00	35 00	55 70	80 30	142 80	223 20	320 40	436 80	571 20
80	34 65	0 04	0 16	0 65	2 60	10 30	23 00	41 20	64 30	92 60	164 40	258 00	370 80	505 20	658 80
100	43 30		0 18	0 75	2 90	11 50	25 90	46 10	72 00	103 70	183 00	288 00	413 00	565 20	738 00
120	51 96		0 19	0 78	3 10	12 60	28 30	50 40	78 80	113 50	201 60	315 60	453 60	624 40	807 60
140	60 64	0 05	0 21	0 85	3 40	13 60	30 60	54 50	85 20	122 40	217 20	340 80	480 80	668 40	872 40
150	64 95		0 22	0 88	3 50	14 10	31 70	56 40	88 20	127 20	225 60	352 80	506 40	691 20	902 40
175	75 80	0 06	0 24	0 95	3 80	15 20	34 20	61 20	95 30	136 80	243 60	380 40	548 40	748 00	975 60
200	86 83	0 06	0 26	1 02	4 10	16 30	36 50	65 20	101 80	146 40	260 40	406 80	588 00	798 00	1042 80
235	101 08	0 07	0 28	1 12	4 50	17 90	41 30	71 50	110 40	158 30	285 20	445 90	641 30	871 30	1140 80

The bottom of the Erie Reservoir is 210 feet above the surface of Presque Isle Bay, from which the water is pumped, and the water in the Reservoir is kept at an average height of nearly 25 feet, or 235 feet above the bay. The pressure at the points named below will give an idea of the average throughout the city: Twenty-fourth and Sassafras streets, 20 lbs.; Twenty-third and Myrtle, 30 lbs.; Twentieth and Chestnut, 40 lbs.; Eighth and Peach, 50 lbs.; Fourteenth and State, 60 lbs.; Eighth and State, 70 lbs.; Third and State, 80 lbs.; Front and State, 100 lbs.

The wire of which pins are made is $\frac{3}{32}$d of an inch in diameter—21, wire gauge. The finest cambric needle is made of wire $\frac{1}{24}$th of an inch in diameter—No. 27, wire gauge. A stream the size of a pin running one year with a head of 235 feet, will flow 147,168 gallons, equaling 4,600 barrels, at a loss—counting at the rate of 10 cents per 1,000 gallons—of $14.71. A stream the size of a cambric needle, running at the same pressure for the same time, will waste 38,792 gallons, a loss

EXHIBIT M.

Advantages Offered in Erie to Manufacturers.

The following are the highest and lowest charges per thousand gallons for water by meter measurement, up to a daily average of fifty thousand gallons, in the cities named; also the charges per horse power for steam engines working ten hours per day. They are taken from official reports direct to this office.

	Hi'h-est.	Low-est.	Steam Engine		Hi'h-est.	Low-est.	Steam Engine
Allegheny City, Pa .	15	.	Spec'l	Lawrence, Mass . .	25	20	3 50
Boston	20	.	6 00	Milwaukee	33½	5	4 00
Chicago	10	8	4 00	Minneapolis	20	10	2 50
Cleveland	18½	6⅔	2 50	Newark, N. J. . . .	15	.	5 00
Columbus, O. . . .	20	9	3 00	New York	13½	.	5 00
Cincinnati	18⅓	.	Meter.	Omaha, Neb. . . .	35	15	2 50
Dayton	40	10	"	Philadelphia . . .	8	.	2 00
Detroit	10	.	"	Pittsburgh	20	6₁₀⁷	2 50
Erie, ...	10	6	2 50	Rochester	30	5₁₀⁴	3 00
Fall River, Mass . .	30	.	Meter.	St. Paul	40	20	4 00
Grand Rapids, Mich	30	9½	6 50	Syracuse	25	6	4 00
Hartford, Conn . .	30	10	6 00	Toledo	20	8	2 50
Indianapolis . . .	40	8	3 00	Utica	30	10	5 50

In most of the above cities the meter is paid for by the consumer, who is also required to keep it in order. Here the meter is set and kept in order by the Department. Below will be found the general charge upon shops and factories in the same cities :

	10 hands or less.	Each ad. hand.		10 hands or less.	Each ad. hand.
Allegheny City . . .	Special	. .	Milwaukee	5 00	25
Boston	5 00	30	Minneapolis	5 00	25
Chicago	F. tax.	25	Newark, N.J.	3 00	25
Cleveland	6 25	31	New York	Special	. .
Columbus,(each empl)	. .	50	Omaha	5 00	25
Dayton, O.	Special	50	Philadelphia	10 00	. .
Detroit	3 00	1 00	Pittsburgh	4 00 to	15 00
Erie	5 00	20	Rochester	Special	30
Fall River, Mass . .	Meter.	. .	St. Paul	10 00	1 00
Grand Rapids, Mich .	Special	. .	Syracuse	10 00	1 00
Hartford, Conn . . .	5 00	50	Toledo	5 00	20
Indianapolis	Meter.	. .	Utica	Special	. .
Lawrence, Mass . . .	Special	. .			

EXHIBIT N.

Cost of Water to the Average Householder in Twenty-five Cities, Compiled from Official Reports to this Department.

CITIES.	Population, 1880.	Family Charge.	Pan Water Closet.	Self-Closing Urinal.	Bath Tub.	Self-Closing Wash Stand.	Permanent Wash Tub.	Two Horses.	Cow.	Street Sprinkler.	Total.
Allegheny City	78,000	8 75	3 00	2 00	3 00	1 00	1 50	1 50	75	3 00	24 50
Boston	302,000	7 00	5 00	2 50	5 00	5 00	5 00	2 00	75	5 00	37 25
Buffalo	156,000	7 20	3 50	3 00	3 00	3 00	2 00	2 40	90	2 50	25 50
Chicago	503,000	6 00	3 00	1 00	4 00	1 00	2 00	2 00	75	3 00	21 75
Columbus, O.	51,000	6 00	3 00	4 00	2 00	·	5 00	4 00	2 00	5 30	32 80
Dayton, O.	38,000	6 00	2 50	3 00	3 00	2 00	2 00	2 50	1 00	4 00	45 30
Detroit	116,000	7 00	4 00	2 00	3 00	1 25	2 00	4 00	1 00	3 00	28 25
Erie	28,000	5 00	3 00	3 00	3 00	1 00	2 00	2 00	75	3 00	21 75
East Saginaw, Mich	19,000	5 00	5 00	2 00	5 00	1 00	2 00	4 00	·	3 00	26 50
Fall River, Mass	49,000	8 00	4 00	3 00	3 50	1 00	2 00	4 00	1 00	6 00	31 00
Grand Rapids, Mich	32,000	5 00	3 00	2 00	3 00	2 50	4 50	2 50	1 00	6 00	33 00
Indianapolis	75,000	5 00	4 00	2 00	3 00	1 00	2 00	5 00	·	10 00	32 00
Lawrence, Mass	39,000	6 00	2 00	7 00	3 00	2 00	1 00	3 00	1 50	3 30	25 80
Milwaukee	115,000	4 00	3 00	2 00	2 00	2 00	·	3 00	1 00	3 00	22 00
Minneapolis	47,000	6 25	2 50	3 00	5 00	1 50	1 00	2 00	1 00	· 30	26 25
Newark, N.J	136,000	6 00	10 00	5 00	3 00	1 00	2 00	2 50	1 50	· 00	26 25
New York	1,200,000	6 75	2 50	1 00	3 00	1 00	2 00	6 00	75	5 00	32 75
Omaha, Neb	30,000	5 00	5 00	2 00	4 00	1 00	2 00	5 00	75	5 00	30 00
Philadelphia	847,000	9 00	3 00	2 00	3 00	1 00	2 00	2 00	75	3 00	28 75
Pittsburgh	156,000	6 00	2 00	2 00	4 00	1 00	1 00	4 50	1 50	2 00	28 50
Sandusky, O.	15,838	8 00	4 00	2 40	3 20	1 00	2 00	4 80	1 50	2 40	25 50
St. Paul	41,000	8 00	2 50	2 00	4 00	·	· 00	8 00	·	6 00	24 80
Syracuse	52,000	5 50	2 50	2 50	3 50	1 00	2 00	5 00	75	5 00	31 75
Toledo	50,000	7 00	6 00	3 00	5 00	1 00	2 00	6 00	1 50	8 00	28 50
Utica	34,000								1 50		31 50

RATES FOR CITY WATER.

All are annual, except as otherwise indicated.

Bath Tub, private .... $	3 00
" " each additional...	1 50
" " public	5 00
Bakery, per barrel of flour used, (but no charge less than $5)	01
Barber Shop, one chair..	4 00
" " each additional chair...............................	2 00
Blacksmith Shop, one fire.........	5 00
" " each additional fire.......................	2 50
Boarding House (in addition to family rates) per room	1 00
Brewery, per barrel brewed	08
Building purposes, per bushel lime............	02
Butcher Stalls.......'.............................	3 00 to 15 00
Charitable Institutions, one-third annual rates ....\.....	
Cow	0 75
Condensing Boiler for Steam Heating, per horse power............	50
Eating Houses..	5 00 to 25 00
Family	5 00
Hand Basin, private, self-closing	1 00
" " " not self-closing........	2 00
" " public, self-closing.....	2 00
" " " not self-closing........	4 00
Hotel, (in addition to family rates) per room....	1 00
Livery Stable, per horse	2 00
Maltster, per 1,000 bushels malted..........	1 75
Offices	3 00 to 10 00
Private Stable, one or two horses	2 00
" " each additional horse.......................	1 00
Printing Offices.......	5 00 to 30 00
Public Halls	5 00 to 25 00
Saloons..\....	5 00 to 25 00
Stores	3 00 to 15 00
School, per pupil..	10
Steam Engine, 10 hours per day, each horse power.............	2 50
Slaughter Houses..	5 00 to 50 00
Sleeping Room	1 00
Sprinkling Streets or Lawns with hose	3 00 and up
Urinal, private, self-closing	2 00
" public "	3 00
" not self-closing..................	3 00 to 10 00
Urinal, continuous flow....................	10 00 to 30 00
Wash Tub, (permanent, with waste)...........	2 00
" " " each additional............	1 00
Watering Trough, public	10 00
Water Closet, (pan) private.....................	3 00
" " " each additional............	1 50
" " " public	5 00
" " (hopper), private..	6 00
" " " public	10 00
Work Shop, 10 employees or less..................	5 00
" " each additional employee	20
All other uses, when not metered, to be assessed by the Department.	

METER RATES, (PER QUARTER.)

Daily Average,	15,000 gallons or less	10 cents.
"	15,000 to 20,000 gallons...	9½ "
"	20,000 to 25,000 "	9 "
"	25,000 to 30,000 "	8½ "
"	30,000 to 35,000 "	8 "
"	35,000 to 40,000 "	7½ "
"	40,000 to 45,000 "	7 "
"	45,000 to 50,000 "	6½ "
"	More than 50,000 gallons..	6 "

GASKILL'S HORIZONTAL COMPOUND PUMPING ENGINE.

ANNUAL REPORT

——OF THE——

Board of Water Commissioners

OF ERIE, PA.,

TO THE

MAYOR AND CITY COUNCILS,

FOR THE

YEAR ENDING DEC. 31, 1886.

ERIE, PENN'A:
Herald Printing & Publishing Co., Limited,
1887.

WATER COMMISSIONERS.

The Water Commissioners are appointed by the Court of Common Pleas of Erie County, Penn'a, for a term of three years, one member being named annually, in May.

EX-MEMBERS OF THE BOARD.

**Wm. L. Scott, 1867 to 1868.
*Henry Rawle, 1867 to 1872.
*Wm. W. Reed, 1867 to 1879.
†John C. Selden, 1868 to 1872.
G. W. F. Sherwin, 1879 to 1885.

John Gensheimer, 1872 to 1878.
Matthew R. Barr, 1872 to 1877.
M. Liebel, 1877 to 1886.
J. M. Bryant, 1878 to 1881.

*Messrs. Scott, Rawle and Reed, the first Commissioners, were appointed respectively for terms of one, two and three years.
†Mr. Selden resigned before the expiration of his second term, Mr. Barr was substituted by the Board and afterward appointed by the Court.

PRESENT BOARD.

Benjamin Whitman, 1881 to 1887.   Geo. W. Starr, 1885 to 1888.
C. Kessler, 1886 to 1889.

OFFICERS OF THE DEPARTMENT, JANUARY 1, 1887.

President of the Board—Benjamin Whitman.
Secretary and Treasurer—B. F. Sloan.
Assistant Secretary—Geo. C. Gensheimer.
Clerk—Allan C. Swalley.
Superintendent of Street Work— Wm. O'Lone.
Inspectors—A. F. Crane, F. W. Koehler.
Mechanical Engineer—F. A. Roth.
Assistant Mechanical Engineers—Geo. R. Miller, John Kelly.
Firemen—R. W. Simons, Joseph Burns, Jacob Mullen.
Watchman at Pumping Works—Thos. Tidman.
Keeper of Reservoir and Grounds—Samuel Pfister.

Office—No. 18 East Seventh Street, between French and State.
Office Hours—From 7:30 A. M. to 5:45 P. M.; Monday Evenings from 7:30 to 9:00 P. M.
Regular Meetings of the Board—Every Saturday at 3:30 P. M.

ANNUAL REPORT.

To the Mayor and City Councils:

GENTLEMEN—We have the honor to submit a series of tables giving in detail the transactions of the Water Department during the year 1886. These show the receipts and expenses to have been as follows:

RECEIPTS.

Balance in office Jan. 1, 1886	$316 26
" City Treasury, same date., ...	1,240 21
From Water Rents...............	58,725 00
For Plumbing, from Sale of Material, &c..............	691 61
	$60,973 08

EXPENSES.

Paid on account of Construction........................	$29,846 32
" " Extraordinary Repairs	1,796 41
" " Maintenance	17,241 03
Balance in City Treasury Dec. 31, 1886	11,756 45
" Office, same date.........................	332 87
	$60,973 08

To the Maintenance account should, however, be added the sum of $246.50 for coal used from the bunker and not yet replaced, which increases the figures to $17,487.53. It is a matter for congratulation, in view of the general tendency of the times, that the cost of Maintenance is the lowest, in proportion to the amount of water pumped and revenue collected, of any year in the history of the Department.

The receipts from Water Rents were $5,174.65 in excess of 1885, being the largest gain that has been reported since 1871, when the benefits of the water system first began to be generally realized by the public. At the average rate of increase of the last five years the revenue from this source will amount to $70,000 by 1890; and, unless some unforeseen event occurs, the Department will soon be able to turn over a handsome sum annually to the city authorities.

Total Receipts and Expenses.

The entire receipts from Water Rents since Jan. 1, 1869, the beginning of collections from that source, have been $596,723.37. The total expenses from the time the erection of the works was commenced, in May, 1867, have been $1,282,733.83, of which $921,394.44 were for Construction and $361,339.39 for Maintenance. From 1867 to 1874 the city advanced $675,955.10 in bonds for the purpose of Construction, which were sold at a discount of $88,033.94, leaving, as the actual proceeds, $587,921.16. Deducting the latter sum from the cost of Construction, and adding the cash on hand, the total net earnings of the Department are shown to have been $345,562.60.

Net Cash Earnings for 1886.

The net cash earnings for 1886, were as follows:

Expended for Construction $29,846 22
Balance in City Treasury 11,756 45
   "   Office 332 87

       Total $41,935 54

It is only fair to add that the statements above presented do not show the full amount of net earnings with which the Department is entitled to be credited. The city water has been supplied, without charge, during the past year, for a variety of public purposes, the value of which, at an estimate much below the sum which most cities allow for similar service, may be placed as follows:

280 Fire Hydrants, at $30 each $8,400 00
Park Fountains 2,000 00
State Fish Hatchery 1,000 00
City Buildings, Drinking Fountains, Flushing Sewers, &c., 500 00

       Total $11,900 00

Adding the latter amount to the net cash earnings, $53,835.54 results as the actual net earnings for 1886, or almost eight per cent. on the original cost of the works, and nearly six per cent. on the total cost of construction, inclusive of the discount on bonds. In a report made in 1874 by Messrs. W. A. Galbraith, J. O. Spencer and G. T. Churchill, a committee appointed by Councils to audit the accounts of the Water

Department up to that date, the position of the Board on this subject was amply sustained, as will be seen by the following extract (page 65.) :

"Nothing is charged the city for water supplied to the several offices, engine and hose houses, park fountains, or for flushing sewers, or for the 120 fire-plugs scattered over the city. Were the works in the hands of a company this service would probably cost the city $20,000 annually, and it is, in fact, a fair offset for so much of the interest paid by the city on the Water Works debt."

In this connection it may be proper to mention that the contract for the supply to the State Fish Hatchery will expire on the 1st of April next. The quantity of water consumed at the Hatchery, as shown by meter, is three times what was anticipated when the arrangement was made for a free supply to the same, and, as the Department will have contributed very liberally for two seasons, it would seem to have given all the encouragement to the enterprise that could be asked.

A NEW PUMPING ENGINE.

In the report for 1885 attention was called to the urgent need for a third Pumping Engine, in order that the works might be able to keep pace with the growing demands of the city. The extraordinary strain upon the old Pumps during the season of 1885 warned the Board that preparations for the new Engine could no longer be safely delayed. To that end, $20,000 were set aside, in April last, from the revenues of 1886, to which $18,000, or so much thereof as may be needed, were afterward added from the receipts of 1887. In May, the Board, accompanied by the Mechanical Engineer, visited a number of Eastern cities for the purpose of ascertaining and examining the most approved pumping machinery. This trip, and the studious investigation given to the matter otherwise, resulted in the drafting of strict specifications describing the kind of Engine wanted and the conditions of its accept-ance, which are believed to cover every point necessary to secure a good, durable and economical machine. Copies of the specifications were sent to the leading builders of pumping machinery throughout the country, nine of whom responded with bids, which were opened on the 8th of July in the presence of a representative of each of the competing parties. The bids and accompanying plans were referred to a committee of three practical mechanics, who, after severe scrutiny, reported unanimously in favor of the Gaskill Horizontal Compound Pumping Engine as the best for the work required, and the offer of its builders, the Holly Manufacturing Co., of Lockport, N. Y., as the lowest, all things considered. Their verdict being in consonance with the judgment of the Board, a contract was made with the Holly Company on July 19th, the price stated being $24,0C0 for the Engine and all fixtures appertaining thereto within the building, besides $850 for the foundation.

DESCRIPTION OF THE ENGINE.

The Gaskill Engine was first introduced to the public notice at Saratoga, N. Y., in 1882, and has since been adopted in Buffalo, Chicago, Boston, Philadelphia and many other important cities. Wherever the Board made inquiry relative to its design and working the responses from Engineers and Water Commissioners were of the most satisfactory nature. The Engine for this city is planned to pump 5,000,000 gallons of water per day (being one-fifth more than the capacity of both the Cornish Pumps) to a height of 237 feet in the Reservoir, but is guaranteed to be capable of running with safety up to 6,000,000 gallons, in case of necessity. Its duty, when operated at the rate first named, is to be 105,000,000-foot pounds for each 100 pounds of good anthracite coal, based upon an evaporation of 10 pounds of water to each pound of coal consumed. As the duty of the old Pumps is scarcely one-half of this, and as the new Engine, if accepted, will not in all likelihood require any important repairs for some years, a great saving in fuel, labor, &c., must inevitably ensue at the Works.

An essential consideration in the choice of a new Engine grew out of the fact that the builder of the present Boilers at the Works, when asked for an opinion on the point, pronounced it unsafe to subject them to a daily steam pressure in excess of 80 pounds. Most of the proposals for Engines offered to the Board called for a higher pressure than this, while the Holly Company guarantee the old Boilers to answer every requirement of their Engine. After the Gaskill Engine is in operation, it is the purpose to use it for doing most of the pumping, simply starting up the Cornish Pumps once or twice a month to keep them ready for an emergency. The increased pumping facilities will enable the Works to shut down for a suitable period whenever severe rains or storms render the bay muddy, thus insuring, if proper care be taken, an abundance of clear and pure water at all seasons of the year.

ADDITIONAL ENGINE ROOM.

To accommodate the new Engine, an additional building has been provided on the east side of the old Engine room, in the planning and construction of which special regard has been had to neatness, convenience and durability. The structure is of sufficient size for two

Engines, but, until another is purchased, a portion of the space will be used as a Coal Bunker, for which it is peculiarly well suited on account of its proximity to the railroad track and boiler room. In preparing the Inlet for the third Engine the Board decided to tap the main conduit at a point outside the building containing the Cornish Pumps, and set a gate for each Engine room, thus enabling the water to be shut off from either without affecting the supply to the other. It is intended, as soon as the funds of the Department will permit, to bring the architecture of the old buildings into harmony with the new edifice. The plan also contemplates that any Engine which may take the place of the Cornish Pumps shall stand on the same floor line as the Gaskill Engine, and that the two rooms shall be connected, and practically made one, by a wide archway.

The contracts called for the completion of the new Building by December 1st, and for the Engine to be in operation by January 1st, but unexpected delays have occurred in both cases, so that the latter will hardly be ready for the tests before the 15th of March. The cost of Building, Engine, Inlet and Delivery Pipe, with their appurtenances, will not be far from $35,000.

CONSUMERS AND CONNECTIONS.

The number of Families and Establishments assessed for water rents has increased from 5,658 to 6,140. The Street Connections put in during the year numbered 411, requiring 1 mile and 2,130 feet of pipe. This is the largest increase that has taken place in many years, but is scarcely a fair index to the growth of the city as no less than eighty Connections were made without the usual applications, to comply with the ordinance regulating street paving. A change in the law is strongly urged, which will enable the Board, in conjunction with such city officers as may be designated, to locate the points where Connections shall be placed when streets are about to be paved. As the ordinance stands, Connections are obliged to be put in, under severe penalties, at intervals of 20 feet, 7½ inches in certain streets, and 41 feet, 3 inches in others, when some of them will never be used and others will lie idle for an indefinite period.

No word has reached the office thus far during the winter of a single frozen Connection, which proves that the Department acted wisely in adopting and enforcing the rule that all pipe should be laid at a depth of five feet.

An Invaluable Work.

The old record of Street Connections was so incomplete that it has been in contemplation for several years to have a survey of the entire city made in order to locate every shut-off and apply the measurement of each one to the proper premises. This important and difficult work was begun by the Inspectors at the close of their spring inspection and occupied most of their time throughout the summer. It was then taken up by the office force, who have entered the information collected in a special book, which will be of permanent and ever-increasing value to the Department. The record shows every Connection in the city, with the premises to which it belongs and the distance from the nearest street intersection, and is so arranged by streets and numbers that it will always be easy to find the various shut-offs without regard to changes in ownership or the condition of the stop boxes. The investigation developed 178 Connections that were not included in recent Annual Reports, and increases the number in the city to 4,513, representing about 18½ miles of pipe. It is not to be expected that so extensive a work should not have been attended with some errors, but with a little care on the part of officers and plumbers to correct them when discovered, the record of Street Connections may, in a few years, be made almost perfect.

Main Pipe, Etc.

The aggregate of Distributing Pipe laid during the year was 2 miles, 1,167 feet and 8 inches, a good proportion of which was 6-inch. The total amount of Main Pipe in the city, inclusive of fire hydrant branches, large private pipe and small temporary pipe, is 53 miles, 1,957 feet and 3 inches. Of this upward of ½ mile is 30-inch, nearly 2 miles, 20-inch ; 2⅝ miles, 12-inch ; and about 15½ miles, 6-inch ; the balance is 4-inch and less in size. The Board have adopted a resolution to lay down no more Distributing Pipe of a smaller size than 6-inch, except in streets near the bay, where the pressure is very strong. It is intended, that, as soon as possible, the 12-inch pipe on Seventh and Twenty-first streets shall be extended to Wallace or Ash, and then connected on the line of one of the latter streets by pipe of similar size, thus serving as a reservoir for the laterals reaching into the extreme eastern part of the city. A balance of $3,721.50 due upon the 30-inch main on Chestnut street, between the Works and Seventh street, was paid during the year, making the total cost of that improvement about $26,000. It is not deemed essential to extend this pipe toward the Reservoir at present.

Stop Valves, Fire Hydrants and Meters.

The Stop Valves set in 1886 numbered 44, making 463 in all. From 40 to 50 Valves should be added each season until enough are in to permit each block to be shut off without interfering with the supply to any other.

The drain upon the resources of the Department to provide adequate pumping facilities has prevented as many Fire Hydrants from being put in as was hoped and intended. The number in the city is now 280, of which 10 were set in new locations during the year. Although much progress has been made in this direction within the last few years, the number of Fire Hydrants here is still scarcely one-half of what is customary in cities the size of Erie. Every street intersection should be provided with a Hydrant as speedily as possible, and, as the city builds up more closely, one should be placed at the centre of each of the long blocks. The old style fixtures, which are clumsy and unreliable, as well as a source of constant expense, should also be got rid of and Hydrants of the most approved pattern substituted in their stead.

The number of Meters in use is 64, a gain of 12 over last year. The rates in Erie, to large consumers, as will be seen by Exhibit N, are below those of most cities; and the practice of charging such parties by measurement is so manifestly fair to all concerned that Meters will continue to be set wherever the use of water seems to warrant their use.

Pumping Statistics.

The Pumpage of the year amounted to 1,117,389,075 gallons, an average of 3,063,423 gallons per diem. or, with an estimated population of 35,000, at the daily rate of 87 gallons to each man, woman and child in the city. Since 1883 the annual consumption has increased over 300,000,000 gallons, or more than one-third of what it was in that year, a quantity out of all proportion to the growth of the corporation or the number of consumers. Besides the regular use of a single pump, the second pump had to be operated in connection therewith 161 days to keep up the supply, and had either one suffered a serious accident, such as has taken a month or two to repair on several occasions, the other would not have been equal to the demands of the city.

Notwithstanding the surprisingly large consumption, the cost of fuel burned under the boilers was only $4,318.64, or about $250 less than last year, a fact due to more economical methods at the Works and to a fortunate coal contract. The duty of the pumps, 165$\frac{2}{3}$ gallons raised to an average height of 233$\frac{1}{2}$ feet for each pound of bituminous slack, is the best in the annals of the Department, with the exception of 1883, when the Works were run under peculiarly favorable conditions. The cost of coal per million gallons was $3.86, the very lowest known to the Department. Encouraging as these results are for our old and out-of-date Cornish Pumps, it is but just to add that they are much below the duty of the improved engines of the present day, and the Board will be sadly disappointed if the introduction of new machinery does not lead to greatly reduced expenses at the Works.

BUILDINGS AND GROUNDS

The policy inaugurated in 1882, of making steady improvements on the buildings and grounds, has met with such decided approval from the public that the Board have felt warranted in continuing it during the year. It is to be hoped that the city authorities will soon find it feasible to grade and sod the portion of the bay front between the Water Works property and Sassafras street. When this is done and the Department makes the proposed improvements west of the pumping station, the ravines at both ends will make a natural stopping place where the work can rest until the city feels able to extend it in either direction.

QUALITY OF THE CITY WATER.

The Board cannot refrain from again calling attention to the excellent quality of the city water, as proven by the results at the State Fish Hatchery. It is well known that the varieties of fish—trout, salmon and white fish—to which the Hatchery has mainly devoted its experiments, will thrive only in water that is cool, fresh and free from sediment or other extraneous matter. Both Mr. Page, the gentleman in charge of the Hatchery last winter, who has had experience in breeding fish in all parts of the country, and Mr. Gay, President of the State Fish Commission, enthusiastically award to the city water in Erie the credit of being the best for their purpose of which they have any knowledge. Nothing is more essential to the health and comfort of a community than an abundant supply of pure water, and the truths here stated should be spread broadcast by our citizens as an extra inducement to the many others Erie affords why people who are seeking homes in a desirable locality should come and settle among us.

Turn the Sewage Into the Lake.

While fully convinced that our city water is almost unequalled, the Board concede that there is something repulsive in the idea of the sewage being poured into the lower portion of the bay, and renew their recommendation that early steps be taken to turn it into the open lake. This is a matter over which they are powerless, except to urge a remedy —having no authority outside of the limited territory under their con-trol—and the people must look wholly to the Councils, who have thus far been strangely indifferent about it. With the sewers emptying their contents beyond the sand beach, and the conduit at the works ex-tended, say two or three hundred feet further, into deeper water, there would be nothing left in regard to the quality of water supplied to our citizens of which the most fastidious could reasonably complain.

Respectfully submitted,

BENJAMIN WHITMAN,
GEO. W. STARR,
C. KESSLER,

Erie, February 1, 1887.   Water Commissioners.

EXHIBIT A.

Receipts of the Erie Water Department for the Year Ending the 31st of December, 1886.

WATER RENTS.			
First quarter—January......................	$5,706 84		
" " —February	4,264 55		
" " —March	2,979 28		
		$12,950 67	
Second quarter—April	5,721 39		
" " —May........................	6,521 19		
" " —June......................	2,491 37		
		$14,733 95	
Third quarter—July	6,592 01		
" " —August	5,398 38		
" " —September.................	2,866 23		
		$14,856 62	
Fourth quarter—October......................	7,031 70		
" " —November.................	6,215 12		
" " —December	2,936 94		
		$16,183 76	$58,725 00
OTHER SOURCES.			
Plumbing and pipe-laying...................	$299 91		
Material sold, etc............................	371 70		
Damage to fire hydrant	20 00		
		$691 61	
Balance last report	....	316 26	
			$1,007 87
Total from all sources.................	....	....	$59,732 87
CR.			
Deposited in Treasury—First quarter....	$13,050 00		
" " Second "	14,800 00		
" " Third "	15,250 00		
" Fourth "	16,300 00		
			$59,400 00
Balance	....	....	$332 87

EXHIBIT B.

Account of Water Department with City Treasurer for the Year Ending December 31, 1886.

DR.			
To balance in Treasury Dec. 31, 1885.....	$1,240 21		
To deposits from Jan. 1 to Dec. 31, 1886..	59,400 00		
			$60,640 21
CR.			
By warrants drawn, 1st quarter—Jan ...	6,051 20		
" " " " " —Feb ...	3,733 65		
" " " " " —Mar...	1,966 08		
		$11,750 93	
By warrants drawn, 2d quarter—April..	2,232 84		
" " " " " —May...	3,449 75		
" " " " " —June ..	2,531 41		
		$8,214 00	
By warrants drawn, 3d quarter—July...	5,861 59		
" " " " " —Aug...	4,194 01		
" " " " " —Sept...	3,051 39		
		$13,106 99	
By warrants drawn, 4th quarter—Oct....	6,797 62		
" " " " " —Nov...	4,528 56		
" " " " " —Dec ...	4,485 76		
		$15,811 84	
			$48,883 76
Balance			$11,756 45

(*Continued on Page* 14.)

EXHIBIT B—Continued.

CONTROLLER'S AUDIT.

Water Commissioners' Cash and Warrant Accounts; also, Account with City Treasurer for Year 1886.

Cash on hand January 1st, 1886... $ 316 26
Received from Water Rents... 58,725 00
Received from other Sources... 691 61

    Total Receipts..$59,732 87
Amount paid City Treasurer 59,400 00

Amount of Cash on hand and in Bank....................................... $332 87

Amount of Warrants outstanding January 1st, 1886....................... $287 10
Total Amount of Warrants issued during 1886 .... 48,883 76

    Total Warrants $49,170 86
Warrants paid during the year 1886... 49,060 78

Amounts of Warrants outstanding January 1st, 1887...................... $110 08

Balance to the Credit of the Water Department in the City Treasury
    January 1st, 1886... $1,527 31
Total Receipts by City Treasurer during the year 1886.................. 59,400 00

    Total $60,927 31
Warrants paid by the Treasurer during 1886................................. 49,060 78

Balance to the Credit of the Water Commissioners in the City Treasury January 1st, 1887 ....$11,866 53

OFFICE OF CITY CONTROLLER, }
ERIE, Pa., Feb. 23, 1887. }

I hereby certify that the above statement has been carefully compared with the records in the office of the City Treasurer and Water Commissioners, and found correct ; and the balance, $11,866.53, was due the Water Commissioners by the City Treasurer January 1st, 1887.

               CHAS. S. CLARKE,
                  City Controller.

· EXHIBIT C.

Expenditures for the Year 1886 ; *also, from the Commencement of the Works in* 1867 *to January* 1, 1886.

FUEL AT WORKS.*	FROM JAN. 1, 1886, TO DEC. 31, 1886.		1867 TO 1886.
From comm't of works to Dec. 31, 1885.	....	....	$112,942 24
Paid Wm. Himrod for 2,972,700 lbs. bituminous slack coal, $1.30 p'r ton.	$1,933 32		
Paid R. J. Saltsman for 3,575,100 lbs. bituminous slack coal, $1.25 p'r ton.	2,234 42		
		$4,167 74	
SALARIES.			
From comm't of works to Dec. 31, 1885.	....	....	$94,254 54
Paid B. F. Sloan, Sec. and Treas........	$1,200 00		
" Geo. C. Gensheimer, Asst. Sec....	830 00		
" A. C. Swalley, Clerk..,..............	360 00		
" Wm. O'Lone, Supt. of St. Work..	950 00		
" A. F. Crane, Inspector.............	390 00		
" F. W. Koehler, "	294 34		
" F. J. Ellison, Tem. Inspector......	363 10		
" Benj. Whitman, Commissioner....	722 00		
" M. Liebel, "	492 00		
" G. W. Starr, "	800 00		
" C. Kessler, "	200 00		
		$6,601 44	
MECHANICAL ENGINEERS AND FIREMEN.			
From comm't of works to Dec. 31, 1885.	....	....	$67,249 61
Paid F. A. Roth, Mech. Eng.............	$1,000 00		
" Geo. R. Miller, Asst. ".............	840 00		
" John Kelly, " "	830 00		
" R. W. Simons, Fireman.............	540 00		
" Joseph Burns, "	540 00		
" Jacob Mullen, "	540 00		
" Extra Firemen......................	125 01		
		$4,415 01	
FIRE HYDRANTS.			
From comm't of works to Dec. 31, 1885.	....	....	$13,493 46
Paid R. D. Wood & Co. for Hydrants..	$1,268 00		
" Empire Line, freight................	26 49		
" Frank Hoffman, cartage...........	18 50		
" Schlosser & Felheim, lumber......	5 67		
" Labor, as per Pay Roll.............	80 98		
		$1,399 64	
Carried forward...................	....	$16,583 83	$287,939 85

*See Exhibits K and L.

	FROM JAN. 1, 1886, TO DEC. 31, 1886.		1867 TO 1886.
Brought forward......................	....	$16,583 83	$287,939 85
CARE AND REPAIR OF HYDRANTS.			
Paid Noble & Hall, sundries.............	$4 85		
" Althof Brothers, lumber............	2 72		
" Humboldt Iron Works, sundries.	15 94		
" Noyes & Sterner, sundries.........	3 00		
" Wm. F. Nick, paints, etc...........	12 80		
" Mehl & Liebel, sundries............	7 59		
" Asphalt Paving Co., repairs........	2 50		
" Cash for sundries.....................	3 18		
" Labor, as per Pay Roll, etc.........	212 39		
		$264 97	
POSTAGE.			
From comm't of works to Dec. 31, 1885.	....	....	$2,800 20
Paid for Envelopes, Postal Cards, &c...	$193 54		
		$193 54	
PLUMBING FOR HIRE.			
From comm't of works to Dec. 31, 1885.	....	....	$3,065 67
Paid Labor as per Supt's Pay Roll......	$48 82		
		$48 82	
DISTRIBUTING MAINS.			
From comm't of works to Dec. 31, 1885.	....	....	$350,193 18
Paid Buffalo Pipe Works, pipe..........	$2,988 93		
" Lake Shore Foundry, "	3,961 19		
" Crouch Bros., "	184 88		
" Cornell Lead Co., for lead..........	868 15		
" Frank Hoffman, dis. pipe..........	19 81		
" W. W. Pierce & Co., et. al., sund.	11 25		
" Adolph Brugger, wooden plugs...	10 55		
" Humboldt Iron Works, sundries..	8 33		
" Erie Gas Co., for coke................	29 18		
" M. Quigley, et. al., old rope.......	27 20		
" Jarecki Mfg. Co., sundries.........	29 05		
" Cash for Inspecting pipe, &c.......	28 00		
" Schlosser & Felheim, lumber......	4 85		
" Geo. Carroll & Bro., "	17 50		
" Noble & Hall, sundries..............	14 08		
" Lake Shore R. R. Co., freight.....	166 19		
" Labor, as per Supt's Pay Roll.....	1,494 23		
" Balance of cost of 30-inch main...	3,721 50		
		$13,584 97	
STOP VALVES, BOXES AND COVERS.			
From comm't of works to Dec. 31, 1885.	....	....	$17,997 35
Paid R. D. Wood & Co., for valves.....	$729 60		
" Humboldt Iron Works, sundries..	235 99		
" Noble & Hall, " ..	84 12		
" Empire Line, et. al., freight.......	17 10		
" Labor, as per Supt's Pay Roll......	122 62		
		$1,189 43	
Carried forward......................	....	$31,865 56	$661,996 25

	FROM JAN. 1, 1886, TO DEC. 31, 1886.		1867 TO 1886.
Brought forward......................	....	$31,865 56	$661,996 25
REPAIRS OF ENGINES AND BOILERS.			
From comm't of works to Dec. 31, 1885.	....	....	$25,648 41
Paid Humboldt Iron Works, sundries..	$290 85		
" D. P. Murphy, for bricklaying...	65 00		
" Noble & Hall, sundries............	67 08		
" South Erie Iron Works, castings..	95 18		
" Erie Lime & Cem't Co., lime, &c.	58 05		
" Jarecki-Hays Co., sundries........	28 59		
" Labor, as per Supt's Pay Roll.....	54 66		
" Cash, as per vouchers...............	54 48		
" R. J. Saltsman, fuel, &c............	26 55		
		$740 44	
REPAIR OF DISTRIBUTING MAINS.			
From comm't of works to Dec. 31, 1885.	....	....	$12,467 85
Paid Labor, as per Pay Roll..............	$166 12		
		$166 12	
CARE AND MAINTENANCE OF RESERVOIR AND KEEPER'S HOUSE.			
From comm't of works to Dec. 31, 1885.	....	....	$7,591 00
Paid Samuel Phister, salary..............	$370 00		
" Mehl & Liebel, sundries............	45 95		
" Samuel Merritt, labor, &c.........	6 75		
" R. J. Saltsman, coal..................	5 25		
" Wm. Nick, paint, &c.................	1 13		
" Wm. Brewster, sundries............	7 00		
" Labor, as per Pay Roll..............	16 38		
" Cash for insurance, &c...............	15 30		
		$467 76	
BUILDINGS, GROUNDS AND STAND PIPE.			
From comm't of works to Dec. 31, 1885.	....	....	$69,622 96
Paid Thos. Tidman, et. al., watchman.	$387 63		
" Labor, as per Supt's Pay Roll......	293 60		
" J. D. Tuohy, contract for fence...	111 75		
" Cash for insurance, &c..............	53 25		
" Beckman & Williams, sundries...	25 07		
" D. P. Murphy, et. al., labor.......	28 40		
" Saltsman & Austin, sundries......	15 15		
" Constable Bros., "	19 11		
" R. W. Russell, "	15 75		
" C. Flickinger "	27 25		
" Dr. P. Hall, et. al., paints.........	10 45		
" H. G. Fink, sundries.................	9 87		
" Penn'a Co., repairs of track.......	25 29		
" Mehl & Liebel, sundries............	25 73		
" N. Murphy & Son, "	11 00		
" P. Osborn, et. al., trees..............	10 10		
		$1,105 40	
Carried forward......................	....	$34,345 28	$777,326 47

	FROM JAN. 1, 1886, TO DEC. 31, 1886.		1867 TO 1886.
Brought forward......................	....	$34,345 28	$777,326 47
SUPERINTENDENT'S SMALL STORES.			
From comm't of works to Dec. 31, 1885.	....	....	$424 94
Paid sundry bills, as per vouchers......	$22 66		
		$22 66	
OFFICE FURNITURE AND EXPENSES.			
From comm't of works to Dec. 31, 1885.	....	....	$11,179 49
Paid T. J. Elliott, rent....................	$250 00		
" Cash for janitor, et. al., and ins...	127 18		
" Labor, as per Pay Roll................	58 62		
" R. J. Saltsman, for fuel.............	82 80		
" G. W. F. Sherwin, maps............	60 00		
" Erie Gas Co..............................	27 31		
" Erie Telephone Exchange...........	150 00		
" Erie Ice Co..............................	16 00		
" Chicago & Erie Stove Co............	10 55		
" Erie Art Novelty Works, case.....	38 00		
" R. M. Johnson, et. al., livery......	6 50		
" Beckman & Williams, mat........	1 25		
" Jarecki-Hays Co., sundries........	1 75		
		$829 96	
WASTE AND PACKING.			
From comm't of works to Dec. 31, 1885.	....	....	$2,344 64
Paid C. W. Parsons, sundries............	$147 63		
" E. S. Greeley & Co., bale of waste.	40 87		
" Mehl & Liebel, sundries............	38 31		
		$226 81	
OIL AND TALLOW.			
From comm't of works to Dec. 31, 1885.	....	....	$5,483 05
Paid C. Kessler, sundry bills in June..	$314 36		
" Eclipse Oil Co., sundry bills.......	81 25		
" Thos. Brown Oil Co., sun'y bills.	104 28		
		$499 89	
CARTAGE.			
From comm't of works to Dec. 31, 1885.	....	....	$480 29
Paid Cash as per vouchers................	$3 25		
		$3 25	
WATER METERS AND CARE.			
From comm't of works to Dec. 31, 1885.	....	....	$6,617 23
Paid Union Water Meter Co., et. al.....	$477 25		
" National Meter Co.....................	62 40		
" Labor, as per Pay Rolls.............	99 66		
" Jarecki Mfg. Co., et. al..............	28 48		
		$667 80	
Carried forward......................	....	$36,595 65	$803,856 11

	FROM JAN. 1, 1886, TO DEC. 31, 1886.		1867 TO 1886.
Brought forward.....................	....	$36,595 65	$803,856 11
SHOP TOOLS AND REPAIRS.			
From comm't of works to Dec. 31, 1885.	....		$3,028 00
Paid Humboldt Iron Works, et. al......	$96 59		
" Mehl & Liebel, et. al., sundry bills	106 84		
" Schlosser & Felheim " " ...	14 84		
" Jarecki-Hays Co., et. al., sundry bills....................................	3 65		
" Wm. F. Nick, sundry bills........	9 04		
" Constable Bros., " "	6 08		
" Cash for insurance, &c...............	13 42		
" Rent of shop...........................	60 00		
		$310 46	
COURT COSTS AND COUNSEL FEES.			
From comm't of works to Dec. 31, 1885.	....		$1,519 88
Paid T. A. Lamb, fees and costs.........	$128 00		
		$128 00	
INLET PIERS AND REPAIRS.			
From comm't of works to Dec. 31, 1885.	....		$42,879 00
INLET FOR NEW PUMP.			
Paid Labor, as per Pay Roll..............	$595 85		
" Noble & Hall, for gate...............	103 50		
" Humboldt Iron Works, sundries..	99 58		
" R. J. Saltsman, fuel...................	166 25		
" Liebel & Duedenheffer..............	122 10		
" Lake Shore Foundry, pipe, &c....	529 06		
" Saltsman & Austin, water lime...	76 50		
" Thos. Dillon, bricklaying..........	18 00		
" Jarecki-Hays Co., pipe, &c........	17 87		
" N. Murphy & Son, sundries.......	18 40		
" Constable Bros., "	9 40		
" Lake Shore R. R. Co., freight......	9 96		
		$1,766 37	
ENGINEER'S SMALL STORES.			
From comm't of works to Dec. 31, 1885.	....		$1,295 75
Paid Wm. F. Nick, sundries..............	$7 77		
" J. R. Cooney, ice for two years...	62 50		
" R. J. Saltsman, fuel...................	16 66		
" Mehl & Liebel, sundries............	7 62		
" Swalley & Warfel, soap..............	15 00		
" C. Kessler, sundries..................	19 76		
" Cash, as per vouchers...............	1 70		
		$131 01	
Carried forward.....................	....	$38,931 49	$852,578 74

	FROM JAN. 1, 1886, TO DEC. 31, 1886.		1867 TO 1886.
Brought forward......................	....	$38,931 49	$852,578 74
PRINTING AND ADVERTISING.			
From comm't of works to Dec. 31, 1885.	....	....	$3,380 55
Paid Erie Dispatch...........................	$75 80		
" " Herald	66 65		
" " Observer...........................	79 15		
" Walker & Gallagher..................	85 14		
" A. P. Durlin & Son....................	31 20		
		$337 94	
BOOKS AND STATIONERY.			
From comm't of works to Dec. 31, 1885.	....	....	$1,313 85
Paid Ashby & Vincent, sundry bills...	$84 90		
" Cash, as per vouchers	14 85		
		$99 75	
ENGINE-ROOM TOOLS AND FURNITURE.			
From comm't of works to Dec. 31, 1885.	....	....	$835 00
Paid Warner Bros., sundries......	$27 28		
" Mehl & Liebel, "	25 50		
" Patterson & Hayes, "	6 58		
" M. A. Sheldon, "	10 00		
" Erie Machine Shop, "	15 50		
" N. Murphy & Son, "	2 30		
" Schlosser & Felheim, "	5 57		
" Dr. P. Hall,	......	4 55		
" J. O. Baker	......	1 50		
		$98 78	
EXPENSE OF HORSE AND WAGON.			
From comm't of works to Dec. 31, 1885.	....	....	$2,910 75
Paid S. S. Caughey, rent of barn	$22 50		
" R. H. Chinnock, shoeing horse ...	11 25		
" Schneider Bros., repairs............	14 63		
" G. L. Siegel & Co., et al., feed....	26 97		
" Henry Mayo, sundries...............	25 90		
" Various parties, for hay, oats, &c	101 62		
" C. Klang. for cart and repairs.....	59 70		
" Mehl & Liebel, sundries............	5 75		
" Wm. J. McCarter, for horse.......	200 00		
" Labor, as per Pay Roll	104 00		
		$572 82	
WATER RENTS RETURNED.			
From comm't of works to Dec. 31, 1885.	....	....	$62 50
Carried forward	....	$40,040 28	$861,081 39

	FROM JAN. 1, 1886, TO DEC. 31, 1886		1867 TO 1886.
Brought forward......................	....	$40,040 28	$861,081 39
STREET CONNECTIONS.			
From comm't of works to Dec. 31, 1885.	....	....	$53,898 65
Paid Jarecki-Hays, et al., sundry bills...	$1,279 90		
" Cornell Lead Co., " " ...	154 81		
" National Tube W'ks, " " ...	330 89		
" Labor, as per Pay Rolls.............	1,078 74		
" Cash, as per vouchers................	5 81		
" Wm. Krueger, et al., street repairs.	47 55		
		$2,897 70	
ON ACC'T OF LOCATING CONNECTIONS.			
Paid Salaries of Inspectors.................	$713 40		
" Labor, as per Pay Roll.............	212 73		
		$926 13	
ON ACC'T OF NEW PUMP.			
Paid F. A. Scheffler, services.............	$100 00		
" J. P. Harrington "	100 00		
" Cash, as per vouchers................	309 57		
" Labor, as per Pay Roll.............	12 73		
		$522 30	
ON ACC'T OF NEW ENGINE-HOUSE.			
Paid S. Kerschner, on contract..........	$3,417 60		
" Jos. Frank, architect...............	50 00		
" D. K. Dean, "	89 62		
" Jarecki Mfg. Co., sundries	19 11		
" Geo. Platt, services..................	15 00		
" Schlosser & Felheim, lumber......	9 03		
" Labor, as per Pay Rolls.............	287 94		
		$3,888 30	
SHOP AND MISCELLANEOUS WORK.			
From comm't of works to Dec. 31, 1885.	....	....	$8,980 07
Paid Labor, as per Pay Rolls	$382 13		
		$382 13	
STATE AND COUNTY TAXES.			
Paid St. and Co. Taxes, 1885 and 1886	$326 92		
		$326 92	
RESERVOIR GROUNDS.			
From comm't of works to Dec. 31, 1885.	....	....	$6,563 99
INTEREST AND EXCHANGE.			
From comm't of works to Dec. 31, 1885.	....	....	$11,031 47
Carried forward	....	$48,883 76	$941,555 57

	FROM JAN. 1, 1886, TO DEC. 31, 1886.	1867 TO 1886.
Brought forward..........................	$48,883 76	$941,555 57
RAILROAD SWITCH AND SCALES.		
From comm't of works to Dec. 31, 1885.		2,840 65
ENGINES AND BOILERS.		
From comm't of works to Dec. 31, 1885.		66,316 95
CIVIL ENGINEERING.		
From comm't of works to Dec. 31, 1885.		7,122 85
GAS WELLS AND CARE.		
From comm't of works to Dec. 31, 1885.		8,148 59
CONSTRUCTION OF RESERVOIR.		
From comm't of works to Dec. 31, 1885.		116,586 84
PARK FOUNTAINS.		
From comm't of works to Dec. 31, 1885.		3,244 68
DISCOUNT ON CITY BONDS.		
From comm't of works to Dec. 31, 1885.		88,033 94
Totals...............................	$48,883 76	$1,233,850 07

RECAPITULATION.
EXPENSES IN 1886.

For Construction	$29,846 32
" Extraordinary Repairs..	1,796 41
" Current Expenses..	17,241 03
Total...	$48,883 76

EXPENSES FROM JULY, 1867, TO DECEMBER 31, 1886.

For Construction	$921,394 44
" Maintenance..	361,339 39
Total...	$1,282,733 83

NET EARNINGS FROM JULY, 1867, TO DECEMBER 31, 1886.

Total Cost of Construction..	$921,394 44
Amount advanced by City ($675,955.10, less discount of $88,-033.94)	587,921 16
Net earnings..	$333,473 28
Add Balance in City Treasury	11,756 45
" " " Office	332 87
Total...	$345,562 60

EXHIBIT D.

Amount of Water Rents Collected each year, with the Increase and Decrease, since the Commencement of the Works.

	Am't Rec'd.	Increase.	Decrease.
From Jan. 1, 1869, to Dec. 31, 1869........	$4,264 47	....	....
" " 1870, " 1870........	9,237 30	$4,972 83	....
" " 1871, " 1871........	18,138 08	8,900 78	....
" " 1872, " 1872........	21,652 68	3,514 60	....
" " 1873, " 1873........	25,560 40	3,907 72	....
" " 1874, " 1874........	27,938 90	2,378 50	....
" " 1875, " 1875........	29,639 38	1,700 48	....
" " 1876, " 1876........	31,048 76	1,409 38	....
" " 1877, " 1877........	32,276 57	1,227 81	....
" " 1878, " 1878........	29,636 01	....	$2,640 56
" " 1879, " 1879........	33,343 20	3,707 19	....
" " 1880, " 1880........	37,385 00	4,041 80	....
" " 1881, " 1881........	40,385 87	3,000 87	....
" " 1882, " 1882........	43,818 73	3,432 86	....
" " 1883, " 1883........	48,269 89	4,451 16	....
" " 1884, " 1884........	51,852 78	3,582 89	....
" " 1885, " 1885........	53,550 35	1,697 57	....
" " 1886, " 1886........	58,725 00	5,174 65	....
Total water rents received	$596,723 37	....	....

INVENTORY

Of Stock, Tools, Material, etc., on hand January 1st, 1887.

Superintendent street work.. $9,061 51
Mechanical engineer 951 65
Keeper at reservoir 50 00
Secretary and Treasurer.. 2,000 00

Total $12,063 16

EXHIBIT E.

Location, Size and Length of Main Pipe, Large Private Pipe and Fire Hydrant Branches Laid in 1886.

LOCATION.	FEET.	IN.
SIX-INCH PIPE.		
Ninth street, between Walnut and Cherry.	266	8
Ninth street, between Ash and Wayne.	1,300	0
Thirteenth street, between Wallace and Ash.	767	6
Thirteenth street, East of Ash.	297	7
Sixteenth street, between Sassafras and Myrtle.	372	......
Sixteenth street, between Holland and Peach.	1,609	......
Seventeenth street, between German and Parade.	788	......
Seventeenth street, West of French.	158	......
Nineteenth street, West of Peach.	421	......
Twenty-sixth street, East of Holland.	160	8
Twenty-sixth street, East of Ash.	225	......
Ash street, South of Eighteenth.	280	4
Wallace street, between Twenty-sixth and Twenty-seventh.	336	......
Parade street, from Twenty-first to Twenty-third.	650	......
Holland street, at intersection of Eighth.	40	......
Holland street, between Twenty-fifth and Twenty-sixth.	127	......
German street, between Tenth and Eleventh.	411	6
State street, North from Twenty-first.	482	3
State street, between Ninth and Tenth.	403	......
State street, North from Tenth.	63	10
Myrtle street, South from Eighth.	46	......
Walnut street, North from Third.	313	......
FOUR-INCH PIPE.	9,518	4
Third street, from Walnut to Cherry.	720	10
Fifth street, between Wallace and Ash.	301	6
Ninth street, between Wallace and Ash.	307	5
German street, from Second northward.	345	......
Holland street, South from Twenty-fifth.	232	8
State street, under bridge at Public Dock.	72	......
Sassafras street, from Fourth to Fifth.	385	4
Walnut street, from Seventeenth to Eighteenth.	328	8
Cherry street, from Third northward.	154	8
ONE-AND-A-HALF-INCH PIPE.	2,848	1
Twelfth street, near Peach (for wagon sprinkler.)	47	6
Carried forward.	12,413	11

LOCATION.	FEET.	IN.
Brought forward..	12,413	11
TEMPORARY ONE-INCH AND THREE-QUARTER-INCH PIPE.		
Short street, from Chestnut westward..	159	10
Second street, between Sassafras and Myrtle.............................	52	......
Eighth street, from Poplar westward.......................................	246	9
Peach street, from Second northward.......................................	341	7
FIRE HYDRANT BRANCHES, (all four-inch.)	800	2
Third street and Cherry...	8	6
Ninth street and Ash..	9	......
Ninth street and Reed..	9	......
Ninth street and Wayne...	8	3
Eleventh street and Reed...	9	6
Thirteenth street and Ash..	8	8
Seventeenth street and Parade...	8	2
Wallace street and Twenty-sixth..	9	3
Wallace street and Twenty-seventh...............	9	2
Holland street and Eighth..	8	8
French street and Sixteenth..	8	3
State street and Sixteenth, (east.)...................................	13	6
	109	11
Total pipe laid in 1886..	13,324	......
PIPE TAKEN UP IN 1886.		
Four-inch.		
Sixteenth street, from French to Holland.............................	712	6
State street, from Ninth to Tenth......................................	403	......
State street, from Tenth northward....................................	63	10
Two-inch.		
State street under bridge at Public Dock.............................	72	......
Three-quarter-inch.		
German street, from Second northward...............................	345	......
Total..	1,596	4
Leaving as the actual gain in main pipe.....................	11,727	8
or 2 miles, 1,167 feet, and 8 inches.		

EXHIBIT F.

Total Amount of Distributing Pipe, Fire Hydrant Branches and Large Private Pipe Laid to December 31, 1886.

STREETS.	LENGTH IN FEET AND INCHES.					
	Less than 4-inch.	4-inch.	6-inch.	12-inch.	20-inch.	30-inch.
EAST AND WEST STS.						
Front and Docks.....	674.8	1,520.4	....	....	147.0	254.7
Short....................	159.10	1,458.0	....	....	....	....
Second	1,301.1	4,360.1	....	....	....	....
Third	237.0	6,501.4	....	....	....	....
Fourth.................	....	3,817.3	4,625.6	....	....	....
Fifth	414.11	6,695.7	....	....	....	....
North Park Row.....	75.0	101.4	820.0	....	....	....
Sixth	152.5	1,910.1	8,290.1	....	....	....
South Park Row.....	182.1	22.7	424.0	....	....	....
Seventh	....	3,316.0	31.2	5,362.2	....	....
Eighth.................	540.8	9,675.8	....	....	....	....
Ninth..................	9.0	7,407.8	1,566.8	....	....	....
Tenth..................	49.0	465.0	9,319.1	....	....	....
Eleventh	275.0	8,500.11	476.1	....	....	....
Twelfth	93.2	1,900.7	13,048.10	....	....	....
Thirteenth	....	3,150.7	1,065.1	....	....	....
Fourteenth............	....	2,988.9	....	....	....	....
Fifteenth..............	358.2	3,180.11	....	....	....	....
Huron.................	....	1,436 10	....	....	....	....
Sixteenth	497.11	1,426.10	3,444.9	....	....	....
Seventeenth...........	....	7,624.8	946.0	....	....	....
Eighteenth............	11.0	2,978.10	12,534.7	....	....	....
Nineteenth	125.8	2,008.4	4,421.0	....	....	....
Twentieth	....	1,043.3	....	....	....	....
Twenty-first.........	....	34.2	5.6	5,178.11	....	....
Twenty-second	....	3,637.8	....	....	....	....
Twenty-third.........	....	2,906.2	....	....	....	....
Twenty-fourth.......	....	2,144.0	....	....	....	....
Twenty-fifth	....	3,099.0	....	....	....	....
Twenty-sixth.........	300.0	965.0	3,008.8	....	1,064,6	....
DIAGONAL STREETS.						
Turnpike	6.6	8.7	795.0	....	....	....
Railroad...............	....	1,780.8	....	....	....	....
Buffalo Road	....	1,168.0	....	....	....	....
Waterford Ave.......	....	910.0	....	....	....	....
Carried forward...	5,463.1	100,144.3	60,822.4	10,541.1	1,211.6	254.7

STREETS.	LENGTH IN FEET AND INCHES.					
	Less than 4-inch.	4-inch.	6-inch.	12-inch.	20-inch.	30-inch.
Brought forward..	5,463.1	100,144.3	60,822.4	10,541.1	1,211.6	254.7
NORTH AND SOUTH STREETS.						
East Ave................	....	593.3	2,830.6	....	....	....
Ash .....'...............	....	1,185.7	1,778.10	....	....	....
Wallace................	391.6	1,358.9	336.0	....	....	....
Vine	....	399.8	....	....	....	....
Parade ....'..	....	5,529.11	3,264.0	....	....	....
German	....	3,'.30.4	411.6	....	....	....
Division	....	317.2	....	....	....	....
Holland	203.4	9,039.7	167.0	....	....	....
French................	262.6	6,635.8	....	....	....	....
State	1,033.9	3,443.4	3,728.9	....	....	....
Peach	352.3	1,087.0	5,974.8	1,996.0	....	....
Sassafras	570.0	10,615.2	....	....	....	....
Myrtle	....	3,931.0	46.0	....	....	....
Hickory...............	....	631.6	....	....	....	....
Chestnut..............	1,206.6	4,714.0	....	24.0	9,222.3	2,457.1
Walnut	....	3,899.8	313.0	....	....	....
Cherry................	....	3,000.8	....	....	....	....
Maple	....	805.0	....	....	....	....
Poplar	....	819.0	....	....	....	....
Liberty................	320.2	1,085.5	....	....	....	....
Plum..................	....	631.1	....	....	....	....
Cascade................	500.0	468.6	2,049.2	....	....	....
Total............	10,303.1	164,065.11	81,721.9	12,561.1	10,433.9	2,711.8

RECAPITULATION.

	Miles.	Feet.	In.
Small pipe..	1	5,023	1
Four-inch pipe	31	385	11
Six-inch pipe...	15	2,521	9
Twelve-inch pipe..	2	2,001	1
Twenty-inch pipe..	1	5,153	9
Thirty-inch pipe	....	2,711	8
Total	53	1,957	3

EXHIBIT G.

Location, Number and Length of Street Connections made in 1886; also, Total Number December 31, 1886.

EAST AND WEST STREETS.	Number.	Length in feet and inches.	Number previous to 1886.	Total Number Dec. 31, 1886.	NORTH AND SOUTH STREETS.	Number.	Length in feet and inches.	Number previous to 1886.	Total Number Dec. 31, 1886.
Front and Docks	1	33.0	36	37	East Avenue			5	5
Short	3	54.3	22	25	Wayne	1	.2		1
Second	9	142.11	94	103	Ash	8	126.7	3	11
Third	13	237.7	110	123	Wallace	2	35.3	17	19
Fourth	10	196.10	168	178	Cedar			1	1
Fifth	5	62.6	133	138	Vine			4	4
Sixth	9	271.10	192	201	Parade	6	152.0	113	119
N. and S. Park Row			31	31	German	6	87.9	64	70
Seventh	5	84.2	166	171	Division			11	11
Eighth	58	1023.9	220	278	Holland	3	65.9	117	120
Ninth	34	480.9	164	198	French	7	74.9	135	142
Tenth	15	555.5	160	175	State	13	222.9	226	239
Eleventh	19	237.7	199	218	Turnpike			19	19
Twelfth	15	465.10	180	195	Peach	15	186.8	269	284
Thirteenth	16	324.11	89	105	Waterford Pike	2	43.6	19	21
Fourteenth	9	108.3	51	60	Sassafras	13	175.3	114	127
Fifteenth	2	19.10	41	43	Myrtle	8	183.9	67	75
Huron	2	35.1	32	34	Hickory			16	16
Sixteenth	30	561.0	62	92	Chestnut	6	107.2	106	112
Seventeenth	16	262.2	97	113	Walnut	7	133.6	44	51
Eighteenth	12	139.11	172	.184	Cherry	4	92.4	18	22
Buffalo Road			3	3	Maple			9	9
Nineteenth	3	51.8	24	27	Poplar	1	25.8	11	12
Twentieth			12	12	Liberty			17	17
Twenty-first	5	35.5	46	51	Plum			3	3
Twenty-second	1	29.8	46	47	Cascade	2	30.6	19	21
Twenty-third	5	96.7	32	37	Raspberry			1	1
Twenty-fourth	1	29.0	21	22	Cranberry			2	2
Twenty-fifth	2	20.6	34	36	Total	104	1753.4	1,430	1,534
Twenty-sixth	6	69.9	35	41	Add North and South streets	307	5656.8	2,672	2,979
Twenty-seventh	1	26.6	....	1					
Total	307	5656.8	2,672	2,979	Total	411	7410.0	4,102	4,513

LENGTH OF CONNECTIONS IN MILES.

	Miles.	Feet.
Connections made in 1886	1	2,130
Previously made, (about)	16	5,549
Total	18	2,399

EXHIBIT H

Location and Style of Fire Hydrants set in 1886, all being 4-inch Steamer and Hose.

HYDRANTS IN NEW LOCATIONS.

Third	street, North-West corner of	Cherry	......	Matthews.
Ninth	" " " "	Wayne	......	"
"	" North-East "	Ash	......	"
"	" " " "	Reed	......	
Eleventh	" North-West "	Reed	......	"
Thirteenth	" " " "	Ash	......	Pittsburgh.
Seventeenth	" " " "	Parade	......	Matthews.
Wallace	" South-East "	Twenty-sixth	......	Pittsburgh.
"	" North-East "	Twenty-seventh	......	"
French	" South-East "	Sixteenth	......	Matthews.

DEFECTIVE HYDRANTS REPLACED WITH OTHERS.

Seventh	street, North-East corner of	German	......	Matthews.
"	" " " "	Reed	......	Bay State.
Eighth	" North-West "	Peach	......	Matthews.
"	" " " "	Myrtle	......	"
"	" South-East "	German	......	"
Tenth	" " " "	French	......	
Eighteenth	" North-East "	Parade	......	

RECAPITULATION.

Fire Hydrants in new locations	10
Defective Fire Hydrants replaced	7
Total in 1886	17

NUMBER AND STYLES OF FIRE HYDRANTS IN USE.

Old style Matthews	11	Ludlow	4
New " "	162	Morris, Tasker & Co	2
Bay State	42	Brown	1
West Jersey	29		
Home-made	7	Total	280
Pittsburgh	22		

HYDRANTS FOR THE SUPPLY OF WAGON SPRINKLERS.

Ninth	street, between State and French	Jarecki, Hays & Co.
*Twelfth	" near South-West corner of Peach	"
Fifteenth	" " " " " "	"
Eighteenth	" " " " " "	
State	" at " " " East Park	
"	" between Tenth and Eleventh	
"	" " Twelfth and Thirteenth	

Total, 7.

*Put in in 1886.

EXHIBIT I.

Location, Size and Kind of Stop Valves Set in 1886.

EAST AND WEST STREETS.					SIZE.	KIND.
Third	street,	West line of	Walnut......................		4	Eddy.
Fifth	"	East "	Wallace......................		4	"
Eighth	"	" "	Myrtle......................		4	"
"	"	" "	Holland......................		4	"
Ninth	"	West "	Ash		4	"
"	"	East "	Wallace, (in place of old			"
one, near centre of block)......................					4	"
Ninth	street,	East line of	Peach, (to replace old one)		4	"
"	"	West "	Walnut......................		6	"
Tenth	"	East "	Holland......................		6	"
"	"	West "	German......................		6	"
Eleventh	"	" "	"		4	"
Twelfth	"	near Peach (for wagon sprinkler).......			1½	J. H. & Co.
Thirteenth	"	East line of	Ash......................		6	Eddy.
"	"	" "	Wallace......................		6	"
Sixteenth	"	West "	Holland, (to replace 4-in).		6	"
"	"	East "	French......................		6	"
"	"	" "	Peach, (to replace 4-in)...		6	"
"	"	West "	Sassafras......................		6	"
Seventeenth	"	East "	German......................		6	"
"	"	West "	French		6	"
"	"	" "	Myrtle		4	"
Nineteenth	"	" "	Peach		6	"
Twenty-sixth	"	East "	Ash......................		6	"
NORTH AND SOUTH STREETS.						
Ash	street,	South line of	Eighteenth......................		6	Eddy.
Wallace	"	" "	Twenty-sixth......................		6	"
Parade	"	" "	Sixteenth......................		4	"
"	"	" "	Twenty-first......................		6	"
"	"	North "	Twenty-third......................		6	"
German	"	" "	Second......................		4	"
"	"	South "	Tenth......................		6	"
Holland	"	North "	Sixteenth......................		4	"
"	"	South "	Twenty-fifth......................		4	"
French	"	" "	Sixteenth......................		4	"
State	"	" "	Ninth......................		6	"
"	"	" "	Tenth, (to replace old one).....		4	"
"	"	" "	Tenth, (to replace 4-inch)......		6	"
"	"	North "	Tenth, " "		6	"
"	"	" "	Sixteenth, (West of State).....		6	"
"	"	" "	Twenty-first......................		6	"

Continued on Page 31.

EXHIBIT I—Continued.

NORTH AND SOUTH STREETS.	SIZE.	KIND.
Sassafras st., South line of Fourth.	4	Eddy.
" " North " Eighteenth, (to replace old one)	4	"
Myrtle " South " Eighth	6	"
Walnut " North " Third	6	"
" " South " Seventeenth	4	"
Cherry " North " Third	4	"

RECAPITULATION.

Six-inch valves set in new locations.. 21
Four-inch " " " .. 14
One-and-a-half-inch valves set in new locations... 1
Six-inch valves to replace four-inch. 4

Four-inch valves to replace old ones... 4

Total set in 1886... 44
Taken out... 1

TOTAL NUMBER AND SIZES OF STOP VALVES IN USE.

Thirty-inch... 3
Twenty-inch... 16
Twelve-inch... 18
Six-inch... 120

Four-inch and less... 307

Total... 463

EXHIBIT J.

Number of Families, Stores, Offices, Manufactories, etc., Supplied with
City Water During the Year 1886.

Breweries	3	Ice Houses	2
Board of Trade	1	Internal Revenue Office	1
Boat Houses	4	Jail and Court House	1
Bakeries	13	Laundries	8
Butcher Shops	53	Lumber Yards	4
Barber Shops	38	Livery Stables	12
Banks	6	Manufactories	75
Billiard Rooms	6	Malt Houses	4
Bottling Works	10	Orphan Asylums	2
Coffee and Spice Mills	1	Opera House	1
Churches	18	Oil Works	5
Cemetery	1	Offices	273
Coal and Iron Dock	1	Photograph Galleries	7
Club House	1	Police Station	1
Custom House	1	Public Halls	38
Convent	1	Printing Offices	8
Driving Park	1	Passenger Depots	2
Dyeing Works	1	Railroads	4
Engine Houses	6	Railroad Shops	2
Express Offices	2	Rink	1
Electric Light Co	1	Soldiers' and Sailors' Home	1
Fish Hatchery	1	Schools	22
Fish Houses	4	Stores	428
Families	4,369	Saloons and Eating Houses	202
" by Special Permits	144	Slaughter Houses	12
Freight Houses	3	Street Railways	1
Fountains—Private	4	Transfer Company	1
" Public	2	U. S. Signal Station	1
" Drinking	2	Work Shops	119
Flouring Mills	4	Watering Troughs	18
Gas Works	1		
Grain Elevators	5	Total	6,140
Greenhouses	3	Last Enumeration	5,658
Hospitals	3		
Hotels and Boarding Houses	70	Increase	484

EXHIBIT K.

PUMPING ENGINE STATISTICS FOR 1886.

The Pumps are two in number, of the kind known as the Cornish Bull Engine. The diameter of each plunger is 20¾ inches, and each pump has a stroke of 10 feet. Allowing for loss, the capacity of each pump is calculated at 165 gallons to every stroke. The Standpipe is 247 feet high. The reservoir is nearly two miles from the pumping works, and the water is pumped to it through a 20-inch pipe, with which all the east and west mains are connected. The bottom of the reservoir is 210 feet above the surface of the bay, and the water has been kept, during the year, at an average depth in the reservoir of about 23⅓ feet. The pumps are run at an average of about 10½ strokes per minute, when operated singly, but when both are used the number of strokes is reduced to about 9 for each pump in the daytime and 8 at night.

MONTHS.	Days a Single Pump was Operated.	Days both Pumps were Operated.	Days both Pumps were Idle.	Strokes of the Pumps.	Gallons Pumped.	Daily Average of Gallons Pumped.	Average Lift in Feet.	Lbs. of Bituminous Slack Coal during the Month.	Cost of Coal for Pumping.
January*	16	14	1	600,060	99,009,900	3,193,867	232.57	590,615	383 90
February*	10	17	1	585,220	96,561,300	3,448,617	232.00	600,353	390 24
March*	17	14		601,793	99,295,945	3,203,095	235.00	536,893	348 99
April	19	8	3	497,327	82,058,955	2,735,298	234.47	809,100	525 92
May	18	9	4	534,288	88,157,420	2,843,787	231.37	344,800	225 17
June‡	17	13		610,062	100,660,230	3,355,341	234.15	450,000	281 25
July‡	20	11		575,619	94,977,135	3,063,778	235.00	472,600	295 37
August	18	13		575,631	94,979,115	3,063,842	234.44	487,000	304 38
September	4	18	8	546,373	90,151,545	3,005,051	231.11	487,600	304 75
October	6	21	4	591,135	97,537,275	3,146,363	233.00	509,900	318 69
November*	14	16		502,342	82,886,430	2,762,881	234.75	571,235	357 01
December*	24	7		552,205	91,113,825	2,939,155	234.26	538,365	336 47
Totals ‖	183	161	21	6,772,055	1,117,389,075	3,063,423	233.35	6,398,461	$4,072 14

* In the above statement a deduction of five per cent., or 149,339 pounds, is made for coal used in keeping the stand pipe clear of ice during the months of January, February, March, November and December.

‡ To the coal used in June and July, 170 tons should be added that were taken from the outside bunker, the latter having been removed to make way for the new Engine House. This coal was bought in 1884 at $1.45 per ton.

‖ The actual amount of coal consumed in pumping was, therefore, 6,738,461 pounds, costing about $4,318.64. (See Exhibit L.)

The average temperature of the feed water during the year has been 180, and the vacuum has been maintained at 25 inches.

The regular employees at the pumping works are 1 mechanical engineer, 2 assistant engineers, 3 firemen and 1 watchman. The mechanical engineer stands a watch of 5 hours, from 7 to 12 every forenoon; the assistants divide the remainder of each day equally between them; each one of the firemen stands a watch of 8 hours. Besides firing, the firemen unload the coal from the cars, except when both pumps are run, in which case they are assisted by the watchman or a laborer. The mechanical engineer gives ten hours daily to the service of the Department, the hours when he is not on watch being employed in repairs, supervision, &c. In addition to standing their regular watch, the assistant engineers aid their superior officer in keeping the machinery in order. The watchman takes care of the buildings and grounds, besides doing such other work as may be required of him.

EXHIBIT L.

Amount of Coal Consumed in Pumping, Gallons of Water Pumped, Average Height Pumped, Cost per Million Gallons, etc., from the First Year the Works were Operated to December 31, 1886.

Year	Tons of coal consumed	Price of coal per ton from May 1st of each year	Cost of coal	Grades of bituminous coal	Gallons of water pumped	Increase or decrease	Number of places supplied	Number of fire hydrants	Average height water in reser- voir above sur- face of bay	Cost of coal per million gallons raised to reser- voir	Cost of coal per million gallons raised 1 foot. (Cts.)	Gallons raised 1 foot by 1 pound of coal	Gallons raised to reservoir by 1 pound of coal
1868	59.1	$5 05	$309 61	Lump.									
1869	544.4	5 05	4,818 48	"									
1870	1,064.5	5 05	5,159 10	"	246,648,960		1,218	97	232.0				
1871	1,422.7	5 05	7,117 00	"	179,368,495	132,719,535 i.	1,727	99	232.0	$18 76	8.0	22,656	98.5
1872	1,306.5	5 05	6,528 65	"	395,076,000	115,708,505 i.	2,140	103	232.0	16 52	7.6	35,092	150.9
1873	1,672.5	4 85	8,412 65	"	384,062,415	11,013,585 d.	2,475	107	232.0	21 90	9.4	26,636	114.8
1874	1,759.0	4 85	7,709 54	"	444,817,395	60,754,980 i.	2,663	107	232.0	17 33	7.1	29,234	126.4
1875	1,836.4	4 00	8,657 61	"	531,005,475	86,181,080 i.	2,700	110	232.0	16 30	6.9	33,772	145.5
1876	2,105.1	3 70	8,925 22	"	670,726,650	139,721,175 i.	2,763	112	232.0	13 30	5.6	36,959	159.3
1877	2,456.6	3 35	8,509 33	"	660,981,810	9,744,840 d.	2,854	114	232.0	12 75	5.4	31,491	135.7
1878	2,463.3	3 09	7,945 37	"	682,392,315	21,390,505 i.	2,915	115	232.0	11 64	4.9	31,665	136.4
1879	2,628.1	1 99	7,428 92	Slack.	807,800,400	125,408,085 i.	3,011	121	232.0	9 19	3.9	35,653	153.6
1880	3,076.1	1 90	6,978 41	"	775,805,250	31,995,150 i.	3,568	126	232.0	8 99	3.8	29,234	126.0
1881	3,430.3	1 75	6,517 58	"	975,640,634	200,235,694 i.	4,110	161	232.0	6 68	2.8	32,990	142.2
1882	2,966.2	1 55	5,355 93	"	829,759,260	145,881,674 d.	4,687	171	234.0	6 45	2.7	32,706	139.7
1883	2,398.2	1 45	3,908 59	"	815,939,685	13,819,575 d.	5,077	197	234.7	4 66	1.9	39,900	170.0
1884	3,010.8	1 30	4,502 61	"	917,781,350	101,841,665 i.	5,395	248	234.3	4 99	2.0	35,712	152.4
1885	3,243.8	1 25	4,575 79	"	1,036,496,665	118,715,315 i.	5,658	270	232.9	4 40	1.8	37,208	159.7
1886*	3,389.0		4,318 64	"	1,117,389,075	80,892,410 i.	6,140	280	233.3	3 86	1.6	39,704	165.8

All coal used from the commencement of the works has been Western Pennsylvania bituminous. The coal contract is awarded annually to the lowest bidder, the coal being delivered in the works at the contract price. The price stated above is per ton of 2,000 lbs. Two gas wells were put down at the pumping works in the spring of 1871, yielding a large supply. The gas was applied to the boilers the same year, and, for some two years, furnished about one-fourth of the fuel at the works. The gas steadily decreased until about 1875, when it failed almost entirely. The wells were pumped out in the summer of 1881, since which time they have supplied the light used at the works and a trifling portion of the fuel.
*See Exhibit K.

EXHIBIT M.

HOW CITY WATER MAY BE WASTED.

Gallons and Hundredths of Gallons of Water that will be Discharged per Minute Through Various Sized Orifices at the Heads Stated.

Head in Feet.	Pressure per Square Inch.	DIAMETER OF ORIFICES IN INCHES AND FRACTIONS OF AN INCH.													
		1/64	1/32	1/16	1/8	1/4	3/8	1/2	5/8	3/4	1	1¼	1½	1¾	2
20	8 66	0 02	0 07	0 30	1 20	5 10	11 70	20 60	32 20	46 20	82 30	128 40	184 80	252 00	328 80
40	17 32	0 02	0 11	0 45	1 40	7 40	16 30	29 60	45 50	65 50	116 50	182 40	261 60	356 40	465 60
60	25 99	0 03	0 14	0 55	2 20	8 90	20 00	35 60	57 70	80 30	142 80	223 20	320 40	436 80	571 20
80	34 65	0 04	0 16	0 65	2 60	10 30	23 20	41 20	64 30	92 60	164 40	258 00	370 80	505 20	658 80
100	43 31	0 04	0 18	0 75	2 90	11 50	25 90	46 10	72 00	103 70	183 60	288 00	415 20	565 20	738 00
120	51 98	0 05	0 19	0 78	3 10	12 60	28 30	50 40	78 80	113 50	201 60	315 60	453 60	624 40	807 60
140	60 64	0 05	0 21	0 85	3 40	13 60	31 70	54 50	85 20	122 40	217 20	340 80	490 80	668 40	872 40
150	64 97	0 05	0 22	0 88	3 50	14 10	31 70	56 40	88 20	127 20	225 60	352 80	507 60	691 20	902 40
175	75 80	0 06	0 24	0 95	3 80	15 20	34 20	61 00	95 30	136 80	243 60	380 40	548 40	748 40	975 60
200	86 83	0 06	0 26	1 02	4 10	16 30	36 60	65 20	101 80	146 40	260 40	406 40	585 00	798 00	1042 80
235	101 08	0 07	0 28	1 12	4 50	17 90	41 30	71 50	111 40	160 40	285 20	445 90	642 20	871 30	1140 80

The bottom of the Erie Reservoir is 210 feet above the surface of Presque Isle Bay, from which the water is pumped, and the water in the Reservoir is kept at an average height of nearly 24 feet, or 234 feet above the bay. The pressure at the points named below will give an idea of the average throughout the city: Twenty-fourth and Sassafras streets, 20 lbs.; Twenty-third and Myrtle, 30 lbs.; Twentieth and Chestnut, 40 lbs.; Eighteenth and Peach, 50 lbs.; Fourteenth and State, 60 lbs.; Eighth and State, 70 lbs.; Third and State, 80 lbs.; Front and State, 100 lbs.

The wire of which pins are made is one-thirty-second of an inch in diameter—No. 21, wire gauge. The finest cambric needle is made of wire one-sixty-fourth of an inch in diameter—No. 27, wire gauge. A stream the size of a pin, running one year with head of 235 feet, will flow 147,168 gallons, equaling 4,600 barrels, the value of which—counting at the rate of 10 cents per 1,000 gallons—is $14.71. A stream the size of a cambric needle, running at the same pressure, for the same time, will flow 36,792 gallons, at a cost of $3.68.

EXHIBIT N.

Advantages Offered in Erie to Manufacturers.

The following are the highest and lowest charges per thousand gallons for water, by meter measurement, up to a daily average of fifty thousand gallons, in the cities named ; also the charges per horse-power for steam engines working ten hours per day.   They are taken from official reports direct to this office, which are open to the examination of interested parties.

	Highest.	Lowest.	Steam Engine.		Highest.	Lowest.	Steam Engine.
Allegheny City, Pa...	5	......	Special.	Lawrence, Mass......	25	20	3 50
Boston......................	20	......	6 00	Milwaukee.............	33½	4¾	4 00
Chicago	10	8	4 00	Minneapolis............	20	10	3 00
Cleveland	....	......	2 50	Newark, N. J..........	15	......	5 00
Columbus, O	20	9	3 00	New York...............	13½	......	5 00
Cincinnati..............	13½	......	Meter.	Omaha, Neb	35	15	2 50
Dayton	40	10	"	Philadelphia	8	......	2 00
Detroit....................	0	......	"	Pittsburgh	20	6	3 50
Erie	0	6	**2 50**	Rochester	13	5⅘	3 00
Fall River, Mass......	30	......	Meter.	St. Paul (1885)	40	20	4 00
Grand Rapids, Mich.	30	9½	6 50	Syracuse...............	25	6	4 00
Hartford, Conn	30	10	6 00	Toledo...................	20	8	2 50
Indianapolis	40	8	3 00	Utica	30	10	5 50

In most of the above cities the meter is paid for by the consumer, who is also required to keep it in order. Here the meter is set and kept in order by the Department.   Below will be found the general charge upon shops and factories in the same cities.

	10 hands or less.	Each ad. hand.		10 hands or less.	Each ad. hand.
Allegheny City.......	Special.	....	Milwaukee...........	5 00	25
Boston	5 00	30	Minneapolis	5 00	25
Chicago.................	F. tax.	25	Newark, N. J	3 00	25
Cleveland	6 25	31	New York	Special.	....
Columbus (each emp)	....	50	Omaha	5 00	25
Dayton, O	Special.	50	Philadelphia.........	10 00	....
Detroit..................	3 00	1 00	Pittsburgh (gen'l charge).............	4 00 } to 15 00	....
Erie (gen'l charge)	3 00 } to 5 00	....	Rochester	Special.	30
Fall River, Mass	Meter.	....	St. Paul	10 00	1 00
Grand Rapids, Mich.	Special.	....	Syracuse.............	10 00	1 00
Hartford, Conn.......	5 00	50	Toledo	5 00	20
Indianapolis..........	Meter.	....	Utica.................	Special.	....
Lawrence, Mass	Special.	....			

EXHIBIT O.

Cost of Water to the Average Householder in Twenty-five Cities, Compiled from Official Reports to this Department.

CITIES.	Population. 1880.	Family Charge.	Pan Water Closet.	Self-Closing Urinal.	Bath Tub.	Self-Closing Wash Stand.	Permanent Wash Tub.	Two Horses.	Cow.	Street Sprinkler.	Total.
Allegheny City	78,000	8 75	3 00	3 00	3 00	1 00	1 50	3 00	75	3 00	24 50
Boston	302,000	7 00	5 00	3 00	3 00	5 00	5 00	2 00	75	5 00	37 25
Buffalo	156,000	7 20	3 50	3 00	3 00	1 00	2 00	2 00	90	3 50	31 50
Chicago	503,000	6 00	3 00	3 00	4 00			4 00	75	3 00	32 80
Columbus, O	51,000	6 00	2 50	1 00	4 00	2 00	2 00	4 00	2 00	3 80	31 75
Dayton, O	38,000	7 00	4 00	4 00	3 00		2 00	2 00	1 00	5 00	45 30
Detroit	116,000	7 00	4 00	3 00	3 00		4 00	2 00	1 00	5 00	28 25
Erie	28,000	5 00	3 00	2 00	3 00	1 00	2 00	2 00	75	3 00	21 75
East Saginaw, Mich	19,000	7 00	2 50	2 00	3 00	1 50	2 00	4 00	1 00		26 50
Fall River, Mass	49,000	5 00	5 00	2 00	5 00	1 00	2 00	4 00	1 00	6 00	31 00
Grand Rapids, Mich	32,000	8 00	4 00	3 50	3 50	2 50	1 50	5 00	1 00	10 00	33 00
Indianapolis	75,000	5 00	3 00	3 00	3 00	1 00	1 00	3 00	1 50	3 30	32 00
Lawrence, Mass	39,000	5 00	2 00	8 00	2 50	2 00	2 00	2 00	1 00	5 00	25 40
Milwaukee	115,000	6 00	2 00	2 00	3 00	1 50	1 50	2 00	1 00	3 00	22 00
Minneapolis	47,000	4 00	3 00	7 00	5 00		2 00	2 00	1 50	5 00	26 00
Newark, N. J	136,000	6 25	2 30	2 50	3 50	1 00	2 00	5 00	75	3 00	25 00
New York	1,200,000	6 00	2 50	3 50	3 00	1 00	2 00	6 00	75	5 00	32 75
Omaha, Neb	30,000	6 75	10 00	2 50	3 50	1 00	2 00	5 00	75	5 00	30 00
Philadelphia	847,000	5 00	5 00	5 00	3 00	1 00	2 00	2 50		3 50	33 00
Pittsburgh	156,000	9 00	3 00	1 50	3 20	1 00	1 00	2 00	1 50	2 40	29 75
Sandusky, O	15,838	6 00	2 00	2 40	4 00		2 00	4 50		3 00	23 50
St. Paul, (1885)	41,000	8 00	5 00	2 50	4 00	1 00		4 80	1 50	6 00	25 50
Syracuse	52,000	6 50	2 30	2 00	3 50		2 00	3 00	75	6 00	31 75
Toledo	50,000	5 00	2 00	3 00	5 00	1 00		5 00	1 50	8 00	28 50
Utica	34,000	7 00	6 00	3 00	5 00	1 00		6 00	1 50	6 00	31 50

RATES FOR CITY WATER.

All are annual, except as otherwise indicated.

Bath Tub, private..$	3 00
" " " each additional...	1 50
" " public...	5 00
Bakery, per barrel of flour used, (but no charge less than $5).......................	
Barber Shop, including Hand Basin, first chair..............................	4 00
" " " " each additional chair...............................	2 00
Blacksmith Shop, one fire..	5 00
" " each additional fire....................................	2 00
Boarding House (in addition to family rates) per room.......................	1 00
Brewery, per barrel brewed..	00
Building purposes, per bushel lime..	02
Butcher Stalls..	3 00 to 15 00
Charitable Institutions, one-third annual rates...............................	
Cow..	0 75
Condensing Boiler for Steam Heating, (per season of six months) per horse	
power..	50
Eating Houses...	5 00 to 25 00
Family..	5 00
Hand Basin, for Dwellings, Hotels and Schools, first basin...................	1 00
" " " " each additional...................	50
" " in Offices, Stores and Blocks, each...........................	1 00
Hotel, (in addition to family rates) per room...................................	1 00
Livery Stable, per horse...	2 00
Maltster, per 1,000 bushels malted...	1 75
Offices...	3 00 to 10 00
Private Stable, one or two horses..	2 00
" " each additional horse.......................................	1 00
Printing Offices..	5 00 to 30 00
Public Halls...	5 00 to 25 00
Saloons...	5 00 to 25 00
Stores...	3 00 to 15 00
Schools, per pupil...	10
Steam Engine, 10 hours per day, each horse power...........................	2 50
Slaughter Houses..	5 00 to 50 00
Sleeping Room..	1 00
Sprinkling Streets or Lawns with hose (per season).......................	3 00 and up
Urinal, private, self-closing	2 00
" public, "	3 00
" not self-closing..	3 00 to 10 00
Urinal, continuous flow..	10 00 to 30 00
Wash Tub, (permanent, with waste)..	2 00
" " " " each additional.....................	1 00
Watering Trough, public..	10 00
Water Closet, (pan) private..	3 00
" " " each additional..............................	1 50
" " " public..	6 00
" " (hopper), private..	6 00
" " " public	10 00
Work Shop, (ordinary use)..	3 00 to 5 00

All other uses, when not metered, to be assessed by the Department.

METER RATES, (PER QUARTER).

Daily Average, 15,000 gallons or less...10	cents
" 15,000 to 20,000 gallons..................................... 9½	"
" 20,000 to 25,000 " 9	"
" 25,000 to 30,000 " 8½	"
" 30,000 to 35,000 " 8	"
" 35,000 to 40,000 " 7½	"
" 40,000 to 45,000 " 7	"
" 45,000 to 50,000 " 6½	"
More than 50,000 gallons... 6	

ANNUAL REPORT

—OF THE—

Board of Water Commissioners,

OF ERIE, PA.,

—TO THE—

MAYOR AND CITY COUNCILS,

—FOR THE—

YEAR ENDING DEC. 31, 1887.

ERIE, PA.
MORNING DISPATCH PRINTING COMPANY.
1888.

WATER COMMISSIONERS

The Water Commissioners are appointed by the Court of Common Pleas of Erie County, Pa., for a term of three years, one member being named annually, in May.

EX-MEMBERS OF THE BOARD.

*WM. L. SCOTT, 1867 to 1868.
*HENRY RAWLE. 1867 to 1872.
*WM. W. REED, 1867 to 1879.
†JOHN C. SELDEN, 1868 to 1872.
MATTHEW R. BARR, 1872 to 1877.

JOHN GENSHEIMER, 1872 to 1878.
M. LIEBEL, 1877 to 1886.
J. M. BRYANT, 1878 to 1881.
G. W. F. SHERWIN, 1879 to 1885.
BENJ. WHITMAN, 1881 to 1887.

*Messrs Scott, Rawle and Reed, the first Commissioners, were appointed respectively for terms of one, two and three years.
†Mr. Selden resigned before the expiration of his second term; Mr. Barr was substituted by the Board and afterward appointed by the Court.

THE PRESENT BOARD.

GEO. W. STARR, 1885 to 1888.   C. KESSLER, 1886 to 1889.
C. J. BROWN, 1887 to 1890.

OFFICERS OF THE DEPARTMENT.

President of the Board—GEO. W. STARR.
Secretary and Treasurer—B. F. SLOAN.
Assistant Secretary—GEO. C. GENSHEIMER.
Clerk—WILL W. REED.
Superintendent of Street Work—WM. O LONE.
Inspectors—A. F. CRANE, F. W. KOEHLER, JOHN D. SPAFFORD.
Mechanical Engineer—F. A. ROTH.
Assistant Mechanical Engineers—GEO. R. MILLER, JOHN KELLY.
Firemen—R. W. SIMONS, JOSEPH BURNS, JACOB MULLEN.
Watchman at Pumping Works—THOS. TIDMAN.
Keeper of Reservoir and Grounds--SAMUEL PFISTER.

OFFICE—No. 18 East Seventh Street, between French and State.
OFFICE HOURS—From 7:30 A. M. to 5:45 P. M.; Monday Evenings from 7:30 to 9.00 P. M.
REG¹   ¶GS OF THE BOARD—Every Saturday at 8:00 P. M.

ANNUAL REPORT.

To the Mayor and City Councils:

GENTLEMEN—In presenting the annual report of the Water Commissioners, it is gratifying to be able to state that the results of the operations of the Department for the year ending December 31, 1887, have proved satisfactory in respect to the working of the force employed, the perfecting of the Machinery, the laying of Mains, and the Receipts for Rents.

Appended are the usual tables showing in detail the Expenses incurred and the Receipts from all sources. A summary of same shows:

RECEIPTS.

Balance in office Jan. 1, 1887	$	332	87
" City Treasury, Jan. 1, 1887		11,756	45
From Water Rents		67,121	92
" all other sources		1,146	88
		$80,358	12

EXPENDITURES.

Paid on account of Construction	$54,251	82
" " Extraordinary Expenses	2,010	74
" " Maintenance	17,492	69
Balance in City Treasury, Dec. 31, 1887	6,251	20
" Office Dec. 31, 1887	351	67
	$80,358	12

The account for Maintenance was necessarily greater for the year than when ordinarily running, by reason of experiments made with the new Pumping Engine. During its trial, both before and after the official tests, various kinds of coal were used with varying prices, as well as the ordinary Bituminous slack heretofore used with the old Cornish Pumps. Through the whole year, except for the last three months, changes have been made in the firing of the boilers, sometimes two or three having been used, as the new or old pumps were in operation. During the building of the new Engine House and the erection of the new Pumping Engine much of the steam generated was used for other needful purposes than driving the Engines, of which no account could possibly be kept, nor the waste ascertained or satisfactorily estimated. Notwithstanding all these changes—experiments and unavoidable losses of steam power —the Maintenance charge, compared with the receipts and amount of water furnished, is less than that of any year of the life of the Works, while the quantity of water lifted exceeds that of last year by more than one hundred millions of gallons.

Eight thousand three hundred and ninety-six dollars and ninety-two cents is the excess of Water Rents of 1887 over the receipts of 1886, accounted for in part as the result of careful inspection, repairs and stoppage of leaks of every kind, and also by reason of a constantly increasing demand for water, which grows with the growth of the City and must annually be provided for.

The Construction account appears large. It is due to the cost of the Engine House, and to the sums paid for the new Pumping Machinery and the new Inlet, and to the 30-inch Pipe laid from the stop on the east side of the Boiler House to the new Engine House to connect the Main with the new Pump. The payments on the contract for the new Engine House were $3,040.23; on the inlet, $375.12; on the new Pumping Engine, $19,362.85, and on the Connections therewith, including Material and Labor, $956.75, making in all the sum of $23,734.95. Deducting this amount from the sum charged to Construction, we have the result of $30,516.87 chargeable to the ordinary account for Construction, as against $29,846.32 for the same item for 1886, or $670.55 more than in 1886.

But during the last year we have laid 13,905 feet of 6-inch Mains alone—more than the whole number of feet of all sizes laid in 1886, besides more than a mile of 4-inch, and more than one-fourth of a mile of 12-inch Main, with several hundred feet of smaller sizes. This result as to extension made and cost of same. we submit, will compare favorably with that of any former report of the Water Department.

NEW PUMPING HOUSE.

The walls of the Engine House are laid upon the rock, are built in the most substantial manner, and the Building adapted in all respects to the purposes for which it is designed. The Foundations of the new Engine are of solid Masonry built from the rock up.

The well in the House is 10 by 6 feet and 18 feet deep, at least
one-half of same cut out of the rock, and built up from the bottom
with hard burned brick one foot in thickness laid in Portland
cement, thus shutting out surface water, and with a heavy woven
copper wire screen of one-eighth of an inch mesh placed in the well
between the Inlet and the suction Pipe of the Engine.

THE GASKILL PUMPING ENGINE.

This new Engine was erected in the early months of the year, but
was not completed in readiness for the tests required until the 26th
day of April, when for three full days it was on trial under the
close scrutiny of Mr. F. A. Scheffler, Mechanical Engineer of this
City, who had been selected by the Board to act for them and report
the results of the trial, and of Mr. Frank Holly, representing the
Holly Manufacturing Company, of Lockport, N. Y., the builders of
the Pumping Engine.

The specifications in the contract called for:

1st.   A Capacity test of 24 hours' continuous duration.

2d.   At conclusion of Capacity test, and without stopping the
Machinery, a duty test of 48 hours' continuous duration, which was
divided into four trials of 12 hours each, at different rates of speed.

3d.   A Working test of 30 days in succession, pumping as the
demands of the City required, and using the slack coal ordinarily
in use at the Works.

The Capacity and Duty tests were made by the two experts above
named and Mr. F. A. Roth, the Engineer at the Works. The Working
test was made by the Mechanical Engineer of the Works and his
Assistants.

Their reports are in the office of this Department and are open
to inspection.

We quote from them as follows:

Mr. Scheffler says: "The first test began at 7 o'clock a. m.
April 26, and as each of the four tests were of 12 hours' duration
the tests concluded at 7 a. m. April 28.

" Two Boilers were found to be ample for the 5,000,000 gallon test,
and no forcing whatever was required, and the steam pressure
throughout the tests was within the limits of the guarantee. *i. e.*,
from 70 to 80 pounds.

· ".The net* duty is shown to exceed the guaranteed duty of 105,-000,000-foot pounds in 5,000,000 gallon test by 17,000,000-foot pounds, which is nearly 17 per cent., and in the other tests an increase of as equally good proportions.

" The coal used during the test was bituminous slack of the usual quality used by you daily.

" The engines have more than fulfilled the duty guaranteed by the contractor in all four tests."

In a circular published by the Holly Manufacturing Company soon after the three days' trial, is the following statement and claim for this engine:

" The engine of a capacity of 5,000,000 gallons daily, at a piston speed of 120 feet per minute, against a head of 237 feet, and the daily consumption being about 3,500,000, a duty guarantee was required while operating at this rate; also, while operating at the rate of 4,000,000 gallons daily, and at the rate of 5,000,000 gallons. The guarantee was made as follows : 95,000,000 at 3,500,000 rate, 100,000,000 at 4,000,000 rate, 105,000,000 at 5,000,000 rate.

" The test was commenced at the higher rate, and at the end of 12 hours the duty was 122,442,491. Without stopping, the speed was lowered to a rate of 3,400,000 and continued 12 hours longer with a result of 117,306,080. Without stopping, the speed was raised to a rate of 4,314,000 and continued for 12 hours, with a result of 121,131,598. Again the speed was lowered to a rate of 3,791,-946 for 12 hours with a result of 118,595,796, thus making an average of 119,868,991-foot pounds for the 48 hours' trial, operating each 12 hours at a different capacity.

" The steam ranged from 70½ to 74 pounds during the test. It is a safe assertion to make that no Pumping Engine has ever made an equal record; and when the low steam pressure and moderate piston speed are taken into account, the result is still more surprising."

The report of our Engineers, on the conclusion of the thirty days' Working test, was favorable, and on the 11th day of June the Board formally accepted the Engine and paid the first instalment of $12,000 required by the contract. Other payments have been made

---

* NOTE—The net duty refers to duty obtained by a deduction for leakage in boilers, spoken of in succeeding pages of this report.

since that time, account of which will be found in the tables published as part of this report.

The reports of the experts show that the Engine was submitted to all the tests required by the specifications, and that the results fully justify the Board in the selection of this particular form of pumping engine.

Since these tests have been made, and dating from the 11th day of June, 1887, the Gaskill Pumping Engine has been running for the greater part of the time, the old Pumps working at intervals both to maintain the required supply of water and to keep them in good working order in case of need.   No attempt has since been made to test the full capacity of the new Pump.   The trial was made by the experts, and the uselessness of repeating it was abundantly demonstrated when, on the first day's Capacity test and several times before its acceptance by the Board, the water was thrown over the Stand-Pipe whenever the quantity lifted much exceeded the rate of 5,000,000 gallons per day, as shown by the number of its revolutions.

Its economy in the use of fuel is shown by comparing the number of gallons pumped in the months of October, November and December (when it was run constantly and with the average quality of slack coal) with the cost of fuel burned.

PUMPAGE.

The number of gallons raised during the year was 1,218,213,688, an average of 3,335,190 gallons per day, an increase over the previous year's supply of 106,824,583, which is about the annual consumption expected in proportion to the increased rents received.

Yet the cost of fuel at the Works for lifting this great number of gallons in excess of the previous year was but $3,589.31, being less than the cost of coal for the year 1886 by the sum of $729.33. The results of the economy of running the new Pumping Engine over the old Pumps in use heretofore will be more fairly shown at the close of another year, when it shall have been in constant use, and all its parts have become perfectly adjusted and in complete working order.

MAINS.

There have been laid of Mains the past year: 13,905 feet of 6-inch, 5,873 feet of 4-inch, 1,381 feet of 12-inch, 585 feet of 4-inch

(Private Mains), 322 feet of 2-inch, 484 feet of 1-inch, 27 feet of 1½-inch for Sprinkling Hydrants, besides 1,033 feet of 4-inch Pipe on State Street, from Front Street to the Dock, in place of 2-inch Pipe taken up, and 336 feet of 6-inch Pipe taken up on Wallace Street and replaced with new Pipe.

The 12-inch Main was laid on Twenty-first Street. It connects Parade Street with Ash Street. It forms part of a plan long since adopted by the Board to produce free circulation, and became necessary to promote a better circulation and a full supply not only to the Water Takers on Twenty-first Street, but also to the numerous Manufactories in that quarter of the City.

HYDRANTS, STOP VALVES AND CONNECTIONS.

Forty fire hydrants were set in new places, and eleven defective ones taken out and replaced with new ones. They are all the Mathews pattern. Whole number now in City, 318.

Of Stop Valves there are now in the city 526. Of these there were set during the year 30 of 6-inch, in new locations; 27 of 4-inch, in new locations; 5 of 4-inch, defective replaced with new; 1 of 6-inch, in place of 4-inch; 1 of 12-inch, in new location; 4 of 1½-inch, for sprinkling purposes.

Four hundred Connections with Mains were made, many of which, being on Streets newly Paved, will not be brought into use for some time to come, but were required to be made at once under the Ordinance of the City relating to newly paved streets.

METERS.

The number of Meters and Counters now in use is 76, a gain of 12 over last year.

We append to this Report a Table—taken from Statistics and Water Rates of the National Meter Co., N. Y., for 1887—published by authority of the Board.

In this Table are the rates charged in 163 Cities and Towns in the United States for 1,000 gallons of water metered. The average rate in these 163 places is shown to be 9$\frac{4}{10}$ cents per 1,000.

Nine only of the whole number charge less than Erie. In one of these, where the charge is but $\frac{11}{100}$ of a cent less than in our City, there is no expense for Pumping Machinery nor for lifting the water, as it is furnished by gravity, and in the remaining eight cases, the loss in the Meter rate is made up by heavier rates than ours on rooms, fixtures and private dwellings, and by payment for Fire Hydrants, or by a constant yearly appropriation by the City to the Department, or by both, showing that the sums lost to the Water Department in those Cities by the decreased Meter Rates are more than made good to the Department by a general tax on the people, not all of whom are Water Takers, for the benefit of the large Manufacturers.

There can be no good ground for objecting to pay for the quantity of water used. The equivalent is given for the price paid. It is a well ascertained fact also that as Meters wear and get out of order they register less, and the gain in such case is in favor of the Consumer and not of the Water Department. A thorough examination will show that in no City (unless supplied by gravity) are the people so well provided with water, at so little cost, where water has to be lifted to such a height.

CONSUMERS.

A gain in number of Families, Manufactories, &c., for the year is 327. Whole number supplied, 6,367.

In testing the Boilers for the trial of the new Pump, a leakage of steam was found of such proportions, on reducing it to its equivalent of coal consumption, as to require prompt attention. This leakage has been stopped and a waste of considerable amount prevented.

The free use of water for the State Fish Hatchery, granted by the Commissioners at the request of the City Councils, for two years has ceased by limitation, and a large drain of revenue in this direction has terminated.

By a recent decision of the Supreme Court the Department will also be relieved from the payment of taxes, imposed and paid for the last two years to the amount of $1,100.83, at the rate of $550.41 annually.

It is understood that the question of Sewers is being agitated in Councils. We respectfully suggest that if the sewerage is to be emptied anywhere into the Bay, the responsibility of polluting the water will not rest upon the Water Department, which has no control over the matter. Whatever system may be devised, there can be no question but that the waste of the City should be turned into the Lake outside the Bay in order to secure the purity of the water now so generally in use by our people.

During the year no complaint has been made of the fishy taste of the water. This unaccountable defect, though of only a few days' duration, and common to all places which obtain their supply from Lakes or Ponds, we have been happily relieved from, and we hope to be able to record its continuous absence in the future.

DEPARTMENT ENTITLED TO CREDIT FOR SERVICES.

The attention of the City Authorities has been for years called to the fact that this Department has never been credited for any use of water by the City.

No money has been asked to be paid, but only the credit given on the books of the City for that which has cost the Water Department a large sum annually.

It is to be noted that since the first issue of Bonds, which netted this Department a little less than $588,000, its whole business has been conducted, and its Mains and Works extended and enlarged, entirely from the rents received; and during the whole time that the Works have been in operation (now 19 years) the Water Department has been charged with the whole expense of delivering water to the City Offices, to the Engine and Hose Houses, to the Public Fountains, for flushing Sewers, and for Hydrants for general fire protection.

For the first time in its existence the Water Department finds that its revenue for the coming year will probably exceed its expenses, and that it will be in condition to appropriate that excess to the partial payment of the maturing Water Bonds issued by the City.

To the requisition of the Finance Committee of Councils, the Commissioners have answered, " That unless extraordinary demands shall be made upon the Department which no prevision can anticipate, they will be able to pay into the City Treasury, from the current year's receipts, towards the redemption of the Water Bonds which will mature in 1888—the sum of $23,000—so much of said sum as may be collected beyond needed expenses, to be paid on or before the first day of July next, and the remainder as soon thereafter as the receipts of the Department will warrant."

Were the just credit given to this Department by the City for the water furnished as above stated, including 318 Fire Hydrants, reckoned at the light sum of $12,500, added to the $23,000 agreed to be paid into the City Treasury, the Works will be seen to have more than paid the interest at the rate of six per cent. for the year on their original cost. The City will, of course, credit the Water Department with the $23,000. Why should credit for only a part be given? and is it not just, as has been repeatedly urged in years past, that the City should give the Department full credit for water supplied on demand and without stint for all City purposes?

Respectfully submitted,

GEO. W. STARR,

C. KESSLER,

C. J. BROWN,

Water Commissioners.

ERIE, February 1, 1888.

EXHIBIT A.

Receipts of the Erie Water Department for the Year Ending the 31st day of December, 1887.

WATER RENTS.			
First quarter—January.........	$6,430 50		
" " —February.............	4,812 10		
" " —March.....	3,180 03		
		$14,372 63	
Second quarter—April	7,399 25		
" " —May.....................	6,288 42		
" " —June.....................	3,661 86		
		$17,349 53	
Third quarted—July.....................	8,396 77		
" " —August	5,712 19		
" " —September...........	3,076 56		
		$17,185 52	
Fourth quarter—October................	8,551 46		
" " —November............	6,164 20		
" " —December.............	3,498 58		
		$18,214 24	
			$67,121 92
From Pipe Laying, Material, etc....	....	$ 1,146 88	
Balance December 31, 1886.............	....	332 87	
			$1,479 75
Total from all sources..............	....	....	$68,601 67
CR.			
Deposits in Treasury, 1st quarter...	$14,200 00		
" " 2d " ...	17,900 00		
" " 3d " ...	18,000 00		
" " 4th " ...	18,150 00		
			$68,250 00
Balance December 31, 1887........	....	....	$ 351 67

EXHIBIT B.

Account of Water Department with City Treasurer for the Year Ending December 31, 1887.

DR.			
To balance in Treasury Dec. 31, '86.	$11,756 45		
" deposits from Jan. 1 to Dec.31,'87.	68,250 00		$80,006 45
CR.			
Warrants drawn, 1st quarter—Jan.	3,875 94		
" " " " —Feb.	2,883 95		
" " " " —Mar.	2,504 23		
		$9,264 12	
Warrants drawn, 2d quarter—Apr.	5,093 46		
" " " " —May.	4,375 24		
" " " " - June	16,161 67		
		25,630 37	
Warrants drawn, 3d quarter—July.	14,693 26		
" " " " —Aug.	4,258 29		
" " " " —Sep.	4,253 28		
		23,204 83	
Warrants drawn, 4th quarter—Oct.	9,378 91		
" " " " —Nov.	2,469 08		
" " " " —Dec..	3,807 94		
		15,655 93	
			73,755 25
Balance December 31, 1887.......	....	....	$6,251 20

(Continued on page 14.)

EXHIBIT B—Continued.

CONTROLLER'S AUDIT.

Water Commissioners' Cash and Warrant Account; also, Account with City Treasurer for the Year 1887.

Cash on hand January 1, 1887..$ 332 87
Received from Water Rents.. 67,121 92
    "   "   other sources.. 1,146 88

    Total..$68,601 67
Amount paid City Treasurer.. 68,250 00

Amount of Cash on hand and in Bank.......................$ 351 67

Warrants outstanding January 1, 1887.........................$ 110 08
Amount of Warrants issued during the year............... 73,755 25

    Total Warrants...$73,865 33
Warrants paid during the year 1887............................. 72,749 34

Warrants outstanding January 1, 1888 ....$ 1,115 99

Balance to the credit of the Water Commissioners in City
    Treasury January 1, 1887......................................$11,866 53
Total Receipts by City Treasurer.................................. 68,250 00

    Total...$80,116 53
Warrants paid by Treasurer during 1887.................... 72,749 34

Balance to the credit of the Water Commissioners in City
    Treasury January 1, 1886.......................................$ 7,367 19

OFFICE OF CITY CONTROLLER, }
ERIE, PA., Feb. 9, 1888. }

    I hereby certify that the above statement has been carefully compared with the Records in the offices of the City Treasurer and Water Commissioners, and found correct; and that the balance, seven thousand, three hundred and sixty-seven $\frac{19}{100}$ dollars ($7,367.19) was due the Water Commissioners by the City Treasurer January 1, 1888.

CHAS. S. CLARK,
City Controller.

EXHIBIT C.

Expenditures for the Year 1887; also, from the Commencement of Works in 1867 to January 1, 1887.

FUEL AT WORKS.	FROM JAN. 1, 1887, TO DEC. 31, 1887.	1867 TO 1887
From com't of works to Dec. 31, 1886	....	$117,109 98
Paid R. J. Saltsman for 2,208,600 lbs. coal, at $1.25 per ton................	$1,442 86	
Paid R. J. Saltsman for 3,318,700 lbs. coal, at $1.15 per ton................	1,908 25	
Paid R. J. Saltsman for 6,000 lbs. coal, at $4.75 per ton................	14 25	
Paid R. J. Saltsman for 563,300 lbs. coal, at $1.12½ per ton...............	316 85	
Paid R. J. Saltsman for 90,500 lbs. coal, at $1.75 per ton................	79 19	
Paid for labor....................	26 25	
	$3,787 65	
SALARIES.		
From com't of works to Dec. 31, 1886	....	$100,855 98
Paid B. F. Sloan, Sec. and Treas....	$1,310 00	
" Geo. C Gensheimer, As't Sec.	895 00	
" Wm. O'Lone. Supt. St. Work..	1,070 00	
" A. F. Crane, Inspector	840 00	
" F. W Koehler, "	660 00	
" A C. Swalley, Clerk..............	475 00	
" B. Whitman, Commissioner....	730 00	
" Geo. W. Starr, "	725 00	
" C. Kessler, "	760 00	
" C. J. Brown, "	475 00	
	$7,940 00	
MECHANICAL ENGINEERS AND FIREMEN.		
From com't of works to. Dec. 31, 1886	....	$71,664 62
Paid F. A. Roth, Engineer	$1,073 33	
" Geo. R. Miller, "	840 00	
" John Kelly, "	840 00	
" R. W. Simmons, Fireman.......	507 00	
" Joseph Burns, "	540 00	
" Jacob Mullen, "	540 00	
" Extra Firemen.....................	49 50	
	$4,389 83	
FIRE HYDRANTS.		
From com't of works to Dec. 31, 1886	....	$15,158 07
Paid R. D. Wood & Co., for Hydrants	$1,256 00	
" Frank Hoffman, labor..........	5 50	
" G. Carroll & Bro., et. al., lumber	15 35	
" Erie Machine Shop, sundries..	3 19	
" Empire Line, freight.............	50 92	
" Labor, as per Pay-Rolls.........	303 54	
	$1,634 50	
Carried forward.	$17,751 98	$304,788 65

	FROM JAN. 1, 1887, TO DEC. 81, 1887.	1867 TO 1887
Brought forward.......	$17,751 98	$304,788 65

CARE AND REPAIR OF HYDRANTS.

Paid Erie Machine Shop, sundries..	$ 29 41	
" Chas. Smith, et. al., labor.......	51 25	
" B. F. Sloan, Sec., sundries......	1 83	
" .Wm. F. Nick, paint, &c..........	10 45	
" Geo. Carroll & Bro., lumber...	8 78	
" Labor, as per Pay-Rolls..........	156 18	
		$257 85

POSTAGE.

From com't of works to Dec. 31, 1886	....	$2,993 74
Paid H. C. Shannon, Postmaster, stamps, envelopes, &c.............	$186 70	
		$186 70

PLUMBING, ETC.

From com't of works to Dec. 31, 1886	....	$3,114 49
Paid labor, as per Pay-Rolls............	$172 21	
		$172 21

DISTRIBUTING MAINS and BRANCHES

From com't of works to Dec 31, 1886	....	$363,778 15
Paid for Pipe and Specials..............	$11,657 84	
" Special Castings, Erie Mach. S.	117 94	
" Freight.............................	340 36	
" R. J. Saltsman, et. al., coke....	42 56	
" Adolph Brugger, sundries......	30 80	
" For Distributing Pipe.............	262 84	
" O. C. Thayer & Son, for clay..	17 50	
" R. W. Russell, for wood........	16 75	
" Martin Quigley, packing.........	37 76	
" J. B. Dwyer, inspecting pipe..	114 00	
" Cash for telegraphs, &c...........	6 32	
" For lumber	42 95	
" National Tube Co., 1-in. pipe..	152 46	
" For lead.........	1,613 08	
" Labor, as per Pay-Rolls..........	3,426 49	
		$17,879 65

STOP VALVES, BOXES AND COVERS.

From com't of works to Dec. 31, 1886	....	$19,186 78
Paid R. D. Wood & Co., et. al., valves	$1,035 00	
" Erie Machine Shop, castings...	675 07	
" Labor as per Pay-Rolls..........	178 68	
" Noble & Hall, sundrie.............	14 15	
" Empire Line, freight..............	33 83	
" F. Dudenhoffer, brick............	6 00	
" Frank Hoffman, cartage........	3 75	
" B. F. Sloan, Sec., cash exp'd..	8 69	
		$1,951 17
Carried forward.....	$38,199 56	$698,861 81

	FROM JAN. 1, 1887, TO DEC. 31, 1887.		1867 TO 1887
Brought forward......................	....	$38,199 56	$693,861 81
REPAIRS OF BOILERS.			
From com't of works to Dec. 31, 1886	....	....	26,388 85
Paid Erie Machine Shop................	$433 17		
" Donnelly & Bro., brick laying	236 75		
" Erie Lime and Cement Co......	178 80		
" D. P. Murphy, labor...............	73 50		
" John Davis, covering pipe......	50 34		
" Noble & Hall, sundries...........	214 78		
" Labor, Supt.'s Pay-Rolls.......	17 86		
" Hays Mfg. Co., sundries........	15 53		
" Michael Leonard, labor.........	12 00		
" B. F. Sloan, Sec., cash exp'd..	1 95		
		$1,234 68	
REPAIRS OF DISTRIBUTING MAINS.			
From com't of works to Dec. 31, 1886	....	....	12,633 97
Paid labor, as per Pay Rolls............	$145 09		
" Chas. Smith, for labor...........	45 50		
" Geo. E. Fry, sundries.............	6 25		
		$196 84	
CARE AND MAINTENANCE OF RESERVOIR AND KEEPER'S HOUSE.			
From com't of works to Dec. 31, 1886	....	....	8,058 76
Paid Samuel Phister, salary...........	$420 00		
" Constable Bros., et. al., sund..	21 00		
" S. S. Burton, for coal.............	5 00		
" Wm. Brewster, for flowers... ..	7 00		
" Mehl & Liebel, sundries..........	4 46		
" Erie Machine Shop................	1 50		
" B F. Sloan, Sec., cash exp'd...	7 41		
" Labor, as per Pay-Rolls...... ...	9 66		
		$476 03	
BUILDINGS, GROUNDS AND STAND-PIPK.			
From com't of works to Dec. 31, 1876	....	....	70,728 36
Paid Thos. Tidman, watchman	$480 00		
" Sebastian Kerschner, sundries	181 88		
" Donnelly Bros., sundries........	143 52		
" Constable Bros., sundries......	87 77		
" Jarecki Mfg. Co., pipe...........	55 01		
" Frank Senger, stone..............	34 30		
" F. Dudenhoffer, brick...........	12 75		
" L. Cummins, et. al , labor.......	23 37		
" Erie Machine Shop, et. al.	5 79		
" Frank Hoffman, cartage.......	11 50		
" Henry Beckman, grass seed...	7 80		
" H. G. Fink, sundries..............	3 25		
" B. F. Sloan, Sec., cash exp'd...	1 50		
" P. Osborne, for trees.............	3 62		
" Wm. F. Nick, paints..............	35 45		
" Labor, as per Pay-Rolls.........	278 07		
		+1,365 08	
Carried forward....................	....	$41,472 14	$811,671 75

	FROM JAN. 1, 1887, TO DEC. 31, 1887.	1867 TO 1887
Brought forward......................	$41,472 14	$811,671 75

OFFICE FURNITURE AND EXPENSES.

From com't of works to Dec. 31, 1886		12,009 45
Paid T. J. Elliott, rent of office......	$250 00	
" Janitor, &c......	123 70	
" G. W F Sherwin, maps, &c...	72 50	
" R. J. Saltsman, for coal.........	51 50	
" Telephone Exchange......	96 00	
" Erie Gas Co......................	16 80	
" Pennsylvania Gas Co.............	14 18	
" R. M. Johnson, et. al., livery...	30 00	
" J. R. Cooney. ice	8 00	
" T. J. Sevin, sundries...............	8 30	
" J. E. Franze, chairs......	2 25	
" B. F. Sloan, Sec., cash exp'd..	35 50	
	$708 73	

SUPERINTENDENT'S SMALL STORES.

From com't of works to Dec. 31, 1886		447 60
Paid Sundry Bills as per vouchers..	$15 22	
	$15 22	

WASTE AND PACKING.

From com't of works to Dec. 31, 1886		2,571 45
Paid C W. Parsons, et. al.............	$50 35	
" E. S. Greeley & Co.,et.al.,waste	82 56	
" H. L. Childs & Co., waste......	47 44	
" Mehl & Liebel, packing.........	24 99	
	$205 34	

OIL AND TALLOW.

From com't of works to Dec. 31, 1886		5,982 94
Paid Thos. Brown Oil Co........	$136 87	
" Eclipse Oil Co.	212 01	
	$348 88	

CARTAGE.

From com't of works to Dec. 31, 1886		483 54
Paid cash as per vouchers...............	$26 50	
	$26 50	

WATER METERS AND CARE.

From com't of works to Dec. 31, 1886		7,285 03
Paid National Meter Co.................	$141 75	
" Union Meter Co......................	256 03	
" Schlosser & Felheim, et. al., lumber......	20 61	
" Jarecki Mfg. Co., sundries	12 18	
" B. F. Sloan, Sec., cash exp'd..	10 06	
" Labor, as per Pay-Rolls.........	132 29	
	$572 92	
Carried forward......................	$43,349 73	$840,451 76

	FROM JAN. 1, 1887, TO DEC. 31, 1887.	1867 TO 1887
Brought forward......................	.... $43,349 73	$840,451 76
SHOP TOOLS AND REPAIRS.		
From com't of works to Dec. 31, 1886	....	3,338 46
Paid Erie Machine Shop, repairs....	$153 82	
" Rent of barn, Peach st...........	55 00	
" Mehl & Liebel, et. al., sundries	43 85	
" C. Flickinger, et. al., sundries.	14 80	
" Keystone Carriage Wks.. et al.	10 25	
" Ashby & Vincent, sundries.....	11 25	
" Hays Mfg. Co., sundries	2 40	
" B. F. Sloan, Sec., cash exp'd..	1 80	
" N. Murphy & Son, sundries....	9 35	
" R. J. Saltsman, coal..............	11 50	
	$314 02	
COURT COSTS AND COUNSEL FEES.		
From com't of works to Dec. 31, 1886	....	1,647 88
Paid Briggs & Fish, rep. testimony	$7 50	
	$7 50	
ENGINEER'S SMALL STORES.		
From com't of works to Dec. 31, 1886	....	1,426 76
" Erie Ice Co., for ice....	$34 06	
" Erie Gas Co., for gas........ ..	37 50	
" R. J. Saltsman, for coal	15 35	
" Mehl & Liebel, et. al..............	30 00	
" J. W. Swalley, for soap...........	13 90	
" James Gaffney, sundries........	8 07	
" P. A. Becker, sundries	10 63	
" Henry Beckman, sundries	8 06	
" Wm. F. Nick, sundries.....	5 25	
" B. F. Sloan, Sec., cash exp'd..	28 35	
	$197 17	
PRINTING AND ADVERTISING.		
From com't of works to Dec. 31, 1886	....	3,718 49
" Erie Herald, for sundries.......	$95 50	
" Erie Observer, for sundries......	31 35	
" Erie Dispatch, for sundries......	29 75	
" J. M. Glazier, for sundries......	14 00	
" Walker & Gallagher, for sun's.	11 50	
	$182 10	
BOOKS AND STATIONERY.		
From com't of works to Dec. 31, 1886	....	1,413 60
Paid Ashby & Vincent, sundry bills.	$67 10	
" E. M. Cole, sundries..............:	2 50	
	$69 60	
Carried forward......................	.... $44,120 12	$851,996 95

	FROM JAN. 1, 1887, TO DEC. 31, 1887.		1867 TO 1887
Brought forward....................	....	$44,120 12	$851,996 95
ENGINE ROOM FURNITURE.			
From com't of works to Dec. 31, 1886	....	....	933 78
Paid Warner Bros , sundries.....	$ 61 18		
" E. Knobloch, for boat	35 00		
" Mehl & Liebel, sundries............	25 01		
" Erie Machine Shop, sundries..	8 56		
" W. H. Dickson, repair'g scales.	8 50		
" August Jarecki, for clock......	8 50		
" F. E. Franze. for chairs.........	12 50		
" Adams Mfg. Co., step ladder...	8 64		
" Thos. M. Hemphill, sundries...	4 50		
" J. O. Baker, sundries.............	2 25		
" B. F. Sloan, Sec., cash exp'd...	6 03		
		$180 62	
EXPENSE OF HORSE AND WAGON.			
From com't of works to Dec. 31, 1886	....	....	3,483 07
" Sundry parties, for hay & oats.	$ 42 67		
" S. S. Caughey, rent....	18 00		
" E. D. Carter, for wagon...	62 00		
" G. L. Siegel & Co., for oats, etc.	38 15		
" Thos. Pickering, sundries	14 50		
" Henry Mayo, sundries.....	26 15		
" R. H. Chinnock, shoeing horse.	18 10		
" G. W. Bell, services...............	4 25		
" A. S. Pinney, sundries.....	4 60		
" Crouch Bros.. feed	5 37		
" Labor as per Pay-Rolls............	72 82		
		$306 61	
STREET CONNECTIONS.			
From com't of works to Dec. 31, 1886	....	....	57,722 48
" Paid National Tub Co., pipe...	$ 413 18		
" Jarecki Mfg. Co., pipe............	407 58		
" Cornell Lead Co., pipe, etc......	154 66		
" Hays Mfg. Co., fittings, etc.....	1,461 59		
" F. R. Simmons, sundries........	5 51		
" Labor for street repairs..........	196 23		
" Cash for freight, etc................	4 64		
" Labor as per Pay-Rolls............	1,431 95		
		$4,094 67	
ON ACCOUNT NEW PUMP.			
From Jan. 1, 1886 to Dec. 31, 1886....	....	....	522 30
Paid Holly Mfg. Co.	$19,720 01		
" Noble & Hall, sundries......	196 22		
" F. A. Scheffler. et. al. services.	165 00		
" Manville Covering Co.........	75 00		
" B. F. Sloan Sec., cash exp'd...	1 50		
" Labor as per Pay-Rolls	155 63		
" Jackson Koehler, sundries......	6 25		
		$20,319 61	
Carried forward.............	....	$69,021 63	$914,658 58

	FROM JAN. 1, 1887, TO DEC. 31, 1887.	1867 TO 1887
Brought forward..........	$69,021 68	$914,658 58
ON ACCOUNT NEW ENGINE HOUSE.		
From Jan. 1, 1886 to Dec. 31, 1886....		3,888 30
Paid S. Kerschner, bal. contract......	$2,413 00	
" W. J. Butler, sundries............	216 00	
" D. K. Dean, services............ ...	118 08	
" Philip Burch, labor, etc........ ..	32 30	
" Saltsman & Austin, sundries...	20 06	
" D. P. Murphy, bricklaying.....	16 00	
" Constable Bros., sundries.......	15 18	
" Donnelly Bros., sundries........	12 50	
" Erie Machine Shop, sundries...	7 96	
" John Mulcahey, stone work....	9 00	
" O. C. Thayer, et. al., sundries.	2 44	
" Labor as per Pay-Rolls...........	177 71	
	$3,040 23	
INLET FOR NEW PUMP.		
From Jan. 1, 1886, to Dec. 31. 1886...		1,766 37
Paid Donnelly Bros., et. al., labor...	$ 67 00	
" Baas & Althof, screen............	182 80	
" Erie Machine Shop, sundries...	35 44	
" Frank Hoffman, sand.....	4 00	
" Labor, as per Pay-Rolls..........	85 88	
	$375 12	
INLET PIERS AND REPAIRS.		
From com't of works to Dec. 31, 1886		42,879 00
Paid Geo. Carroll & Bro. et. al.......	$12 10	
	$12 10	
STATE, COUNTY AND SCHOOL TAXES.		
Paid State and County taxes 1885 and 1886....................		326 92
Paid State, County and School tax.	$773 91	
	$773 91	
INSURANCE.		
Paid for policies on buildings, etc...	$186 58	
	$186 58	
SHOP AND MISCELLANEOUS WORK.		
From com't of works to Dec. 31, 1886		9,362 20
Paid Labor, as per Pay-Rolls........	$267 41	
	$267 41	
INTEREST AND DISCOUNT.		
From com't of works to Dec. 31, 1886		99,065 41
WATER RENTS RETURNED.		
From com't of works to Dec. 31, 1886		62 50
RAILROAD SWITCH AND SCALES.		
From com't of works to Dec. 31, 1886		2,840 65
Paid Pennsylvania Co , repairs.......	$78 27	
	$78 27	
Carried forward.....................	$73,755 25	$1,074,749 92

	FROM JAN. 1, 1887, TO DEC. 31, 1887.	1867 TO 1887
Brought forward	....	$73,755 25	$1,074,749 93
RESERVOIR AND GROUNDS.		
From com't of works to Dec. 31, 1886	....	....	123,150 88
ENGINES AND BOILERS.		
From com't of works to Dec. 31, 1886	....	....	66,816 95
CIVIL ENGINEERING.		
From com't of works to Dec. 31, 1886	....	.. ..	7,122 85
GAS WELLS AND CARE.		
From com't of works to Dec. 31, 1886	....	....	8,148 59
PARK FOUNTAINS.		
From com't of works to Dec. 31, 1886	....	....	3,244 68
Totals......	....	$73,755 25	$1,282,733 83

RECAPITULATION.

EXPENSES IN 1887.

For Construction $54,251 82
  " Extraordinary repairs.. 2,010 74
  " Current expenses 17,492 69

    Total $73,755 25

EXPENSES FROM JULY 1867, TO DEC. 31, 1887.

For Construction...... .... $975,646 26
  " Maintenance................................... .... 380,842 82

    Total $1,356,489 04

NET EARNINGS FROM JULY 1867, TO DEC. 3, 1887.

Total cost of construction................... .... $975,646 26
Advanced by City in bonds......................... $675,000 00
Advanced by City to sink gas wells................ 955 10
                                   675,955 10

    Balance $299,691 16
Add balance in City Treasury............... .... 6,251 20
  "   "   " Office 351 67

    Total net earnings..... .... *$306,294 03

*NOTE—As the Department realized but $586,966.06 from the $675,000 Bonds advanced by the city, the discount on the Bonds, $88,093.94, should be added to the net earnings. This would make that sum $394,327.97.

EXHIBIT D.

Amount of Water Rents Collected each year, with the Increase and Decrease, since the Commencement of the Works.

	Am't Rec'd.	Increase.	Decrease.
From Jan. 1, 1869, to Dec. 31, 1869	$4,264 47	....	....
" " 1870, " 1870......	9,237 30	$4.972 83	....
" " 1871, " 1871......	18,138 08	8,900 78	....
" " 1872, " 1872	21,652 68	3,514 60	....
" " 1873, " 1873......	25,560 40	3,907 72	....
" " 1874, " 1874......	27.938 90	2,378 50	....
" " 1875, " 1875......	29,639 38	1,700 48	....
" " 1876, " 1876......	31,048 76	1,409 38	....
" " 1877, " 1877......	32,276 57	1,227 81	....
" " 1878, " 1878.....	29,636 01	....	$2,640 56
" " 1879, " 1879......	33,343 20	3.707 19	....
" " 1880, " 1880......	37,385 00	4,041 80	....
" " 1881, " 1881......	40,385 87	3,000 87	....
" " 1882, " 1882	43,818 73	3.432 86	....
" " 1883, " 1883	48.269 89	4,451 16	....
" " 1884, " 1884	51,852 78	3.582 89	....
" " 1885, " 1885......	53,550 35	1,697 57	....
" " 1886, " 1886......	58,725 00	5,174 65	....
" " 1887, " 1887......	67,121 92	8,396 92	....
	$663,845 29	....	....

EXHIBIT E.

Location, Size and Length of Main Pipe, Large Private Pipe and Fire Hydrant Branches Laid in 1887.

LOCATION.	FEET.	IN.
SIX-INCH PIPE.		
Fifth street, across Sassafras...	51	......
Fifth street, West from Sassafras...	53	......
Sixth street, from 383 feet west of Cherry to Plum..............	1,121	7
Tenth street, from 277.8 feet east of Wayne to East.............	1,010	6
Eleventh street, from Cherry to near Liberty......................	1,038	......
Eleventh street, between Wayne and Perry......................	565	3
Fourteenth street, from French east.............................	328	......
Seventeenth street, between Chestnut and Hickory.............	301	......
Nineteenth street, from Chestnut west..........................	260	5
Twenty-first street, from East avenue to Ash..........	2,714	......
Twenty-sixth street, between Ash and Reed......	402	6
Twenty-sixth street, from Maple west.........................	324	6
East street, from Buffalo road south......	210	......
Wayne street, between Twelfth and Fifteenth....................	858	......
Ash street, from Tenth south..................................	185	8
Ash street, from Ninth north..................................	71	......
German street, from Ninth to Tenth............................	403	4
French street, from Twenty-second south......................	218	2
French street, from Seventeenth to Eighteenth	312	......
State street, from Eighteenth south............................	176	......
Wallace street, from Twenty-sixth to Twenty-seventh.........	336	......
Myrtle street, from Nineteenth south..........................	216	10
Myrtle street, from Twenty-first south........................	151	8
Myrtle street, between Nineteenth and Twentieth..............	115	6
Myrtle street, from Twenty-sixth south........................	350	2
Walnut street, from Fifth north...............................	110	9
Cherry street, from Eighth to south of Ninth....................	464	6
Poplar street, from Eleventh to 179 feet north of Tenth..	629	11
Plum street, from Sixth north.................................	182	2
Scott street, from Myrtle southeast.........	541	.. ..
Hazel street, from Twenty-sixth south.........................	203	......
	13,905	5
FOUR-INCH PIPE.		
East from new Pump House...................................	65	11
Short street, corner Myrtle........	7	10
Short street, corner Sassafras.................................	7	11
Second street, west from Walnut..............................	317	5
Second street, between State and French......................	393	11
Second street, corner Chestnut..	12	5
Second street, corner Parade.................................	9	10
Third street, west of Cherry..................................	172	3
Third street, corner Myrtle.	8	9
Carried forward..	996	3

LOCATION.	FEET.	IN.
FOUR-INCH PIPE.		
Total 6-inch and 4-inch brought forward........	14,901	8
Third street, corner Sassafras.....................................	9	5
Fifth street, corner Myrtle......................................	9	4
Sixth street, corner Sassafras...................	1	2
Sixth street, corner Poplar...................	7	7
Sixth street, corner Plum.....	8	3
Seventh street, from Ash street west...........	206	8
Tenth street, corner Perry.......................	9	10
Tenth street, corner East Avenue.....................,.......	6	8
Eleventh street, corner Poplar..................................	7	6
Eleventh street, corner Wayne........	7	3
Eleventh street, between Wayne and Perry......	8	7
Eleventh street, corner Myrtle....................	6	1
Thirteenth street, corner Holland	9	6
Fourteenth street, corner Peach................................	5	4
Fifteenth street, corner Wallace...................	7	6
Seventeenth street, corner Cherry........	7	3
Twentieth street, between Chestnut and Myrtle..............	686	6
Twentieth street, corner Myrtle........	8	3
Twenty-first street, corner Ash.......	8	......
Twenty-first street, corner Reed..............................	8	......
Twenty-first street, corner Wayne............................	6	6
Twenty-first street, corner Perry..............................	6	6
Twenty-fifth street, between Holland and French..............	182	8
Twenth-sixth street, corner Reed.....	8	2
Ash street, corner Eighteenth..............................	8	3
Holland street, between Seventh and Eighth.....................	154	......
'French street, from Eighteenth south............................	194	11
French street, corner Thirteenth..............	8	7
French street, corner Eighteenth........	7	10
State street, from Second to Public Dock	1,687	......
Sassafras street, between Tenth and Eleventh	9	......
Sassafras street, between Eleventh and Twelfth	9	......
Sassafras street, between Twelfth and Thirteenth...	21	6
Sassafras street, between Thirteenth and Fourteenth.........	21	4
Sassafras street, between Fifteenth and Sixteenth..............	22	4
Sassafras street, corner Seventeenth......	7	4
Myrtle street, from Sixth to Seventh.............................	310	5
Myrtle street, corner Sixth....................	8	6
Myrtle street, from Second to Short......	220	9
Chestnut street, north of Thirteenth...............	2	1
Walnut street, from Fifth to Sixth............................	363	....
Walnut street, from Second south...	79	6
Cherry street, corner Ninth.....	8	....
Poplar street, corner Tenth.................	9	8
Liberty street, corner Seventeenth...............................	10	5
Plum street, corner Fourth..	6	7
Scott street, 515 feet east of Myrtle.............	25	......
	19,279	2
THIRTY-INCH PIPE.		
At Water Works................	75	8
Carried forward....	19,354	10

LOCATION.	FEET.	IN.
Brought forward.	19,854	10
TWELVE-INCH PIPE.		
Twenty-first street, from Ash to Parade...........….........	1,881	1
PRIVATE PIPE, FOUR-INCH.		
Stearns Mfg. Co., Wayne street.......................	322	......
Erie Forge Works, Cascade street....................	263	......
TWO-INCH PIPE.	585	......
Public Dock, from State street west...............	322	......
ONE-INCH PIPE.		
Front street, between Holland and German.....	165	9
Second street, between Holland and German.....................	319	......
ONE-AND-ONE-HALF-INCH PIPE.	484	9
State street, corner Twelfth (for cart sprinkler).................	10	......
Myrtle street, corner Eighteenth (for cart sprinkler).....	8	3
Walnut street, north of Eighteenth (for cart sprinkler)......	9	......
	27	3
Total pipe laid in 1887..........	22,154	11
PIPE TAKEN UP IN 1887.		
Six-inch.		
Wallace street, from Twenty-sixth to Twenty-seventh.........	336	......
Two-inch.		
State street, from Front to Public Dock...........	1,033	9
Total.....................	1,369	9
Leaving as the actual gain in pipe............................	20,785	2
Or 3 miles, 4,945		

NOTE.—All 4-inch pipe, 10 feet or less, was laid for new Fire Hydrants; also **25 feet** on Scott street.

EXHIBIT F.

Total Amount of Distributing Pipe, Fire Hydrant Branches and Large Private Pipe Laid to December 31, 1887.

STREETS.	LENGTH IN FEET AND INCHES.					
	Less than 4-inch.	4-inch.	6-inch.	12-inch.	20-inch.	30-inch.
Docks and Front.	1,182 5	1,586.2			147.0	330.3
Short	159.10	1,473 9				
Second	1,555.8	5,160.8				
Third	237.0	6,691 9				
Fourth		8,817 8	4,625.6			
Fifth	414.11	6,704.11	104.0			
North Park	75.0	101.4	820.0			
Sixth	152 5	1,927.1	9,650.0			
South Park	182.1	22.7	424.0			
Seventh		8,506.6	31 2	5,362.2		
Eighth	540.8	9,666.8				
Ninth	9.0	7,398.8	1,566.8			
Tenth	49.0	481.11	10,329.7			
Eleventh	275.0	8,521.11	2,079.4			
Twelfth	47.6	1,900 7	13,037.10			
Thirteenth		8,160.1	1,065.1			
Fourteenth		2,994.1	328.0			
Fifteenth	358.2	8,187.5				
Huron		1,436.10				
Sixteenth	497.11	1,418.8	3,372.5			
Seventeenth		7,440.1	1,247.0			
Eighteenth	11.0	2,971.10	12,534.7			
Buffalo Road		1,168.0				
Nineteenth	125.8	2,008.4	689.5			
Twentieth		1,788.0				
Twenty-first		63 2	2,719.6	6,560.0		
Twenty-second		3,637.8				
Twenty-third		2,906.2				
Twenty-fourth		1,634.0				
Twenty-fifth		3,281.8				
Twenty-sixth	300.0	973.2	3,735 8		1,064.6	
Railroad		1,780 0				
Carried forw'd.	6,072.3	97,759.10	68.031.9	11,922.2	1,211.6	330.3

LENGTH IN FEET AND INCHES.

STREETS.	Less than 4-inch.	4-inch.	6-inch.	12-inch.	20-inch.	30-inch.
Brought forw'd	6,072.3	97,759.10	68.031.9	11,922.2	1,211.6	380.0
East Ave............	....	593.3	3,040.6			
Wayne...............			858.0			
Ash...................		1,193.10	2,035.6			
Wallace.............	391.11	1,358.9	336.0			
Vine..................		399.8				
Parade..............		5,529.11	3,343.10			
German..........		3,729.11	814.10			
Division............		317.2				
Holland	203.4	9,351.1	167.0			
French.............	262.6	5,525.6	1,740.2			
State	20.0	5,077.6	4,077.3			
Turnpike..........	6.6	8.7	795.0			
Peach	352.3	1,087.0	5,931.8	1,996.0		
Waterford 'Pike..		910.0				
Sassafras...........	570.0	9,608.4				
Myrtle.	8.3	4,446.3	880.2			
Hickory.............		631.6				
Chestnut...........	1,206.6	4,722.8		24.0	9,222.3	2,457.1
Walnut.............	9.0	4,843.1	423.9			
Cherry.............		2,883.8	464.6			
Poplar..............		829.2	629.11			
Liberty	320.2	1,095.10				
Plum		623.8	182.2			
Cascade............	500.0	475.10	2,620.8			
Maple..............		805.0				
Scott		25.0	541.0			
Hazel...............			203.0			
Total............	10,023.11	166,335 1	97,444.8	13,942.2	10,433.9	2,787.4

RECAPITULATION.

	FEET.	IN.
Less than four-inch pipe..................................	10,023	11
Four-inch pipe.............................	166,335	1
Six-inch pipe................................	97,444	8
Twelve-inch pipe...........................	13,942	2
Twenty inch pipe...........................	10,433	9
Thirty-inch pipe...........................	2,787	4
Total	300,965	11

Total in miles, 57. From this deduct pipe taken up and replaced
1,369 feet, 9 inches—and we have 56 miles, 2,916 feet.

EXHIBIT G.

Location, Number and Length of Street Connections Made During the Year 1887.

EAST AND WEST STREETS.	Number of Connections	FEET.	IN.	NORTH AND SOUTH STREETS.	Number of Connections	FEET.	IN.
Front and Docks....	5	163	2	Wayne................	4	54	7
Second.......	11	242	9	Ash	7	66	7
Third......................	10	188	6	Parade....................	4	110	5
Fourth..................	6	101	11	German.	7	151	2
Fifth......................	24	396	1	Holland.................	4	55	10
North Park...........	2	53	10	French.................	5	132	11
Sixth	6	188	8	State...........	12	323	7
Seventh.	12	213	6	Peach.	4	43	3
Eighth....................	6	158	......	Sassafras, ...	25	425	8
Ninth.....................	8	92	4	Myrtle.	7	157	9
Tenth	20	710	4	Chestnut................	7	80	9
Eleventh................	41	584	5	Walnut...................	8	212	4
Twelfth..................	18	422	3	Cherry...................	4	62	......
Thirteenth	11	190	......	Poplar....................	4	64	......
Fourteenth............	8	92	7	Liberty.............	1	14	9
Fifteenth	2	84	3	Cascade.	3	27	4
Sixteenth	3	14	2	Scott.....................	6	90	8
Seventeenth...........	11	207	7	Hazel	1	10	......
Eighteenth...	17	229	8				
Nineteenth	9	170	10	Total.....	113	2,083	7
Twentieth..............	12	189	4	Add East and West			
Twenty-first	32	621	8	streets................	287	5,484	5
Twenty-second	4	68	8				
Twenty-third	......	....	......	Total................	400	7,568	0
Twenty-fourth	2	37	......				
Twenty-fifth	1	10	......				
Twenty-sixth	11	152	11				
Total................	287	5,484	5				

LENGTH OF CONNECTIONS IN MILES.

	Miles.	Feet.
Connections made in 1887...	1	2,288
Previously made...	18	2,399
Total...	19	4,687

EXHIBIT H.

Location and Style of Fire Hydrants Set in 1887, all being 4-inch Steamer and Hose.

HYDRANTS IN NEW LOCATIONS.

Street		Corner		Cross street	Maker
Front	street,	at new Pumping House			Mathews.
Short	"	Northwest corner of Sassafras			"
"	"	Northeast	"	Myrtle	"
Second	"	Noithwest	"	Chestnut	..
"	"	"	"	Parade	
Third	"	Northeast	"	Sassafras	
"	"	"	"	Myrtle	
Fifth	"	"	"	Myrtle	
Sixth	"	"	"	Sassafras	
"	"	Northwest	"	Cherry	
"	"	Northeast	"	Poplar	
"	"	"	"	Plum	"
Tenth	"	Northwest	"	Perry	Bay State.
"	"	"	"	East Avenue	"
Eleventh	"	Northeast	"	Poplar	Mathews.
"	"	Northwest	"	Wayne	Bay State.
"	"	"	"	Perry	"
Thirteenth	"	"	"	Holland	Mathews.
"	"	Northeast	"	French	"
Fourteenth	"	Northwest	"	Peach	"
Fifteenth	"	"	"	Wallace	Bay State.
Seventeenth	"	"	"	Cherry	Pittsburgh.
Twentieth	"	"	"	Myrtle	Mathews.
Twenty-first	"	Northeast	"	Ash	"
"	"	"	"	Reed	"
"	"	"	"	Wayne	Bay State.
"	"	"	"	Perry	"
Twenty-sixth	"	Northwest	"	Reed	West Jersey
Wayne	"	Between Fourteenth and Fifteenth			Bay State.
French	"	Southeast corner of Eighteenth			Mathews.
State	"	At Public Dock			"
Peach	"	West Park and Sixth street			"
Sassafras	"	Northeast corner of Seventeenth			
Chestnut	"	"	"	Thirteenth	
Walnut	"	Southeast	"	Second	
Cherry	"	Northeast	"	Ninth	
Poplar	"	"	"	Tenth	Pittsburgh.
Liberty	"	"	"	Seventeenth	Bay State.
Plum	"	Southeast	"	Fourth	Mathews.
Scott	"	East from Myrtle street			Bay State.

DEFECTIVE HYDRANTS REPLACED WITH OTHERS.

Street		Corner		Cross street	Maker
Sassafras	street	Southeast corner of Twelfth			Mathews.
"	"	Northeast	"	Sixteenth	"
"	"	"	"	Eighteenth	"
Peach	"	Southeast	"	Seventeenth	
Myrtle	"	Northeast	"	Sixth	
Holland	"	Southeast	"	Eleventh	
German	"	"	"	Eleventh	"
Ash	"	"	"	Eighteenth	Bay State.
Short	"	Northeast	"	Chestnut	Mathews.
Sixth	"	"	"	Chestnut	"
Tenth	"	Southeast	"	Sassafras	"

EXHIBIT H- Continued.

RECAPITULATION.

Fire Hydrants in new locations...40
Defective Fire Hydrants replaced..11

    Total in 1887...51

NUMBER AND STYLES OF FIRE HYDRANTS IN USE.

New style Mathews..............187	Morris, Tasker & Co..............	2
Old " " 11	Union.................................	1
Bay State............................... 29		—
West Jersey........................ 32	Total	290
Pittsburgh 21	Private Fire Hydrants............	28
Home-made............................. 3		—
Ludlow. 4	Grand total.................	318

HYDRANTS FOR THE SUPPLPY OF WAGON SPRINKLERS.

Ninth   street, between State and French...........Jarecki, Hays & Co.
Twelfth   " near Southwest corner of Peach.   "
Fifteenth   " " " Peach.   "
Eighteenth " " Northwest " Peach.
State   " at East Park.................................
" " between Tenth and Eleventh.....
" " Southeast corner of Twelfth ......
Myrtle   " " " Eighteenth.
Walnut   " Northeast " Eighteenth.

EXHIBIT I.

Location, Size and Kind of Stop Valves Set in 1887.

EAST AND WEST STREETS	SIZE.	KIND.
Front and Dock, at Pumping Works, on pipe lead- ing to Fire Hydrant.....	4	Eddy.
Front and Dock, west line of Holland.......................	4	"
Short street, east line of Myrtle.........................	4	"
Second street, 295.6 feet E. of east line of Holland...	1	J., H. & Co.
" " west line of Walnut...........................	4	Eddy.
" " east " State.........................	4	"
" " west " French.....∴..................	4	"
Third " " " Cherry.	4	"
Fifth " " " Walnut........................	4	"
Sixth " east " Sassafras....................	4	"
" " west " Myrtle	4	"
" " east " Poplar	6	"
" " " " Liberty......................	6	"
Seventh " west " Ash........	4	"
Eighth " east " Cherry. ...∙...........	4	"
Ninth " " " Sassafras....................	4	"
" " " " Myrtle	4	"
Tenth " west " Sassafras....................	6	"
" " " " Perry	6	"
" " east " Reed	6	"
Eleventh street, west line of Cherry...................	6	"
" " " " Poplar	6	"
" " " " Sassafras.....................	4	"
" " " " Wayne....................	6	"
Twelfth " " " Sassafras..	6	"
Fourteenth street, east line of French................	6	"
Seventeenth " " " Sassatras................	4	"
Twentieth " west " Myrtle	4	"
Twenty-first " " " Perry	6	"
" " " " Wayne..	6	"
" " " " Reed	6	"
" " east " Ash	6	"
" " " " Wallace..................	12	"
Twenty-sixth street, west " Maple...............	6	"

NORTH AND SOUTH STREETS.

	SIZE	KIND
East street, south line of Buffalo Road...............	6	Eddy.
Wayne " " " Twelfth	6	"
" " " " Fourteenth.................	6	"
Ash " " " Tenth....................	6	"
" " north " Ninth....................	6	"
Parade " " " Eighteenth..............	6	"
German " south " Ninth	6	"
French " " " Twenty-second............	6	"
" " " " Eighteenth......	4	"
State " " " Eighteenth......	6	"

NORTH AND SOUTH STREETS.			SIZE.	KIND.
State	street	11.10 feet S. of south line of Twelfth‡	1½	J., H. & Co.
"	"	north line of Second	4	Eddy.
"	"	" " Front.	4	"
"	"	south " Eleventh*....................	4	"
"	"	north " Eleventh*....................	4	"
Peach	"	" " Fourth*................:...........	4	"
"	"	" " Seventh*	6	"
Sassafras	"	south " Eighth	4	"
"	"	north " Tenth*	4	::
"	"	165 ft. S. of south line of Tenth†	4	
"	"	165 " " " " Eleventh†	4	"
"	"	140 " " " " Twelfth†	4	..
"	"	184 N. north " Fourteenth †	4	"
"	"	126.5 S. south " Fifteenth†	4	"
Myrtle	"	south line of Nineteenth..................	6	".
"	"	15 feet S. of south line of Eighteenth‡	1½	J., H. & Co.
"	"	south line of Twenty-first.	6	Eddy.
"	"	" " Twenty-sixth.........	6	"
"	"	" " Short.	4	"
"	"	" " Second	4	"
Walnut	"	north " Fifth	6	"
"	"	17.6 ft. N. of north line of Eighteenth‡	1½	J., H. & Co.
Cherry	"	south line of Eighth..........	6	Eddy.
Poplar	"	north " Eleventh	6	"

‡On pipe leading to cart sprinkling hydrant.
*In place of old one.
†On account of recent street paving.

RECAPITULATION.

Six-inch valves in new locations..30
Four-inch " " " 27
" " in place of old ones...... 5
Six-inch " " four-inch.......................... 1
Twelve-inch valve in new location.... 1
One-and-a-half-inch valves in new locations.................................... 4

————

Total 68

TOTAL NUMBER AND SIZE IN USE.

Four-inch and less. 339		Thirty-inch........ 3
Six-inch......... ... .151		———
Twelve-inch 17		Total 526
Twenty-inch........................... 16		

EXHIBIT J.

Number of Families, Stores, Offices, Manufacturers, &c., Supplied with City Water During the Year 1887.

Breweries	8	Jail and Court House	1
Board of Trade	1	Laundries	7
Boat Houses	5	Lumber Yards	4
Bakeries	13	Livery Stables	15
Butcher Shops	51	Manufactories	75
Barber Shops	35	Malt Houses	3
Banks	6	Orphan Asylums	2
Billiard Rooms	5	Opera House	1
Bottling Works	7	Oil Works	2
Coffee and Spice Mills	1	Offices	273
Churches	13	Old Folks Home	1
Cemeteries	1	Photograph Galleries	7
Coal and Iron Docks	1	Police Station	1
Club House	1	Public Halls	30
Custom House	1	Packing Houses	2
Convent	1	Printing Offices	9
Driving Park	1	Passenger Depots	2
Dyeing Works	1	Railroads	4
Engine Houses	6	Railroad Shops	2
Express Offices	2	Rink	1
Electric Light Co	1	Soldiers' Home	1
Fish Hatchery	1	Schools	22
Fish Houses	4	Stores	420
Families	4,829	Saloons and Eating Houses	201
Families, by permits	77	Slaughter Houses	16
Freight Houses	3	Street Railway	1
Fountains, private	6	Transfer Co	1
" public	2	U. S. Signal Station	1
" drinking	2	Work Shops	79
Flouring Mills	4	Watering Troughs	16
Gas Works	1	U. S. Steamer Michigan	1
Grain Elevators	3		
Green Houses	3	Total	6,867
Hospital	2	Last Enumeration	6,040
Hotels and Boarding Houses	70		
Ice Houses	2	Increase	827
Internal Revenue Office	1		

EXHIBIT K.

PUMPING ENGINE STATISTICS FOR 1887.

The Pumps are three in number. Two are known as the Cornish Bull
Pumps. The diameter of each plunger is 20¾ inches, and each has
a stroke of 10 feet. The capacity of each pump is estimated to be
165 gallons to every stroke. The third pump is a new one, put in
operation in the early part of the year, and known as the Gaskill
Horizontal Pumping Engine, of a guaranteed capacity of 5,000,000
gallons daily at a piston speed of 120 feet per minute against a head
of 237 feet. The stand-pipe is 251 feet high. The reservoir is nearly
two miles from the Pumping Works, the bottom of which is 210 feet
above the surface of the bay, and the water has been maintained
during the year at an average depth in the reservoir of about 24
feet.

MONTHS.	Days a single Cornish Pump was opera'd.	Days both Cornish Pumps were opera'd.	Days Gaskill Pump was operated.	Strokes of Cornish Pumps.	Revolutions of Gaskill Pump.	Gallons Pumped.	Daily Average of Gallons Pumped.	Average Lift in Feet.	Lbs. of Slack Coal each Month.	Cost of Coal for Pumping.
Jan'y ..	15	16	....	604,898	....	99,725,670	3,216,957	232.91	635,700	$397 81
Feb'y ..	4	19	....	531,045	....	87,622,425	3,129,372	233.81	651,765	402 75
Mar....	15	8	8	413,062	88,115	84,192,160	2,715,876	239.13	571,970	395 63
Apr....	....	....	30	....	471,500	85,813,000	2,860,433	232.32	400,850	316 90
May....	2	....	29	10,660	570,713	105,628,666	3,407,376	235.37	397,600	262 75
June...	9	14	9	458,351	133,919	100,086,173	3,336,205	235.00	505,980	290 88
July ...	2	15	14	377,461	227,608	121,905,721	3,932,443	235.35	577,710	332 18
Aug....	....	....	31	....	654,530	119,124,460	3,842,724	234.57	408,805	335 07
Sept...	....	....	30	....	565,530	102,926,460	3,430,883	235.14	377,580	216 53
Oct	3	....	28	23,367	539,825	102,103,705	3,293,668	234.98	384,030	221 16
Nov....	....	....	30	....	570,565	103,842,830	3,461,428	235.40	361,850	207 11
Dec....	....	1	29	1,882	576,594	105,242,388	3,394,915	234.49	367,090	211 04
	80	73	238	2,415,176	4,503,899	1,218,213,658	3,335,190	234.23	5,641,470	$3,589 81

The regular employees at the pumping works are 1 mechanical engineer, 2 assistant engineers, 3 firemen and 1 watchman. The mechanical engineer stands a watch of 5 hours, from 7 to 12 every forenoon; the
assistants divide the remainder of each day equally between them; each
one of the firemen stands a watch of 8 hours. Besides firing, the firemen unload the coal from the cars, except when both pumps are run,
in which case they are assisted by the watchman or a laborer. The
mechanical engineer gives 10 hours daily to the service of the Department, the hours when he is not on watch being employed in repairs,
supervision, etc. In addition to standing their regular watch, the assistant engineers aid their superior officer in keeping the machinery in
order. The watchman takes care of the buildings and grounds, besides
doing such other work as may be required of him.

EXHIBIT L.

Amount of Coal Consumed in Pumping, Gallons of Water Pumped, Average Height Pumped, Cost per Million Gallons, etc., from the First Year the Works were Operated to December 31, 1887.

Year	Tons of coal consumed.	Price of coal per ton from May 1st of each year.	Cost of coal.	Grades of bituminous coal.	Gallons of water pumped.	Increase or decrease.	Number of places supplied.	Number of fire hydrants.	Average height of water in reservoir above surface of bay.	Cost of coal per million gallons raised to reservoir.	Cost of coal per million gallons raised 1 foot.	Gallons raised 1 foot by 1 pound of coal.	Gallons raised to reservoir by 1 pound of coal.
											Cts.		
1868	59.1	$5 05	$ 309 61	Lump									
1869	544.4	5 05	4,818 48	"									
1870	1,064.5	5 05	5,159 10	"	246,648,960		1,218	97	232.0				
1871	1,422.7	5 05	7,117 00	"	179,363,495	132,719,585 i.	1,727	99	232.0	$18 76	8.0	32,656	98.5
1872	1,308.5	5 05	6,528 50	"	395,076,000	115,708,505 i.	2,140	103	232.0	16 52	7.6	35,092	150.9
1873	1,672.5	5 05	8,412 65	"	384,062,415	11,013,585 d.	2,475	107	232.0	21 90	9.4	26,636	114.8
1874	1,759.0	4 85	7,709 54	"	444,817,395	60,754,980 i.	2,663	107	232.0	17 33	7.1	29,294	126.4
1875	1,836.4	4 85	8,657 61	"	531,005,475	86,181,080 i.	2,700	110	232.0	16 30	6.9	33,772	145.5
1876	2 105.1	4 00	8,925 22	"	670,726,650	139,721,175 i.	2,763	112	232.0	13 30	5.6	36,969	159.8
1877	2,456.6	3 70	8,509 83	"	660,981,810	9,744,840 d.	2,854	114	232.0	12 75	5.4	31,491	135.7
1878	2,463.3	3 35	7,945 37	"	682,392,315	21,390,505 i.	2,915	115	232.0	11 64	4.9	31,065	136.4
1879	2,628.1	3 09	7,488 92	"	807,800,400	125,408,085 i.	3,011	121	233.0	9 19	3.9	35,633	153.6
1880	3,076.1	1 99	6,978 41	"	775,805,250	31,995,150 i.	3,568	126	232.0	8 99	3.8	39,284	126.0
1881	3,490.3	1 90	6,517 58	Slack	975,640,634	200,235,684 i.	4,110	161	233.0	6 68	2.8	32,590	143.2
1882	2,968.2	1 75	5,355 93	"	829,759,260	145,881,674 d.	4,687	171	234.0	6 45	2.7	32,700	189.7
1883	2,398.2	1 55	3,906 59	"	815,989,685	13,819,575 d.	5,077	197	234.7	4 66	1.9	39,900	170.0
1884	3,010.8	1 45	4,502 61	"	917,781,350	101,841,665 i.	5,395	248	234.3	4 99	2.0	35,712	152.4
1885	3,243.8	1 30	4,575 79	"	1,036,496,665	118,715,815 i.	5,658	270	232.9	4 40	1.8	37,208	159.7
1886	3,369.0	1 25	4,818 64	"	1,117,389,075	80,892,410 i.	6,140	280	233.3	3 86	1.6	39,704	165.8
1887	2,820.4	1 15	3,589 31	"	1,218,213,688	106,824,588 i.	6,368	318	234.1	2 95	1 2	50,544	216.0

EXHIBIT M.

HOW CITY WATER MAY BE WASTED.

Gallons and Hundredths of Gallons of Water that will be Discharged per Minute Through Various Sized Orifices at the Heads Stated.

Head in Feet.	Pressure per Square Inch.	DIAMETER OF ORIFICES IN INCHES AND FRACTIONS OF AN INCH.													
		1/64	1/32	1/16	1/8	1/4	3/8	1/2	5/8	3/4	1	1¼	1½	1¾	2
20	8 66	0 02	0 07	0 30	1 20	5 10	11 70	20 60	32 20	46 20	82 30	128 40	184 80	252 00	338 80
40	17 32	0 02	0 11	0 45	1 80	7 40	16 30	29 60	45 50	65 50	116 50	182 40	261 60	356 40	465 60
60	25 99	0 03	0 14	0 55	2 20	8 90	20 00	35 60	57 70	80 30	142 80	223 20	320 40	436 80	571 20
80	34 65	0 04	0 16	0 65	2 60	10 30	23 80	41 20	64 30	92 60	164 40	258 00	370 80	505 20	658 80
100	43 31	0 04	0 18	0 75	3 10	11 50	25 90	46 10	72 00	103 70	183 70	288 60	415 20	565 20	738 00
120	51 98	0 05	0 19	0 78	3 10	12 60	28 80	50 40	78 80	113 50	201 60	315 60	453 60	624 40	807 60
140	60 64	0 05	0 21	0 85	3 40	13 60	30 60	54 50	85 20	122 40	217 90	340 80	490 80	668 40	872 40
150	64 97	0 05	0 22	0 88	3 50	14 10	31 70	56 40	88 20	127 90	225 60	352 80	507 60	691 20	902 40
175	75 80	0 06	0 24	0 95	3 80	15 20	34 20	61 00	95 30	136 80	243 60	380 40	548 40	748 80	975 60
200	86 83	0 06	0 26	1 02	4 00	16 30	36 60	65 20	101 80	146 40	260 40	406 00	588 00	798 00	1043 80
235	101 08	0 07	0 28	1 12	4 50	17 90	41 30	71 50	137 70	185 80	285 20	445 90	642 20	871 80	1140 80

The bottom of the Erie Reservoir is 210 feet above the surface of Presque Isle Bay, from which the water is pumped, and the water in the Reservoir is kept at an average height of nearly 24 feet, or 234 feet above the bay. The pressure at the points named below will give an idea of the average throughout the city: Twenty-fourth and Sassafras streets, 20 lbs.; Twenty-third and Myrtle, 30 lbs.; Twentieth and Chestnut, 40 lbs.; Eighteenth and Peach, 50 lbs.; Fourteenth and State, 60 lbs.; Eighth and State, 70 lbs.; Third and State, 80 lbs.; Front and State, 100 lbs.

The wire of which pins are made is one-sixty-fourth of an inch in diameter—No. 27, wire gauge. A stream the size of a cambric needle is made of wire one-thirty-second of an inch in diameter—No. 21, wire gauge. The finest cambric needle, running one year with head of 235 feet, will flow 147,168 gallons, equaling 4,600 barrels, the value of which—counting at the rate of 10 cents per 1,000 gallons—is $14.71. A stream the size of a cambric needle, running at the same pressure, for the same time, will flow 36,792 gallons, at a cost of $3 68.

EXHIBIT L.

Amount of Coal Consumed in Pumping, Gallons of Water Pumped, Average Height Pumped, Cost per Million Gallons, etc., from the First Year the Works were Operated to December 31, 1887.

Year.	Tons of coal consumed.	Price of coal per ton from May 1st of each year.	Cost of coal.	Grades of bituminous coal.	Gallons of water pumped.	Increase or decrease.	Number of places supplied.	Number of fire hydrants.	Average height of water in reservoir above surface of bay.	Cost of coal per million gallons raised to reservoir.	Cost of coal per million gallons raised 1 foot.	Gallons raised 1 foot by 1 pound of coal.	Gallons raised to reservoir by 1 pound of coal.
											Cts.		
1868	59.1	$5 05	$309 61	Lump	246,648,960								
1869	544.4	5 05	4,818 48	"	179,369,495	132,719,585 i.							
1870	1,064.5	5 05	5,159 10	"	395,076,000	115,708,505 i.	1,218	97					
1871	1,422.7	5 05	7,117 00	"	384,062,415	11,018,585 d.	1,727	99	232.0	$18 76	8.0	22,656	98.5
1872	1,308.5	5 05	6,528 50	"	444,817,395	60,754,980 i.	2,140	103	232.0	16 52	7.6	35,092	150.9
1873	1,672.5	4 85	8,412 65	"	531,005,475	86,181,080 i.	2,475	107	232.0	21 90	9.4	26,036	114.8
1874	1,759.0	4 85	7,709 54	"	670,726,650	139,721,175 i.	2,663	107	232.0	17 33	7.1	29,294	126.4
1875	1,836.4	4 00	8,657 61	"	660,981,810	9,744,840 d.	2,700	110	232.0	16 30	6.9	33,772	145.5
1876	2,105.1	3 70	8,925 23	"	682,392,815	21,390,505 i.	2,763	112	232.0	13 30	5.6	36,959	159.8
1877	2,456.6	3 35	8,509 33	"	807,800,400	125,408,085 i.	2,854	114	232.0	12 75	5.4	31,491	135.7
1878	2,463.3	3 09	7,945 37	"	775,805,250	31,995,150 i.	2,915	115	232.0	11 64	4.9	31,665	136.4
1879	2,628.1	1 99	7,428 92	"	975,640,694	200,285,684 i.	3,011	121	232.0	9 19	3.9	35,658	163.6
1880	3,076.1	1 90	6,978 41	Slack	829,759,260	145,881,674 d.	3,568	126	232.0	8 99	3.8	29,234	126.0
1881	3,490.3	1 75	6,517 58	"	815,939,685	13,819,575 d.	4,110	161	232.0	6 68	2.8	32,990	143.2
1882	2,968.2	1 55	5,255 93	"	917,781,350	101,841,665 i.	4,687	171	234.0	6 45	2.7	32,706	139.7
1883	2,398.2	1 45	3,908 59	"	1,036,496,665	118,715,315 i.	5,077	197	234.7	4 66	1.9	32,900	170.0
1884	3,010.8	1 30	4,502 61	"	1,118,715,315	80,892,410 i.	5,395	248	234.3	4 99	2.0	35,712	152.4
1885	3,243.8	1 25	4,575 79	"	1,117,389,075	106,824,583 i.	5,658	270	232.9	4 40	1.8	37,208	159.7
1886	3,369.0	1 15	4,318 64	"	1,218,213,688		6,140	280	233.3	3 86	1.6	39,704	165.8
1887	2,820.4	1 15	3,589 31	"			6,868	318	234.1	2 95	1.2	50,544	216.0

EXHIBIT O.

Cost of Water to the Average Householder in Twenty-five Cities, Compiled from Official Reports to this Department.

CITIES.	Population 1880.	Family Charge	Pan Water Closet.	Self-closing Urinal.	Bath Tub.	Self-closing Wash-stand	Permanent Wash Tub	Two Horses	Cow.	Street Sprinkler.	Total
Allegheny City	78,000	8 75	3 00	2 00	3 00	1 00	1 50	1 50	75	8 00	24 50
Boston	302,000	7 00	5 00	2 50	5 00	5 00	5 00	2 00	75	5 00	87 25
Buffalo	156,000	7 20	3 50	3 00	8 00	1 00	2 00	2 40	90	2 50	25 50
Chicago	503,000	6 00	3 00	1 00	8 00	......	2 00	4 00	......	8 00	21 75
Columbus, Ohio	51,000	6 00	3 00	3 00	4 00	2 00	5 00	3 50	3 00	5 80	82 80
Dayton, Ohio	38,000	6 00	2 50	4 00	2 00	1 25	2 00	3 00	1 00	3 00	45 30
Detroit	116,000	7 00	4 00	3 00	2 00	1 00	2 00	4 00	1 00	4 00	28 85
Erie	35,000	6 00	3 00	8 00	3 00	......	2 00	4 00	......	3 00	21 75
East Saginaw, Mich	19,000	7 00	2 50	2 00	8 00	1 00	2 00	4 00	75	8 00	26 50
Fall River, Mass	49,000	5 00	5 00	2 00	5 00	1 00	2 00	4 00	1 00	6 00	31 00
Grand Rapids, Mich	32,000	8 00	4 00	3 00	8 50	......	2 00	2 50	1 00	6 00	88 00
Indianapolis	75,000	5 00	3 00	3 00	3 00	2 50	4 50	5 00	......	6 00	82 00
Lawrence, Mass	39,000	5 00	4 00	2 00	3 00	1 00	1 00	8 00	1 50	10 00	85 90
Milwaukee	115,000	6 00	2 00	7 50	3 00	1 50	......	3 00	1 00	3 80	22 00
Minneapolis	47,000	4 00	3 00	2 50	3 00	1 00	1 50	2 00	1 00	5 00	26 00
Newark, N. J	136,000	6 25	2 50	2 50	2 50	1 00	2 00	2 50	1 50	3 00	28 85
New York	1,200,000	6 00	10 00	3 00	5 00	1 00	2 00	2 00	75	8 00	88 75
Omaha, Neb	30,000	6 75	2 50	5 00	8 00	1 00	2 00	5 00	75	......	80 00
Philadelphia	847,000	5 00	5 00	1 50	3 00	1 00	1 00	2 00	75	5 00	28 75
Pittsburgh	156,000	9 00	3 00	2 50	4 00	1 00	2 00	2 50	1 50	5 00	28 50
Sandusky, Ohio	15,838	6 00	2 50	2 50	3 00	1 00	......	4 50	1 50	8 00	25 50
St. Paul (1885)	41,000	8 00	4 00	2 40	3 20	1 00	2 00	4 80	......	2 40	24 80
Syracuse	52,000	8 00	4 00	2 50	4 00	1 00	2 00	3 00	75	6 00	81 75
Toledo	50,000	5 50	2 50	2 50	3 50	1 00	2 00	5 00	1 50	5 00	28 50
Utica	34,000	7 00	6 00	3 00	5 00	1 00	......	6 00	1 50	8 00	81 50

RATES FOR CITY WATER.

All are annual, except as otherwise indicated.

Bath Tub, private...$	3 00
" " " each additional..	1 50
" " public..	5 00
Bakery, per barrel of flour used, (but no charge less than $5)............	01
Barber Shop, including Hand Basin, first chair............................	4 00
" " " " " each additional chair................	2 00
Blacksmith Shop, one fire..	5 00
" " each additional fire..................................	2 50
Boarding House (in addition to family rates), per room...................	1 00
Brewery, per barrel brewed...	03
Building purposes, per bushel lime.......................................	02
Butcher Stalls...........	3 00 to 15 00
Charitable Institutions, one-third annual rates..........................	
Cow..	75
Condensing boiler for steam heating, (per season of six months) per horse power...	50
Eating Houses..	5 00 to 25 00
Family...	5 00
Hand Basin, for Dwellings, Hotels and Schools, first basin...............	1 00
" " " " each additional...................	50
" " in Offices, Stores and Blocks, each............	1 00
Hotel (in addition to family rates), per room............................	1 00
Livery Stable, per horse...	2 00
Maltster, per 1,000 bushels of malt......................................	1 75
Offices..	3 00 to 10 00
Private Stable, one or two horses..	2 00
" " each additional horse.............................	1 00
Printing Offices...	5 00 to 30 00
Public Halls...	5 00 to 25 00
Saloons..	5 00 to 25 00
Stores...	3 00 to 15 00
Schools, per pupil...	10
Steam Engine, 10 hours per day, each horse power.........................	2 50
Slaughter Houses...	5 00 to 50 00
Sleeping Room..	1 00
Sprinkling Streets or Lawns with hose (per season).......................	3 00 and up.
Urinal, private, self-closing..	2 00
" public, "	3 00
" not self-closing...	3 00 to 10 00
" continuous flow..	10 00 to 50 00
Wash Tub, (permanent, with waste)..	2 00
" " " " " each additional..................	1 00
Watering Trough, public..	10 00
Water Closet, (pan) private..	3 00
" " " " each additional........................	1 50
" " " public...................................	5 00
" " (hopper), private................................	6 00
" " " public.................................	10 00
Work Shop, (ordinary use)..	3 00 to 5 00

All other uses, when not metered, to be assessed by the Department.

METER RATES (PER QUARTER.)

Daily Average, 15,000 gallons or less..	10	cents.
" 15,000 to 20,000 gallons..................................	9½	"
" 20,000 to 25,000 "	9	"
" 25,000 to 30,000 "	8½	"
" 30,000 to 35,000 "	8	"
" 35,000 to 40,000 "	7½	"
" 40,000 to 45,000 "	7	"
" 45,000 to 50,000 "	6½	"
" More than 50,000 gallons...................................	6	"

——OF THE——

ARD OF WATER COMMISSIONERS,

OF ERIE, PA.,

——TO THE——

MAYOR AND CITY COUNCILS,

——FOR THE——

YEAR ENDING DEC. 31, 1888.

ERIE, PA.
HERALD PRINTING & PUBLISHING CO., LTD.
1889.

WATER COMMISSIONERS

The Water Commissioners are appointed by the Court of Common Pleas of Erie County, Pa., for a term of three years, one member being named annually, in May.

EX-MEMBERS OF THE BOARD.

*WM. L. SCOTT, 1867 to 1868.
*HENRY RAWLE, 1867 to 1872.
*WM. W. REED, 1867 to 1879.
†JOHN C. SELDEN, 1868 to 1872.
MATTHEW R. BARR, 1872 to 1877.

JOHN GENSHEIMER, 1872 to 1878.
M. LIEBEL, 1877 to 1886.
J. M. BRYANT, 1878 to 1881.
G. W. F. SHERWIN, 1879 to 1885
BENJ. WHITMAN, 1881 to 1887.

*Messrs. Scott, Rawle and Reed, the first Commissioners, were appointed respectively for terms of one, two and three years.
†Mr. Selden resigned before the expiration of his second term; Mr. Barr was substituted by the Board and afterward appointed by the Court.

THE PRESENT BOARD.

GEO. W. STARR, 1885 to 1891.   C. KESSLER, 1886 to 1889.
C. J. BROWN, 1887 to 1890.

OFFICERS OF THE DEPARTMENT.

President of the Board—GEO. W. STARR.
Secretary and Treasurer—B. F. SLOAN.
Assistant Secretary—GEO. C. GENSHEIMER.
Clerk—WILL W. REED.
Superintendent of Street Work—WM. O'LONE.
Imspectors—A. F. CRANE, F. W. KOEHLER, JOHN D. SPAFFORD
Mechanical Engineer—F. A. ROTH.
Assistant Mechanical Engineers—GEO. R. MILLER, JOHN KELLY.
Firemen—R. W. SIMONS, JOSEPH BURNS, JACOB MULLEN.
Watchman at Pumping Works—THOS. TIDMAN.
Keeper of Reservoir and Grounds—SAMUEL PFISTER.

OFFICE—No. 18 East Seventh Street, between French and State.
OFFICE HOURS From 7:30 A. M. to 5:45 P. M.; Monday Evenings from 7:30 to 9:00 P. M.
REGULAR MEETINGS OF THE BOARD—Every Saturday at 3:00 P. M.

ANNUAL REPORT.

To the Mayor and Councils of the City of Erie:

GENTLEMEN—The administration of the Water Department for the year just closed, has presented no new features. Its business has been transacted quietly, but none the less effectively, the revenues slightly increasing as its work has extended. Its principal outlays beyond the ordinary expenses in the extension of mains, connections, etc., have been in repairs to the Reservoir, and the works at the foot of Chestnut street, rendered necessary at the Reservoir by the abrasion of the sides of the basin by the ice, and at the works by the decaying roof of the boiler house, and the leakage of water during storms through the outside sloping walls in the third story of the original pumping house, keeping it damp with dripping water, loosening the plaster from the inside walls and rapidly tending to their disintegration. These repairs are believed to have been thoroughly made, and after the buildings have been painted in the coming Spring, will require no more than the ordinary attention for many years.

The results of the year's work are given in detail in the succeeding pages of this report, and may thus be briefly stated, viz: 423 tons less of coal consumed than in 1887, a reduction in cost of fuel of $1,043.85, over 9 per cent increase of water rents, and over 123½ millions of gallons pumped and delivered more than in any twelve months before since the works were erected.

The following is a summary of receipts and expenses:—

RECEIPTS.

Balance in office Jan. 1, 1888	$ 351 67
" City Treasury Jan. 1, 1888	6,251 20
From Water Rents	73,197 03
" all other sources	1,579 82
Total	$81,379 72

Paid on account of Construction..................$31,096 54
"   "   Maintenance................. 17,640 56
"   "   Extraordinary expenses...... 3,267 09
" Sinking Fund Commissioners towards redemp- ·
tion of Water Bonds........................ 23,000 00
Balance in City Treasury Dec. 31, 1888........... 5,697 01
"   "   Office, Dec. 31, 1888............... 678 52

Total.....................................$81,379 72

Under the head 'Construction,' is included $6,007.75 which
represents the last instalment and interest due on the new Gaskill pump, and which was paid in January. Deduct this sum,
and we have $24,888,79 as the amount strictly chargeable to that
account. There have been no losses by the bursting of pipes,
and but slight repairs to connections, those of the latter being
necessary only to replace old ones laid many years ago, which
were of inferior iron and had rusted out.

The difference in the cost of fuel is owing, besides the economy
of the new pumping engine, to a lessened price for coal—the
continued use of the same quality, (no experiments having been
tried) and the contract requiring a given number of gallons of
water to be lifted by a given weight of coal. The outcome is
eminently satisfactory, inasmuch as it is believed that the true
solution of the problem—how to obtain the best results in the use
of steam fuel—has been found.

THE GASKILL PUMPING ENGINE.

The new Gaskill Pumping Engine has fully met the expectations of the Board, and has proved to be all that was guaranteed by
the builders, economical in its workings and altogether superior
in its simplicity and power and ease of management for the
heavy work needed to lift large quantities of water to the height
required to supply the City. There has been no necessary stoppage of the engines for any length of time. Its economy in fuel
was shown in 1887, when the new pump had been run for only
a part of the year. Its constant use in 1888, resulted, under the

conditions hereinbefore stated, in a saving in cost of fuel to the amount of $1,043.85 less by that sum than in any former year when the whole work was done by the old pumps, and without taking into account the added millions of gallons of water raised. The last year's service proves to be a saving of over 40 per cent on cost of coal in 1886, when the old pumps alone were used, and a gain of over 10 per cent on number of gallons of water raised in 1887.

PUMPAGE.

There have been raised and delivered during the year 1,341,-708,002 gallons, an increase over the supply of any previous year of 123,494,314 gallons. This is an average supply per day to the City of 3,675,912 gallons, or an average daily increase over the year previous of 340,722 gallons, showing a gradual but steady progress in the demand for water, no large quantity having been diverted from ordinary use by extensive fires or by losses in breakage of mains.

STOP VALVES, CONNECTIONS, METERS, WATER TAKERS.

Thirty-six new Stop Valves have been added to the number heretofore in use, to wit: thirty of 6 inches, and six of 4 inches. Three of 6 and 4 inches were taken out and replaced by three of 12 inches. Whole number, 562.

Four hundred and sixty-three connections with mains have been made, most of them for immediate use, the remainder laid in streets newly paved, as required by ordinance.

The number of meters and counters is 80, a gain of four from last year.

Of water takers, including manufactories, families, &c., 231 have been added to those of previous year.

Whole number of consumers in the city, 6598.

MAINS.

Three miles and 255 3-12 feet of mains were laid in 1888, 1436 feet of small pipe has been taken up, 13,425 feet of 6-inch, 1391 feet of 4-inch, and 1420 feet of 12-inch have been laid in the streets, besides 1200 feet of 3-inch and 96 feet of 4-inch, laid in private grounds.

The 1420 feet of 12 inches was laid in 26th street west of the Reservoir, and extended to Poplar street, replacing the smaller pipe found insufficient to furnish supply for fire purposes, on account of light pressure and want of connection with mains in the cross streets to effect circulation. It is believed that this large pipe will be ample for all purposes, and when connected with mains in other streets, will serve as a feeder for all property lying on either side of the ridge on which it is laid.

HYDRANTS.

Thirteen hydrants have been set along the streets, in addition to those before placed. Four old ones have been removed and new ones substituted. All of them are of the Mathews pattern, Whole number now in the City, including 30 on private property, 333. Each one of these hydrants is connected with the mains by a four-inch pipe, and notwithstanding the difference of pressure, they are all available for use at fires without the aid of a fire engine.

This was clearly shown at the fire in November last, at the corner of Fifth and Sassafras streets, when of the eight streams playing, four were from the hydrants direct, and were very effective. In no other city known to the department, is there ready means so efficient for fire protection without the aid of an expensive apparatus. Connected with a sprinkler only a $\frac{3}{4}$-inch hose may prevent a great disaster, as its prompt application has often proved, and it is ever at hand for use. The lightest pressure at any hydrant is sufficient to throw a stream through a $2\frac{1}{4}$ inch hose, with an inch nozzle, a distance of twenty feet, and (as the pressure varies with the elevation of the streets,) at its greatest force, a solid stream will reach from 100 to 120 feet. These statements are reliable, as trials were made some time since, by order of the Board, and were verified by actual experiment. at every hydrant then fixed in place. The advantage of such ready means of protection in an emergency, is but little regarded, but its benefits can hardly be overestimated.

CREDITS.

The sum credited by the City to the Water Department for water furnished city offices, fire engine and hose houses, public fountains, for over 300 hydrants, and for all public uses is—nothing. The City Controller in his report makes mention of this supply to the city, and places his estimate of its value at the small sum of $13,000.

The Department is thankful for this, the first recognition of its general service without pay or credit for 20 years, ever made by any City official in a public report.

He also acknowledges the "contribution," by this Department, of the sum of $23,000 towards the redemption of the Water Bonds of the City.

It may be in the course of time, that justice so long prayed for, will be done the Water Department, by the opening of an account with it, and giving it credit not only for the money received, but for services rendered.

Attention is respectfully called to the fact that a large and populous part of the City lying between Wayne street and East Avenue north of Sixth street, is entirely without fire protection and water for domestic use. Applications have been repeatedly made to the Board by the Taxpayers of that district, for relief, but until Perry street shall be opened from 6th to 5th street, extensions of the necessary water mains are impracticable.

The question of Sewerage is of great interest to this Department as it bears directly on the source of supply of water to our people. Last year it was understood that plans had been drawn to sewer a large portion of the City, and to take the sewerage of the section proposed to be drained, away from and outside of the Bay. On examination, it was ascertained that such drainage was to have been carried into the old canal basin. Fortunately no such scheme was carried out. This Board has repeatedly called attention to this subject, and again reiterates the views so often expressed, that whenever the City shall undertake such work, inasmuch as the health of our citizens and the growth of our population, depends greatly upon the purity of the water so generally used in our dwellings, too great care cannot be exercised in securing perfect drainage, WITHOUT POLLUTING THE SOURCE FROM WHICH WATER IS DRAWN FOR GENERAL SUPPLY. Strangers are attracted to our growing City by reason of its location on the Bay, by the facilities for transacting business by land or water carriage, by its generally admitted healthfulness, its delightful summer climate, and its cheap and abundant supply of water. Put in question the quality of the water furnished, by refusing or neglecting to take every means possible to secure its purity, and one of the principal inducements to an increased immigration or settlement here, has been lost. If this loss shall be due to the indifference of those who are elected to represent the people the responsibility will rest on a few in number, but the resulting effects will be felt by our whole community. The Board therefore respectfully but earnestly urges the City Government to adopt some plan by which the Sewerage of the City shall be carried outside the Bay, and to require that in future all proposed Sewers shall be made to conform with that plan.

However unpleasant it is to repeatedly urge such action in this matter, the Board are unanimous in the opinion that they will not have done their duty to the public, unless they persist in calling the attention of the City Authorities (the only persons having control over the subject) to the necessity of such action as shall result in a general and complete remedy for evils which threaten to impair, if not eventually to destroy, the usefulness of this Department.

Respectfully Submitted,

GEO. W. STARR,

C. KESSLER,

C. J. BROWN,

Water Commissioners.

Erie, February 16, 1889.

EXHIBIT A.

Receipts of the Erie Water Department for the Year Ending December 31, 1883.

WATER RENTS.				
First quarter—January	$7,523 44			
" " —February	6,626 95			
" " —March	2,411 53			
		$16,561 92		
Second quarter—April	6,706 19			
" " —May	7,655 63			
" " —June	3,507 24			
		17,869 06		
Third quarter—July	7,755 76			
" " —August	8,231 88			
" " —September	2,937 54			
		18,925 18		
Fourth quarter—October	8,671 12			
" " —November	7,741 65			
" " —December	3,428 10			
		19,840 87		
			$73,197 03	
From Plumbing, Sale of Material, etc		1,579 82		
Balance December 31, 1887		351 67		
			1,931 49	
Total from all scources			$75,128 52	
CR.				
Deposits in Treasury, 1st quarter		16,800 00		
" " 2d "		17,900 00		
" " 3d "		19,250 00		
" " 4tb "		20,500 00		
			74,450 00	
Balance December 31, 1888			$ 678 52	

EXHIBIT B.

Account of Water Department with City Treasurer for the Year Ending December 31, 1888.

DR.			
To balance in Treasury Dec, 31, 1887.	$6,251 20		
" deposits to " 31, 1888	74,450 00		$80,701 20
CR.			
Warrants drawn 1st quarter—Jan.	6,869 19		
" " " " —Feb	1,880 04		
" " " " —Mar	2,212 91		
		$10,962 14	
Warrants drawn, 2nd quarter Apr.	2,674 25		
" " " " —May	4,327 77		
" " " " —June	21,645 31		
		28,647 33	
Warrants drawn, 3rd quarter—July.	5,560 14		
" " " " —Aug.	7,199 96		
" " " " —Sept.	6,136 85		
		18,896 95	
Warrants drawn, 4th quarter—Oct.	8,511 02		
" " " " —Nov.	3 835 85		
" " " " —Dec..	4,150 90		
		16,497 77	
Total deposits...........			$75,004 19
Balance in Treasury, Dec. 31, 1888.	....	....	$5,697 01

(*Continued on page* 11).

EXHIBIT B--Continued.

CONTROLLER'S AUDIT.

Water Commissioners' Cash and Warrant account, also account with City Treasurer for the year 1888.

Cash on hand January 1, 1888......	$	351 67
Received from Water Rents..		73,197 03
" " other sources..		1,579 82
Total...	$75,128 52	
Amount paid City Treasurer...		74,450 00
Amount Cash on hand and in Bank..	$	678 52

Warrants outstanding January 1, 1888..	$	1,115 99
Amount of Warrants issued during the year............................		75,004 19
Total Warrants...	$76,120 18	
Warrants paid during the year...		75,556 53
Warrants outstanding January 1, 1889..	$	563 65

Balance to the credit of Water Commissioners in City Treasury January 1, 1888.........	$	7,367 19
Total Receipts by City Treasurer...		74,450 00
Total........	$81,817 19	
Warrants paid by Treasurer during 1888		75,556 53
Balance to the credit of Water Commissioners in City Treasury January, 1, 1889...		$ 6,260 66

OFFICE OF CITY CONTROLLER,
ERIE. Pa., Feb. 4, 1889.

I hereby certify that the above statement has been carefully compared with the Records in the offices of the City Treasurer and Water Commissioners and found correct, and that the balance, six thousand two hundred and sixty dollars and $\frac{66}{100}$ dollars, ($6,260.66) was due the Water Commissioners by the City Treasurer, January 1, 1889.

CHAS. S. CLARKE,
City Controller.

EXHIBIT C.

Expenditures for the year 1888. also from Commencement of Works in 1867 to January 1. 1888.

FUEL AT WORKS.	FROM JAN. 1, 1888 TO DEC. 31, 1888.		1867 TO 1888
From Com't of works to Dec. 31. 1887			$120,897 63
Paid R. J. Saltsman, 2,161,300 lbs. coal at $1.15	$1,260 10		
Paid R. J. Saltsman, 86,100 lbs. coal at $1.80	77 49		
Paid R. J. Saltsman, 75,400 lbs. coal at $1.65	62 21		
Paid F. P. Coal Co., 3,087,000 lbs. coal 92.8	1,426 93		
Paid for labor	14 25		
		$2,840 98	
SALARIES.			
From Com't of works to Dec. 31. 1887.			$108,795 98
Paid B. F. Sloan Sec. & Treas	$1,320 00		
" Geo. C. Gensheimer, Asst. Sec	1,010 00		
" Wm O'Lone, Supt. St. Work	1,080 00		
" A. F. Crane, Inspector	840 00		
" F. W. Koehler, "	660 00		
" John D. Spafford "	500 00		
" Will W. Reed, et al Clerk	470 00		
" Geo. W. Starr, Commissioner	650 00		
" C. Kessler, "	650 00		
" C. J. Brown, "	675 00		
		$7,855 00	
ENGINEERS AND FIREMEN.			
From Com't of works to Dec. 31. 1887.			$76,054 45
Paid F. A. Roth, Engineer	$1,080 00		
" Geo. R. Miller, "	840 00		
" John Kelley, "	840 00		
" R. W. Simons, Fireman	555 00		
" Jos. Burns, "	555 00		
" Jacob Mullen, "	555 00		
		$4.425 00	
FIRE HYDRANTS.			
From Com't of works to Dec. 31, 1887.			$17,050 42
Paid R. D. Wood & Co., for Hydrants	660 00		
" Erie Machine Shop	3 18		
" Labor, as per Pay-Rolls	56 82		
		$720 00	
CARE AND REPAIR OF HYDRANTS.			
Paid Labor, as per Pay-Rolls	69 89		
" Erie Machine Shop, Sundries	15 84		
" Chas. Smith, Labor	49 44		
		$135 17	
Carried forward		$15 976 15	$322,798 48

	FROM JAN. 1. 1888, TO DEC. 31, 1888.		1867 TO 1888.
Brought forward............................	....	$15,976 15	$322,798 48
DISTRIBUTING MAINS AND BRANCHES.			
From Com't of works to Dec. 31, 1887.	....	....	$381,657 80
Paid Lake Shore Foundry, Pipe. &c.....	$10,297 05		
" Cornell Lead Co., Lead..............	1,502 96		
" Freight on Lead.....	17 16		
" Labor, as per Pay-Rolls..............	3,029 47		
" Frank Hoffman, Distributing Pipe	126 43		
" Erie Machine Shop, Castings........	100 50		
" Labor as per Pay-Rolls, Unl'd Pipe	40 94		
" J. B. Dwyer, et al. Inspect'g Pipe	90 95		
" R. J Saltsman, for Water Lime...	33 50		
" A. Schuster, Packing.	29 60		
" A. Brugger, for Sundries............	12 85		
" Erie Forge Co., Sundries...........	9 80		
" Thayer & Son, Clay........	7 50		
STOP VALVES, BOXES AND COVERS.		$15,298 71	
From Com't of works to Dec. 31, 1887.	....	....	$21,137 95
Paid R. D. Wood & Co., Stop Valves...	694 96		
" Erie Machine Shop, Boxes...........	477 35		
" Labor, as per Pay-Rolls..............	100 65		
" Frank Dudenhoffer, Brick..........	27 00		
" P. C. Thayer, et. al., Bricklaying	21 00		
" Freight.............................	3 84		
" Barber Asphalt Co., Repairs........	3 75		
REPAIRS OF BOILERS.		$1,328 55	
From Com't of works to Dec. 31. 1887.	....	....	$27,623 48
Paid Erie Machine Shop.....................	517 03		
" Donnelly Bros, Bricklaying.......	8 00		
" Eddy Valve Co............................	17 50		
" Jarecki Mfg. Co.......................	3 25		
" J. W. Hardwick, Steam Indicator	28 00		
" B. F. Sloan, Sec., Cash exp'd.....	4 00		
REPAIRS OF DISTRIBUTING MAINS.		$577 78	
From Com't of works to Dec 31. 1887.	....	....	$12,830 81
Paid Labor, as per Supt's. Pay-Rolls...	356 62		
CARE AND REPAIRS OF RESERVOIR.		$356 62	
From Com't of work to Dec. 31. 1887.	....	....	$8.534 79
Paid Sam'l Pfister, salary..................	420 00		
" Saltsman & Austin, Lime........	58 32		
" Geo. Waidley, moving barn........	20 00		
" A. S. Pinney. Sundries.............	6 08		
" F. Dudenhoffer, Brick..............	48 00		
" M. R. Barr, for Clay...............	11 75		
" H. Hamburger, Rep. of Barn.......	30 55		
" W. F. Nick, for Paints, &c........	57 95		
" Wm. Brewster, for Plants, &c......	7 00		
" Jarecki Mfg. Co., Sundries.........	3 96		
" B. F. Sloan, Sec., Cash Ex..........	1 80		
" Labor, as per Pay-Rolls..............	314 10		
" C. Flickinger, Repairs	14 80		
		$994 31	
Carried forward...........................	....	$34,532 12	$774,583 31

	FROM JAN. 1, 1888 TO DEC. 31, 1888.		1867 TO 1888.
Brought forward............................	....	$34,532 12	$774,583 31
BUILDINGS AND GROUNDS.			
From Com't of works to Dec. 31. 1887.	..............;	....	$79,021 97
Paid Thomas Tidman, Watchman	$ 480 00		
" Ed. Donnelly, on Contract..........	2.274 00		
" Constable Bros., Bill Rendered...	124 18		
" D.K. Dean & Son "	56 74		
" R. T. Williams & Co, " ...	51 05		
" Jas. P. Dailey, " ...	51 07		
" Labor, as per Pay-Rolls..............	42 69		
" Wm F. Nick, Sundries........	3 10		
" Erie Machine Shop...................	*1 35		
" B. F. Sloan, Sec., Cash Ex	4 50		
		$3,088 86	
OFFICE EXPENSES.			
From Com't of works to Dec. 31. 1887.	....	....	$12,718 18
Paid T. J. Elliott, rent.................. ...	$250 00		
" Janitor.................................	104 00		
" B. F. Sloan, Sec., Sundries.........	30 27		
" Erie Gas Co.	24 15		
" Penn'a Gas Co.	58 30		
" Telephone Exchange...................	84 00		
" Jas. M. Sherwin, Maps	54 00		
" Erie Ice Co............................	8 00		
" R. T. Williams & Co., Sundries...	7 48		
" Hays Mf'g Co., Sundries........ ..	1 75		
" N. Murphy & Son, "	4 40		
		$626 35	
SUPERINTENDENT'S SMALL STORES.			
From Com't of works to Dec. 31, 1887.	....	....	$462 82
Paid Sundry Bills, as per Vouchers......	$ 29 70		
		$29 70	
WASTE AND PACKING.			
From Com't of works to Dec. 31, 1887.	....	....	$2,776 79
Paid E. S. Greeley & Co., Sundry Bills.	$114 38		
" Mehl & Co., " "	39 70		
" Erie Machine Shop....................	11 00		
" Erie Rubber Co.......................	8 57		
" A. S. Pinney..........................	3 24		
" B. F. Sloan, Sec., Cash Ex.........	5 24		
		$185 13	
OIL AND TALLOW.			
From Com't of works to Dec. 31, 1887.	....	....	$6,331 82
Paid Eclipse Oil Co., Bills Rendered...	$461 16		
		$461 16	
Carried forward	....	$38,920 14	$875,894 89

	FROM JAN. 1, 1888 TO DEC. 31, 1888.	1867 TO 1888.
Brought forward............................	$38,920 14	$874,894 89

POSTAGE.

From Com't of works to Dec. 31, 1887.		
Paid H. C. Shannon, P. M..................		$3,180 44
	$209 74	
		$209 74

SHOP TOOLS AND REPAIRS.

From Com't of works to Dec. 31, 1887.		$3,652 48
Paid Erie Machine Shop......................	$126 13	
" Julia A. Teil, Rent....................	60 00	
" Mehl & Co., Bills Rendered.........	28 48	
" A. S. Pinney " "..........	7 70	
" Thos. Watkins, 3 Pipe Jointers...	17 50	
" R. J. Saltsman, Fuel................	6 00	
" C Klang, Bill Rendered............	2 45	
" Jacob Simon, "............	2 40	
" N Murphy & Son, "............	3 45	
" Jarecki Mf'g Co , et. al............	3 90	
" F. R. Simmons, for Leather........	2 40	
" B. F Sloan, Sec., per Vouchers....	7 15	
" R T. Williams & Co................	4 68	
		$272 24

COURT COSTS AND COUNSEL FEES

From Com't of works to Dec. 31, 1887.		$1,655 38

ENGINEER'S SMALL STORES.

From Com't of works to Dec. 31, 1887.		$1,623 93
Paid Erie Gas Co...........................	$103 06	
" N. Murphy & Son, et. al.........	7 27	
" J. W. Swalley, Soap.................	10 00	
" J. R. Cooney, for Ice..............	27 60	
" P. A. Becker, et. al	29 68	
" Wm. F. Nick, Sundries............	5 08	
" B. F. Sloan, Sec., per Vouchers...	5 82	
		$188 51

PRINTING AND ADVERTISING.

From Com't of works to Dec. 31, 1887.		$3,900 59
Paid Erie Dispatch Co......................	$204 60	
" Erie Herald, et. al.................	33 40	
" Daily Times. et. al.................	9 92	
" J. M. Glazier......................	31 00	
" B. F. Sloan, Sec , Cash Exp'd.	1 00	
		$282 92
Carried forward........................	$39,873 55	$889,907 71

	FROM JAN. 1, 1888 TO DEC. 31, 1888.		1867 TO 1888.
Brought forward......................		$39.873 55	$839,907 71
BOOKS AND STATIONERY.			
From Com't of works to Dec. 31, 1887.	....	....	$1,483 20
Paid Ashby & Vincent.	$40 24		
" B. F. Sloan, Sec., Cash Exp'd	20 75		
		$60 99	
ON ACCOUNT OF NEW PUMP.			
From Jan. 1. 1886, to Dec. 31, 1887.	....	....	$20,841 91
Paid Balance of Contract..................	$6,207 75		
		$6,207 75	
INSURANCE.			
From Com't of works to Dec. 31, 1887.	....	....	$186 58
Paid Van Anden, et. al........	$125 00		
		$125 00	
ENGINE ROOM FURNITURE			
From Com't of works to Dec. 31, 1887.	....	....	$1,114 40
Paid Mehl & Co., Bills Rendered...	$24 97		
' A. S. Pinney, " "	34 25		
" Erie Machine Shop....................	14 45		
" F. A. Roth. Bill Rendered.........	50 00		
" B. F. Sloan, Sec., Cash Exp'd.....	1 85		
		$125 52	
HORSE AND WAGON.			
From Com't of works to Dec. 31. 1887.	....	....	$3,789 68
Paid Keystone Carriage Works....	$28 80		
" Geo. L. Siegel & Co. Bills Rend'd	111 42		
" A. S. Pinney, " "	24 25		
" S. S. Caughey, Rent....................	14 00		
" Geo. L. Wood, et. al.............. .	46 96		
" John M. Cormick. Sundries........	16 80		
" Geo. Schlindwein, "	4 95		
" Mehl & Co.............................	1 10		
" B. F. Sloan, Sec., Cash Exp'd.....	1 50		
		$249 78	
STREET CONNECTIONS.			
From Com't of works to Dec. 31, 1887.	....	....	$61,817 15
Paid Jarecki Mf'g Co.. Bills Rendered.	$1,408 30		
" Cornell Lead Co., " "	218 89		
" National Tube Works, "	337 57		
" F. R. Simmons, "	10 11		
" Freight on Sundries..................	10 83		
" B. F. Sloan, Sec., Cash Exp'd......	4 75		
" Sundry Bills for St. Repairs......	13 76		
" R. T. Williams & Co., Sundries...	2 04		
" Labor, as per Pay-Rolls............	1,471 14		
		$3,477 39	
Carried forward............................	....	$50,119 98	$979,140 63

	FROM JAN 1, 1888 TO DEC. 31, 1888.		1867 TO 1888.
Brought forward...............	....	$50,119 98	$979,140 63
WATER METERS AND CARE.			
From Com't of works to Dec. 31, 1887.	....	....	$7,857 95
Paid Union Meter Co., Bill Rendered...	$460 00		
" H. R. Worthington " " ...	35 40		
" Crown Meter Co., " " ...	33 85		
" Jarecki Mf'g Co., Sundries......	10 10		
" David Schlosser, Lumber............	29 12		
" A. S. Pinney Sundries.	1 05		
" Labor, as per Pay-Rolls............	305 78		
		$875 30	
SHOP AND MISCELLANEOUS WORK.			
From Com't of works to Dec. 31, 1887	....	....	$9,529 49
Paid Labor, as per Pay-Rolls............	$335 20		
		$335 20	
REDEMPTION OF BONDS.			
Paid Finance Committee of Councils..	$23.000 00	$23,000 00	
PLUMBING.			
From Com't of works to Dec. 31, 1887.	....	....	$3,286 70
Paid R. D. Wood & Co., for Pipe........	$225 31		
" Jarecki Mf'g Co., Sundries........	78 05		
" R. T Williams & Co., "	5 15		
" Labor as per Pay-Rolls............	251 81		
		$560 32	
LOWERING MAINS.			
Paid Labor, as per Pay-Rolls..............	$113 39		
		$113 39	
INLET PIERS AND REPAIRS.			
From Com't of works to Dec. 31, 1887.	....	....	$45,032 59
STATE, COUNTY AND SCHOOL TAXES.			
From 1885 to 1887............	....	....	$1,100 83
INTEREST AND DISCOUNT.			
From Com't of works to Dec. 31, 1887.	....	....	$99,065 41
RAILROAD SWITCH AND SCALES.			
From Com't of works to Dec. 31, 1887.	....	....	$2,918 92
WATER RENTS RETURNED.			
From Com't of works to Dec. 31, 1887.	....	....	$62 62
RESERVOIR AND GROUNDS.			
From Com't of works to Dec. 31, 1887.	....	....	$123,150 83
ENGINES AND BOILERS.			
From Com't of works to Dec. 31, 1887	....	....	$66,316 95
Carried forward.................	....	$75,001 19	$1,337,463 92

	FROM JAN. 1, 1888 TO DEC 31, 1888.	1867 TO 1888.
Brought forward	$75,004 19	$1,337,463 92
CARTAGE.		
From Com't of works to Dec. 31, 1887.		510 04
CIVIL ENGINEERING.		
From Com't of works to Dec. 31, 1887.		7,122 85
GAS WELLS AND CARE.		
From Com't of works to Dec. 31, 1887.		8,148 59
PARK FOUNTAINS		
From Com't of works to Dec. 31, 1887.		3,244 68
Totals	$75,004 19	$1,356 489 08

RECAPITULATION.
EXPENSES IN 1888.

For Construction	$31.096 54
" Extraordinary Repairs	3,267 09
" Redemption of Water Bonds	23 000 00
" Current Expenses	17,363 63
Total	$75,004 19

EXPENSES FROM JULY 1867 TO DEC. 31, 1888.

For Construction	$1,006,742 80
" Maintenance	401,750 47
Total	$1,408,493 27

NET EARNINGS FROM JULY 1867 TO DEC. 31, 1888.

Total cost of Construction		$1 006,742 80
Advanced by City in Bonds	$675,000 00	
" " " to sink Gas Wells	955 10	
		$675,955 10
Balance		$430,787 70
Add Balance in City Treasury		5,697 01
" " " Office		678 52
Total Earnings		$437,163 23

EXHIBIT D.

Amount of Water Rents Collected each year, with the Increase and Decrease, since the Commencement of the Works.

	Am't Rec'd.	Increase.	Decrease.
From Jan. 1, 1869, to Dec. 31, 1869......	$ 4,264 47	....	....
" " 1870, " 1870......	9,237 30	$4,972 83	....
" " 1871, " 1871.....	18,138 08	8,900 78	....
" " 1872, " 1872......	21,652 68	3,514 60	....
" " 1873, " 1873......	25,560 40	3,907 72	....
" " 1874, " 1874......	27,938 90	2,378 50	....
" " 1875, " 1875......	29,639 38	1,700 48	....
" " 1876, " 1876......	31,048 76	1,409 38	....
" " 1877, " 1877......	32,276 57	1,227 81	....
" " 1878, " 1878......	29,636 01	....	$2,640 56
" " 1879, " 1879......	33,343 20	3,707 19	....
" " 1880, " 1880......	37,385 00	4,041 80	....
" " 1881, " 1881......	40,385 87	3,000 87	....
" " 1882, " 1882......	43,818 73	3,432 86	....
" " 1883, " 1883......	48,269 89	4,451 16	....
" " 1884, " 1884......	51,852 78	3,582 89	....
" " 1885, " 1885......	53,550 35	1,697 57	....
" " 1886, " 1886......	58,725 00	5,174 65	....
" " 1887, " 1887......	67,121 92	8,396 92	....
" " 1888, " 1888......	73,197 03	6,075 11	....
	$737,042 23	....	....

EXHIBIT E.

Location, Size and Length of Main Pipe, Large Private Pipe and Fire Hydrant Branches Laid in 1888.

LOCATION.	SIZE	FEET.	IN.
Fifth street, east of Ash..	6	558	8
" " west of Sassafras..............................	6	368	3
Sixth " west of Plum...............................	6	94	......
Seventh street, west of Cherry.............................	6	719	......
Tenth street, west of Walnut...............................	6	339	8
Tenth street, west of Walnut...............................	6	164	4
Eleventh street, west of Peach............................	4	200	......
Eleventh street, east of Wayne.............................	6	806	6
Eleventh street, north to State to Hydrant.............	4	8	2
Thirteenth street, west of Wayne.........................	6	341	......
Thirteenth street, east of Ash..............................	6	105	......
Fourteenth street, west of Wayne.........................	6	320	11
Fourteenth street, east of Ash..............................	6	104	6
Fifteenth street, west of Myrtle............................	6	138	6
Seventeenth street, east of Parade........................	6	391	6
Nineteenth street, west of Walnut........................	6	259	......
Twentieth street, east of Cascade.........................	6	494	......
Twentieth street, north of Cascade to Hydrant........	4	8	4
Twenty-fourth street, west of Sassafras.................	6	205	......
Twenty-fifth street, north on Reed to Hydrant........	4	7	4
Twenty-fifth street, east of Ash............................	6	631	......
Twenty-sixth street, east of Holland.....................	6	454	......
Twenty-sixth street, west of Holland.....................	6	178	......
Twenty-sixth street, north on Holland to Hydrant....	4	6	6
Twenty-sixth street, west from Reservoir, (relaid)....	12	1420	6
Twenty-sixth street, north on Poplar to Hydrant......	4	8	8
Twenty-ninth street, west of Waterford Avenue.......	6	377	8
Wallace street, between Eleventh and Twelfth........	6	398	10
Wallace " " Ninth and Tenth..............	6	400	......
Wallace " north of Sixth to Hydrant..............	4	8	......
French " " "Twenty-first.........	6	93	......
Myrtle " " "Fifteenth............................	6	20	......
Myrtle " " "Short............	4	321	9
Myrtle " Crossing Eleventh........................	6	51	......
Myrtle " north of Twenty-third....................	6	118	......
Walnut street, between Eighteenth and Nineteenth....	6	326	......
Walnut " Crossing Eleventh.	6	51	......
Cherry " from Third to Fourth....................	4	388	......
Cherry " between Second and Third........	4	75	6
Poplar " south of Eighteenth to Hydrant........	4	8	2
Poplar street, from Eighteenth south.....................	6	857	8
Poplar street, south of Twentieth to Hydrant..........	4	8	......
Poplar street, south of Twenty-third to Hydrant......	4	8	6
Poplar street, between Twenty-sixth and Twenty-third........	6	982	......
Poplar street, between Ninth and Tenth.................	6	89	......
Carried forward.......................................	......	12913	7

LOCATION.	SIZE	FEET.	IN.
Brought forward	......	12,913	7
Poplar street, between Seventh and Eighth	6	93	......
Poplar street, from Eighth street north	6	298	.....
State street, south of Eighteenth	6	22	4
Plum street, north of Twelfth	6	244	2
Plum street, north of Twelfth to Hydrant	4	7	8
Cascade street, between Eighteenth and Twenty-first	6	954	2
Cascade street, north of Twenty-first	4	8	6
Waterford Avenue, south of Twenty-ninth	6	502	8
Waterford Avenue, south of Twenty-sixth	6	397	6
Cascade street, south of Twenty-ninth to Hydrant	4	11	6
Scott street, north of Twenty-ninth	6	313	6
Scott street, north of Twenty-ninth to Hydrant	4	6	6
Hazel street, south of Twenty-sixth	6	162	......
Front street, from Myrtle east	4	300	.....
Total	......	16,236	1

RECAPITULATION.

6-in Pipe Laid ....13425 feet
4-in "   "   .... 1391 "
12-in "   "   .... 1420 "

| | | 16,236 | 1 |

PRIVATE PIPE LAID IN 1888.

For Erie Cemetery, 3-in..1200 feet.
"   Erie Rubber Works 4-in................................. 96 "

| | | 1,296 | ...... |

| Total public and private | ...... | 17,532 | 1 |

PIPE TAKEN UP IN 1888.

On Twenty-sixth street, 912-4 4-in pipe..................... 912-4
On Eleventh street, 200 4-in pipe.......................... 200
On Twenty-sixth street, 324-6 6-in pipe................... 324-6

| | | 1,436 | 10 |

| Actual gain in 1888 | ...... | 16,095 | 3 |
| In Miles, 3 $\frac{255}{5280}$ 3. | | | |

EXHIBIT F.

Total Amount of Distributing Pipe. Fire Hydrant Branches and Large Private Pipe Laid to December 31, 1888

STREETS.	Less than 4-inch.	4-inch.	6-inch.	12-inch.	20-inch.	30-inch.
		LENGTH IN FEET AND INCHES.				
Dock and Front	1,182.5	2,186.2			147.	330.3
Short	1,591.0	1,473.9				
Second	1,558.8	5,160.8				
Third	237.0	6,691.9				
Fourth		3,817.3	4,625.6			
Fifth	4,141.1	6,704.11	791.4			
North Park	75.0	101.4	820.0			
Sixth	152.5	1,927.1	9,744.0			
South Park	182.1	22.7	424.0			
Seventh		3,506.6	740.2	5,362.2		
Eighth	540.8	9 666.8				
Ninth	9.0	7,398.8	1,566.8			
Tenth	49.0	481.11	10,833 7			
Eleventh	275.0	8,530.2	2.885.10			
Twelfth	47.6	1,900.7	13,371.10			
Thirteenth		3,160.1	1,511.1			
Fourteenth		2,994.1	750.5			
Fifteenth	358.2	3,187.5	138.6			
Huron		1,436.10				
Sixteenth	4,971.1	1,418.8	3,372.5			
Seventeenth		7,440.1	1,638.6			
Eighteenth	11.0	2,971 10	12,534.7			
Buffalo Road		1,168.0				
Nineteenth	125.8	2,008.4	948 5			
Twentieth.		1,746.4	494.0			
Twenty-first		63.2	2,719.6	6,560.0		
Twenty-second		3,637.8				
Twenty-third		2,906.2				
Twenty-fourth		1,634.8	205.0			
Twenty-fifth		3,281.8	631.0			
Twenty-sixth	30.0	979.8	4,467.8	1,420.6		
Twenty-ninth			377.8			
Railroad		1,780.0				
East Avenue		593.3	3,040.6			
Wayne			858.0			
Ash		1,193.10	2,035.6			
Wallace	391.11	1,366.9	1,134.10			
Vine		399.8				
Parade		5,529.11	3,343.10			
German		3,729.11	814.10			
Division		317.2				
Holland	203.4	9,351.1	167.0			
Carried forward	6,886.6	117,810.1	90,468.5	13,342.8	147.0	330.3

STREETS.	LENGTH IN FEET AND INCHES.					
	Less than 4-inch.	4-inch.	6-inch.	12-inch.	20-inch.	30-inch
Brought forward..	6,886.6	117,810.1	90,468.5	13,342.8	147.0	330.3
French	262.6	5,525.6	1,833.2			
State	20.0	5,077.6	4,099.7			
Turnpike	6.6	8.7	795.0			
Peach....................	352.3	1,087.0	5,931.8	1,996.0		
Waterford Avenue..		910.0	900.2			
Sassafras...............	570.0	9,608.4				
Myrtle	8.3	4,768.2	1,068.0			
Hickory		631.6				
Chestnut...............	1,206.6	4,722.8		24.0	9,222.3	2,457.1
Walnut.............:....	9.0	4,343.1	800.9			
Cherry...........		3,347.2	464.6			
Poplar..................		853.10	2,949.7			
Liberty	320.2	1,095.10				
Plum.....................		623.8	426.4			
Cascade................	500.0	486.10				
Maple		805.0	25.0			
Scott		31.6	854 6			
Hazel			365.			
Total........... ...	10,132.8	167,726.1	110,869.8	15,362.8	10,433.9	2,787.4

RECAPITULATION.

	FEET	IN.
Less than four inches...	10,132	8
Four-inch pipe...	167,726	1
Six-inch pipe...	110 869	8
Twelve-inch pipe..	15,362	8
Twenty-inch pipe..	10,433	9
Thirty-inch pipe..	2,787	4
Add private pipe laid in 1888..	1,296	1
Total in feet................	318,608	3

Total in feet..	318,608.3	
Deduct amount taken out and relaid	1,436.10	
Total gain in feet...	317,171.4	
Total in miles...............	60$\frac{3}{5}\frac{7}{2}\frac{1}{4}\frac{1}{0}$	

EXHIBIT G.

Location, Number and Length of Street Connections Made During the Year 1888.

STREETS.	Number of Connections	FEET.	IN.	STREETS.	Number of Connections	FEET.	IN.
Front and Dock.....	4	30	......	Brought forward..	354	6,471	2
Short.....................	1	12	......	East Avenue........	2	53	3
Second....................	2	35	......	Wayne....................	1	9	6
Third 1D	13	218	1	Reed	1	10	....
Fourth..................	16	329	3	Ash	2	32	3
Fifth......................	10	151	5	Wallace	4	86	....
North Park...........	5	86	1	Parade..................	5	120	6
Sixth 1D	10	287	......	German	10	158	6
South Park............	4	77	6	Holland 1D	4	80	4
Seventh	13	275	10	French..................	8	107	10
Eighth...................	3	65	2	State	12	334	5
Ninth 1D	6	83	11	Peach	5	43	4
Tenth 3D	12	357	6	Sassafras...............	3	46	5
Eleventh 4D	82	1270	9	Myrtle..................	9	105	1
Twelfth 1D	22	586	5	Scott	3	33	9
Thirteenth	11	246	7	Chestnut...............	4	39	11
Fourteenth 1D	11	124	10	Walnut..................	4	93	....
Fifteenth	4	53	5	Cherry...................	8	122	....
Huron....................	2	36	3	Hazel	3	37	....
Sixteenth 1D	4	70	....	Poplar...................	11	227	6
Seventeenth	15	228	9	Liberty..................	2	36	8
Eighteenth'.........2D	20	346	9	Plum.....................	4	105	4
Buffalo Road......1D	6	97	5	Cascade.................	4	83	8
Nineteenth.............	7	69	1				
Twentieth..............	20	410	11	Total	463	8,437	5
Brown's Avenue.....	1	23	6				
Twenty-first..........	11	170	10				
Twenty-second	4	55	4				
Twenty-third	4	89	2				
Twenth-fourth.......	6	53	2				
Twenty-fifth	9	150	3				
Twenty-sixth	10	232	11				
Twenty-seventh	2	67	10				
Twenty-ninth........	4	78	3				
Total................	354	6471	2				

LENGTH OF CONNECTIONS IN MILES.

	MILES	FEET
Connections made in 1888...	1	3.157
Previously made..	19	4,687
Total	21	3,157

EXHIBIT H.

Location and Style of Fire Hydrants Set in 1888, all being 4-inch Steamer and Hose.

STREET.	WHERE LOCATED.	NAME.
Seventh	street, Northeast corner of Poplar	Mathews.
Ninth	" " " " German	"
Eleventh	" Northwest " " Cherry	"
Eleventh	" Northeast " " Perry	Bay State.
Eleventh	" Northwest " " East Avenue	Mathews.
Twentieth	" 47 feet east of Cascade	"
Twenty-fifth	" Northwest corner of Reed	Bay State.
Twenty-sixth	" " " " Holland	Mathews.
Twenty-sixth	" Northeast " " Poplar	"
Wallace	" " " " Sixth	"
Plum	" " " " Twelfth	
Poplar	" Southeast " " Eighteenth	
Poplar	" " " " Twentieth	
Poplar	" " " " Twenty-third	
Cascade	" Northeast " " Twenty-first	"
Scott	" " " " Twenty-ninth	Bay State.
Waterford Avenue, 500 ft. south of Twenty-ninth		Mathews.

RECAPITULATION.

Fire Hydrants in new location 13
" " renewed 4
Total 17
Net gain in 1888 13

NUMBER AND STYLES OF FIRE HYDRANTS IN USE.

New style Mathews............ 201
Old " " 11
Bay State............ 27
West Jersey............ 32
Pittsburgh............ 21
Home-made............ 3
Ludlow............ 4

Morris, Tasker & Co............ 2
Union............ 1
Total............ 303
Private Fire Hydrants............ 30
Grand total............ 333

HYDRANTS FOR THE SUPPLY OF WAGON SPRINKLERS.

Ninth | street, between State and French | Jarecki, Hays & Co.
Twelfth | " near Southwest corner of Peach | "
Fifteenth | " " " " " Peach | "
Eighteenth | " " Northwest " " Peach |
State | " at East Park |
" | " between Tenth and Eleventh |
" | " Southeast corner of Twelfth |
Myrtle | " " " Eighteenth |
Walnut | " Northeast " Eighteenth |

EXHIBIT I.

Location, Size and Kind of Stop Valves Set in 1888.

STREETS.	WHERE LOCATED.	KIND.	SIZE
Fifth	East line of Ash	**Eddy.**	6
Sixth	West line of Plum	" "	6
Tenth	West line of Walnut	" "	6
Seventh	West line of Cherry	" "	4
Eleventh	West line of Walnut	" "	4
Eleventh	East line of Perry	" "	6
Fourteenth	West line of Wayne	" "	6
Fifteenth	West line of Myrtle	" "	6
Thirteenth	West line of Wayne	" "	6
Sixteenth	East line of German	" "	6
Seventeenth	East line of Parade	" "	6
Eighteenth	East line of Liberty	" "	6
Twentieth	East line of Cascade	" "	6
Twenty-fifth	East line of Ash	" "	6
Twenty-sixth	West line of Holland	– –	6
Twenty-sixth	East line of Cherry		12
Twenty-sixth	East line of Poplar		12
Twenty-sixth	55 feet west of Stop House	" "	12
Twenty-ninth	West of the west line of 29th	::	6
Wallace	South line of Eleventh	" "	6
Wallace	South line of Ninth	" "	6
French	North line of Twenty-first	" "	6
Myrtle	North line of Short	" "	4
Myrtle	South line of Short	" "	4
Myrtle	South line of Eleventh	" "	6
Walnut	South line of Eighteenth	" "	6
Walnut	South line of Eleventh	" "	6
Cherry	South line of Third	" "	4
Poplar	South line of Eighteenth	" "	6
Poplar	South line of Twenty-third	" "	6
• Poplar	North line of Twenty-fifth	" "	6
Poplar	North line of Twenty-sixth	" "	6
Poplar	South line of Seventh	" "	6
Plum	West line of Twelfth	" "	6
Cascade	South line of Eighteenth	" "	6
Cascade	North line of Twentieth	" "	6
Waterford Ave.	South line of Twenty-sixth	" "	4
Waterford Ave.	South line of Twenty-ninth	" "	6
Scott	North line of Twenty-ninth	" "	6

RECAPITULATION.

Total number of all kinds in 1887	526
Six-inch put in, in 1888	30
Four-inch put in, in 1888	6
Twelve-inch put in, in 1888	3
Total	565
Taken out and replaced with 12	3
Balance, Dec. 31, 1888	562

EXHIBIT J.

Number of Families, Stores, Offices, Manufacturers, &c., Supplied with City Water During the Year 1888.

Breweries	3	Jail	1
Board of Trade	1	Laundries	6
Boat Houses	5	Lumber Yards	4
Bakeries	14	Livery Stables	17
Butcher Shops	57	Manufactories	84
Banks	6	Malt Houses	4
Barber Shops	38	Orphan Asylums	2
Billiard Rooms	5	Opera Houses	2
Bottling Works	8	Oil Works	1
Coffee and Spice Mill	1	Offices	331
Churches	17	Old Folks' Homes	2
Cemeteries	1	Photograph Galleries	8
Coal and Iron Docks	1	Police Stations	1
Club Houses	1	Paint Works	1
Custom House	1	Public Halls	26
Court House	1	Packing Houses	2
Convent	1	Printing Offices	11
Driving Park	1	Passenger Depots	2
Dyeing Works	2	Rail Roads	4
Engine Houses	6	Rail Road Shops	2
Express Offices	2	Rink	1
Electric Light Co	1	Soldiers' Home	1
Fish Hatchery	1	Schools	22
Families	5055	Stores	417
Families by permit	58	Saloons and Eating Houses	143
Fish Houses	5	Slaughter Houses	10
Freight Houses	5	Street Railway	1
Fountains, Private	6	Transfer Co	1
Fountains, Public	2	U. S. Signal Station	1
Fountains, Drinking	2	Work Shops	126
Flouring Mills	4	Watering Troughs	17
Gas Works	1	U. S. Steamer Michigan	1
Grain Elevators	3	U. S. Court House	1
Gas Offices	2	U. S. Post Office	1
Green Houses	4		
Hospitals	2		6,636
Hotels and Boarding Houses	36	Last Enumeration	6,367
Ice Houses	2		
Internal Revenue Offices	1	Increase	269

EXHIBIT K.

PUMPING ENGINE STATISTICS FOR 1888.

The Pumps are three in number. Two are known as the Cornish Bull Pumps. The diameter of each plunger is 20¾ inches, and each has a stroke of 10 feet. The capacity of each pump is estimated to be 165 gallons to every stroke. The third pump is a Gaskill Horizontal Pumping Engine, of a guarranteed capacity of 5,000,000 gallons daily at a piston speed of 120 feet per minute against a head of 237 feet. The stand-pipe is 251 feet high. The Reservoir is nearly two miles from the Pumping Works, the bottom of which is 210 feet above the surface of the Bay, and the water has been maintained during the year at an average depth in the Reservoir of about 24 feet.

MONTHS	Days single Cornish pump.	Days both Cornish Pumps Run.	Days Gaskill Pump Run.	Strokes of Cornish Pump.	Revolutions of Gaskill Pump.	Gallons Pumped.	Daily Average.	Average Lift in Feet.	Lbs of Coal per Month.	Cost of Coal.
Jan'y....	5	.....	27	61,845	465,916	113.209,387	3,651,915	236,00	478,000	$274 85
Feb	3	.....	27	33,340	610,800	116,666,700	4,022,089	286.00	437,680	251 67
Mar......	......	...	31	....	663.148	120,692,936	3,893,302	237.50	417,200	286 71
Apr......	......	5	19	91,855	335,052	76,135,538	2.537,850	232.00	214,200	123 16
May......	......	......	31	....	647,529	117,851,278	3,801,654	228.00	377,850	186 65
June.....	......	......	24	....	619,671	112.780,122	3,759,337	230.00	387,150	191 25
July.....	......	......	30	....	620,628	112,954,206	3,643,686	236.00	401,730	198 45
Aug.....	2	1	28	36,978	660,422	126,298,174	4,074,134	235.00	453,050	223 81
Sept	......	......	30	....	651,235	118,524,770	3,950,825	236.00	408,550	201 82
Oct	......	......	27	....	608,615	110,658,730	3,569,636	235.00	382,750	189 87
Nov ...	6	......	25	65,478	515,350	104,597,570	3,486,585	236.00	393,400	194 33
Dec......	......	......	31	....	611,750	111,338,500	3,591,564	236.50	444,550	222 82
	16	6	330	289,546	7,009,516	1,341,708,092	3,675,912	234.60	4,796,110	$2,545 46

The regular employees at the pumping works are 1 mechanical engineer, 2 assistant engineers, 3 firemen and 1 watchman. The mechanical engineer stands a watch of 5 hours, from 7 to 12 every forenoon; the assistants divide the remainder of each day equally between them; each one of the firemen stands a watch of 8 hours. Beside firing, the firemen unload the coal from the cars, except when both pumps are run, in which case they are assisted by the watchman or a laborer. The mechanical engineer gives 10 hours daily to the service of the Department, the hours when he is not on watch being employed in repairs, supervision, etc In addition to standing their regular watch, the assistant engineers aid their superior officer in keeping the machinery in order. The watchman takes care of the buildings and grounds, besides doing such other work as may be required of him.

EXIHIBIT L.

Amount of Coal Consumed in Pumping, Gallons of Water Pumped, Average Height Pumped, Cost per Million Gallons, etc., from the First Year the Works were Operated to December 31, 1888.

YEAR.	Tons of coal consumed.	Price of coal per ton from May 1st of each year.	Cost of coal from Jan. 1st to Dec. 31st.	Grades of bituminous coal.	Gallons of water pumped.	Increase or decrease.	Number of places supplied.	Number of fire hydrants.	Average height of water in reservoir above surface of bay.	Cost of coal per million gallons raised to reservoir.	Gallons raised to reservoir by 1 pound of coal.
1868	59.1	$5 05	$ 309 61	Lump							
1869	544.4	5 05	4,818 48	"							
1870	1,064.5	5 05	5,159 10	"	246,648,960		1,218	97			
1871	1 432.7	5 05	5,117 00	"	179,368,495	132,719 585 i.	1,727	99	232.0	$18 76	98.5
1872	1,308.5	5 05	6,528 50	"	395,076,000	115,708,505 d	2,140	103	232.0	16 52	150.9
1873	1,672.5	4 85	8,412 65	"	384,062,415	11,013,585 d	2,475	107	232.0	21 90	114.8
1874	1,759.0	4 85	7,709 54	"	444,817,395	60,754,980 i.	2,663	107	233.0	17 33	126.4
1875	1,836.4	4 00	8,657 61	"	531,005,475	86,181,080 i.	2,700	110	232.0	16 30	145.5
1876	2,105.1	3 70	8,925 22	"	670,726,650	139,721,175 i.	2,763	112	232.0	13 30	159.3
1877	2,456.6	3 35	8,509 33	"	660,981,810	9,744,840 d	2,854	114	232.0	12 75	135.7
1878	2,463.3	3 09	7,945 37	"	682,392,315	21,390,505 i.	2,915	115	232.0	11 64	136.4
1879	2,628.1	1 99	7,428 92	Slack	807,800,400	125,408,085 i.	3,011	121	232.0	9 19	153.6
1880	3,076.1	1 90	6,978 41	"	775,805,250	31,995,150 i.	3,568	126	232.0	8 99	126.0
1881	3,430.3	1 75	6,517 58	"	975,640,634	200,235,684 i.	4,110	161	232.0	6 68	142.2
1882	2,968.2	1 55	5,355 93	"	829,759,260	145,881,674 d	4,687	171	234.0	6 45	139.7
1883	2,398.2	1 45	3,908 59	"	815,939,685	13,819,575 d	5,077	197	234.7	4 66	170.0
1884	3,010.8	1 30	4,502 61	"	917,781,350	105 841,665 i.	5,395	248	234.3	4 99	152.4
1885	3,243.8	1 25	4,575 79	"	1,036,496,665	118,715,315 i.	5,658	270	232.9	4 40	159.7
1886	3,369.0	1 15	4,318 64	"	1,117,389,075	80,892,410 i.	6,140	280	233.3	3 86	165.8
1887	2,820.4	1 09	3,589 31	"	1,218,213,688	106,824,583 i.	6,368	318	234.1	2 95	216.0
1888	2,393.3		2,545 46	"	1,341,708,002	123,494,314 i.	6,600	233	234.6	1 15	292.1

EXHIBIT M.

HOW CITY WATER MAY BE WASTED.

Gallons and Hundredths of Gallons of Water that will be Discharged per Minute Through Various Sized Orifices at the Heads Stated.

Head in Feet	Pressure per Square Inch	DIAMETER OF ORIFICES IN INCHES AND FRACTIONS OF AN INCH													
		$\frac{1}{64}$	$\frac{1}{32}$	$\frac{1}{16}$	$\frac{1}{8}$	$\frac{1}{4}$	$\frac{3}{8}$	$\frac{1}{2}$	$\frac{5}{8}$	$\frac{3}{4}$	1	$1\frac{1}{4}$	$1\frac{1}{2}$	$1\frac{3}{4}$	2
20	8 66	0 02	0 07	0 30	1 20	5 10	11 70	20 60	32 20	46 20	82 30	128 40	184 80	252 00	328 80
40	17 32	0 02	0 11	0 45	1 80	7 40	16 30	29 60	45 50	65 50	116 50	182 40	261 60	356 80	465 60
60	25 99	0 03	0 14	0 55	2 20	8 90	20 20	35 60	57 70	80 30	142 40	223 20	320 40	436 80	571 20
80	34 65	0 04	0 16	0 65	2 60	10 30	23 20	41 20	64 30	92 60	164 40	258 00	370 40	505 20	658 80
100	43 31	0 04	0 18	0 75	2 90	11 50	25 90	46 10	72 00	103 70	183 60	288 00	415 20	565 20	738 00
120	51 98	0 05	0 19	0 78	3 10	12 60	28 30	50 40	78 80	113 50	201 60	315 60	453 60	624 40	807 60
140	60 64	0 05	0 21	0 85	3 40	13 60	30 60	54 50	85 20	122 40	217 20	340 80	490 80	668 40	868 80
150	64 97	0 05	0 22	0 88	3 50	14 10	31 70	56 40	88 20	127 20	225 60	352 80	507 60	691 20	902 40
175	75 80	0 06	0 24	0 95	3 80	15 20	34 20	61 00	95 30	136 80	243 60	380 60	549 40	748 80	975 60
200	86 83	0 06	0 26	1 02	4 10	16 30	36 60	65 20	101 80	146 40	260 40	406 80	588 00	798 00	1042 80
235	101 08	0 07	0 28	1 12	4 50	17 90	41 30	71 50	111 40	160 40	285 20	445 90	642 20	871 30	1140 80

The bottom of the Erie Reservoir is 210 feet above the surface of Presque Isle Bay, from which the water is pumped, and the water in the Reservoir is kept at an average height of nearly 24 feet, or 234 feet above the bay. The pressure at the points named below will give an idea of the average throughout the city: Twenty-fourth and Sassafras Streets, 20 lbs.; Twenty-third and Myrtle, 30 lbs.; Twentieth and Chestnut, 40 lbs.: Eighteenth and Peach, 50 lbs.; Fourteenth and State, 60 lbs.; Eight and State, 70 lbs.; Third and State, 80 lbs.; Front and State, 100 lbs.

The wire of which pins are made is one-thirty-second of an inch in diameter—No. 21, wire gauge. The finest cambric needle is made of wire one-sixty-fourth of an inch in diameter—No. 27, wire gauge. A stream the size of a pin, running one year with head of 235 feet, will flow 147,168 gallons, equaling 4,600 barrels the value of which—counting at the rate of 10 cents per 1,000 gallons—is $14.71. A stream the size of a cambric needle, running at the same pressure, for the same time, will flow 36,792 gallons, at the cost of $3.68.

EXHIBIT N.

Table Showing the Water Rates Per 1,000 Gallons in 162 Cities Where Meters are used.

MAINE.	Cents.
Bangor	30
Portland	20 to 40
NEW HAMPSHIRE.	
Manchester	20
Nashua	15 to 30
VERMONT.	
St. Albans	10 to 30
Burlington	12 to 50
MASSACHUSETTS.	
Amesbury	30 to 50
Boston	20
Clinton	15 to 50
Cambridge	10 to 20
Fall River	30
Haverhill	15 to 20
Hingham	25
Lawrence	20 to 25
Lowell	15
Lynn	17½to20
New Bedford	2½ to 15
Northampton	10 to 20
North Adams	10 to 15
Quincy	12½to30
Peabody	20
Pittsfield	10
Salem	13½to20
Springfield	10 to 20
Taunton	12½to25
Waltham	25 to 30
Westboro	50
Worcester	15 to 25
CONNECTICUT.	
Bridgeport	20 to 30
Hartford	7½to 30
Meriden	10 to 25
New Britain	10
New Haven	10 to 35
New London	20 to 30
Norwich	15 to 30
Stonington	10 to 20
RHODE ISLAND.	
Providence	15 to 30
Pawtucket	6 to 30
Woonsocket	30
Waterbury	10 to 30
NEW YORK.	
Albany	5 to 40
Amsterdam	6 to 30
Binghamton	6 to 25
Brooklyn	10⅓
Buffalo	3
Catskill	12 to 25
Cortland and Homer	20 to 50
Corning	10 to 30
Elmira	9 to 45
Flushing	20 to 60
Johnstown	25
Kingston	30
Mt. Morris	10 to 30
New York	13⅗
Owego	30
Oneonta	20 to 50
Oneida	20 to 50
Rochester	5 to 13
Saratoga	15
Syracuse	6 to 25
Troy	10 to 20

NEW YORK—*Continued.*	Cents.
Utica	15 to 30
Waverly	20
Waterford	5 to 20
Whitehall	6 to 20
Yonkers	16 to 40
NEW JERSEY.	
Bridgeton	20
Hackensack	13 to 23
Jersey City	21 to 27
Morristown	33
Newark	15
New Brunswick	12½to50
Trenton	15 to 20
PENNSYLVANIA.	
Allegheny City	15
Bloomsburg	10 to 35
Conshohocken	15
Easton	16¼to40
ERIE	**6 to 10**
Franklin	60
Hazelton	10 to 15
Lebanon	5 to 15
Meadville	8 to 30
McKeesport	4½to30
Philadelphia	8
Pittsburgh	5 to 20
Reading	10¾to21½
OHIO.	
Cleveland	6⅔to13⅜
Cincinnati	9
Columbus	7 to 20
Dayton	8 to 40
Norwalk	10
Sandusky	6 to 20
Springfield	10 to 40
Toledo	8 to 20
Wooster	15
INDIANA.	
Indianapolis	12 to 40
Terre Haute	11
ILLINOIS.	
Bloomington	10 to 15
Chicago	8 to 10
Joliet	15 to 30
Jacksonville	13 to 40
Quincy	15 to 50
MICHIGAN.	
Bay City	5 to 10
Detroit	10
East Saginaw	6 to 12
Flint	6 to 30
Grand Rapids	9½to30
Kalamazoo	10
Port Huron	5 to 20
WISCONSIN.	
Kenosha	10 to 15
Milwaukee	4½to20
Madison	20 to 50
IOWA.	
Council Bluffs	15 to 35
Cedar Rapids	15 to 40
Dubuque	30 to 60
Davenport	10 to 40
Des Moines	15 to 20
Ottumwa	10 to 30
Muscatine	35 to 60
Sioux City	13 to 40

MINNESOTA.	Cents.
Minneapolis	10 to 20
Winona	8
St. Paul	15 to 40
MISSOURI.	
Hannibal	20 to 50
Kansas City	10 to 35
Springfield	25
St. Louis	12½to30
KANSAS.	
Abilene	30 to 50
Atchison	20
COLORADO.	
Denver City	30
Gunnison	10
NEBRASKA.	
Lincoln	10 to 20
CALIFORNIA.	
Los Angeles	30
Oakland	30 to 55
San Francisco	23½to46
Vallego	40 to $1
DELAWARE.	
Wilmington	10
MARYLAND.	
Baltimore	8
Hagerstown	8 to 60
VIRGINIA.	
Norfolk	20 to 40
Richmond	15
NORTH CAROLINA.	
Charlotte	30 to 50
Wilmington	10 to 20
SOUTH CAROLINA.	
Charleston	25 to 60
GEORGIA.	
Atlanta	17
ALABAMA.	
Birmingham	6 to 40
Montgomery	25
LOUISIANA.	
New Orleans	15 to 30
TEXAS.	
Fort Worth	20 to 45
San Antonio	25 to 50
KENTUCKY.	
Maysville	15 to 30
Newport	10
Owensboro	10 to 20
Lexington	17½to25
Louisville	6 to 35
TENNESSEE.	
Chattanooga	6 to 33
Knoxville	10 to 30
Nashville	7 to 15
CANADA.	
Brantford	12 to 20
Hamilton	12½
Halifax	30
London	20 to 33⅓
St. Catharine	14
Average Minimum Price,	9¼
" Maximum "	28

EXHIBIT O.

Cost of Water to the Average Householder in Twenty-five Cities, Compiled from Official Reports to this Department.

CITIES.	Population, 1880.	Family Charge.	Pan Water Closet.	Self-closing Urinal.	Bath Tub.	Self-closing Wash-stand.	Permanent Wash Tub.	Two Horses.	Cow.	Street Sprinkler.	Total.
Allegheny City	78,000	8 75	3 00	2 00	3 00	1 00	1 50	1 50	75	3 00	24 50
Boston	302,000	7 00	5 00	2 50	5 00	5 00	5 00	2 00	75	5 00	37 25
Buffalo	156,000	7 20	3 50	3 00	3 00	1 00	2 00	2 40	90	2 50	25 50
Chicago	503,000	6 00	3 00	1 00	3 00	1 00	2 00	2 00	75	3 00	21 75
Columbus, Ohio	51,000	6 00	3 00	3 00	4 00		5 00	4 00	2 00	5 00	32 80
Dayton, Ohio	38,000	6 00	2 50	4 00	2 00	2 00	2 00	2 50	1 00	8 30	45 30
Detroit	116,000	7 00	4 00	3 00	2 00	1 25	2 00	4 00	1 00	4 00	28 25
ERIE	35,000	5 00	3 00	3 00	3 00	1 00	2 00	2 00	75	3 00	21 75
East Saginaw, Mich	19,000	7 00	2 50	3 00	3 00	1 00	2 00	4 00	1 00	3 00	26 50
Fall River, Mass	49,000	5 00	5 00	2 00	5 00	1 00	2 00	4 00	1 00	6 00	31 00
Grand Rapids, Mich	32,000	8 00	4 00	2 00	3 50	2 50	4 50	2 50	1 00	6 00	33 00
Indianapolis	75,000	5 00	10 00	3 00	3 00	2 00	1 00	5 00		10 00	32 80
Lawrence, Mass	39,000	5 00	4 00	3 00	3 00	1 00		3 00	1 50	3 00	25 80
Milwaukee	115,000	6 00	2 00	3 00	3 00	1 50	1 50	2 00	1 00	5 00	22 00
Minneapolis	47,000	4 00	3 00	2 00	2 50	1 00	2 00	2 00	1 50	3 00	26 00
Newark, N. J	136,000	6 25	2 50	7 50	5 00	1 00	2 00	2 50	1 00	3 00	26 25
New York	1,200,000	6 00	5 00	2 00	3 00	1 00	2 00	6 00	1 50		32 75
Omaha, Neb	30,000	6 75	3 00	2 50	3 00	1 00	2 00	5 00	75	5 00	30 00
Philadelphia	847,000	5 00	2 50	3 50	4 00	1 00	1 00	2 00	75	5 00	28 75
Pittsburgh	156,000	9 00	4 00	5 00	3 00	1 00	2 00	2 00	1 50	3 00	23 50
Sandusky, Ohio	15,838	6 00	5 00	1 50	3 00	1 00		4 50	1 50	3 00	25 50
St. Paul (1885)	41,000	8 00	2 50	2 00	4 00	1 00		4 80		2 40	24 70
Syracuse	52,000	8 00	4 00	2 40	3 20	1 00	2 00	3 00	75	6 00	31 75
Toledo	50,000	5 50	2 50	2 50	3 50	1 00	2 00	5 00	1 50	5 00	28 50
Utica	34,000	7 00	6 00	3 00	5 00	1 00		6 00	1 50	8 00	31 50

RATES FOR CITY WATER.

All are annual, except as otherwise indicated.

Bath Tub, private...$	3 00
" " each additional..	1 50
" " public	5 00
Bakery, per barrel of flour used. (but no charge less than $5).....	01
Barber Shop, including Hand Basin, first chair.....	4 00
" " " " each additional chair..............	2 00
Blacksmith Shop, one fire..	5 00
" " each additional fire......................................	2 50
Boarding House (in addition to family rates), per room.............	1 00
Brewery, per barrel brewed...	03
Building purposes, per bushel lime......................................	02
Butcher Stalls...	3 00 to 15 00
Charitable Institutions, one-third annual rates........................	
Cow...	75
Condensing boiler for steam heating, (per season of six months) per horse power...••••	50
Eating Houses..	5 00 to 25 00
Family...	5 00
Hand Basin, for Dwellings, Hotels, and Schools, first basin...........	1 00
" " " " " " each additional..............	50
" " in Offices, Stores and Blocks, each.......	1 00
Hotel (in addition to family rates), per room.........................	1 00
Livery Stable, per horse...	2 00
Maltster, per 1,000 bushels of malt.....................................	1 75
Offices..	3 00 to 10 00
Private Stable, one or two horses..	2 00
Private Stable, each additional horse....................................	1 00
Printing Offices..	5 00 to 30 00
Public Halls..	5 00 to 25 00
Saloons...	5 00 to 25 00
Stores..	3 00 to 15 00
Schools, per pupil...	10
Steam Engine, 10 hours per day, each horse power.......................	2 50
Slaughter Houses	5 00 to 50 00
Sleeping Rooms..	1 00
Sprinkling Streets or Lawns with hose (per season).....................	3 00 and up.
Urinal, private, self closing..	2 00
" public,...	3 00
" not self-closing..	3 00 to 10 00
" continuous flow...	10 00 to 30 00
Wash Tub, (permanent, with waste)..	2 00
" " " " each additional.....	1 00
Watering Trough, public..	10 00
Water Closet, (pan) in private houses....................................	3 00
" " " each additional..................................	1 50
" " " public...	5 00
" " (hopper), private..	6 00
" " " public	10 00
Work Shop, (ordinary use)..	3 00 to 5 00

All other uses, when not metered, to be assessed by the Department.

METER RATES (PER QUARTER.)

Daily Average, 15,000 gallons or less....................................	10	cents.
" 15,000 to 20,000 gallons.................................	9½	"
" 20,000 to 25,000 "	9	"
" 25,000 to 30,000 "	8½	"
" 30,000 to 35,000 "	8	"
" 35,000 to 40,000 "	7½	"
" 40,000 to 45,000 "	7	"
" 45,000 to 50,000 "	6½	"
" More than 50,000 gallons................................	6	"

OF ERIE, PA.,

TO THE

R AND CITY COUNCILS

AR ENDING DEC. 31, 1889.

ERIE, PA.
THE GAZETTE.
1890.

ANNUAL REPORT

—OF THE—

Board of Water Commissioners,

OF ERIE, PA.,

—TO THE—

MAYOR AND CITY COUNCILS

—FOR THE—

YEAR ENDING DEC. 31, 1889.

ERIE, PA.
THE GAZETTE.
1890.

WATER COMMISSIONERS.

The Water Commissioners are appointed by the Court of Common Pleas of Erie County, Pa., for a term of three years, one member being named annually, in May.

EX-MEMBERS OF THE BOARD.

*WM. L. SCOTT, 1867 to 1868.
*HENRY RAWLE, 1867 to 1872.
*WM. W. REED, 1867 to 1879.
†JOHN C. SELDEN, 1868 to 1872.
MATTHEW R. BARR, 1872 to 1877.

JOHN GENSHEIMER, 1872 to 1878.
M. LIEBEL, 1877 to 1886.
J. M. BRYANT, 1878 to 1881.
G. W. F. SHERWIN, 1879 to 1885.
BENJ. WHITMAN, 1881 to 1887.

*Messrs. Scott, Rawle and Reed, the first Commissioners, were appointed respectively for terms of one, two and three years.
†Mr. Selden resigned before the expiration of his second term; Mr. Barr was substituted by the Board and afterward appointed by the Court.

THE PRESENT BOARD.

GEO. W. STARR, 1885 to 1891.   C. KESSLER, 1886 to 1892.
C. J. BROWN, 1887 to 1890.

OFFICERS OF THE DEPARTMENT.

President of the Board—GEO. W. STARR.
Secretary and Treasurer—B. F. SLOAN.
Assistant Secretary—GEO. C. GENSHEIMER.
Clerk—WILL W. REED.
Superintendent of Street Work—WM. O'LONE.
Inspectors—A. F. CRANE, F. W. KOEHLER, JOHN D. SPAFFORD.
Mechanical Engineer—F. A. ROTH.
Assistant Mechanical Engineers—GEO. R. MILLER, JOHN KELLY.
Firemen—R. W. SIMONS, JOSEPH BURNS, JACOB MULLEN.
Watchman at Pumping Works—THOS. TIDMAN.
Keeper of Reservoir and Grounds—SAMUEL PFISTER.

OFFICE—City Hall.—OFFICE HOURS.—From 7:30 A. M. to 5:45 P. M.; Monday Evenings from 7:30 to 9:00.

REGULAR MEETINGS OF THE BOARD—Every Saturday at 3:00 P. M.

ANNUAL REPORT.

To the Mayor and Councils of the City of Erie:

The Board of Water Commissioners respectfully present their report for the year ending December 31, 1889, as follows:

RECEIPTS.

Balance in office Jan. 1, 1889	$ 678	52
" " City Treasury Jan. 1, 1889	5,697	01
From Water Rents	81,110	68
From all other sources.	599	13
Total	**$88,085**	**34**

EXPENDITURES.

Paid for Construction	$33,141	80
" Maintenance.	16,292	18
" Extraordinary expenses	2,707	13
" Sinking Fund for Redemption of Bonds.	33,500	00
Balance in City Treasury Dec. 31, 1889	1,955	90
" " Office " " "	488	33
Total	**$88,085**	**34**

The year 1889 to this Department has in no particular been unusually eventful. No work has been done of an extraordinary character.

The city having required an increased amount of the expected surplus, the expenses have been kept within such limit that it has prevented the making of certain extensions of mains and connections, which, if continued, would increase circulation by leaving fewer "dead ends," or pipes which have no outlet, and the result is, as our accounts will show, a smaller sum left in the Treasury at the end. of the last twelve months' operations than has been reported in many years previous—a sum so small as to be considered unsafe in the event of great breakage of mains or pumps, or damage at the reservoir.

The extraordinary expenses have been principally in painting and necessary changes at the pumping and boiler house and in repairs at the reservoir. The bursting of one length of the 30-inch main near Twelfth street, which occurred in September last and for which no satisfactory reason can be found, is also to be added to this account.

The item "Construction," includes, of course, the extension of the 30-inch main. This main will be further extended to Twenty-first street during the coming season. The constant demand for more water convinces the Board that this main cannot too soon be completed to connect with the reservoir. It will relieve the pumps and enable them to continue the full supply required for a longer term with the present pumping facilities. Yet it should be ever in mind that if the city shall continue its growth, at the same rate of progress shown in the last two years, an additional pump of greater capacity and power will be required, and it would seem to be but prudent to provide for such contingency by maintaining a reserve fund which shall be at command when such emergency occurs.

The Gaskill engine is doing the principal part of the work, but its capacity, as well as that of the other pumps, is limited. It has lifted for many days in succession full five millions of gallons daily, the largest quantity ever before needed, but its full power cannot be exercised to its limit all the year round. Put at its full strain it cannot work on forever. Like man, it must have rest. It is liable to, and does get out of order. To fall back upon the old pumps is to increase the expense of running full 40 per cent. in the cost of fuel. Consulting economy in this department, which is economy also for the city, should we not provide for increasing demand by enlarged facilities of supply?

The quantity of water lifted during the year was 1,475,358,-220 gallons; average per day, 4,040,908 gallons; increase over the previous year, 133,650,218 gallons. This large quantity with its increase has been delivered at a less cost per million than in the year before, the cost of raising a million gallons to the reservoir in 1888 having been $1.89, this year for the same service being $1.80.

MAINS.

2,069 7-12 feet of 30-inch pipe was laid along Chestnut street, extending same from a point 48 7-12 feet south of south line of Seventh street to a point 82 6-12 feet south of the south line of Twelfth street. 1,422 feet of 12-inch pipe was laid on Twelfth street from Chestnut street to Cherry street, connecting with a 6-inch main running westwardly to Cascade street, and replacing a 4-inch pipe for that distance.

12,074 feet of 6-inch, and 1,092 8-12 feet of 4-inch, laid in various sections of the city, completes the list and adds 16,-658 3-12 feet to the mains heretofore laid, making a total of mains of all sizes laid in our streets of 65, 629–5,280 miles.

HYDRANTS.

Thirteen new Hydrants have been attached to the mains. Three old ones were taken out and replaced with new. One of the latter was on private premises. Three hundred and fifteen hydrants are now in use on the public streets. Whole number of hydrants set, 346, of which 31 are for fire protection on private grounds.

STOP VALVES.

One on 30-inch main, two on 20-inch main, three on 12-inch main, twenty-five on 6-inch main and thirteen on 4-inch mains have been set. One of 6-inch taken out and replaced with new one, one of 4-inch taken out and replaced with 12-inch and two of 4-inch taken out and replaced with others of same size—a gain of 40.

METERS.

Whole number now in use—80.

Three hundred and fifty-five connections have been made with mains. Of water takers 488 have been added to those heretofore supplied.

Whole number of consumers in city 7,086.

The so-called "fishy taste" in the water was noticeable a less number of days than usual during the last season. It is not peculiar to our city. In fact we are only afflicted with it for a week or two in each year, and then only in a mild form. It is present every year, not only at our Lake cities, but in the interior towns of the west, in New England and throughout the east. It is found in all places where water is taken from large ponds, from lakes or running streams, and even in water drawn from artesian wells, which is not aerated by constant contact with the open air.

This subject has been carefully investigated by scientists in different sections of the country, and is generally believed to be a vegetable growth, or water plant, which for a few days in the spring, or at a certain degree of temperature is developed, and impregnates the water with its peculiar odor, harmless, though unpleasant to the senses of taste and smell. It is short-lived, and disappears, to be renewed only at the recurrence of the same conditions, twelve months afterwards. For it there has never yet been found a prevention or a remedy.

This Department had occasion in its last report to call attention to the proposed sewer for the western section of the City and to deprecate the plan of emptying its contents into the Bay. Again near the close of last year this Board sent into Councils a remonstrance against the construction of a sewer down the Little Cascade, the outlet of which is less than a hundred rods west of the Water Works pier. Notwithstanding this remonstrance and a second one since made by this Board, the petition for this same sewer has again been taken up, referred to a committee and by them recommended to be constructed ; when the facts as represented by the Water Board showed that the outlet of this sewer would be far within the limit of distance within which any deleterious matter is, under the rules of this Department, approved by Councils, and thus having the force and effect of an ordinance of the city, *prohibited* from being thrown into the bay, and which, if passed, (and it were law) would deprive the Water Commissioners of all control over the inlet of the Water Works, of the pier leading to it, and the shore adjoining.

Every year for more than a decade, or for more than half the life of this Department, have its officers in the line of their duty to the public, been compelled to remonstrate against the contamination of the water in the Bay, no matter from what source it came, nor by what authority it was permitted.

That no heed has been paid to these appeals by the only authorities having power over such constructions, it is not within our province to account for. With the fact alone we have to deal.

It naturally leads to a review of the action of the City on the matter of sewers, in connection with the water supply, and has become the more necessary on account of the frequent changes in the personnel of Councils. Acts of their predecessors in office are often unknown, disregarded or forgotten.

Than the matter referred to, there is none of greater interest, nor any demanding more serious consideration.

As the furnishing of a water supply for the City, includes the question of sewers and requires their construction, and both are necessary for the convenience, comfort and health of a large community, it follows that a wise foresight would have established a well digested and matured plan for the mutual and harmonious working of each system. Unfortunately no general plan has ever been adopted.

Since the construction of the Water Works the City, in the absence of a general sewer system, has gone on under direction of different engineers, building sewers where demanded, in many locations apparently without regard to the place of deposit, or their effect upon the City's supply of water.

The first effective action towards adopting a general system was taken in 1879, when a plan was proposed by a former City Engineer to carry the sewage from Mill Creek outside the Bay. It was the initiatory step towards the care of the sewage of the whole city.

Councils then approved the plan because it presented a solution of the whole difficulty of drainage and the supply of pure water, at a small outlay of money.

They appropriated half the sum estimated to be needed for that purpose, and agreed to hold said sum, (between $5,000 and $6.000,) intact for a twelve-month, and to provide a like sum the following year, when the work was to have been begun and pushed to completion.

Unfortunately the next year found a new Council in power holding different views, and instead of appropriating the second half of the amount agreed upon to be used for that specific purpose, they ignored the previous action, and they and their successors found other use for the first half set aside, which, had it all been legitimately applied as originally intended and expressly agreed, would have relieved the greater part of the City, have saved many thousands of dollars towards the work of sewerage, and there would to-day have been no complaint of the quality of the water.

There should be to-day the whole of the sum first raised, as before stated, in the City Treasury, due to said fund, and yet available for the work for which said fund was designated. The city is committed by its own acts to the enterprise and no subsequent legislation should be allowed to interfere with the completion of a work for which the people have been taxed, and which, it is as evident now as when the tax was levied and collected, is greatly in their interest.

That plan has apparently been abandoned, and until a recent date no substitute proposed. Meantime the Water Mains have been extended until more than 65 miles have been laid, and over 7,000 families and business firms have been supplied.

The quality of the water has to the public, with a few exceptions, been satisfactory, and only tentatively questioned, since the offer of over a million dollars for the works and its franchises.

Although this proposition was not favorably received by the public nor the press, yet the City newspapers have at times since, called attention to the purity of the water, and the Water Commissioners, without acquainting any one with their proceedings, but determined to give the exact state of its conditition to the public, procured an analysis of the water to be made by the State Board of Health, who printed the result, *before it was reported to this Department*, in the "Annals of Hygiene," a publication issued under the sanction of this Board.

Copied from that issue into our City newspapers, it has for the time silenced the clamor of speculators, and in a great degree lessened the demand that the in-take should be changed to a different source of supply.

A few persons, however, are yet found, who, ignoring this analysis, without a thorough inquiry into the subject, neither regarding the financial ability of the City nor the Water Department, and with no knowledge as to whether the proposed change will result in obtaining purer water, insist on the extension of the water inlet into the Lake. These few are reinforced by the City Engineer's Department in a special report to Councils, and afterwards repeated in an annual report.

The recommendations in these reports are somewhat startling. A complete change has taken place in the formerly expressed views of that Department, which were, even during the term of service of its present head, that all the sewage of the City should be carried outside the Bay and into the Lake beyond. It is a reversal of all previous opinions held by engineers and civilians. It is nothing more or less than that ALL THE CITY'S SEWAGE SHOULD BE CARRIED INTO AND DEPOSITED IN THE BAY. The proposition would seem to require no argument to prove it a dangerous scheme. . It refutes itself by its mere statement. Every impulse of self-preservation would seemingly condemn it. But, as we find that Councils have entertained it by instructing the Engineer to submit plans, the subject seems to be thrust upon the Water Department and to challenge its attention. It will not do to pass it by without notice and in silence.

Looking into these reports to learn upon what grounds such recommendations are based, we find it stated that "the topography of the City is such that it indicates itself at once to the Engineer," meaning from what follows that the Bay is the natural place of deposit of the detritus of the present City, and all the accumulations of a dense population ; and, therefore, this must be the dumping ground. As if this earth was formed ready and complete for all the needs of man, and that all he had to do to enjoy it to the full, was to use it as he finds it, without an effort on his part to change its face or adapt it to his wants.

The plan (we say it with all deference) is but a cheap solution of the question. It avoids labor and persistent study and experiment ; it renders work so far as one Department of the City is concerned an easy task ; it answers the purpose for the time being, but takes no account of results for the future.

As this project, if carried out, would, as the Engineer's report admits, so seriously affect the water in the Bay as to render it "unfit for drinking purposes," and of necessity therefore unfit for domestic use, another plan is furnished for the benefit of the Water Department, and that is, to carry the inlet of the Water Works from the pumping station to a point in the locality of the Whallon Pier or near the Land Light House, and to lay the inlet pipe under docks, railroads, Mill Creek and Sand Beach intervening, and to protect the outer end by bulkheads or piers. Nothing is said as to cost, and it is stated without comment, as if it were a simple and inexpensive thing to do, and would answer the purposes intended for all time. Now, what is the necessity for all this work? It is not shown in the paper submitted, as that asserts that "the water " in the Bay is surprisingly pure, owing to extreme change " to and fro going on at all times, the difference of level be- " tween Lake and Bay of only one inch meaning a change of " many millions of gallons."

A careful calculation has been made of the rise and fall of water in the Bay for the last twelve months, taken from the daily record in the pumping house. It verifies the statement in the above mentioned report, and proves that the whole volume of water in the Bay, estimated by an able engineer some years ago, to equal 24,000,000,000 of gallons, must of necessity be changed in its whole bulk many times during the year. These facts, taken in connection with the analysis of the Bay water by a citizen for the sole purpose of satisfying himself, published in a city paper in 1888, and the analysis of the water by the State Board of Health in January last, would seem to answer the question as to its character, purity and fitness for use.

Then why this demand for change?

The reason given in this report is "to submit a plan for *better water* and dispose of sewage at the same time." May we not reasonably doubt whether any plan for better water would have been suggested were the question of sewage eliminated from the calculation?

The first requisite of a water supply is the purity of the water. Shall we abandon a reasonably pure supply for one less pure or one of doubtful character? What is its quality at the point proposed for the inlet? It is not demonstrated; it is assumed. If it were proved to be better it would save discussion. What are the probabilities?

It is a well-known fact that the outward current on leaving the piers is diverted towards the South, forming a great curve along and in which vessels of much draught have for many years steered their way because of its greater depth. The trend of this curve is towards the Whallon Dock and the Light House.

If, then, the sewage now emptied into the Bay in a degree pollutes the water, what would be the condition as to purity of the water supply when the whole sewage of a city of many times our present population is discharged directly upon the locality from which the supply is proposed to be taken?

As to the work itself and what will be its cost? It involves a contest with quicksands, excavation in leaking rock, tunneling under railroad tracks and through the shifting lake sands outside the pier, under shelter of coffer-dams or caissons, at a depth of ten or more feet below the ordinary level of the Bay, for a distance of more than two miles, and the construction of piers at the terminus of strength sufficient to resist the impact of the storms and drifting ice of the open Lake.

It is not required of us to estimate its cost. That matter has been referred to the City Engineer, and we shall await with interest his report.

We have given this much attention to this proposition because, as citizens and as a Board, we are entirely and without qualification, opposed to any scheme for further polluting the waters of the Bay, whether the water supply for the City is taken from it or not.

To make of the beautiful sheet of water of which our people have boasted in the pride of their surroundings, ever since the smallest craft sailed over it, a cesspool teeming with the seeds of pestilence, is in the extreme revolting. Nor does it require a too vivid imagination to foresee at no distant day under such conditions, our once healthful City almost a pest house, reeking with the germs of epidemics, our hospitals filled, and our water front deserted.

We have said nothing of the financial ability either of the City or of the Water Department to construct this newly proposed inlet. The only revenues of the Water Department are its rents. The surplus, if any, after payment of its yearly expenses, extensions, etc., is, by the act creating the Department, required to be used toward the redemption of the bonds from the proceeds of which the works were built.

This is the situation: The Water Board forbidden by the constitution to incur a debt. The City already in debt to an amount exceeding the limit fixed by the same supreme authority.

Heie, then, is an effectual bar to any present progress towards even the commencement of this questionable scheme.

Let it be understood that no objection is raised here to sewers in any part of the City. They are needed, particularly on the West Side, and this Department is far from opposing their construction. They produce a demand for water, and a consequent revenue to this Department. The objection is solely to *the discharge of their contents into the Bay*, the result of which, it must be admitted, would be seriously injurious to the whole City, including the people who ask for their construction.

What then can be done? The Water Board has no purpose other than to furnish within the means at its command, a full supply of pure and wholesome water. But it has a vital interest in seeing that no action is taken by which its work may be crippled or neutralized through misdirected efforts.

City legislation, *so far as it relates to this Department*, has in many cases been embarrassing. Questions seriously affecting its revenues have been decided without consultation with the Board. Except in the matter of surplus, hardly an inquiry, even for information, has for years been made.

Each Department of the City Government seems to have a policy of its own. It is noteworthy when two of them agree. The present state of affairs, so far as they affect this Department, may thus be summarized: The City, through its Finance Committee, demands every year an increasing proportion of the surplus of the Water Department to be paid into the Sinking Fund. The Mayor suggests the partial lowering of rates, which means lessening of revenue, and, of course, less of surplus. Sewers turned into the Bay by order of Councils induce complaint against the Water Board. They first roil the stream, as in the fable, and then charge upon the Department that it furnishes impure water. The City Engineer proposes to pollute it still more by turning the whole sewage of the City into the Bay and then, as a remedy for foul water so defiled, requires a change of inlet, and locates that inlet with no certainty of getting purer water, if as pure. Official reports refer to the Water Works as a very valuable part of the City's assets, and City officers recommend a plan which will not only lessen its annual rents, but if carried out will absorb the whole of its revenues for years to come, leaving no funds with which to redeem the water bonds, the City meantime paying their accruing interest.

Is it not plain that a better understanding should exist, not only between the City as a corporation and the Water Department, but also between the responsible heads of the different departments of the City? Unity and uniformity of action would be far more effective and produce better results.

While this Department is strenuously opposed to the fouling of the Bay, it is anxious to do all within its power to satisfy the public. If the general sentiment should demand it (notwithstanding the analyses heretofore made) and it shall be found that a purer water can be had by extending the present inlet some hundreds of feet further north, this Board will make the necessary preparations for it, provided no objections which are insurmountable shall be offered by those navigating the waters of the Bay. Any proposition which will bear the test of examination will be gladly welcomed and carefully considered. We all have the same aim and purpose.

We recur again to the proposition that a general system of sewers ought to be adopted which should harmonize with the work of the Water Department, and that both the City and this Department should act in concert.

Is it not self-evident that the time has come to decide upon such a system for all the future? It is a serious problem, but the longer action is deferred the more difficult will it be to determine. It is of great interest to this Department to have it settled. Applications are daily made for extensions of mains, even where there are no sewers, and some idea of the demand made upon it may be learned

from the fact that of over 13,000 feet of six-inch pipe purchased for consumption the coming season, more than one-third
has already been asked for in this early part of the year—a demand greater by far than ever before known in its history.
Were sewers built more generally in accordance with a well-
defined system (as they would be were such system adopted),
the Water Department would be still more busied with extensions, and its revenues with corresponding surplus would be
larger, thus adding to the comfort of the individual citizen,
while aiding at the same time in the decrease of the public debt.

The rapid increase of manufacturing establishments, spread-
ing over a large area east and west, and the steady growth of
our population, calls for City legislation which shall keep pace
with private enterprise. The question is daily assuming
greater magnitude, including larger and more varied interests.
It is of grave import to every citizen. Until some plan shall
be agreed upon, the Water Commissioners claim that no
further pollution of the waters of the Bay should be permitted, and that all applications for emptying of sewers into
it should be discountenanced and refused.

To adopt a proper system and carry it into effect, belongs
solely to the City Authorities, and inasmuch as the surplus
funds of the Water Department inure to the benefit of the
City towards the payment of its bonded water debt, we believe the City Government is equitably, if not legally, bound
to exert its influence and authority to enable this Department
to furnish a full supply of water as nearly pure as nature
made it, uncontaminated by foul foreign matter discharged
into the Bay through artificial constructions like sewers.

Permit us to refer again to the plan of 1879. In the absence of any other feasible system why should not this be
again considered? It seems to answer all the necessary conditions, and to promise the best results at the least expense.
It need not be condemned because it is an old project. It is
not outlawed. The expense of constructing an intercepting
sewer as part of said plan would be far within the cost of ex-

tending the water inlet to the same terminus.   **Furthermore** it is within the power and means of the City to construct it.   A fraction of a mill in the tax levy set aside every year and expended yearly, would be sufficient to complete it in a comparatively short time and without being burdensome upon the people.

Let us suppose the plan for Mill Creek completed.   Supplement it with an intercepting sewer along the bluff on Front street discharging through the same outlet.   Substitute iron pipe for brick in its material, with man-holes for overflow in great storms and for flushing when necessary.   Compare this with the lately proposed scheme or with any other project yet suggested, as to their probable effect upon the healthfulness of our City.   Contrast them each with the other as to practicability, economy and efficiency, and it would seem that there could be but one conclusion.

That some definite action looking to a settlement of the question of sewers will soon be taken by the City, we must confidently expect.   Were the Councils closer in contact with the people they would better know what they require.   It is brought to the notice of the Water Office every week day in the year, and is one reason why this Board so earnestly directs attention to it.   The final decision of this vexed matter will induce settlement in all directions, will invite immigration of a desirable class to seek homes here and become citizens, and tend greatly to the importance and rapid growth of the City.   Respectfully submitted,

                         GEO. W. STARR,
                         C. KESSLER,
                         C. J. BROWN,   .
                                   Water Commissioners.

ERIE, March 1, 1890.

EXHIBIT A.

Receipts of the Erie Water Department for the Year End-
ing December 31, 1889.

WATER RENTS.		
Receipts for the Month—January...............	$7,880 02	
February.............	6,182 16	
March...............	4,449 53	
April................	7,825 46	
May.................	7,780 40	
June.................	4,251 14	
July.................	8,019 72	
August...............	8,712 42	
September............	3,323 25	
October	10,492 51	
November............	6,928 90	
December	5,265 17	
Total Water Rents........................	$81,110 68	
Balance December 31, 1888.....................	678 52	
Pipe laying, sale of material, &c	599 13	
Total from all sources.....................		$82,388 33
Deposited in Treasury........................		81,900 00
Balance		$488 33

EXHIBIT B.

Account of Water Department with City Treasurer for the Year Ending December 31, 1889.

DR.		
To balance in the Treasury December 31, 1888....	$ 5,697 01	
To deposits to Treasury to December 31, 1889.....	81,900 00	
		$87,597 01
CR.		
Warrants Drawn in—January...................	2,243 03	
February.................	2,482 76	
March....................	3,771 92	
April....................	2,711 87	
May.....................	7,742 22	
June.....................	7,125 57	
July.....................	5,317 39	
August...................	28,363 52	
September................	2,7c7 59	
October	6,384 10	
November................	2,530 57	
December	4,260 57	
		85,641 11
Balance in Treasury December 31, 1889...........		1,955 90
Total..................................		$87,597 01

EXHIBIT C.

Expenditures for the Year 1889; also, from Commencement of Works in 1867 to January 1, '89.

	FROM JAN. 1, 1889, TO DEC. 31, 1889.		1867 TO 1889.
FUEL AT WORKS.			
From Com't of works to Dec. 31, 1888.	....	....	$123,738 61
Paid Fort Pitt Coal Co., for 1,732,100 lbs. of coal at $.917 per ton......	795 10		
Paid R. J. Saltsman for 47,800 lbs. coal at $1.80 per ton.............	43 02		
Paid R. J. Saltsman for 132,900 lbs. of coal at $1.70..............	112 96		
Paid R. J. Saltsman 3,060,550 lbs. at $1.15.......................	1,759 78		
Paid for labor......................	20 88		
		$2,731 74	
SALARIES.			
From Com't of works to Dec. 31, 1888.	....	....	116,650 98
Paid—B. F. Sloan, Sec. & Treas.....	1,365 00		
Geo. C. Gensheimer, Ass't. Sec.	1,065 00		
Wm. O. Lone. Sup't. St. Work	1,080 00		
A. F. Crane, Inspector........	840 00		
F. W. Koehler, do	660 00		
J. D. Spafford, do	600 00		
Will W. Reed, Clerk..........	510 00		
Geo. W. Starr, Commissioner..	650 00		
C. Kessler, do ..	700 00		
C. J. Brown, do ..	725 00		
		8,195 00	
ENGINEERS AND FIREMEN.			
From Com't of works to Dec. 31, 1888.	....	....	80,479 45
Paid—F. A. Roth, Engineer........	1,080 00		
George R. Miller, do	840 00		
John Kelly, do	840 00		
R. W. Simons, Fireman.......	600 00		
Jos. Burns, do	600 00		
Jacob Mullen, do	600 00		
Extra Fireman..............	50 50		
		4,610 50	
FIRE HYDRANTS.			
From Com't of works to Dec. 31, 1888.	....	....	17,905 59
Paid—R. D. Wood & Co., for hydrants	372 00		
Labor as per pay rolls........	63 29		
		435 29	
CARE OF HYDRANTS.			
Paid—Labor as per supts. pay roll...	61 13		
John Applebee for labor.......	17 50		
		78 63	
Carried forward................		$16,051 16	$338,774 63

	FROM JAN. 1, 1889, TO DEC. 31, 1889.	1867 TO 1889.
Brought forward	$16,051 16	$338,774 63

DISTRIBUTING MAINS AND BRANCHES.

From com't of works to Dec. 31, 1888.		396,956 51
Paid—Lake Shore Foundry, pipe, &c.	$14,589 20	
L. S. & M. S. Ry., freight	576 47	
J. B. Dwyer, insp. pipe	144 77	
R. J. Saltsman, coke, &c.	72 87	
Humboldt Iron Works, et al	94 86	
R W. Russell, wood	11 25	
Martin Quigley, rope packing	45 84	
David Schlosser, lumber	38 33	
Adolph Brugger, bills rendered	26 75	
Cornell Lead Co., lead	1,594 80	
Labor as per Supts. pay roll	5,664 79	
	22,859 16	

STREET CONNECTIONS.

From com't of works to Dec. 31, 1888.		65,294 54
Paid—Labor as per Supts. pay rolls	1,196 59	
Hays Manf. Co., sundries	928 93	
National Tube Wks, service pipe	460 27	
Cornell Lead Co., lead pipe	156 44	
Jarecki Manf. Co., sundries	10 00	
L. S. & M. S. Ry., freight	8 38	
B. F. Sloan, sec., cash expended	3 69	
	2,764 30	

BUILDINGS AND GROUNDS.

From com't of works to Dec. 31, 1888.		82,110 83
Paid—E. Donnelly, bal. of contract	925 89	
T. Tidman, services watchman	480 00	
E. M. White, contract for paint'g	428 45	
D. K. Dean & Son, services	42 55	
D. P. Murphy, bills rendered	37 00	
Saltsman & Austin, do	6 00	
J. E. Patterson, do	15 67	
Murphy Bros., do	9 20	
Wm. F. Nick, do	13 32	
Geo. Carroll & Bro., lumber	15 29	
J. O. Baker, labor	34 72	
Lyman Felheim, lumber	12 50	
Larry Cummins, labor	5 00	
Constable Bros., sundries	2 85	
Jacob Bing, labor	5 00	
Humboldt Iron Works	2 00	
B. F. Sloan, secretary, cash	1 25	
F. W. Miller, repairs	15 83	
Labor as per Supts. pay roll	50 34	
John McCormick	3 75	
	2,106 61	
Carried forward	$43,781 23	$883,136 51

	FROM JAN. 1, 1889, TO DEC. 31, 1889.	1867 TO 1889.
Brought forward.....................	.... $43,781 23	$883,136 51
REPAIRS OF DIS. MAINS AND BRANCHES.		
From Com't of works to Dec. 31, 1888.	....	13,187 43
Paid—Labor as per Supts. Pay Rolls..	$361 46	
Mich Lynch, Bill Rendered....	5 50	
Saltsman & Austin Sundries...	2 75	
B. F. Sloan, Sec., Sundries....	2 00	
	371 71	
CARE AND REPAIR OF RESERVOIR.		
From Com't of works to Dec. 31, 1888.	....	9,529 10
Paid—Samuel Phister, Keeper	420 00	
Labor as per Supts. Pay Rolls..	521 31	
R. J. Saltsman. Sundry Bills...	20 91	
Lyman Felheim, " " ...	47 37	
James P. Daily, Sundries......	13 50	
John Applebee, Labor	10 50	
W. F. Nick, Paint and Oil.....	18 77	
M. R. Barr, Bill Rendered	30 90	
David Schlosser, do ·........	7 04	
A. S. Pinney, do	3 45	
B. A. Smith, paints and oil....	154 95	
Wm. Brewster, plants.........	7 00	
Tim Lynch, bill for sodding...	34 50	
Wm. Morgan, mason work.....	20 76	
B. F. Sloan, Sec., cash expended	1 00	
C. Mong, bill rendered	3 55	
	1,315 51	
SHOP TOOLS AND REPAIRS.		
From Com't of Works to Dec. 31, 1888.	....	3,924 72
Paid—Erie Machine Shop............	108 74	
Edward Donnelly, rent........	90 00	
Humboldt Iron Works, sundries	79 11	
Thomas Watkins, pipe jointers.	31 00	
Julia A. Teel, rent............	35 00	
B.F. Sloan, Sec.,cash for sund..	12 45	
Mehl & Sapper, bills rendered..	16 85	
Keystone Carriage Works, do..	11 39	
R. T.Williams & Co., sundries..	10 50	
Solomon Loeb, do	5 75	
James P. Dailey, do	16 00	
Edward Zieser, do	4 35	
A. S. Pinney, do	8 64	
W. J. Christian, do	8 25	
Ashcroft Mfg. Co., water gage..	12 00	
Constable Bros., sundries......	3 20	
Edward Diehl, do	6 80 ·	
J. H. Williams, wrenches......	10 10	
Martin Quigley, sundries......	1 12	
R. J. Saltsman, coal...........	17 50	
	488 75	
Carried forward.................	$45,957 20	$909,777 76

	FROM JAN. 1, 1889, TO DEC. 31, 1889.	1867 TO 1889.
Brought forward	$45,957 20	$909,777 76

STOP VALVES.

From Com't of works to Dec. 31. 1888.	....	22,466 50
Paid—Labor as per Supts. Pay Rolls.. $ 175 57		
D. Murphy, for Brick Laying.. 25 93		
R. D. Wood & Co., Valves.... 1,052 44		
Penn R. R. Co., Freight...... 30 83		
Humboldt Iron Works......... 287 84		
Selden Brick Co.,............. 6 50		
B. F. Sloan Sec., Cash Exp'd.. 5 57		
F. Dudenhoffer, for Brick...... 37 80		
P. C. Thayer for Brick Laying. 12 75		
Erie Machine Shop Sundries. ... 38 63		
Saltsman & Austin........... 13 30		
	1,687 16	

PRINTING AND ADVERTISING.

From Com't of work to Dec. 31, 1888.	....	4,183 51
Paid—Erie Herald Printing Co. 152 80		
John J. O'Brien............... 34 90		
Hugo Held 12 90		
Erie Daily Times............. 6 70		
Erie Gazette 11 25		
Erie Graphic................. 5 10		
B. F. Sloan, Sec., Cash Exp'd.. 5 10		
	228 75	

REPAIRS OF ENGINES AND BOILERS.

From Com't of works to Dec. 31, 1888.	....	28,201 26
Paid—Humboldt Iron Works 128 95		
Erie Machine Shop........... 45 02		
Hays Mf'g Co................ 5 68		
D. P. Murphy 80 75		
B. F. Sloan, Sec., Cash Exp'd.. 1 50		
Saltsman & Austin........... 1 50		
	263 40	

REPAIRS OF ENGINES.

Paid—Humboldt Iron Works 22 19		
Erie Machine Shop........ ..... 8 35		
	30 54	
Carried forward......................	$48,167 05	$964,629 03

	FROM JAN. 1, 1889, TO DEC. 31, 1889.	1867 TO 1889.
Brought forward.................................	$48,167 05	$964,629 03

OFFICE EXPENSES.

From Com't of works to Dec. 31, 1888.		13,544 53
Paid—T. J. Elliott, Rent..............	125 00	
Pennsylvania Gas Co , Fuel....	29 50	
Erie Gas Co...................	18 85	
Erie Telephone Exchange......	83 68	
James M. Sherwin, Mapping..	36 50	
C. Kessler, Ex. of Com........	22 50	
A. McVicker, Clock...........	10 00	
B. F. Sloan, Cash Expended...	101 46	
Cold Spring Ice Co..........	10 00	
Erie Electric Light Co..........	20 00	
Warner Bros., Carpets.........	62 14	
Bauschard Bros., Furniture....	73 65	
R. T. Williams & Co., Sundries	40 08	
Labor, as per Supt.'s Pay Rolls	13 11	
	646 47	

SUPERINTENDENT'S STORES.

From Com't of works to Dec. 31, 1888.		492 52
Paid—Erie Telephone Exchange	11 00	
B. F. Sloan,Sec.,Cash Expended	2 65	
Murphy Bros. Bill Rendered....	8 40	
Mehl & Sapper, Bill Rendered.	1 84	
Wm. F. Nick.................	3 40	
	27 29	

HORSE AND WAGON.

From Com't of works to Dec. 31, 1888.		4,039 46
Paid—R. H. Chinnock, bill rendered..	18 25	
E. L. Dunn, Bill for Oats......	6 96	
G. L. Siegel, Bill for Feed......	36 97	
B. F.Sloan,Sec., Cash Expended	30	
Keystone Carriage Works......	70 35	
Willis Ripley, for Hay.........	10 23	
	143 06	

WATER METERS AND CARE.

From Com't of works to Dec. 31, 1888.		8,733 25
Paid—Union Meter Co., meters & rep.	606 18	
Labor as per Supts. Pay Rolls..	145 07	
Jarecki Mf'g Co., Fittings......	5 00	
David Schlosser, for Lumber...	23 24	
National Meter Co., Repairs ...	40 58	
B. F.Sloan,Sec., for Cash Exp'd	4 97	
L. S. & M. S.,R. R............	3 64	
	828 68	

Carried forward....................	$49,812 55	$991,438 79

	FROM JAN. 1, 1889, TO DEC. 31, 1889.	1867 TO 1889.
Brought forward...............	$49,812 55	$991,438 79
LOWERING MAINS.		
From Jan. 1. 1888, to Dec. 31, 1888....		113 39
Paid for labor as per Supts. pay rolls.. $177 66		
	177 66	
COURT COSTS AND COUNSEL FEES.		
From com't of works to Dec. 31, 1888.		1,655 38
Paid S. A. Davenport, services...... 150 00		
	150 00	
PLUMBING AND PIPE LAYING.		
From com't of works to Dec. 31, 1888.		3,847 02
Paid for labor as per Supts. pay rolls.. 98 95		
	98 95	
REDEMPTION OF BONDS.		
From com't of works to Dec. 31, 1888.		23,000 00
Paid Sinking Fund Commissioners... 33,500 00		
	33,500 00	
OIL AND TALLOW.		
From com't o work to Dec. 31, 1888..		6,792 98
Paid—Eclipse Co. bi ls rendered.. 443 38		
W. A. Crawford, do........... 141 70		
	585 08	
POSTAGE.		
From com't of works to Dec. 31, 1888.		3.390 18
Paid—H. C. Shannon, Postmaster.... 79 80		
J. C. Hilton, Postmaster....... 133 40		
B. F. Sloan, Secretary......... 2 00		
	215 20	
INSURANCE.		
From com't of works to Dec. 31, 1888.		311 58
Paid L. J. Van Anden, T. M. Hemp- hill, et al..................... 130 25		
	130 25	
ENGINEERS' STORES.		
From com't of works to Dec. 31, 1888.		1,812 44
Paid—Erie Gas Co................. 131 26		
J. W. Swalley, soap........... 16 00		
Mehl & Sapper, sundries....... 5 61		
Erie Ice Co................. 22 00		
P. A. Becker & Son......... 17 95		
A. S. Pinney, sundries........ 5 44		
Wm. F. Nick, do........... 2 63		
Hays Manf. Co.............. 1 69		
B. F. Sloan, Sec., cash ex...... 91		
	203 49	
BOOKS AND STATIONERY.		
From com't of works to Dec. 31, 1889..		1,544 19
Paid Ashby & Vincent, bills rendered. 94 13		
Paid B F. Sloan, Sec., cash ex....... 7 03		
	101 16	
Carried forward...............	$84,974 34	$1,033,905 95

	FROM JAN 1, 1889, TO DEC. 31, 1889.	1867 TO 1889.
Brought Forward................	$84,974 34	$1,033,905 95
ENGINE ROOM FURNITURE.		
From com't of works to Dec. 31, 1888. ....,.....		1,239 92
Paid—Mehl & Sapper sundries...... $10 15		
Erie Machine Shop........... 4 00		
	14 15	
CARTAGE.		
From com't of works to Dec. 31, 1888. ....,....		510 04
Paid sundry bills rendered.......... 12 75		
	12 75	
SHOP AND MISCELLANEOUS WORK.		
From com't of works to Dec. 31, 1888.		9,864 69
Paid—Labor as per Supts. pay rolls.. 406 93		
	406 93	
PAVING AND ST. REPAIRS.		
Paid—James P. Daily.............. 3 30		
Labor as per Supts. pay roll... 3 26		
Barber Asphalt Paving Co.,... . 27 00		
Edword Driscoll, labor........ 14 00		
Peter Wessler, labor.......... 11 92		
	59 48	
WASTE AND PACKING.		
From com't of works to Dec. 31, 1888.		2,961 91
Paid E. S. Greely & Co.,............. 80 83		
Mehl & Sapper............... 22 85		
Erie Machine Shop........... 65 60		
B. F. Sloan, Sec. Cash Ex..... 4 18		
	173 46	
INLET PIERS AND REPAIRS.		
From Com't of works to Dec. 31, 1888.		45,032 59
STATE, COUNTY AND SCHOOL TAXES.		
From 1885 to 1887...................		1,100 83
INTEREST AND DISCOUNT.		
From com't of works to Dec. 31, 1887.		99,065 41
RAILROAD SWITCH AND SCALES.		
From com't of works to Dec. 31, 1887.		2,918 92
WATER RENTS RETURNED.		
From com't of works to Dec. 31, 1887.		62 62
RESERVOIR AND GROUNDS.		
From com't of works to Dec. 31, 1887.		123,150 83
Carried forward................	$85,641 11	$1,319,812 50

	FROM JAN. 1, 1889, TO DEC. 31, 1889.	1867 TO 1889.
Brought forward	$85,641 11	$1,319,812 50
ENGINES AND BOILERS.		
From Com't of works to Dec. 31, 1887.	....	93,336 61
CIVIL ENGINEERING.		
From com't of works to Dec. 31, 1887.	....	7.122 85
GAS WELLS AND CARE.		
From com't of works to Dec. 31, 1887	....	8,148 59
PARK FOUNTAINS.		
From com't of works to Dec. 31, 1887.	———	3,244 68
	$85,641 11	———
		$1,431,665 23

RECAPITULATION.

EXPENSES OF 1889.

For construction.............................	$33,141 80	
For extraordinary repairs	2,707 13	
For current expenses	16,292 18	
For redemption of bonds......................	33,500 00	
		$85,641 11

EXPENDITURES FROM JULY, 1867, TO DECEMBER 31, 1889.

For construction...............................,	1,040.233 59	
For maintenance..............................	420,572 85	
For redemption of Water Works bonds.........	56,500 00	
Total expenditures........................,	....	1.517.306 44
Add balance in Treasury......................	....	1,955 90
Add balance in Office........................	....	488 33
Total	....	1.519,750 67
Advanced by the City in bonds................	675,000 00	
Advanced by the City in cash.................	955 10	
		675,955 10
Balance to credit of Works.....................	....	$843.795 75

EXHIBIT D.

Amount of Water Rents Collected Each Year, with the Increase and Decrease since the Commencement of the Works.

	Am't Rec'd.	Increase.	Decrease.
From Jan. 1, 1869, to Dec. 31, 1869....	$4,264 47	....	....
" " 1870, " 1870.....	9,237 30	$4,972 83	....
" " 1871, " 1871....	18,138 08	8,900 78	....
" " 1872, " 1872....	21,652 68	3,514 60	....
" " 1873, " 1873....	25,560 40	3,907 72	....
" " 1874, " 1874....	27,938 90	2,378 50	....
" " 1875, " 1875....	29,639 38	1,700 48	....
" " 1876, " 1876....	31,048 76	1,409 38	....
" " 1877, " 1877....	32,276 57	1,227 81	....
" " 1878, " 1878....	29,636 01	....	$2,640 56
" " 1879, " 1879....	33,343 20	3,707 19	....
" " 1880, " 1880....	37,385 00	4,041 80	....
" " 1881, " 1881....	40,385 87	3,000 87	....
" " 1882, " 1882....	43,818 73	3,432 86	....
" " 1883, " 1883....	48,269 89	4,451 16	....
" " 1884, " 1884....	51,852 78	3,582 89	....
" " 1885, " 1885....	53,550 35	1,697 57	....
" " 1886, " 1886....	58,725 00	5,174 65	....
" " 1887, " 1887....	67,121 92	8,396 92	....
" " 1888, " 1888....	73,197 03	6,075 11	....
" " 1889, " 1889....	81,110 68	7,913 65	....
	$818,152 91	....	

EXHIBIT E.

*Location, Size and Length of Main Pipe, Large Private Pipe
and Fire Hydrant Branches Laid in 1889.*

LOCATION.	SIZE	FEET	IN.
Second street. between Sassafras and Myrtle	4	354	8
Fifth street, between Wallace and Ash	6	184	....
Fifth street, between Parade and Wallace	6	51	6
Fifth street, corner of Ash	4	7	7
Fifth street, east of Parade	4	7	4
Seventh street, east of Reed	6	83	....
Ninth street, west of Walnut	6	90	....
Tenth street, between Walnut and Cherry	6	191	6
Twelfth street, between Chestnut and Cherry	12	1422	....
Thirteenth street, between Ash and Reed	6	48	....
Thirteenth street, between Reed and Wayne	6	43	4
Thirteenth street, between Division and Holland	6	194	....
Fourteenth street, between Ash and Reed	6	323	5
Fifteenth street, between Wallace and Ash	6	574	....
Sixteenth street, between Parade and Wallace	6	472	7
Sixteenth street, between Chestnut and Walnut	6	729	....
Sixteenth street, between Walnut and Cherry	6	723	6
Eighteenth street, east of Raspberry	4	8	6
Eighteenth street, between Cascade and Cranberry	6	1441	9
Nineteenth street, between Chestnut and Walnut	6	459	....
Nineteenth street, between Peach and Sassafras	6	292	....
Twentieth street, from Myrtle eastward	6	96	....
Twenty-first street, east of Chestnut	4	8	5
Twenty-fourth street, between Sassafras and Chestnut	6	860	2
Twenty-fourth street, from Ash westward	6	322	7
Twenty-fifth street, between Sassafras and Myrtle	6	62	10
Twenty-fifth street, between Sassafras and Myrtle	6	143	2
East avenue, from Twelfth street north	6	263	....
Reed street, from Eleventh street south	6	166	2
Reed street, from Twenty-first to Twenty-third	6	634	....
Reed street, north of Twenty-third	4	9	6
Ash street, between Twenty-fourth and Twenty-fifth	6	166	....
Parade street, north of Nineteenth	4	16	....
Parade street, south of Eighth	1½	......	....
Parade street, north of Twelfth	1½	......	....
German street, between Twenty-third and Twenty-fourth	6	385	....
Holland street, from Ninth street south	6	149	....
French street, south of Twenty-third	4	8	4
French street, between Twenty-second and Twenty-fourth	4	481	....
French street, between Twentieth and Twenty-first	6	149	6
French street, south of Twentieth	4	7	10
Myrtle street, between Eleventh and Twelfth	6	137	....
Myrtle street, from Eighth to Ninth	6	347	....
Myrtle street, from Twenty-fifth south	6	55	....
Carried forward		12,168	2

LOCATION.	SIZE	FEET.	IN.
Brought forward..	....	12,168	2
Chestnut street, between Seventh and Thirteenth..........	30	2069	7
Walnut street, between Fourth and Fifth..................	6	277	....
Cherry street, between Fourth and Fifth,.................	6	162	....
Cherry street, between Tenth and Eleventh...............	6	229	6
Cherry street, corner of Thirteenth......................	4	31	....
Poplar street, between Twentieth and Twenty-second......	6	260	....
Poplar street, between Ninth and Tenth..................	6	63	....
Poplar street, corner of Ninth...........................	4	8	....
Liberty street, between Fourth and Fifth.................	6	307	3
Plum street, between Seventeenth and Eighteenth.........	6	124	3
Cascade street, from Third street north..................	4	633	6
Cranberry street, from Eighteenth to Ninteenth...........	6	325	....
Total..	....	16,658	3

RECAPITULATION.

Four-Inch Pipe laid....................	1100 feet 8 inches			
Six-Inch Pipe laid.....................	12066 feet			
Twelve-Inch Pipe laid..................	1422 feet			
Thirty-inch Pipe laid..................	2069 feet 7 inches		16658	3

PIPE TAKEN UP IN 1889.

On Second street, 52 feet of ¾-inch......	52			
On Twelfth street, 1422 feet of 4-inch pipe.	1422			
On Liberty street, 320 ft. 2 in., ¼-inch pipe	320–2		1794	2
Actual gain in 1889...................................	....		12,723	6
In miles............................	2 2163–5280			

EXHIBIT F.

Total Amount of Distributing Pipe, Fire Hydrant Branches and Large Private Pipe Laid to December 31, 1889.

LENGTH IN FEET AND INCHES.

STREETS.	Less than 4-inch.	4-inch.	6-inch.	12-inch.	20-inch.	30-inch.
Front and Dock..	1,182.5	2.186.2	....	....	147	330.3
Short street	159.10	1.473.9	....	....	....	....
Second	1.558.8	5,515.4	....	....	....	....
Third	237	6.691.9	....	....	....	....
Fourth	....	3.817 3	4.625.6	....	....	....
Fifth	4.141.1	6,719.10	1 026.10	....	....	....
North Park	75	101.4	820	....	....	....
Sixth	152.5	1 927.1	9.744	....	....	....
South Park	182.1	22.7	424	....	....	....
Seventh	....	3.506.6	823.2	5.362.2	....	....
Eighth	540.8	9,666.8	....	....	....	....
Ninth	9	7.398.8	1,656 8	....	....	....
Tenth	49	481.11	11,025.1	....	....	....
Eleventh	275	8.530.2	2,885.10	....	....	....
Twelfth	47.6	1.900.7	13.371.10	1.422	....	....
Thirteenth	....	3 160.1	1.796.5	....	....	....
Fourteenth	....	2.994.1	1,073.10	....	....	....
Fifteenth	358.2	3.187.5	712.6	....	....	....
Huron	....	1.436.10	....	....	....	....
Sixteenth	....	1.418.8	5.297.6	....	....	....
Seventeenth	....	7.440.1	1,638.6	....	....	....
Eighteenth	11	2.980.4	13 976.4	....	....	....
Buffalo Road	....	1,168	....	....	....	....
Nineteenth	125.8	2.008.4	1,699.5	....	....	....
Twentieth	....	1.746.4	590	....	....	....
Twenty-first	....	71 7	2,719.6	6.560	....	....
Twenty-second	....	3.637.8	....	....	....	....
Twenty-third	....	2,906.2	....	....	....	....
Twenty-fourth	....	1,634 8	1.387.9	....	....	....
Twenty-fifth	....	3,281.8	837	....	....	....
Twenty-sixth	30	979.8	4,467.8	1.420.6	1.064.6	....
Twenty-ninth	....	....	377.8	....	....	....
Railroad	....	1,780	....	....	....	....
East avenue	....	593.3	3.303.6	....	....	....
Wayne	....	....	858	....	....	....
Reed	....	9.6	800.2	....	....	....
Carried forw'd..	9,134.6	102,373.11	87,938.8	14,764.8	1,211.6	330.3

LENGTH IN FEET AND INCHES.

STREETS.	Less than 4-inch.	4-inch.	6 inch.	12-inch.	20-inch.	30-inch.
Brought forw'd	9.134.6	102,373.11	87,938.8	14 764.8	1,211.6	330.3
Ash			1,193.10	2.201.6		
Wallace	391.11		1,366 9	1.134.10		
Vine			399.8			
Parade			5.545 11	3,343.10		
German			3.729.11	1.199.10		
Division			317.2			
Holland	203.4		9.351.1	316		
French	262.6		5.541.8	2,463 8		
State	20		5.077.6	4.099.7		
Turnpike	6.6		8.7	795		
Peach	352.3		1,087	5.931.8	1,996	
Waterford ave			910	900.2		
Sassafras	570		9.608.4			
Myrtle	8.3		4,768.2	1,607		
Hickory			631.6			
Chestnut	1.206.6		4,722.8	24	9,222.3	4.526.8
Walnut	9		4,343.1	1,077.9		
Cherry			3.378.2	856		
Poplar			861.10	3,272.7		
Liberty	320.2		1,095.10	307.3		
Plum			623.8	550.7		
Cranberry				325		
Cascade	500		1,120.4			
Maple			805			
Scott			31.6	854.6		
Hazel				365		
Total	12.984.11	168,885.1	119,477.3	16,784.8	10.433.9	4,856.11

RECAPITULATION.

	FEET.	IN.
Less than four inches	12,984	11
Four-inch pipe	168,885	1
Six-inch pipe	119,477	3
Twelve-inch pipe	16,784	8
Twenty-inch pipe	10,433	9
Thirty-inch pipe	4,856	11
Total	333.422	7
Total in feet	333,422	9
Deduct amount taken out and relaid	2,292	1
Total gain in feet	331,130	8
Total in miles ....62 miles—	3.770	8

EXHIBIT G.

Location, Number and Length of Street Connections Made During the Year 1889.

STREETS.	Number of Connections.	FEET.	IN.	STREETS.	Number of Connections.	FEET.	IN.
Front and Docks....	4	87	6	Brought forw'd....	235	4,276	125
Short	1	26	11				
Second.............	5	82	....	Twenty-fifth........	8	119	2
Third	9	177	6	Twenty-sixth........	7	102	8
Fourth	5	97	....	East avenue	6	175	2
Fifth	7	128	8	Reed...............	3	32	4
South Park.........	1	8	....	Ash................	2	34	3
Sixth..............	8	227	....	Wallace	2	44	9
Seventh............	12	220	9	Parade	9	280	9
Eighth	13	169	....	German	9	163	4
Ninth	11	146	3	Division............	2	9	6
Tenth..............	10	350	3	Holland............	10	187	1
Eleventh...........	10	126	7	French	7	130	1
Twelfth	16	361	10	State...............	11	189	4
Thirteenth..........	13	244	6	Peach	3	34	4
Fourteenth	13	113	11	Waterford avenue...	2	40	9
Fifteenth...........	5	50	3	Sassafras	3	42	....
Huron..............	2	40	....	Myrtle.............	10	155	9
Sixteenth...........	10	227	2	Chestnut...........	3	75	8
Seventeenth	12	177	10	Walnut.............	3	44	6
Eighteenth..........	17	310	5	Cherry	10	212	11
Nineteenth	9	68	2	Maple	1	20	6
Twentieth.	7	187	10	Poplar.............	4	87	4
Twenty-first	13	291	....	Liberty	2	62	4
Twenty-second......	4	64	2	Plum	2	7	10
Twenty-third.......	7	106	8	Cascade	1	7	5
Twenty-fourth......	11	215	3				
				Total.............	355	6,546	10
Carried forward...	235	4,276	125				

LENGTH OF CONNECTIONS IN MILES.

	MILES	FEET.
Connections made in 1889......................................	1	266
Previously made...	21	3,157
Total..	22	3,423

EXHIBIT H.

*Location and Style of Fire Hydrants set in 1889, all Being
Four-Inch Steamer and Hose.*

STREET.	WHERE LOCATED.	NAME.
Fifth street........	Northeast corner of Ash....................	Matthews.
Fifth street........	Northeast corner of Parade.................	"
Eighth street......	Northwest corner of Walnut.................	"
Twelfth street.....	Northwest corner of Perry..,,.............	"
Eighteenth street..	Northeast corner of Myrtle.................	"
Eighteenth street..	Northeast corner of Raspberry..............	"
Twenty-first street..	Northeast corner of Chestnut...............	"
Reed street........	Northeast corner of Twenty-third	"
Railroad street.....	Corner of Twenty-third....................	"
Parade street	Southeast corner of Eighth.................	"
Parade street	Northeast corner of Nineteenth.............	"
French street......	Southeast corner of Twenty-third...........	"
French street......	Southeast corner of Twentieth.............	"
Myrtle street.......	Southeast corner of Twenty-fifth............	"
Cherry street......	Northwest corner of Thirteenth.............	"
Poplar street.......	Southeast corner of Ninth.................	"

RECAPITULATION.

Fire Hydrants in new location.. 13
Fire Hydrants renewed... 3
—16
    Net gain in 1889.. 13

NUMBER AND STYLE OF FIRE HYDRANTS IN DAILY USE.

New style Mathews.............	217	Morris, Tasker & Co............	2
Old style Matthews.............	11	Union.........................	1
Bay State.....................	27		
West Jersey...................	30	Total	315
Pittsburg.....................	21	Private Fire Hydrants..........	31
Home-made....................	2		
Ludlow.......................	4	Grand total................	346

HYDRANTS FOR THE SUPPLY OF WAGON SPRINKLERS.

Ninth street, between State and French.................Jarecki, Hays & Co.
Twelfth street, near southwest corner of Peach.........   "
Fifteenth street, near southwest corner of Peach........   "
Eighteenth street, near northwest corner of Peach......
State street, at East Park...............................
State street, between Tenth and Eleventh...............
State street, southeast corner of Twelfth...............
Myrtle street, southeast corner of Eighteenth...........
Walnut street, northeast corner of Eighteenth..........
Parade street, southeast corner of Eighth..............
Parade street, northeast corner of Twelfth.............

EXHIBIT I.
Location, Size and Kind of Stop Valves Set in '89.

STREET.	WHERE LOCATED.	KIND.	SIZE
Second street	Between State and Peach	Eddy.	4
Fifth street	West line of Ash	"	6
Seventh street	East line of Reed	"	6
Twelfth street	East line of Chestnut	"	6
Twelfth street	West line of Chestnut	"	12
Twelfth street	West line of Walnut	"	12
Twelfth street	Between Sassafras and Myrtle	"	4
Twelfth street	Between Walnut and Cherry	"	4
Thirteenth street	East line of Holland	"	6
Fourteenth street	East line of Wallace	"	4
Fifteenth street	East line of Wallace	"	6
Sixteenth street	East line of Parade	"	4
Sixteenth street	West line of Chestnut	"	6
Sixteenth street	West line of Walnut	"	6
Eighteenth street	West line of Sassafras	"	6
Eighteenth street	East line of Myrtle	"	6
Eighteenth street	West line of Cascade	"	6
Eighteenth street	West line of Raspberry	"	6
Buffalo Road	West line of East avenue	"	4
Twenty-first street	East line of Myrtle	"	12
Twenty-fourth street	West line of Myrtle	"	6
Twenty-fourth street	West line of Ash	"	6
Twenty-fifth street	East line of Wallace	"	4
East avenue	North line of Twelfth	"	6
Reed street	South line of Eleventh	"	6
Reed street	South line of Twenty-first	"	6
Parade street	Twenty feet south of Eighth	"	.....
Parade street	Fourteen feet north of Twelfth	"	.....
German street	South line of Twenty-third	"	6
Holland street	South line of Ninth	"	6
Holland street	South line of Fourteenth	"	4
Holland street	South line of Twelfth	"	4
French street	North line of Twenty-fourth	"	6
Myrtle street	North line of Ninth	"	6
Chestnut street	South of Twelfth	"	20
Chestnut street	South of Twelfth	"	20
Chestnut street	South of Twelfth	"	30
Walnut street	South line of Sixteenth	"	4
Walnut street	South line of Eighth	"	4
Cherry street	South line of Sixteenth	"	4
Cherry street	South line of Fourth	"	6
Cherry street	North line of Eleventh	"	6
Liberty street	South line of Fourth	"	6
Plum street	North line of Eighteenth	"	6
Cascade street	North line of Third	"	4
Cranberry street	South line of Eighteenth	"	6

EXHIBIT I—Continued.

RECAPITULATION.

Total number of kinds in 1888 562
Four-inch put in in 1889 13
Six-inch put in in 1889. 25
Twelve-inch put in in 1889 3
Twenty-inch put in in 1889 2
Thirty-inch put in in 1889 1

Total 606

REPLACED.

Six-inch 1
Four by Twelve 1
Four by Four 2

—4   4

Balance December 31, 1889 602

EXHIBIT J.

Number of Families, Stores, Offices, Manufactories, &c., Supplied with City Water During the Year '89

Breweries	3	Internal Revenue Office	1
Board of Trade	1	Jail	1
Boat Houses	5	Laundries	6
Bakeries	15	Libraries	1
Butcher Shops	59	Lumber Yards	4
Brick Yards	1	Livery Stables	17
Banks	6	Manufacturers	73
Barber Shops	45	Malt Houses	4
Billiard Rooms	3	Orphan Asylums	2
Bottling Works	7	Opera Houses	2
City Hall	1	Oil Works	1
Coffee and Spice Mill	1	Offices	203
Churches	19	Old Folks' Homes	2
Cemeteries	1	Photograph Galleries	8
Coal and Iron Docks	1	Police Station	1
Club Houses	2	Public Halls	28
Custom House	1	Packing Houses	3
Court House	1	Printing Offices	12
Convent	1	Passenger Depots	2
Driving Park	1	Railroads	4
Dyeing Works	2	Railroad Shops	2
Engine Houses	6	Rink	1
Express Offices	2	Soldiers' Home	1
Electric Light Company	1	Schools	22
Fish Hatchery	1	Stores	408
Families	5,700	Saloons and Eating Houses	115
Families by permit and other uses	56	Slaughter Houses	13
Fish Houses	5	Street Railway	1
Freight Houses	5	Transfer Company	2
Fountains, Private	5	United States Signal Station	1
" Public	2	Work Shops	83
" Drinking	2	Watering Troughs	18
Flouring Mills	4	U. S. Steamer Michigan	1
Gas Works	1	U. S. Court House	1
Grain Elevators	3	U. S. Postoffice	1
Gas Offices	2		
Green Houses	5	Total	7,086
Hospitals	2	Last Enumeration	6,636
Hotels and Boarding Houses	61		
Ice Houses	2	Increase	450

EXHIBIT K.

Pumping Engine Statistics for '89.

The Pumps are three in number. Two are known as the Cornish Bull Pumps. The diameter of each plunger is 20¼ inches, and each has a stroke of 10 feet. The capacity of each Pump is estimated to be 165 gallons to each stroke. The third Pump is a Gaskill Horizontal Pumping Engine, of a guaranteed capacity of 5,000,000 gallons daily at a piston speed of 120 feet per minute against a head of 237 feet. The Stand Pipe is 251 feet high. The Reservoir is nearly two miles from the Pumping Works, the bottom of which is 210 feet above the surface of the Bay, and the water has been maintained during the year at an average depth in the Reservoir of about 24 feet.

MONTHS	Days single Cornish Pump run.	Days both Cornish Pumps run.	Days Gaskill Pump run.	Strokes of Cornish Pump.	Revolutions of Gaskill Pump.	Gallons Pumped.	Daily average.	Average Lift in Feet.	Pounds of Coal per Month.	Cost of Coal.
Jan.			29		554,930	100,997,260	3,257,976	235.50	363,775	$200 07
Feb			29		642,330	116,904,060	4,175,145	236.50	424,025	223 21
March			31		658,290	119,808,780	3,864,799	237.00	436,210	239 91
April			30		574,675	104,590,850	3,486,361	236.40	408,250	224 53
May	2		28	8,760	654,164	120,503,248	3,887,201	234.00	390,309	214 66
June			29		607,811	110,621,602	3,687,386	233.00	322,800	177 54
July			31		842,429	153,322,078	4,945,873	233.00	408,200	224 51
Aug.	4	12	20	276,008	539,321	143,697,742	4,635,411	236.00	551,400	303 27
Sept	1	6	23	139,678	545,518	122,331,146	4,077,704	237.00	446,350	225 49
Oct.			28		723,577	133,210,004	4,297,096	231.00	376,150	206 88
Nov.			30		675,505	123,341,910	4,111,397	237.00	371,550	204 35
Dec.			31		692,470	126,029,540	4,065,469	237.00	394,000	216 70
	7	18	339	424,446	7,811,020	1,475,358,220	4,040,908	235.28	4,893,019	$2,661 12

The regular employes at the Pumping Works are one mechanical engineer, two assistant engineers, three firemen and one watchman. The mechanical engineer stands a watch of five hours, from 7 to 12 every forenoon; the assistants divide the remainder of each day equally between them; each one of the firemen stands a watch of eight hours. Beside firing, the firemen unload the coal from the cars, except when both Pumps are run, in which case they are assisted by the watchman or a laborer. The mechanical engineer gives ten hours daily to the service of the Department. the hours when he is not on watch being employed in repairs, supervision, etc. In addition to standing their regular watch. the assistant engineers aid their superior officer in keeping the machinery in order. The watchman takes care of the buildings and grounds, besides doing such other work as may be required of him.

EXHIBIT L.

Amount of Coal consumed in Pumping, Gallons of Water Pumped, Average Height Pumped, Cost per Million Gallons, &c., from the First Year the Works were Operated to December 31, '89.

YEAR.	Tons of coal consumed.	Price of coal per ton from May 1 of each year.	Cost of coal from Jan. 1st to Dec. 31st.	Grades of bituminous coal.	Gallons of water pumped.	Increase or Decrease.	Number of places supplied.	Number of Fire Hydrants.	Average height of water in Reservoir above bay.	Cost of coal per million gallons raised to Reservoir.	Gallons raised to Reservoir by 1 pound of coal.
1868	59.1	$5 05	$309 61	Lump.							
1869	544.4	5 05	4,818 48	"							
1870	1,064.5	5 05	5,159 10	"	246,648,960		1,218				
1871	1,422.7	5 05	7,117 00	"	179,368,495	132,719,535 i.	1,727	97	232.0	$18 76	98.5
1872	1,308.5	5 05	6,528 50	"	395,076,000	115,708,505 i.	2,140	99	232.0	16 52	150.9
1873	1,672.5	5 05	8,412 65	"	384,062,415	11,013,585 d.	2,475	103	232.0	21 90	114.8
1874	1,759.0	4 85	7,709 54	"	444,817,395	60,754,980 i.	2,663	107	233.0	17 33	126.4
1875	1,836.4	4 85	8,657 61	"	531,005,475	86,181,680 i.	2,700	110	232.0	16 30	145.5
1876	1,105.1	4 00	8,925 22	"	670,726,650	139,721,175 i.	2,763	112	232.0	13 30	159.3
1877	2,456.6	3 70	8,509 33	"	660,981,810	9,744,840 d.	2,854	114	232.0	12 75	135.7
1878	2,463.3	3 35	7,945 37	"	682,399,315	21,390,505 i.	2,915	115	232.0	11 64	136.4
1879	2,628.1	3 09	7,428 92	"	807,800,400	125,408,085 i.	3,011	121	232.0	9 19	153.6
1880	3,076.1	1 99	6,978 41	Slack.	775,805,250	31,995,150 i.	3,568	126	232.0	8 99	126.0
1881	3,430.3	1 90	6,517 58	"	975,640,634	200,235,684 i.	4,110	161	232.0	6 68	142.2
1882	2,968.2	1 75	5,355 93	"	829,759,260	145,881,674 d.	4,687	171	234.0	6 45	139.7
1883	2,398.2	1 55	3,908 59	"	815,939,685	13,819,575 d.	5,077	197	234.7	4 66	170.0
1884	3,010.8	1 45	4,502 61	"	917,781,350	105,841,665 i.	5,395	248	234.3	4 99	152.4
1885	3,243.8	1 30	4,575 79	"	1,036,496,665	118,715,315 i.	5,658	270	232.9	4 40	159.7
1886	3,369.0	1 25	4,318 64	"	1,117,389,075	80,892,410 i.	6,140	280	233.3	3 86	165.8
1887	2,820.4	1 15	3,589 31	"	1,218,213,688	106,824,583 i.	6,368	318	234.1	2 95	216.0
1888	2,393.3	1 09	2,545 46	"	1,341,708,002	123,494,314 i.	6,600	333	234.6	1 89	292.1
1889	2,446.0	1 08	2,661 12	"	1,475,358,220	133,650,218 i.	7,086	346	335.2	1 80	301.5

EXHIBIT M.

Table Showing the Water Rates Per 1,000 Gallons in 162 Cities Where Meters are Used.

MAINE.	Cents.	NEW YORK—Continued.	Cents.	MINNESOTA.	Cents.
Bangor	30	Utica	15 to 30	Minneapolis	10 to 20
Portland	20 to 40	Waverly	20	Winona	8
NEW HAMPSHIRE.		Waterford	5 to 20	St. Paul	15 to 40
Manchester	20	Whitehall	6 to 20	MISSOURI.	
Nashua	15 to 30	Yonkers	16 to 40	Hannibal	20 to 50
VERMONT.		NEW JERSEY.		Kansas City	10 to 35
St. Albans	10 to 30	Bridgeton	20	Springfield	25
Burlington	12 to 50	Hackensack	13 to 23	St. Louis	12½ to 30
MASSACHUSETTS.		Jersey City	21 to 27		
Amesbury	30 to 50	Morristown	33	Abilene	30 to 50
Boston	20	Newark	15	Atchison	20
Clinton	15 to 50	New Brunswick	12½ to 50	COLORADO.	
Cambridge	10 to 20	Trenton	15 to 20	Denver City	30
Fall River	30	PENNSYLVANIA.		Gunnison	10
Haverhill	15 to 20	Allegheny City	15	NEBRASKA.	
Hingham	25	Bloomsburg	10 to 35	Lincoln	10 to 20
Lawrence	20 to 25	Conshohocken	15	CALIFORNIA.	
Lowell	15	Easton	16½ to 40	Los Angeles	30
Lynn	17½ to 20	ERIE	6 to 10	Oakland	30 to 55
New Bedford	2½ to 15	Franklin	60	San Francisco	23½ to 46
Northampton	10 to 20	Hazleton	10 to 15	Vallego	40 to $1
North Adams	10 to 15	Lebanon	5 to 15	DELAWARE.	
Quincy	12½ to 30	Meadville	8 to 30	Wilmington	10
Peabody	20	McKeesport	4½ to 30	MARYLAND.	
Pittsfield	10	Philadelphia	8	Baltimore	8
Salem	13½ to 20	Pitsburg	5 to 20	Hagerstown	8 to 60
Springfield	10 to 20	Reading	10¾ to 21½	VIRGINIA.	
Taunton	12½ to 25	OHIO.		Norfolk	20 to 40
Waltham	25 to 30	Cleveland	6⅔ to 13⅔	Richmond	15
Westboro	50	Cincinnati	9	NORTH CAROLINA.	
Worcester	15 to 25	Columbus	7 to 20	Charlotte	30 to 50
CONNECTICUT.		Dayton	8 to 40	Wilmington	10 to 20
Bridgeport	20 to 30	Norwalk	10	SOUTH CAROLINA.	
Hartford	7½ to 30	Sandusky	6 to 20	Charleston	25 to 60
Meriden	10 to 25	Springfield	10 to 40	GEORGIA.	
New Britain	10	Toledo	8 to 20	Atlanta	17
New Haven	10 to 35	Wooster	15	ALABAMA.	
New London	20 to 30	INDIANA.		Birmingham	6 to 40
Norwich	15 to 30	Indianapolis	12 to 40	Montgomery	25
Stonington	10 to 20	Terre Haute	11	LOUISIANA.	
RHODE ISLAND.		ILLINOIS.		New Orleans	15 to 30
Providence	15 to 30	Bloomington	10 to 15	TEXAS.	
Pawtucket	6 to 30	Chicago	8 to 10	Fort Worth	20 to 45
Woonsocket	30	Joliet	15 to 30	San Antonio	25 to 50
Waterbury	10 to 30	Jacksonville	13 to 40	KENTUCKY.	
NEW YORK.		Quincy	15 to 50	Maysville	15 to 30
Albany	5 to 40	MICHIGAN.		Newport	10
Amsterdam	6 to 30	Bay City	5 to 10	Owensboro	10 to 25
Binghamton	6 to 25	Detroit	10	Lexington	17½ to 25
Brooklyn	10½	East Saginaw	6 to 12	Louisville	6 to 35
Buffalo	3	Flint	6 to 30	TENNESSEE.	
Catskill	12 to 25	Grand Rapids	9½ to 30	Chattanooga	6 to 33
Cortland & Homer	20 to 50	Kalamazoo	10	Knoxville	10 to 15
Corning	10 to 30	Port Huron	5 to 20	Nashville	7 to 15
Elmira	9 to 45	WISCONSIN.		CANADA.	
Flushing	20 to 60	Kenosha	10 to 15	Brantford	12 to 20
Johnstown	25	Milwaukee	4⅓ to 20	Hamilton	12½
Kingston	30	Madison	20 to 50	Halifax	30
Mt. Morris	10 to 30	IOWA.		London	20 to 33½
New York	13⅔	Council Bluffs	15 to 35	St. Catharine	14
Owego	30	Cedar Rapids	15 to 40		
Oneonta	20 to 50	Dubuque	30 to 60		
Oneida	20 to 50	Davenport	10 to 40		
Rochester	5 to 13	Des Moines	15 to 20		
Saratoga	15	Ottumwa	10 to 30	Average Minimum Price, 9¼	
Syracuse	6 to 25	Muscatine	35 to 60	Average Maximum Price, 28	
Troy	10 to 20	Sioux City	13 to 40		

EXHIBIT N.

Cost of Water to the Average Householder in Twenty-five Cities, Compiled from Official Reports to this Department.

CITIES.	Population 1880.	Family Charge.	Pan Water Closets.	Self-closing Urinal.	Bath Tub.	Self-closing Wash stand.	Permanent Wash Tub.	Two Horses.	Cow.	Street Sprinkler.	Total.
Allegheny	78,000	$8 75	$3 00	$2 00	$3 00	$1 00	$1 50	$1 50	$ 75	$3 00	$24 50
Boston	302,000	7 00	5 00	2 50	5 00	5 00	5 00	2 00	75	5 00	37 25
Buffalo	156,000	7 20	3 50	3 00	3 00	1 00	2 00	2 40	90	2 50	25 50
Chicago	503,000	6 00	3 00	1 00	4 00		5 00	2 00	75	3 00	21 75
Columbus, Ohio	51,000	6 00	3 00	3 00	2 00	2 00	2 00	4 00	2 00	5 80	32 80
Dayton, Ohio	38,000	6 00	2 50	3 00	3 00	1 25	2 00	2 50	1 00	3 30	45 30
Detroit	116,000	7 00	4 00	3 00	3 50	1 00	2 00	2 00	75	4 00	28 25
ERIE (1890)	**40,000**	**5 00**	**3 00**	**2 00**	**3 00**	**1 00**	**2 00**	**2 00**	**75**	**3 00**	**21 75**
East Saginaw, Mich.	19,000	7 00	2 50	3 00	3 50		2 00	4 00	1 00	3 00	26 50
Fall River, Mass.	49,000	5 00	5 00	2 00	3 00		4 50	4 00	1 00	6 00	31 00
Grand Rapids, Mich.	32,000	8 00	4 00	3 00	3 00	2 50	2 00	2 50		6 00	33 00
Indianapolis	75,000	5 00	3 00	3 00	5 00	1 00	1 00	5 00		10 00	32 00
Lawrence, Mass.	39,000	6 00	4 00	3 00	3 00	2 00		3 00	50	3 30	25 80
Milwaukee	115,000	6 00	3 00	75	3 00	2 00	1 50	3 00	1 00	5 00	22 00
Minneapolis	47,000	4 00	3 00	2 00	3 00	50	1 50	2 00	1 00	3 00	26 25
Newark, N. J.	136,000	6 25	2 50	3 50	3 00	50	2 00	2 50	50	3 00	26 25
New York	1,200,000	6 75	10 00	5 00	5 00		2 00	6 00	75		32 75
Omaha, Neb.	30,000	6 75	2 50	2 00	3 00	1 00	2 00	5 00	75	5 00	30 00
Philadelphia	847,000	5 00	5 00	2 50	4 00	1 00	1 00	2 00	75	5 00	28 75
Pittsburg	156,000	9 00	5 00	2 40	3 20		2 00	2 50	1 50	3 00	23 50
Sandusky, Ohio	15,838	9 00	2 00	2 00	4 00	1 00	1 00	4 50	1 50	3 50	25 50
St. Paul (1885)	41,000	8 00	4 00	2 40	3 00		2 00	4 80		2 40	24 70
Syracuse	52,000	8 00	5 00	3 00	3 00	1 00	2 00	3 00	75	6 00	31 75
Toledo	50,000	5 50	2 50	2 50	3 50		3 00	6 00	1 50	5 00	28 50
Utica	34,000	7 00	6 00	3 00	5 00			6 00	1 50	8 00	31 50

EXHIBIT O.

Report of the State Board of Health on 12 Samples of Water Submitted for Analysis December 10, 1889.

ED. ANNALS OF HYGIENE:—I have this day sent you twelve samples of water, by direction of the Board of Water Commissioners of this city. It is desired that you make a complete statement of the analysis in the forthcoming number of the *Annals of Hygiene*—the official organ of the State Board of Health.   B. F. SLOAN, Secretary.

These samples were forwarded to Dr. Chas. M. Cresson, who thus reports : Waters received from the State Board of Health, marked " Erie, Nos. 1 to 12." Locations not given :

Result of chemical and microscopical examinations as follows :

Samples Marked.	Results Expressed in Parts per Million.				Remarks.
	Free Ammon	Alb. Ammon	Nitrates.	Chlorine.	
Erie, Pa., "No. 1,"...	0.137	0.055	0.285	1.937	Fair condition for drink'g purposes
" "No. 2,"...	0.027	0.055	trace.	1.772	" " "
" "No. 3,"...	0.027	0.083	0.171	3.188	" " "
" "No. 4,"...	0.055	0.165	trace.	2.828	" " "
" "No. 5,"...	0.027	0.083	20.560	17.720	Contains cesspool drainage. Unfit for use.
" "No. 6,"...	0.027	0.027	2.742	4.251	Contains cesspool drainage. Typhoid bacillus.
" "No. 7,"...	0.055	0.687	2.742	386.300	Contains cesspool drainage. Typhoid bacillus.
" "No. 8,"...	0.027	0.055	6.856	8.433	Contains cesspool drainage. Unfit for use.
" "No. 9,"...	trace.	0.137	0.343	61.930	Doubtful, probably contaminated and dangerous to use.
" "No. 10,"...	0.055	0.165	41.136	73.342	Contains cesspool drainage. Typhoid bacillus.
" "No. 11,"...	0.055	0.220	8.227	97.094	Contains cesspool drainage. Typhoid bacillus.
" "No. 12,"...	0.055	0.083	1.714	103.980	Contains cesspool drainage. Dysentery.

Waters Nos. 1, 2, 3 and 4 are in fit condition for drinking purposes. They contain minute amounts of decaying animal and vegetable matter, but not enough to affect their utility for household purposes. They are to be classed with waters fit for city use.

No. 9 is in doubtful condition for household use. I find nothing in it to absolutely condemn it, but indications require that it should be examined frequently for the presence of hurtful material.

Sources Nos. 5 and 8 have been badly contaminated by cesspool drainage and contain sufficient nitrates to forbid their use for household purposes.

Nos. 6, 7, 10 and 11 are sources that should be abandoned at once, as there is evidently free communication with cesspools, and each of them contains large numbers of typhoid bacilli.

No. 12 contains drainage, such as I have found to come from cesspools used by dysenteric cases.   CHARLES M. CRESSON, M. D.

KEY TO ABOVE REPORT.

No. 1, from Channel Piers.
No. 2, from Lake, north of Whallon's Piers.
No. 3, from inlet at Water Works.
No. 4, from Water Office.
No. 5, from private well, Seventh street, between French and Holland.
No. 6, from private well, Nineteenth street, between Walnut and Cherry.
No. 7, from private well, 431 Thirteenth street, east of Parade.
No. 8, from private well, —— Fourth street, west of Chestnut.
No. 9, from private well, —— Second street, east of Hospital.
No. 10, from private well, 133 Eighth street, west of Peach.
No. 11, from private well, 15 and 17 Seventh street, between State and Peach.
No. 12, from private well, 405 State street.

It must be stated that this "key," which was sent *sealed* to the editor of this journal, was not opened until after the analyses were made, when the seal was broken in the presence of Dr. Cresson and the editor.

RATES FOR CITY WATER.

All are Annual, Except as Otherwise Indicated.

Bath Tub, private...$		3 00
" " each additional..		1 50
" " public...		5 00
Bakery, per barrel of flour used (but no charge less than $5).............		01
Barber Shop, including Hand Basin, first chair.................................		.4 00
" " " " each additional chair.................		2 00
Blacksmith Shop, one fire...		5 00
" " each additional fire................................		2 50
Boarding House (in addition to family rates), per room.....................		1 00
Brewery, per barrel brewed...		03
Building purposes, per bushel lime...		02
Butcher Stalls...	3 00 to	15 00
Charitable Institutions, one-third annual rates...............................		
Cow...		75
Condensing Boiler for steam heating (per season of six months), per horse power		50
Eating Houses...	5 00 to	25 00
Family..		5 00
Hand Basin, for Dwellings, Hotels, and Schools, first basin..............		1 00
" " " " each additional.................		50
" " in Offices, Stores and Blocks, each..........		1 00
Hotel (in addition to family rates), per room.................................		1 00
Livery Stable, per horse..		2 00
Maltster, per 1,000 bushels of malt..		1 75
Offices...	3 00 to	10 00
Private Stable, one or two horses...		2 00
" " each additional horse...................................		1 00
Printing Offices..	5 00 to	30 00
Public Halls...	5 00 to	25 00
Saloons..	5 00 to	25 00
Stores..	3 00 to	15 00
Schools, per pupil...		10
Steam Engine, ten hours per day, each horse power........................		2 50
Slaughter Houses..	5 00 to	50 00
Sleeping Rooms..		1 00
Sprinkling Streets or Lawns with hose, per season.........................	3 00 and up.	
Urinal, private, self-closing..		2 00
" public, ...		3 00
" not self-closing..	3 00 to	10 00
" continuous flow..	10 00 to	30 00
Wash Tub (permanent, with waste)..		2 00
" " " " each additional..................................		1 00
Watering Trough, public..		10 00
Water Closet (pan), in private houses..		3 00
" " " " each additional....................		1 50
" " public...		5 00
" " (hopper), private..		6 00
" " " public..		10 00
Work Shop (ordinary use)..	3 00 to	5 00
All other uses, when not metered, to be assessed by the Department.		

METER RATES (Per Quarter.)

Daily Average, 15,000 gallons or less...	10	cents.
" 15,000 to 20,000 gallons............................	9½	"
" 20,000 to 25,000 "	9	"
" 25,000 to 30,000 "	8½	"
" 30,000 to 35,000 "	8	"
" 35,000 to 40,000 "	7½	"
" 40,000 to 45,000 "	7	"
" 45,000 to 50,000 "	6½	"
" More than 50,000 gallons............................	6	"

—OF THE—

ard of Water Commissioners,

OF ERIE, PA.,

—TO THE—

MAYOR AND CITY COUNCILS

—FOR THE—

YEAR ENDING DEC. 31, 1890.

ERIE, PA.:
DISPATCH PUBLISHING COMPANY, LIMITED.
1891.

WATER COMMISSIONERS.

The Water Commissioners are appointed by the Court of Common Pleas of Erie County, Pa., for a term of three years, one member being named annually, in May.

EX-MEMBERS OF THE BOARD.

*WM. L. SCOTT, 1867 to 1868.   JOHN GENSHEIMER, 1872 to 1878.
*HENRY RAWLE, 1867 to 1872.   M. LIEBEL, 1877 to 1886.
*WM. W. REED, 1867 to 1879.   J. M. BRYANT, 1878 to 1881.
+JOHN C. SELDEN, 1868 to 1872.   G. W. F. SHERWIN, 1879 to 1885.
MATTHEW R. BARR, 1872 to 1877.   BENJ. WHITMAN, 1881 to 1887.

*Messrs. Scott, Rawle and Reed, the first Commissioners, were appointed respectively for terms of one, two and three years.
+Mr. Selden resigned before the expiration of his second term ; Mr. Barr was substituted by the Board and afterward appointed by the Court.

THE PRESENT BOARD.

GEO. W. STARR, 1885 to 1891.   C. KESSLER, 1886 to 1892.
C. J. BROWN, 1887 to 1893.

OFFICERS OF THE DEPARTMENT.

President of the Board— GEO. W. STARR.
Secretary and Treasurer— B. F. SLOAN.
Assistant Secretary - GEO. C. GENSHEIMER.
Clerks JOHN KOLB, DAVID W. HARPER.
Superintendent of Street Work—WM. O'LONE.
Inspectors—A. F. CRANE, F. W. KOEHLER, JOHN D SPAFFORD.
Mechanical Engineer F. A. ROTH.
Assistant Mechanical Engineers—GEO. R. MILLER, JOHN KELLY.
Firemen—R. W. SIMONS, JOSEPH BURNS, JACOB MULLEN.
Watchman at Pumping Works— MICHAEL FLYNN.
Keeper of Reservoir and Grounds—SAMUEL PFISTER.

OFFICE City Hall.
OFFICE HOURS From 7:30 A. M. to 5:45 P. M. ; Monday evenings from 7:30 to 9:00.
REGULAR MEETINGS OF THE BOARD—Every Saturday at 3:00 P. M.

ANNUAL REPORT.

To the Mayor and Councils of the City of Erie:

The Commissioners of Water Works of the City of Erie herewith respectfully present their Annual Report for the year ending December 31, 1890, to-wit:

RECEIPTS.

Balance in Office, January 1, 1890,	$ 486 33	
" Treasury " " "	1,955 90	
Water Rents collected in year 1890,	87,279 96	
From other sources,	1,910 14	
Total,		$91,634 33

EXPENDITURES.

Paid for Construction,	$48,305 48	
" " Maintenance,	19,231 58	
" " Extraordinary Expenses,	537 46	
" Sinking Fund Commissioners,	20,000 00	
Balance in Treasury,	2,858 07	
" " Office,	701 74	
Total,		$91,634 33

The record of this department for the year 1890, shows an amount of work done in the extensions of its mains and the connections therewith, far beyond that of any other year since the works were established. The extension of the thirty-inch main has been continued, and the main has been laid from Twelfth street south, underneath the railroad tracks to a point 112 feet south of Twenty-first street, a distance of 3,047 feet. It is a gratifying fact, that though laid under many railroad tracks the work was completed without accident to any person. It is intended, and contracts have been made, for the pipe needed, to carry this main in the coming year to its connection with the reservoir. When this work is completed, it will enable the department to furnish a full supply of water to all parts of the city, with less strain upon the pumps and with greater certainty of constant and uninterrupted delivery, as there then will be a double connection between the pumping engines and the reservoir. In case of failure of either one of the mains, resort can be had to the other. The demand for water in the city has been greater than ever before known. This is owing mainly to the erection of new manufactories, the enlargement of others, and to the great number of new buildings constructed in all parts of the city, requiring water supply and protection against fire. A large district lying north of Sixth street, on the east side, a locality heretofore wholly without access to the city supply, was this year included in the water limits.

More than five and one-half miles of mains of all sizes have been laid—twice as much in length as was ever before laid in any one year—making the number of miles of main now in use over sixty-eight, or more than one-half the length of all the streets now laid out in the city. Attention has been largely given to connecting the mains where comparatively short distances intervened, thus making them as far as practicable continuous, and consequently more effective as to pressure, and more satisfactory by reason of better circulation. In the first years of the works, with the limited means at their command, the Commissioners were unable to place stop valves in the mains as frequently as were desirable. In consequence, whole districts including many blocks, were of necessity cut off temporarily from use of water, whenever a break occurred, or a main was to be repaired or connected with another. Sixty-five of these stops have been put into the mains during the year. The department intends to continue this work of connecting mains and putting in stop-valves year by year, until the whole net work of pipes shall have become bound together, and so arranged as to the volume of water to be delivered or altogether to be cut off, as to be under complete control, with as little disturbance to the water taker as is possible.

MAINS.

There have been laid during the year, of mains 85$\frac{4}{12}$ feet of three-fourths inch; 323 feet of one inch; 3,856$\frac{7}{12}$ of four inch; 20,968$\frac{1}{12}$ feet of six inch, and 3,047 feet of thirty inch, or 28,875$\frac{1}{12}$ feet : and of

STOP VALVES,

One of one inch; 14 of four inch; 48 of six inch; 1 of twelve inch, and one of thirty inch, or 65 in all.

HYDRANTS,

Three hundred and seventy-two are now connected with the mains: 26 have been put in place during the last year. Of the whole number, 33 are on private premises.

Besides all this necessary work, 703 connections with the
mains have been made, and 642 permits granted, from which
latter number only can the Department at present derive any
benefit. The remainder, or 61, are placed in streets ordered
paved, and are opposite vacant lots. These, with many others
laid in the last few years, are a dead and decaying capital, and
will be of no use or revenue to the Department until the lots
fronting them shall be built upon, yet all are required to be laid
by the city ordinance.

METERS.

Seventy-five meters are now in use. 8 have been discontinued, and 3 new ones have been set during the year.

WATER TAKERS.

Six hundred and forty-two persons and companies have applied for and are now furnished with water, in addition to the
former number of consumers. Whole number supplied, 7,728.

The Gaskill Pump has proved as effective as heretofore, the
old Cornish Pumps having been used singly or with the Gaskill,
but 28 days altogether. The number of gallons of water delivered in 1890 was 1,659,625,551. Average per day, 4,546,919. Increase over last year, 184,267,331 gallons. This constant yearly
increase is a perpetual reminder of the future needs of the Department, and that ere long a heavy outlay for additional pumping power will be required.

Should the number of consumers increase in the same ratio as
in previous years, one twelve month more will tax the capacity
of the Gaskill engine operated day and night for the whole number of days of the year. As no pump can be worked to its full
capacity for such length of time and strain of service, this
will compel the use of the old engines the greater part of the
time, resulting in a heavy loss of economy in coal, greater strain
upon the boilers, and the necessity of constant personal supervision for every minute of time their power is applied, a sudden
break in a main being liable to cause great damage and expense
to the works by the fall of either of the plungers, a contingency
which can never be foreseen or guarded against. These facts are
mentioned because neither the city authorities nor the public
generally are aware of the necessity of preventing waste. A
prudent use of the quantity actually needed may defer the pur-

chase of another pumping engine for some time to come. When, however, such purchase shall become a necessity, the expense will be heavy, for an engine double the capacity of the present Gaskill will be required, and the cost of setting same with its foundation and connections must be defrayed from the receipts of the water rents. For some time after, the city will have to provide for the payment or refunding of such of its bonds as shall mature, without recourse to the Water Board for aid in that direction.

The old battery of boilers has been re-inforced by two others made under contract, each 6 feet in diameter and 18 feet long, of steel and of most approved construction, with all necessary attachments. They were needed to relieve the old boilers, which have been in constant use day and night for many years, and in anticipation of a new pump. They are ready for use and will prove a valuable addition to the works.

It seems almost useless to again call attention to the fact that no credit has as yet been given this Department for furnishing water to the hydrants in our streets, and for other public uses. Very few cities have better protection against fire. The height to which the water is lifted gives a pressure so great that hydrants in nearly all parts of the city, when properly connected with hose, skilfully handled, are as effective as fire engines. This fact should not be overlooked in estimating the advantages and value of the Water Works.

Demands are made upon the Department at times far beyond its resources. It will have been seen that the extensions of mains in the city has added largely to the construction account. When water is asked for under usual conditions, it must be granted. All that the Department can require is, that the call is reasonable and within its means. The out-lying districts which are being rapidly built upon, and which bear their proportion of the expenses of the city government, are entitled to their share of its benefits, including fire protection.

Suggestions, too, are occasionally made, that the inlet pipe should be lengthened out and carried to some distant point or place as yet undefined. The certainty of getting better water is not shown, nor are the many obstacles to be encountered taken into account. Neither the cost nor the limited amount of money in control of the Department applicable to such purpose is con-

dered. Even were it possible to extend the pipe across the Bay
ithin the coming twelve months, it would necessarily defer for
ears to come the purchase of additional pumping power, the
irly and absolute necessity of which is daily brought to notice.
i this connection we beg leave to call attention again to the
ialysis of water (Exhibit O) made by the State Board of Health.
 is worthy of study, coming, as it does, from the highest author-
y in the State on that subject.

During the last year the Councils, with the Health Officer, the
ity Engineer, and the Water Commissioners, have given time
id attention to the subject of an intercepting sewer. The peo-
e of our city are to be congratulated that this long neglected
roject is now in a fair way of being carried on. The action of
ouncils has and will continue to have the public approval, and
ie persistency of the Water Department in urging forward this
heme, begun at the time of starting the Water Works, and fol-
wed up to date, promises to result in the completion, next to
ie Water Works themselves, of the most important and most
eded public work that has been attempted by the city in a
neration.   Respectfully submitted,

                          GEO. W. STARR,
                          C. KESSLER,
                          C. J. BROWN,
Erie, Pa., April 1, 1891.   Water Commissioners.

EXHIBIT A.

Receipts of the Erie Water Department for the Year Ending December 31, 1890.

WATER RENTS.		
Receipts for Month—January	$ 8,280 72	
February	5,748 82	
March	6,180 81	
April	10,160 20	
May	7,933 08	
June	3,480 60	
July	10,341 35	
August	6,994 68	
September	3,589 84	
October	11,243 74	
November	7,246 17	
December	6,079 95	
Total Water Rents	$87,279 96	
Balance December 31, 1889	488 33	
Pipe Laying, Material Sold, &c	1,910 14	
Total from all sources		$ 89,678 43
Deposited in Treasury		88,976 69
Balance		$ 701 74

CR.

rawn in January	2,742 50
February	2,560 95
March	6,054 11
April	7,833 98
May	6,556 28
June	13,567 05
July	10,182 76
August	9,525 83
September	3,189 36
October	7,659 84
November	4,389 25
December	13,813 61

Treasury December 31, 1890

EXHIBIT C.

Expenditures for the Year 1890; also, from Commencement of Works in January, 1867, to January 1, 1891.

	FROM JANUARY 1, 1890, TO DECEMBER 31, 1890.		1867 TO 1890.
FUEL AT WORKS.			
From Com't of works to Dec. 31, 1890..			$ 126,470 35
Paid—R. J. Saltsman, for 2,075,100 lbs. of Coal at $1.15	$ 1,191 19		
Paid—R. J. Saltsman, for 3,350,900 lbs. of Coal at $1.20	2,010 34		
		$ 3,201 53	
SALARIES.			
From Com't of works to Dec. 31, 1890..			124,845 9|
Paid—B. F. Sloan, Sec. and Treas	1,500 00		
Geo. C. Gensheimer, Ass't Sec	1,000 00		
Wm. O. Lone, Supt. of St. Work.	1,080 00		
A. F. Crane, Inspector	840 00		
A. F. Koehler, "	660 00		
John D. Spafford, "	650 00		
Will W. Reed, Clerk	640 00		
Otto Lutje, Ass't Clerk	40 00		
Geo. W. Starr, Commissioner	800 00		
C. Kessler, "	700 00		
C. J. Brown, "	675 00		
		8,585 00	
FIRE HYDRANTS.			
From Com't of works to Dec. 31, 1890..			18,419 5:
Paid—Labor as per Supt. pay roll	89 17		
R. D. Wood & Co	750 70		
Penn'a R. R. Co	24 30		
Frank Hoffman	2 25		
		866 42	
DISTRIBUTING MAINS AND BRANCHES.			
From Com't of works to Dec. 31, 1890..			419,851 67
Paid—Buffalo Cast Iron Pipe Co	7,401 72		
L. S. & M. S. R. R. Co	515 96		
Frank Hoffman	137 85		
A. J. Schuster.	98 44		
R. J. Saltsman	73 00		
E. Funk, Buffalo inspecting pipe.	69 90		
Globe Iron Foundry	66 75		
Adolph Brugger.	30 10		
Humboldt Iron Works	22 11		
O. Thayer & Son	20 42		
Henry Beckman.	5 44		
Cornell Lead Co	1,647 05		
Laying Mains.	4,328 33		
		14,417 07	
Carried forward		$27 070 02	$ 689,587 51

		From January 1, 1890, to December 31, 1890.		1867 to 1889.
ht forward	....		$27,070 02	$ 689 587 51
INEERS AND FIREMEN.				
n't of works to Dec. 31, 1890	....		....	85,089 95
A. Roth, Engineer	$ 1,080 00			
R. Miller, "	895 00			
Kelley, "	895 00			
V. Simons, Fireman	600 00			
ph Burns, "	600 00			
b Mullen, "	600 00			
			4,670 00	
ARE OF HYDRANTS.				
or as per Supt. pay roll	30 78		30 78	
THIRTY INCH MAIN.				
D. Wood & Co	13,410 60			
or as per Supt. pay roll	4,586 34			
. & M. S. R. R. Co	807 63			
nk Hoffman	146 57			
id Schlosser	104 60			
c Albertson	106 80			
Saltsman	41 00			
ard Donnelly	39 60			
nell Lead Co,, lead	1,020 52			
pire Line	39 51			
en Brick Co	26 00			
C. Thayer & Son.	8 00			
na R. R. Co	7 54			
sman & Austin	5 85			
Steam Bending Works	3 06			
			20,353 62	
TREET CONNECTIONS.				
nt of works to Dec. 31, 1890	....		....	68,058 84
or as per Supt. pay roll	2,253 61			
s Manufacturing Co	1,642 26			
onal Tube Works	831 19			
nell Lead Co	181 40			
ki Manufacturing Co.	158 26			
. & M. S. R. R. Co	19 37			
. Butler	6 78			
immons	6 18			
'. Williams & Co.	3 80			
. Sloan, Sec., cash expended.	45			
			5,103 30	
F DIS. MAINS AND BRANCHE .				
n't of works to Dec. 31, 1890	....		....	13,618 62
or as per Supt's pay roll	559 39			
k Hoffman	14 00			
Walker Tool Co.	5 12			
			578 51	
d forward	....		$57,806 23	$ 856 354 92

	FROM JANUARY 1, 1890, TO DECEMBER 31, 1890.	1867 TO 1890.
Brought forward.....................	$57,806 23	$ 856,354 9²

BUILDINGS AND GROUNDS.

From Com't of works to Dec. 31, 1890..		84,217 44
Paid—Labor as per Supt. pay roll......	348 46	
F. W. Miller & Son..............	240 19	
Thos. Tidman, service as watchm'n	200 00	
Penn'a R. R. Co................	35 50	
Erie Gas Co...................	34 62	
James P. Dailey...............	32 50	
Erie Steam Bending Works......	11 52	
Moore, Winchel & Co..........	19 00	
Saltsman & Austin.............	12 62	
C. H. Nunn	9 00	
John O. Baker.................	7 83	
Larry Cummings...............	5 00	
Constable Bros.................	2 67	
Florence Lynch,...............	2 66	
B. F. Sloan, Sec., cash expended.	2 00	
	963 97	

CARE AND REPAIR OF RESERVOIR.

From Com't of works to Dec. 31, 1890..		10,844 6
Paid—Samuel Phister..................	420 00	
Frank Hoffman..................	46 25	
Erie Steam Bending Works......	8 30	
Wm. Brewster..................	7 50	
B. F. Sloan, Sec., cash expended.	5 25	
Henry Beckman & Son..........	1 15	
	488 45	

SHOP, TOOLS AND REPAIRS.

From Com't of works to Dec. 31, 1890..		4,413 4
Paid—F. Walker Tool Co.............	569 07	
Edward Donnelly..............	130 00	
Boston & Lockport Block Co.....	79 60	
Globe Iron Foundry.............	22 94	
Thomas Watkins................	22 50	
A. S. Pinney..................	24 91	
Edison Electric Light Co........	20 98	
Labor as per Supt. pay roll......	14 88	
L. J. Fitzgerald...............	13 73	
R. J. Saltsman................	16 15	
Erie Machine Shop.............	15 22	
Murphy Bros..................	13 75	
Mehl & Sapper.................	14 43	
B. F. Sloan, Sec., cash expended	15 22	
Fred Dehl....................	12 00	
R. W. Simmons................	4 77	
Jarecki Manufacturing Co.......	9 80	
David Schlosser...............	8 75	
South Erie Iron Works..........	2 46	
Constable Bros.................	2 23	
Humboldt Iron Works...........	2 31	
	1,011 30	
Carried forward....................	$602,269 95	$ 955,830 4

Brought forward......................		$69,269 95	$ 955,830 44

STOP VALVES.

rom Com't of works to Dec. 13, 1890..		....	24,153 66
aid—R. D. Wood & Co...............	1,486 26		
Globe Iron Foundry.............	429 62		
Labor as per Supt. pay roll......	272 96		
Penn'a R. R. Co.................	44 91		
Selden Brick Co.................	22 80		
O. C. Thayer....................	12 00		
Frank Hoffman...................	6 75		
Erie Machine Shop..............	2 70		
B. F. Sloan, Sec., cash expended.	1 51		
		2,179 51	

PRINTING AND ADVERTISING.

rom Com't of works to Dec. 31, 1890..		....	4,412 26
aid—F. D. Mallory..................	140 00		
Herald Printing and Pub. Co....	50 85		
Erie Morning Dispatch..........	44 75		
John J. O'Brien.................	32 40		
Erie Sunday Graphic............	11 75		
Erie Daily Times................	3 00		
B. F. Sloan, Sec., cash expended.	9 75		
		292 50	

REPAIR OF ENGINES AND BOILERS.

rom Com't of works to Dec. 31, 1890..		....	28,495 20
aid—E. Walker Tool Co.............	222 14		
Holly Manufacturing Co.........	67 20		
Erie Machine Shop.............	55 88		
Lake Shore Rubber Works......	23 00		
B. F. Sloan, Sec., cash expended.	1 10		
		369 32	

REPAIR OF BOILERS.

or the year 1890....................			
aid—E. Walker Tool Co.............	414 24		
Erie Lime and Cement Co.......	75 00		
South Erie Iron Works..........	66 25		
D. P. Murphy...................	51 12		
P. T. Donnelly.................	38 50		
Noble & Hall...................	6 48		
		651 59	

SUPERINTENDENT'S STORES.

rom Com't of works to Dec. 31, 1890..		....	519 81
aid—Henry Beckman.................	49 35		
Murphy Bros....................	5 46		
B. F. Sloan, Sec., cash expended.	17 36		
Solomon Levi...................	3 80		
R. T. Williams & Co...........	2 41		
Erie Soap Co...................	2 50		
A. S. Pinney...................	2 85		
		83 73	

Carried forward.....................		$63,846 60	$1,013,411 37

	FROM JANUARY 1, 1890, TO DECEMBER 31, 1890.		1867 TO 1890.
Brought forward......................		$63,846 60	$1,013 411 37
OFFICE EXPENSES.			
From Com't of works to Dec. 31, 1890..		....	14,191 00
Paid—N. Y. & Pa. Tel. and Teleph. Ex. $	84 00		
State Board of Health...........	72 00		
James M. Sherwin..............	48 75		
E. J. Riblet....................	41 90		
B. F. Sloan, Sec., cash expended.	52 28		
Moore, Winschel Co...........	11 27		
Union Ice Co..................	9 90		
Bauschard Bros................	9 15		
Erie Morning Dispatch.........	8 00		
		337 25	
HORSE AND WAGON.			
From Com't of works to Dec. 31, 1890..	....	....	4,182 5:
Paid—Geo. L. Siegel, feed.............	144 04		
Wm. O. Lone, barn rent........	100 00		
Dr. John Brice.................	43 00		
George Schleindwein...........	34 40		
R. H. Chinnock, blacksmith work	32 35		
John Dugan....................	24 15		
W. H. Hyke...................	13 75		
Dr. G. W. Bell................	7 75		
W. A. Roberts................	7 50		
C. A. Bell....................	7 20		
Keystone Carriage Works.......	5 65		
A. S. Pinney..................	1 23		
B. F. Sloan, Sec., cash expended.	1 05		
		422 07	
WATER METERS AND CARE.			
From Com't of works to Dec. 31, 1890..	....	....	9,561 9:
Paid—Union Water Meter Co., met & rep	336 02		
David Schlosser................	20 67		
Jarecki Manufacturing Co........	3 86		
Superintendent pay roll........	90 99		
Erie Steam Bending Works......	1 40		
L. S. & M. S. R. R. Co........	1 35		
B. F. Sloan, Sec., cash expended.	2 39		
Constable Bros................	2 50		
		459 18	
LOWERING MAINS.			
From Jan. 1, 1888, to Dec. 31, 1890.....		....	291 05
Paid Labor as per Supt. pay roll......	14 40		
		14 40	
PLUMBING AND PIPE LAYING.			
From Com't of works to Dec. 31, 1890..	....	....	3,945 97
Paid Labor as per Supt. pay roll......	552 88		
Miller Bros....................	14 18		
Jarecki Manufacturing Co........	1 13		
		568 19	
Carried forward.....................		$65,647 69	$1 045 583 84

	December 31, 1890.	1887 to 1890.
ht forward....................	....	$65 647 69	$1 045 583 84

COSTS AND COUNCIL FEES.

n't of works to Dec. 31, 1890..	....	....	1,805 38
V. Loomis....................	$ 9 60		
		9 60	

OIL AND TALLOW.

n't of Works to Dec. 13, 1890..	....	....	7,378 06
ipse Oil Co., bills rendered ..	307 21		
A. Crawford, " " ...	273 28		
iry Beckman, " " ...	1 48		
		581 97	

POSTAGE.

n't of works to Dec. 31, 1890..	....	....	3,605 38
. Hilton, postmaster.........	227 25		
. Sloan, Secretary..........	7 36		
		234 61	

INSURANCE.

n't of works to Dec. 31, 1890..	....	....	441 83
J. VanAnden, T. M. Hemp-			
t al.........................	120 50		
		120 50	

ENGINEERS' STORES.

n't of works to Dec. 31, 1890..	....	....	2,015 93
Gas Co....................	138 13		
on Ice Co...................	36 65		
. Swalley, soap.............	16 84		
l & Sapper...................	36 59		
. Pinney....................	9 30		
. Fitzgerald................	6 84		
. Williams & Co............	5 86		
iry Beckman................	4 75		
phy Bros....................	3 50		
. Sloan, Sec., cash expended.	5 40		
F. Nick....................	1 70		
		265 56	

INE ROOM FURNITURE.

't of works to Dec. 31, 1890..	....	....	1,254 07
. Pinney....................	9 00		
		9 00	

CARTAGE.

n't of works to Dec. 31, 1890..	....	....	522 79
nk Hoffman.................	16 46		
		16 46	

ND MISCELLANEOUS WORK.

n't of works to Dec. 31, 1890..	....	....	10,271 62
or as per Supt. pay roll......	355 35		
		355 35	

d forward.....................	....	$67 240 74	$1 072,878 90

	FROM JANUARY 1, 1890, TO DECEMBER 31, 1890.	1867 TO 1890.
Brought forward..................	$67 240 74	$1 072 878 90

BOOKS AND STATIONERY.

From Com't of works to Dec. 31, 1890..		1,645 35
Paid—Ashby & Vincent.............. $	52 27	
John J. O'Brien..............	13 50	
Herald Print. & Pub. Co.........	19 45	
Erie Sunday Graphic...........	4 25	
B. F. Sloan, Sec., cash expended.	19 10	
	108 57	

PAVING AND STREET REPAIRS.

Paid—Barber Asphalt Paving Co......	210 87	
Peter Wessler..................	46 75	
Erie Paving Co................	25 17	
Wessler & Stuhle..............	5 25	
B. F. Sloan, Sec., cash expended.	1 50	
	389 54	

WASTE AND PACKING.

From Com't of works to Dec. 31, 1890..		3,135 38
Paid—E. S. Greeley & Co............	134 04	
Erie Machine Shop..............	109 80	
Mehl & Sapper..................	87 07	
Penn'a R. R. Co................	1 74	
Henry Beckman.................	2 50	
B. F. Sloan, Sec., cash expended.	3 72	
	338 87	

REDEMPTION OF BONDS

From Com't of works to Dec. 31, 1890..		56,500 00
Paid—Sinking Fund Commissioners ...	20 000 00	
	20 000 00	

INLET PIPE AND REPAIRS.

From Com't of works to Dec. 31, 1890..		45,032 59

STATE, COUNTY AND SCHOOL TAXES.

From 1885. to Dec. 31, 1890..............		1,100 83

INTEREST AND DISCOUNT.

From Com't of works to Dec. 31, 1890..		99,065 41

RAILROAD SWITCH AND SCALES.

From Com't of works to Dec. 31, 1890 ..		2,918 92

WATER RENTS RETURNED.

From Com't of works to Dec. 31, 1890..		62 62

RESERVOIR AND GROUNDS.

From Com't of works to Dec. 31, 1890 ..		123,150 83

Carried forward.................	$88 074 53	$1,405 453 61

rom Com't of works to Dec. 31, 1890.. .... |.......... 93,336 61

CIVIL ENGINEERING,

Com't of works to Dec. 31, 1890.. .... |.......... 7,122 85

GAS WELLS AND CARE.

·om Com't of works to Dec. 31, 1890.. .... 8,148 59

PARK FOUNTAINS.

·om Com't of works to Dec. 31, 1890.. .... |............ 3,244 68

|$88,074 12 ||$1,517 306 34

RECAPITULATION.

EXPENSES IN 1890.

>r construction	$ 48,305 48	
>r maintenance...........................,	19,231 58	
r extraordinary expenses..................	537 46	
>r redemption of bonds...................	20,000 00	
		$ 88,074 52
PENDITURES FROM JULY, 1867, TO DECEMBER 31, 1890		
>r construction...........................	$ 1,088.539 07	
r maintenance............................	439 804 43	
r extraordinary expenses, 1890...........	537 46	
>r redemption of bonds to Dec. 31, 1890....	76 500 00	
r balance in Treasury, Dec. 31, 1890......	2,858 07	
r balance in Office, Dec. 31, 1890	701 74	
Total.......................	....	1 608.940 77
vanced by city in bonds..................	675 000 00	
vanced by city in cash..................	955 10	
		675.955 10
lance to credit of Works...................	....	$ 932,985 67

EXHIBIT D.

Amount of Water Rents Collected Each Year, with the Increase and Decrease since the Commencement of the Works.

			Am't Rec'd.	Increase.	Decrease.
From Jan. 1. 1869, to Dec. 31,	1869....	$	4,264 47	....	....
" " 1870,	" 1870....		9,237 30	$ 4,972 83	....
" " 1871,	" 1871....		18,138 08	8,900 78	....
" " 1872,	" 1872....		21,652 68	3,514 60	....
" " 1873,	" 1873....		25,560 40	3,907 72	....
" " 1874,	" 1874....		27,938 90	2,378 50	....
" " 1875,	" 1875....		29,639 38	1,700 48	....
" " 1876,	" 1876....		31,048 76	1,409 38	....
" " 1877,	" 1877....		32,276 57	1,227 81	....
" " 1878,	" 1878....		29,636 01	....	$ 2,640 56
" " 1879,	" 1879....		33,343 20	3,707 19	....
" " 1880,	" 1880....		37,385 00	4,041 80	....
" " 1881,	" 1881....		40,385 87	3,000 87	....
" " 1882,	" 1882....		43,818 73	3,432 86	....
" " 1883.	" 1883....		48,269 89	4,451 16	....
" " 1884,	" 1884....		51,852 78	3,582 89	....
" " 1885,	" 1885....		53,550 35	1,697 57	....
" " 1886,	" 1886....		58,725 00	5,174 65	....
" " 1887,	" 1887....		67,121 92	8,396 92	....
" " 1888.	" 1888....		73,197 03	6,075 11	....
" " 1889,	" 1889....		81,110 68	7,913 65	....
" " 1890,	" 1890....		87,279 96	6,169 28	....
		$	905,432 87	....	....

EXHIBIT E.

Location, Size and Length of Main Pipe, Large Private Pipe and Fire Hydrant Branches Laid in 1890.

STREET.	BETWEEN.	LESS THAN 4 INCH.	4 INCH.	6 INCH.	20 INCH
Third.........	Cherry and Poplar............	125.9			
"	State and French.............	135.6			
Fourth	In Cascade...................	9			
Fifth.........	Corner of Ross...........H. B.	10.7			
"	" " Newman.......H. B.	8.10			
"	East Avenue and Wayne.......			1,305	
"	Parade and Wallace..........			31	
"	Wayne and East Avenue.......			87.7	
"	Cascade and Raspberry........			587.8	
"	" " " ...H. B.	9.4			
Seventh	Corner of Perry..............	9.6			
"	Perry and East Avenue			1,046.6	
"	Corner of East Avenue........	9.6			
Eighth	Poplar and Liberty...........			356	
"	Perry and East Avenue........			178	
Ninth	" " "			410	
"	Poplar and Liberty...........			361	
"	Corner of Perry..........H. B.	9.10			
"	Cherry and Poplar.			314.5	
"	Perry and East Avenue........			334	
Tenth	From 19½ West of West Line of East, Eastward.............			93	
"	Poplar and Plum........... ..			662.3	
Eleventh	Plum and Cascade...........			515	
"	Poplar and Liberty...........			24	
Twelfth.......	East Avenue and Pennsylvania Avenue...................			789.6	
"	Cor. Pennsylvania Avenue.H.B.	10.11			
"	East Avenue and Pennsylvania Avenue...................			503	
Thirteenth.....	French and Holland...........			111	
Fourteenth	Ash and Reed.................			163.8	
Sixteenth......	Myrtle and Chestnut..........			104	
"	" " "			134.8	
Seventeenth ...	Parade and Wallace..........			266	
" ...	Corner of Wallace........H. B.	9			
Twentieth	Sassafras and Myrtle.........			333.6	
Twenty-third ..	Poplar and Liberty...........			397.10	
" " ..	Reed and Wayne.............			435.6	
" " ..	French and Holland...........			721.2	
Twenty-fourth .	German and Parade...........			157.10	
" " .	Ash and Reed................			147.7	
" " .	Wayne and Perry.............			66	
" " .	Corner of Wayne.........H. B.	9.10			
Twenty-fifth ...	East Avenue and Pennsylvania Avenue...................			663.3	

246 ft. ⅝-in. removed.

STREET.	BETWEEN	LESS THAN 4 INCH.	4 INCH.	6 INCH.	30 INCH
Twenty-fifth ...	Cor. Pennsylvania Avenue H.B.		9.8		
Twenty-sixth ..	Holland and German..........			106.7	
Twenty-seventh	State and Peach.			115	
East Avenue...	Ninth and Tenth.............			406.7	
" " ...	Sixth and Eighth.............			755	
" " ...	Twenty-first and Twenty-seventh			1,861.5	
" " ...	Eighth and Ninth............			53.10	
" " ...	Fifth and Sixth.............			405.6	
" " ...	Corner Twenty-third.....H. B.		6.6		
" " ..	" Twenty-fifth......H. B.		8		
" " ...	Fourth and Fifth.............		122		
.. " "	" " " ....H. B.		11		
" " ...	Twelfth and Thirteenth...H. B.		8.9		
" " ...	Eighth and Ninth............			49	
" " ...	" "			75	
Newman	North of Fifth...............		601.2		
Wilson	" "		452.6		
"	" " ....H. B.		8.5		
Wayne	From Fifth Street North.......		1,306.6		
"	North of Second..........H. B.		7.7		
"	Eleventh and Twelfth.........			194	
"	Corner o Twenty-second.H. B.		8.2		
"	Twenty-first to Twenty-fourth..			990	
Perry	Eighth and Ninth............			198	
Reed	Twenty-third and Twenty-fourth			293	
"	Tenth and Eleventh			165	
"	Twenty-third and Twenty-fourth			64.8	
Wallace	Sixth and Seventh............			181	
Parade	Fifth and Sixth..............			402	
German	Corner of Nineteenth.....H. B.		9.2		
"	Twenty-fourth and Twenty-sixth			634	
Holland	Ninth and Tenth.............			237	
"	Fifth and Sixth.............			398	
"	Ninth and Tenth............			25.6	
WaterfordPlank Road........	From Twenty-sixth South......			230.8	
State	Fifteenth and Sixteenth........	85.6			
"	Thirteenth and Fourteenth.....			204	
Peach	North of Front...............	323			
Myrtle........	Twentieth and Twenty-first.....			142	
"	From Twelfth South..........		529.3		
"	Twenty-fifth and Twenty-sixth..			96.6	
Chestnut	Twelfth and Twenty-second....				3047
Walnut........	Eleventh and Twelfth			349.5	
Cherry........	Eighteenth and Nineteenth.....			272.8	
"	Tenth and Eleventh			72.6	
Poplar	Crossing Twenty-third Street...			39	
"	" Ninth Street..........			47.3	
"	" Eighteenth Street.....			29 8	
Liberty	From Twenty-third North......			174 2	
"	Twenty-third and Twenty-fourth			306	
"	Corner of Twenty-fourth..H. B.		11.6		
Cascade	Fourth and Fifth.............		390		
"	Corner of Fifth..........H. B.		8.10		
Hazel..........	South of Twenty-sixth........			94.6	
Total feet.................		408.6	3 856.7	20,968.4	3047

ON.

	FEET.	IN.	MS.	FEET.	IN.
sizes reported to Dec. 31, 1889...........			62	3 770	8
irty inch laid in 1890.....................	3 047	0			
inch " "	20 968	4			
ur inch " "	3,856	2			
ss than 4 inch, temporary.................	408	6			
ivate pipe, 4 and 6 inch..................	595	6			
Total in feet...........................	28,875	6			
Total in miles........................			5	2,476	2
and total in miles to Dec. 31, 1890.........			68	966	6

EXHIBIT F.

Location, Number and Length of Street Connections Made During the Year 1890.

STREETS.	Number of Connections.	FEET.	IN.	STREETS.	Number of Connections.	FEET.	IN.
Front and Dock....	2	27	6	Bro't forward.....	506	9,339	1
Short	....	....	....	Twenty-sixth	13	267	6
Second............	7	80	6	Twenty-seventh	2	16	....
Third	16	301	3	East Avenue........	18	362	6
Fourth	9	164	7	Reed	3	39	....
Fifth	23	347	....	Ash	3	43	....
North Park........	2	31	6	Wallace	6	161	4
Sixth	13	433	....	Parade.............	10	337	8
Seventh	21	281	7	German	8	103	5
Eighth	22	273	....	Holland	16	256	10
Ninth	65	1,093	....	French	3	81	....
Tenth	9	359	6	State	16	447	2
Eleventh	14	319	2	Sassafras	14	287	....
Twelfth	67	1,583	....	Myrtle	13	263	....
Thirteenth	5	78	....	Chestnut	4	65	6
Fourteenth	15	243	7	Walnut.............	7	140	10
Fifteenth	4	33	....	Cherry.............	8	93	7
Sixteenth	6	118	10	Maple..............	1	20	6
Seventeenth	23	333	6	Poplar	6	115	....
Eighteenth	112	1,944	....	Liberty............	7	351	....
Nineteenth	5	66	4	Plum...............	1	21	10
Twentieth	8	106	1	Wilson.............	5	56	....
Twenty-first......	14	319	3	Newman.............	4	64	10
Twenty-second	9	98	9	Ross	1	8	6
Twenty-third	19	360	6	Perry	2	18	....
Twenty-fourth	8	117	6	Wayne	22	332	....
Twenty-fifth	8	120	7	Hazel	4	59	6
Carried forward...	506	9,339	1	Total.............	703	13,451	7

LENGTH OF CONNECTIONS IN MILES.

	MILES	FEET.
Connections made in 1890.........	2	1,891
Previously made.................	22	3,423
Total...........................	25	34

STREET.	WHERE LOCATED.	NAME.
Twelfth street...........	Northwest corner of Penn Avenue....	Matthews.
Seventeenth street......	Southwest corner of Wallace.........	"
Nineteenth street.......	Northwest corner of German.........	"
Fifth street.............	Northeast corner of Ross.............	"
Fifth street.............	Northwest corner of Newman........	"
Fifth street.............	North side of Wayne.................	"
Wilson street...........	North side of Fifth..................	"
East Avenue.............	Southeast corner of Twenty-third.....	Pittsburgh.
East Avenue.............	Southeast corner of Twenty fifth......	"
East Avenue.............	North line of Fifth..................	Matthews.
East Avenue.............	South line of Twelfth................	"
Wayne street...........	North line of Second................	"
Tenth street.............	East line of Raspberry...............	"
Tenth street.............	Northeast corner of Cascade..........	"
Sixth street.............	Northeast corner of Perry............	"
Wayne street...........	Southeast corner of Twenty-second...	"
Twenty-fourth street....	Northeast corner of Wayne..........	"
Seventh street..........	Southwest corner of Perry...........	"
Twenty fifth street......	Northwest corner of Penn Avenue....	"
Seventh street..........	Northeast corner of East Avenue.....	"
Twenty-fourth street....	Northeast corner of Liberty..........	"
Twelfth street..........	Between Penn Avenue and Brandes st.	"
Seventh street..........	Southeast corner of Sassafras........	"
Fifth street.............	Northwest corner of Holland.........	"
East Avenue.............	Erie City Iron Works...............	"
Ninth street.............	Northeast corner of French..........	"
Ninth street.............	Corner of Holland..................	"

RECAPITULATION.

Fire Hydrants in new location.. 23
Fire Hydrants renewed... 4
— 27
Net gain in 1890... 23

NUMBER AND STYLE OF FIRE HYDRANTS IN DAILY USE.

New style Matthews............	239	Morris, Tasker & Co...........	2
Old style Matthews.............	11	Union......................	1
By State......................	27		
West Jersey...................	30	Total.....................	339
Pittsburgh....................	23	Private Fire Hydrants.........	33
Jones-made...................	2		
Mellow.......................	4	Grand total..............	372

HYDRANTS FOR THE SUPPLY OF WAGON SPRINKLERS.

Ninth street, between State and French................Jarecki, Hays & Co.
Twelfth street, near southwest corner of Peach.........   "
Fifteenth street, near southwest corner of Peach........   "
Eigteenth street, near northwest corner of Peach........
State street, at East Park..............................
State street, between Tenth and Eleventh..............
Myrtle street, southeast corner of Eighteenth...........
Walnut street, northeast corner of Eighteenth..........
Parade street, southeast corner of Eighth..............
Parade street, northeast corner of Twelfth.............

EXHIBIT H.

Location, Size and Kind of Stop Valves Set in 1890.

STREET.	WHERE LOCATED.	KIND.	SIZE
fth street.	East line of East Avenue............	Eddy.	6
fth street.........	East line of Penn. Avenue...........	"	6
h street...........	West line of East Avenue...........	"	6
Avenue...........	North side of Tenth..............	"	6
1 street...........	West line of East Avenue...........	"	6
Avenue...........	South line of Sixth..............	"	6
Avenue...........	South line of Twenty-third..........	"	6
t Street...........	East line of French..............	"	4
street...........	South line of Twenty-third..........	"	6
ry street.........	South line of Eighteenth...........	"	6
ity-third street....	West line of Poplar...............	"	6
ty street.........	North line of Twenty-third..........	"	6
ifras street.......	South line of Sixth..............	"	4
1 street...........	West line of Poplar...............	"	6
street...........	West line of Holland.............	"	4
:nth street.......	East line of Cascade.............	"	6
le street..........	South line of Twentieth...........	"	6
th street.........	West line of Poplar...............	"	6
ind street........	South line of Fifth..............	"	6
1 street..........	West line of Holland.............	"	4
ity-third street....	West line of Reed..............	"	6
rford Plank Road..	South line of Twenty-sixth..........	"	6
le street..........	South line of Twelfth.............	"	4
1 street..........	East line of French.............	"	4
Avenue..........	North line of Sixth..............	"	6
street..........	West line of East Avenue...........	"	6
ity-fourth street..	East line of German.............	"	6
street..........	East line of Perry..............	"	6
teenth street......	East line of Poplar.............	"	6
tr street.........	North line of Eighteenth...........	"	6
teenth street......	West line of Walnut..............	"	6
>n...............	North line of Fifth.............	"	4
ace street........	North line of Seventh.............	"	6
nan street.......	North line of Fifth.............	"	4
street..........	East line of Parade.............	"	6
le street..........	North line of Sixth..............	"	6
Avenue..........	North line of Fifth.............	"	4
ian street.......	North line of Twenty-fifth..........	"	6
ity-sixth street....	West line of German.............	"	6
ty-fifth street.....	East line of East Avenue...........	"	6
1e street.........	North line of Third.............	"	4
1e street.........	North line of Fifth.............	"	4
street..........	East line of Wayne..............	"	6
tnut street.......	South of South line of Twelfth.......	"	4
t street..........	North of North line of Front.........	"	1
ide street........	South line of Fourth.............	"	4
l street..........	East line of State.............	"	4

STREET.	WHERE LOCATED.	KIND.	SIZE
Chestnut street........	Southwest corner of Seventeenth.....	Eddy.	6
Fifth street............	West line of Cascade................	"	6
Tenth street...........	West line of Poplar..................	'	6
Wayne street..........	South line of Eleventh...............	--	6
Twenty-third street....	East line of French..................	"	6
Chestnut street........	South of South line of Twenty-first...	"	30
Sixteenth street........	West line of Myrtle..................	"	6
Twenty-fourth street...	West line of Reed....................	"	6
Chestnut street........	Northwest corner of Twenty-first.....	"	12
Wayne street..........	South line of Twenty-first...........	"	6
Eighth street..........	West line of East Avenue............	"	6
Wayne street..........	South line of Twenty-third..........	"	6
Seventh street.........	West line of Perry...................	"	6
Ninth street...........	East line of Poplar..................	"	6
Seventh street.........	West line of East Avenue............	"	6
East Avenue...........	South line of Eighth................	"	6
Liberty street..........	South line of Twenty-third..........	"	6
Hazel street...........	South line of Twenty-sixth..........	"	6

Total number of Stop Valves set in 1890......................... 65

Previously reported.. 606

 Total..——— 671

EXHIBIT I.

*mber of Families. Stores, Offices, Manufactories, Etc., Supplied
with City Water During the Year 1890.*

weries	3	Jail	1
rd of Trade	1	Laundries	8
t Houses	5	Libraries	1
eries	15	Lumber Yards	5
cher Shops	62	Livery Stables	14
k Yards	1	Manufacturers	78
ks	6	Malt Houses	4
ber Shops	48	Orphan Asylums	2
iard Rooms	4	Opera Houses	2
ling Works	9	Oil Works	3
Hall	1	Offices	220
fee and Spice Mill	1	Old Folks Home	1
rches	25	Photograph Galleries	8
eteries	1	Police Station	1
l and Iron Docks	1	Public Halls	30
b Houses	7	Packing Houses	3
tom House	1	Printing Offices	12
rt House	1	Passenger Depots	2
vent	1	Railroads	4
ing Park	1	Railroad Shops	2
ing Works	2	Rink	1
ine Houses	6	Soldiers Home	1
ress Offices	2	Schools	26
tric Light Co	1	Stores	406
Hatchery	1	Saloons and Eating Houses	116
ilies	6,322	Slaughter Houses	12
Houses	6	Street Railway	1
ght Houses	5	Transfer Company	1
ntains, Private	4	United States Signal Station	1
" Public	2	Work Shops	94
" Drinking	2	Watering Troughs	15
ring Mills	4	U. S. Steamer Michigan	1
Works	1	U. S. Court House	1
n Elevators	3	U. S. Post Office	1
Offices	2		
n Houses	5	Total	7,728
pitals	2	Last Enumeration	7,086
ls and Boarding Houses	83		
louses	2	Increase	642
rnal Revenue Office	1		

EXHIBIT J.

Pumping Engine Statistics for 1890.

The Pumps are three in number. Two are known as the Cornish Bull Pumps. The diameter of each plunger is 20¼ inches, and each has a stroke of 10 feet. The capacity of each pump is estimated to be 165 gallons to each stroke. The third pump is a Gaskill Horizontal Pumping Engine, of a guaranteed capacity of 5,000,000 gallons daily at a piston speed of 120 feet per minute against a head of 237 feet. The Stand Pipe is 251 feet high. The Reservoir is nearly two miles from the Pumping Works, the bottom of which is 210 feet above the surface of the Bay, and the water has been maintained during the year at an average depth in the Reservoir of about 24 feet.

MONTHS	Days Single Cornish Pump run.	Days Both Cornish Pumps run.	Days Gaskill Pump run.	Strokes of Cornish Pump.	Revolutions of Gaskill Pump.	Gallons Pumped.	Daily Average.	Average lift in feet.	Pounds of Coal per Month.	Cost of Coal.
Jan	2	..	29	26,044	612,950	121,314,164	3,913,360	237.00	382,350	$219 85
Feb......	..	..	28	......	623,350	113,149,700	4,051,775	236.00	341,350	196 37
Mar......	1	9	23	181,268	528,965	126,180,685	4,070,344	236.00	427,300	245 69
Apr......	..	..	30	......	689,035	125,404,370	4,180,145	236.05	375,700	216 01
May......	..	..	31	......	722,750	131,510,500	4,243,242	236.06	398,800	229 31
June......	..	..	29	......	780,445	142,041,090	4,734,703	236.00	422,930	253 75
July......	3	..	31	18,511	895,840	166,097,195	5,357,974	236.00	457,030	271 21
Aug......	5	1	28	109,074	778,275	159,643,260	5,149,782	236.17	516,150	309 69
Sept......	..	3	29	37,190	780,275	148,195,900	4,939,863	236.00	477,580	286 54
Oct......	..	..	31	......	799,575	145,522,650	4,694,279	237.20	435,900	261 54
Nov......	1	..	30	252	773,200	140,762,160	4,692,072	237.00	450,900	270 54
Dec	..	..	30	......	766,340	139,473,880	4,199,157	236.10	480,670	289 39
	12	16	349	372,639	9,662,275	1,659,625,554	4,546,594	236.90	5,166,640	$3,052 89

The regular employes at the Pumping Works are one mechanical engineer, two assistant engineers, three firemen and one watchman. The mechanical engineer stands a watch of five hours, from 7 to 12 every forenoon; the assistants divide the remainder of each day equally between them; each one of the firemen stands a watch of eight hours. Besides firing, the firemen unload the coal from the cars, except when both pumps are run, in which case they are assisted by the watchman or a laborer. The mechanical engineer gives ten hours daily to the service of the Department, the hours when he is not on watch being employed in repairs, supervision, etc. In addition to standing their regular watch, the assistant engineers aid their superior officer in keeping the machinery in order. The watchman takes care of the buildings and grounds, besides doing such other work as may be required of him.

YEAR	Tons of Coal consumed	Price of Coal per ton from May 1st of each year	Cost of Coal from Jan. 1st to Dec. 31st	Grades of Bituminous Coal	Gallons of Water Pumped	Increase or Decrease	Number of places supplied	Number of Fire Hydrants	Average height of Water in Reservoir above surface of Bay	Cost of Coal per million gallons raised to Reservoir	Gallons raised to Reservoir by 1 pound of Coal
1868	59 1	$5 05	$309 61	Lump.							
1869	544 4	5 05	4,818 48	"							
1870	1,064 5	5 05	5,159 10	"	246,648,960		1,218	97	232.0		
1871	1,427 7	5 05	7,117 00	"	179,368,495	132,719,535 i.	1,727	99	232.0	$18 76	98.5
1872	1,308 5	5 05	6,528 50	"	395,076,000	115,708,505 i.	2,140	103	232.0	16 52	150.9
1873	1,672 5	5 05	8,412 65	"	384,062,415	11,013,585 d.	2,475	107	232.0	21 90	114.8
1874	1,759 0	4 85	7,709 54	"	444,817,395	60 754 980 i.	3,663	107	233 0	17 33	126.4
1875	1,836 4	4 85	8,657 61	"	531,005,475	86 181,080 i.	2,700	110	232.0	16 30	145.5
1876	1,105 1	4 00	8,925 22	"	670,726,650	139 721,175 i.	2,763	112	232.0	13 30	159.3
1877	2,456 6	3 70	8,509 33	"	660,981,810	9,744,840 d.	2,854	114	232.0	12 75	135.7
1878	2,463 3	3 35	7,945 37	"	682,399,315	21 390,505 i.	2,915	115	232.0	11 64	136.4
1879	2,628.1	3 09	7,428 92	Slack.	807,800,400	125,408 085 i.	3,011	121	232.0	9 19	153.6
1880	3,076 1	1 99	6,978 41	"	775,805,250	31,995 150 i.	3,568	126	232.0	8 93	126.0
1881	3,430 3	1 90	6,517 58	"	975,640,634	200 235 684 d.	4,110	161	232.0	6 68	142.2
1882	2,968 2	1 75	5,355 93	"	829,759,260	145,881 674 d.	4,687	171	234.0	6 45	139.7
1883	2,398 2	1 55	3,908 59	"	815,939,685	13 819 575 d.	5,077	197	234.7	4 66	170 0
1884	3,010 8	1 45	4,502 61	"	917,781,350	105 841 665 i.	5,395	248	234.3	4 99	152.4
1885	3,243 8	1 30	4,575 79	"	1,036,496,665	118,715 315 i.	5,658	270	232.9	4 40	159.7
1886	3,369 0	1 25	4,318 64	"	1,117,389,075	80,892,410 i.	6,140	280	233.3	3 86	165.8
1887	2,820 4	1 15	3,589 31	"	1,218,213,688	106,824,583 i.	6,368	318	234.1	2 95	216.0
1888	2,393 3	1 09	2,545 46	"	1,341,708,002	123 494 314 i.	6,600	333	234.6	1 89	292.1
1889	2,446 0	1 08	2,661 12	"	1,475,358,220	133,650 218 i.	7,086	346	235.2	1 80	301.5
1890	2,583 6	1 20	3 052 89	"	1,659,625,551	184 267,331 i.	7,728	372	236.9	1 81	322.4

EXHIBIT L.

Table Showing the Water Rates Per 1,000 Gallons in 162 Cities Where Meters are Used.

MAINE. Cents.
Bangor.......... 30
Portland ....20 to 40

NEW HAMPSHIRE.
Manchester....... 20
Nashua ....15 to 30

VERMONT.
St A[....] . . . . to 30
Burlington . . . . 5 to 50

MASSACHUSETTS.
Amesbury ....30 to 50
Boston 20
Clinton...........15 to 50
Cambridge ....10 to 20
Fall River........ 30
Haverhill ....15 to 20
Hingham.......... 25
Lawrence........ 20 to 25
Lowell 15
Lynn ....17½ to 20
New Bedford.....2½ to 15
Northampton .....10 to 20
North Adams.....10 to 15
Quincy...........12½ to 30
Peabody.......... 20
Pittsfield 10
Salem...........13½ to 20
Springfield ....10 to 20
Taunton.........12½ to 25
Waltham ....25 to 30
Westboro 50
Worcester........15 to 25

CONNECTICUT.
Bridgeport ....20 to 30
Hartford ....7½ to 30
Meriden.........10 to 25
New Britain...... 10
New Haven.......10 to 35
New London.....20 to 30
Norwich.........15 to 30
Stonington.......10 to 20

RHODE ISLAND.
Providence.......15 to 30
Pawtucket........ 6 to 30
Woonsocket 30
Waterbury ....10 to 30

NEW YORK.
Albany .... 5 to 10
Amsterdam ..... 6 to 30
Binghamton ..... 6 to 25
Brooklyn 10½
Buffalo........... 3
Catskill ....12 to 25
Cortland & Homer.20 to 50
Corning ....10 to 30
Elmira........... 9 to 45
Flushing ....20 to 60
Johnstown........ 25
Kingston......... 30
Mt. Morris..... 10 to 30
New York 13½
Owego........... 30
Oneonta ....20 to 50
Oneida...........20 to 50
Rochester .... 5 to 15
Saratoga 15
Syracuse .... 6 to 25
Troy.............10 to 20

NEW YORK--Continued. Cents.
Utica ....15 to 30
Waverly 20
Waterford......... 5 to 20
Whitehall......... 6 to 20
Yonkers..........16 to 40

NEW JERSEY.
Bridgeton 20
Hackensack.......13 to 23
Jersey City .....21 to 27
Morristown........ 33
Newark 15
New Brunswick ..12½ to 50
Trenton ....15 to 20

PENNSYLVANIA.
Allegheny City.... 15
Bloomsburg ....10 to 35
Conshohocken.... 15
Easton ....16½ to 40
ERIE....... 6 to 10
Franklin 60
Hazleton .... 10 to 15
Lebanon......... 5 to 15
Meadville .... 8 to 30
McKeesport.... 4½ to 30
Philadelphia 8
Pittsburg .... 5 to 20
Reading ....16½ to 21½

OHIO.
Cleveland .... 6½ to 13½
Cincinnati......... 9
Columbus ..... 7 to 20
Dayton ...... 8 to 40
Norwalk 10
Sandusky .. 6 to 40
Springfield .....10 to 40
Toledo ....8 to 20
Wooster......... 15

INDIANA.
Indianapolis......12 to 40
Terre Haute..... 11

ILLINOIS.
Bloomington. .. .10 to 15
Chicago ...... 8 to 10
Joliet ....15 to 30
Jacksonville.....13 to 40
Quincy ....15 to 50

MICHIGAN.
Bay City.......... 5 to 10
Detroit 10
East Saginaw ..... 6 to 12
Flint .... 6 to 30
Grand Rapids..... 9½ to 30
Kalamazoo 10
Port Huron ..... 5 to 20

WISCONSIN.
Kenosha ....10 to 15
Milwaukee .... 14½ to 20
Madison.........20 to 50

IOWA.
Council Bluffs.... 15 to 35
Cedar Rapids.....15 to 40
Dubuque ....30 to 60
Davenport.......10 to 40
Des Moines.......15 to 20
Ottumwa.........10 to 30
Muscatine.......35 to 60
Sioux City........35 to 40

MINNESOTA. Cents.
Minneapolis......10 to 20
Winona........... 8
St. Paul.........15 to 40

MISSOURI.
Hannibal........20 to 50
Kansas City......10 to 35
Springfield.. ... 25
St. Louis.........12½ to 30

KANSAS.
Abilene...........30 to 50
Atchison......... 20

COLORADO.
Denver City...... 30
Gunnison......... 10

NEBRASKA.
Lincoln..........10 to 20

CALIFORNIA.
Los Angeles....... 30
Oakland ....30 to 55
San Francisco......23½ to 46
Vallejo........40 to 81

DELAWARE.
Wilmington....... 10

MARYLAND.
Baltimore......... 8
Hagerstown ...... 8 to 60

VIRGINIA.
Norfolk..........20 to 40
Richmond......... 15

NORTH CAROLINA.
Charlotte..........30 to 50
Wilmington......10 to 30

SOUTH CAROLINA.
Charleston ....25 to 60

GEORGIA.
Atlanta 17

ALABAMA.
Birmingham .. .. 6 to 40
Montgomery...... 25

LOUISIANA.
New Orleans ......15 to 30

TEXAS.
Fort Worth.....20 to 45
San Antonio......25 to 50

KENTUCKY.
Maysville........15 to 30
Newport 10
Owensboro ....10 to 25
Lexington ....17½ to 25
Louisville ..... 6 to 25

TENNESSEE.
Chattanooga....... 6 to 33
Knoxville.........10 to 30
Nashville....... 7 to 15

CANADA.
Brantford ....12 to 20
Hamilton 12½
Halifax 30
London ....20 to 33½
St. Catharine...... 14

Average Minimum Price, 9½
Average Maximum Price, 28

CITIES.	Family Charge.	Pan Water Closet.	Self-closing Urinal.	Bath Tub.	Self-closing Wash stand.	Permanent Wash Tub.	Two Horses	Cow.
Allegheny	$ 8 75	$ 3 00	$ 2 00	$ 3 00	$ 1 00	$ 1 50	$ 1 50	$ 75
Boston	7 00	5 00	2 50	5 00	5 00	5 00	2 00	75
Buffalo	7 20	3 50	3 00	3 00	1 00	2 00	2 40	90
Chicago	6 00	3 00	1 00	3 00	......	2 00	2 00	75
Columbus, Ohio	6 00	3 00	3 00	4 00	2 00	5 00	4 00	2 00
Dayton, Ohio	6 00	2 50	4 00	2 00	1 25	2 00	2 50	1 00
Detroit	7 00	3 00	2 00	3 00	1 00	2 00	2 00	1 00
ERIE	**8 00**	**3 00**	**2 00**	**3 00**	**1 00**	**2 00**	**2 00**	**75**
East Saginaw, Mich	7 00	2 50	3 00	3 00	1 00	2 00	4 00	1 00
Fall River, Ms.	5 00	5 00	2 00	5 00	1 00	2 00	4 00	1 00
Grand Rapids, Mich.	8 00	4 00	3 00	3 50	2 50	4 50	2 50	1 00
...apolis	5 00	3 00	3 00	3 00	1 00	1 00	5 00	......
Lawrence, Mass.	5 00	4 00	2 00	3 00	2 00	......	3 00	1 50
Milwaukee	6 00	2 00	2 00	3 00	1 00	1 50	2 00	1 00
Minneapolis	4 00	3 00	7 50	2 50	1 50	2 00	2 00	1 00
New York	6 00	10 00	2 00	3 00	1 00	2 00	6 00	75
Omaha, Neb.	6 75	2 50	3 50	3 00	1 00	2 00	5 00	75
Philadelphia	5 00	5 00	5 00	3 00	1 00	1 00	2 00	75
Pittsburg	9 00	3 00	1 50	4 00	1 00	2 00	2 50	1 50
Sandusky, Ohio	8 00	2 50	2 50	3 20	1 00	......	4 50	1 50
St. Paul	8 00	4 00	2 40	4 00	......	2 00	4 80	......
Syracuse	8 00	5 00	2 00	3 00	1 00	2 00	3 00	75
Toledo	5 50	2 50	2 50	3 50	1 00	2 00	5 00	1 50
Utica	7 00	6 00	3 00	5 00	1 00	......	6 00	1 50

EXHIBIT N.

Report of the State Board of Health on 12 Samples of Water Submitted for Analysis December 10, 1889.

Ed. Annals of Hygiene:—I have this day sent you twelve samples of water, by direction of the Board of Water Commissioners of this city. It is desired that you make a complete statement of the analysis in the forthcoming number of the *Annals of Hygiene*—the official organ of the State Board of Health. B. F. Sloan, Secretary.

These samples were forwarded to Dr. Chas. M. Cresson, who thus reports: Waters received from the State Board of Health, marked "Erie, Nos. 1 to 12." Locations not given.

Result of chemical and microscopical examinations as follows:

Samples Marked.	Results expressed in Parts per Million.				Remarks.
	Free Ammon	Alb. Ammon	Nitrates.	Chlorine.	
Erie, Pa., "No. 1,"..	0.137	0.055	0.285	1.637	Fair condit'n for drink'g purposes
"No. 2,"..	0.027	0.055	trace.	1.772	" " "
"No. 3,"..	0.027	0.083	0.171	3.188	" " "
"No. 4,"..	0.055	0.165	trace.	2.828	" " "
"No 5,"..	0.027	0.085	25.560	17.720	Contains cesspool drainage. Unfit for use.
"No. 6,"..	0.027	0.027	2.742	4.251	Contains cesspool drainage. Typhoid bacillus.
"No 7,"..	0.055	0.687	2.742	386.300	Contains cesspool drainage. Typhoid bacillus.
"No. 8,"..	0.027	0.055	6.856	8.433	Contains cesspool drainage. Unfit for use.
"No. 9,"..	trace.	0.137	0.343	61.930	Doubtful, probably contaminated and dangerous to use.
"No. 10,"..	0.055	0.165	11.136	73.342	Contains cesspool drainage. Typhoid bacillus.
"No. 11,"..	0.055	0.220	8.227	97.694	Contains cesspool drainage. Typhoid bacillus.
"No. 12,"..	0.055	0.083	1.714	103.980	Contains cesspool drainage. Dysentery.

Waters Nos. 1, 2, 3 and 4 are in fit condition for drinking purposes. They contain minute amounts of decaying animal and vegetable matter, but not enough to affect their utility for household purposes. They are to be classed with waters fit for city use.

No. 9 is in doubtful condition for household use. I find nothing in it to absolutely condemn it, but indications require that it should be examined frequently for the presence of hurtful material.

Sources Nos. 5 and 8 have been badly contaminated by cesspool drainage and contain sufficient nitrates to forbid their use for household purposes.

Nos. 6, 7, 10 and 11 are sources that should be abandoned at once, as there is evidently free communication with cesspools, and each of them contains large numbers of typhoid bacilli.

No. 12 contains drainage, such as I have found to come from cesspools used by dysenteric cases. Charles M. Cresson, M. D.

KEY TO ABOVE REPORT.

No. 1, from Channel Piers.
No. 2, from Lake, north of Whallon's Piers.
No. 3, from inlet at Water Works.
No. 4, from Water Office.
No. 5, from private well, Seventh street, between French and Holland.
No. 6, from private well, Nineteenth street between Walnut and Cherry.
No. 7, from private well, 131 Thirteenth street, east of Parade.

No. 8, from private well, —— Fourth street, west of Chestnut.
No. 9. from private well, —— Second street, east of Hospital.
No. 10, from private well, 133 Eighth street, west of Peach.
No. 11, from private well, 15 and 17 Seventh street, between State and Peach.
No. 12, from private well, 105 State street.

It must be stated that this "key," which was sent *sealed* to the editor of this journal, was not opened until after the analysis were made, when the *seal was* broken in the presence of Dr. Cresson and the editor.

RATES FOR CITY WATER.

All are Annual, Except as Otherwise Indicated.

Bath Tub, private..$	3 00
" " each additional..	1 50
" " public..	5 00
Bakery, per barrel of flour used (but no charge less than $5).............	01
Barber Shop, including Hand Basin, first chair...........................	4 00
" " " " " each additional chair.....................	2 00
Blacksmith Shop, one fire..	5 00
" " each additional fire....................................	2 50
Boarding House (in addition to family rates), per room.................	1 00
Brewery, per barrel brewed..	03
Building purposes, per bushel lime...................................	02
Butcher Stalls..	3 00 to 15 00
Charitable Institutions, one-third annual rates........................	
Cow..	75
Condensing Boiler for steam heating (per season of six months), per horse power	50
Eating Houses..	5 00 to 25 00
Family...	5 00
Hand Basin, for Dwellings, Hotels, and Schools, first basin.............	1 00
" " " " " " each additional.............	50
" " in Offices, Stores and Blocks, each......	1 00
Hotel (in addition to family rates), per room.........................	1 00
Livery Stable, per horse..	2 00
Malster, per 1,000 bushels of malt...................................	1 75
Offices...	3 00 to 10 00
Private Stable, one or two horses.....................................	2 00
" " each additional horse...............................	1 00
Printing Offices..	5 00 to 30 00
Public Halls...	5 00 to 25 00
Saloons..	5 00 to 25 00
Stores...	3 00 to 15 00
Schools, per pupil...	10
Steam Engine, ten hours per day, each horse power.....................	2 50
Slaughter Houses...	5 00 to 50 00
Sleeping Rooms...	1 00
Sprinkling Streets or Lawns with hose, per season.....................	3 00 and up.
Urinal, private, self-closing...	2 00
" public, "	3 00
" not self-closing...	3 00 to 10 00
" continuous flow...	10 00 to 30 00
Wash Tub, (permanent, with waste)....................................	2 00
" " " " " each additional..................	1 00
Watering Trough, public..	10 00
Water Closet (pan), in private houses................................	3 00
" " " " " each additional..............	1 50
" " " public...............................	5 00
" " (hopper), private..............................	6 00
" " " public..............................	10 00
Work Shop (ordinary use)...	3 00 to 5 00
All other uses, when not metered, to be assessed by the Department.	

METER RATES (Per Quarter.)

Daily Average, 15,000 gallons or less	10 cents.
" 15,000 to 20,000 gallons...........................	9½ "
" 20,000 to 25,000 "	9 "
" 25,000 to 30,000 "	8½ "
" 30,000 to 35,000 "	8 "
" 35,000 to 40,000 "	7½ "
" 40,000 to 45,000 "	7 "
" 45,000 to 50,000 "	6½ "
" More than 50,000 gallons..........................	6 "

ANNUAL REPORT

—OF THE—

COMMISSIONERS

—OF—

WATER ╫ WORKS,

OF ERIE, PA.,

—TO THE—

MAYOR AND CITY COUNCILS,

—FOR THE—

YEAR ENDING DECEMBER 31, 1891.

ERIE, PA.:
DISPATCH PUBLISHING COMPANY, LIMITED,
1892.

ANNUAL REPORT

—OF THE—

COMMISSIONERS

Compliments

C. J. BROWN,

President Water Works.

MAYOR AND CITY COUNCILS,

—FOR THE—

YEAR ENDING DECEMBER 31, 1891.

ERIE, PA.:
DISPATCH PUBLISHING COMPANY LIMITED
1892.

The Commissioners are appointed by the Court of Comm
of Erie County, Pa., for a term of three years, one member bein
annually, in May.

EX-COMMISSIONERS.

‡*Wм. L. Scott, 1867 to 1868.   John Gensheimer, 1872 t
*Henry Rawle, 1867 to 1872.   M. Liebel, 1877 to 1886.
*Wм. W. Reed, 1867 to 1879.   ‡J. M. Bryant, 1878 to 188
‡†John C. Selden, 1868 to 1872.   ‡G. W. F. Sherwin, 1879 t
Matthew R. Barr, 1872 to 1877.   Benj. Whitman, 1881 to 1
Geo. W. Starr, 1885 to 1891.

*Messrs. Scott, Rawle and Reed, the first Commissioners, were appointed resp
terms of one, two and three years.
†Mr. Selden resigned before the expiration of his second term; Mr. Barr was
by the other Commissioners, and afterward appointed by the Court.
‡Dead.

THE PRESENT COMMISSIONERS.

C. J. Brown, 1887 to 1893.   C. Kessler, 188
Wм. Hardwick, 1891 to 1894.

OFFICERS OF THE WATER WORKS.

President—C. J. Brown.
Secretary and Treasurer—Wм. Himrod.
Assistant Secretary—Geo. C. Gensheimer.
Clerks—John Kolb, M. L. Whitley.
Superintendent of Street Work—R. T. Walker.
Inspectors—F. W. Koehler, John D. Spafford, Wм. Mc
Mechanical Engineer—F. A. Roth.
Assistant Mechanical Engineers—Geo. R. Miller, John Ke
Firemen—R. W. Simons, Joseph Burns, Jacob Mullen.
Watchman at Pumping Works—Michael Flynn.
Keeper of Reservoir and Grounds—Samuel Phister.

Office—City Hall.
Office Hours—From 7:30 a. m. to 5:45 p. m.; Monday eveni
7:30 to 9:00.
Regular Meetings of the Commissioners—Every Satu
3:00 p. m., and the first day of each month at 10:00 a. m., excep
occurs on Sunday; then they meet the following day.

ANNUAL REPORT.

To the Honorable Mayor and Members of the Councils, of the City of Erie, Pa.:

GENTLEMEN:—We herewith hand you report of our official transactions for the year 1891.

The receipts for use of water this year amounted to $93,891.55, being an increase over the previous year of $6,611.59, and making the total receipts for water rents from the commencement of the Works to December 31st, 1891, almost $1,000,000.

The Statement of Accounts with the Treasurer of the City of Erie, Pa., shows our deposits with him, during the year, to have been $95,775.03; after deducting warrants drawn on him for various purposes, shows a balance in our favor of $2,261.83.

That a fair and equitable showing of the financial condition of the Water Works might be had, it was deemed advisable to present you with a statement of the Bonds and Cash furnished us by the City, and of the material furnished the City by the Water Works, adding compound interest to each. The Statement of Bonds and Cash, together with compound interest on the same, was prepared by the Honorable City Controller. These show that the Water Works owe the City the sum of $718,322.06, which sum deducted from our resources, shows a balance in our favor of $421,546.78.

Arrangements have been made with the Commissioners of the Sinking Fund, to pay them on or before July 1st, 1892, the sum of 24,000, to enable them to retire the Water Works Bonds maturing at that time.

In the Report of the Commissioners for 1890, they congratulated themselves on having laid more mains and branches than had ever been done in any one year since the commencement of the Works. The same condition holds good for the year 1891, for we laid 50 per cent. more this year than last. The increase in the mains and branches being almost nine miles. The 30-inch main is completed, which gives us two lines of mains between the Pumping Engines and the Reservoir, making a valuable addition to our plant.

Our mains and branches are now laid in nearly 77 miles of the streets of the City, leaving about 28 miles of mains to lay, to occupy all the streets now open. Connections from these mains and branches to the curb line of the streets, form a large part of the outlay of the Works, and one that is not done in any other city that we are acquainted with. We laid this year 13,753 feet of connections, making the total amount laid to date 27 miles, 3,227 feet, at a cost of $93,890.35.

Fire Hydrants, Meters, Stop Valves, Etc , enter largely into the construction account, and the care of same is considerable.

The construction account for the year amounts to $65.943.99.

Demands for water are increasing, and the pumping facilities for meeting the demand is taxed to its maximum. The average daily consumption of water was almost 5,000,000 gallons, an increase of over 400,000 gallons over the previous years' record.

To meet this growing demand for water, it will be necessary to have another pumping engine of a daily capacity of not less than 10,000,000 gallons.

This engine should be in place, ready for duty, on or before January 1st, 1893.

The water in the lake lowering each year, increases the duty of the engines now in use, and if it does not soon change for the better, it will be necessary to lower the present inlet pipe.

Obtaining permission from the City Hall Committee, we, at the expense of Water Works, removed the brick partition between the two north rooms in the City Building, assigned to us, moved the wood and glass partitions adding thereto, which changes make the office more convenient. In our credits to the City we estimated the annual rental of the same to be $1,200.

In our reports for the year 1889 and 1890, we called your attention to the necessity of constructing an intercepting sewer, to take the sewerage outside of the bay into the open lake.

We cannot close our report without again calling your attention to the urgent necessity of the early completion of this much needed improvement. We are aware that $10,000 has been appropriated to commence the work, and we hope that a much larger amount will be added from this years' appropriation, so that at least that part of the sewer west of the canal sewer can be pushed to a speedy completion.

Respectfully submitted,
C. J. BROWN,
C. KESSLER,
WM. HARDWICK,
Commissioners of Water Works.

Receipts of the Water Works from all Sources for the Year Ending December 31, 1891.

MONTH.	PLUMBING, WARRANT No. 4,752 &c.	WATER RENTS.	TOTAL.
January..	$217 37	$9,726 32	$9,943 69
February......................................	117 70	7,459 73	7,577 43
March...	22 25	4,095 59	4,117 84
April..	26 40	11 271 96	11,298 36
May...	83 65	7,101 53	7,185 18
June...	80 53	3,306 42	3,386 95
July...	20 32	12,063 85	12,084 17
August	50 35	8,415 37	8,465 72
September.....................................	59 88	3,307 18	3,367 06
October.......................................	417 99	15,325 72	15,743 71
November.....................................	136 32	7,826 25	7,962 57
December	123 98	3,991 63	4,115 61
Total...	$1,356 74	$93,891 55	$95,248 29

Cash Account of Treasurer of Water Works for Year Ending December 31, 1891.

DR.

Amount on hand January 1, 1891........................... $ 701 74
Receipts for the year 1891...................................... 95,248 29
                                                                    ———— $95,950 03

CR.

Deposited with the Treasurer of the City of Erie, Pa...$95,775 03
Balance on hand...   175 00
                                                                    ———— $95,950 03

Amount of Water Rents Collected Each Year, with the Increase and Decrease since the Commencement of the Works.

	Am't Rec'd.	Increase.	Decrease.
From Jan. 1, 1869 to Dec. 31, 1869	$ 4.264 47	....	....
" " 1870, " 1870	9,237 30	$ 4,972 83	....
" " 1871, " 1871	18.138 08	8 900 78	....
" " 1872, " 1872...	21.652 68	3,514 60	....
" " 1873. " 1873	25 560 40	3 907 72	....
" " 1874, " 1874	27,938 90	2.378 50	....
" " 1875, " 1875	29.639 38	1,700 48	....
" " 1876, " 1876...	31,048 76	1,409 38	....
" " 1877. " 1877	32,276 57	1,227 81	....
" " 1878, " 1878.........	29 636 01	....	$ 2,640 56
" " 1879, " 1879	33 343 20	3,707 19	....
" " 1880, " 1880...	37,385 00	4,041 80	....
" " 1881, " 1881.........	40,385 87	3,0⊃0 87	....
" " 1882 " 1882	43,818 73	3,432 86	....
" " 1883, " 1883	48,269 89	4,451 16	....
" " 1884, " 1884	51,852 78	3,582 89	....
" " 1885, " 1885...	53,550 35	1,697 57	....
" " 1886, " 1886.........	58,725 00	5,174 65	....
" " 1887, " 1887	67.121 92	8,396 92	....
" " 1888, " 1888.........	73.197 03	6,075 11	....
" " 1889, " 1889	81,110 68	7 913 65	....
" " 1890, " 1890	87,279 96	6,169 28	....
" " 1891, " 1891.........	93,891 55	6,611 59	....
	$ 999,324 51	....	....

Statement of Account with the Treasurer of the City of Erie, Pa., for the Year Ending Dec. 31, 1891.

DR.

To balance January 1, 1891.		$	2,857 07
To deposits—			
January	$ 9,200 00		
February	8.200 00		
March	4,550 00		
April	11,250 00		
May	7,200 00		
June	3,326 33		
July	11,693 15		
August	8,886 07		
September	3,495 99		
October	15,190 89		
November	8,537 17		
December	4,245 43		
		$95,775 03	
			$98,633 10

CR.

By Warrants for—			
Construction Department	$65,943 99		
Maintenance "	5,925 79		
Operating "	10,927 58		
Accounting "	7,775 90		
City of Erie, Pa	5,000 00		
Legal—Seven years	. 795 25		
		$96,368 51	
Warrant No. 4752	2 75		
Amount to make accounts agree	01		
		2 76	
Balance		2,261 83	
			$98.633 10

WARRANTS ISSUED DURING THE YEAR 1891.

January, 1891—		
B. F. Sloan, Secretary	$ 125 00	
Geo. C. Gensheimer, Asst. Sec'y	88 33	
William O'Lone	90 00	
A. F. Crane	70 00	
F. W. Koehler	55 00	
John D. Spafford	55 00	
Will W. Reed	70 00	
Otto Lutje	40 00	
F. A. Roth	90 00	
George R. Miller	75 00	
John Kelly	75 00	
R. W. Simons	50 00	
Joseph Burns	50 00	
Jacob Mullen	50 00	
Samuel Phister	35 00	
B. F. Sloan, Secretary	17 54	
J. C. Hilton, P. M	10 90	
Weekly pay roll, street work	52 63	
L. S. & M. S. R'y Co	4 58	
R. J. Saltsman	204 52	
E. Walker Tool Co	61 41	
William O'Lone	60 00	
Weekly pay roll, street work	50 88	
The Erie Gas Co	29 67	
Edward Donnelly	15 00	
Henry Shenk	15 00	
C. Flickinger	8 68	
A. Brugger	7 15	
Penn's Boiler Works	6 00	
Edward Driscoll	4 00	
John L. Kelley	2 25	
Union Iron Works	750 00	
Buffalo Cast Iron Pipe Co	3,905 18	
Cornell Lead Co	126 24	
Weekly pay roll, street work	40 75	
Weekly pay roll, street work	47 75	
Eclipse Lubricating Oil Co	33 15	
Herald Printing & Pub. Co., L't'd	25 70	
Ashby & Vincent	15 83	
George L. Siegel	11 60	
John J. O'Brien	8 50	
Valentine Schultz	2 80	
City of Erie Sinking Fund Com'n'rs.	5,000 00	
Weekly pay roll, street work	57 39	
Erie Machine Shop	20 80	
N.Y. & Pa. Telephone & Telegraph Co	21 00	
L. J. Fitzgerald	2 90	
Dispatch Publishing Co	18 00	
C. J. Brown	200 00	
	$11,200 18	
February, 1891—		
B. F. Sloan, Necretary	125 00	
Geo. C. Gensheimer, Asst. Sec'y	100 00	
William O'Lone	100 00	
A. F. Crane	70 00	
F. W. Koehler	55 00	
John D. Spafford	55 00	
Will W. Reed	70 00	
Otto Lutje	40 00	
Fred A. Roth	100 00	
George R. Miller	75 00	
John Kelly	75 00	
R. W. Simons	50 00	
Joseph Burns	50 00	
Jacob Mullen	50 00	
Michael Flynn	50 00	
Samuel Phister	35 00	
R. J. Saltsman	403 67	
Weekly pay roll, street work	58 88	
P. A. Becker	15 92	
B. F. Sloan, Secretary	15 48	
L. S. & M. S. R'y Co	9 39	
E. Walker Tool Co	9 25	
Union Iron Works	750 00	
Frank Hoffman	529 00	
Hays Manufacturing Co	337 91	
Cornell Lead Co	139 19	
Weekly pay roll, street work	55 18	
W. A. Crawford & Co	33 80	
The Erie Gas Co	18 06	
Edward Donnelly	15 00	
Carey & Campbell	5 63	
J. C. Hilton, P. M	5 00	
George W. Starr	200 00	
Union Water Meter Co	208 00	
H. C. Dunn	106 22	
Weekly pay roll, street work	62 32	
Eclipse Lubricating Oil Co	32 84	
Union Iron Works	43 65	
Henry B Worthington	26 08	
Murphy Bros	15 49	
Hardwick & Himrod	12 76	
Geo. L Siegel	8 05	
P. T. Donnelly	254 02	
John Meyerhoeffer	14 00	
C. Kessler	200 00	
Globe Iron Foundry Co	109 85	
Weekly pay roll, street work	70 51	
A. S. Pinney	6 45	
Herald Printing & Pub. Co., L't'd	4 55	
	$4,928 15	
March, 1891—		
B. F. Sloan, Secretary	125 00	
Geo. C. Gensheimer, Asst. Sec'y	100 00	
William O'Lone	100 00	
A. F. Crane	70 00	
F. W. Koehler	55 00	
John D. Spafford	55 00	
F. A. Roth	100 00	
George R. Miller	75 00	
John Kelly	75 00	
R. W. Simons	50 00	
Joseph Burns	50 00	
Jacob Mullen	50 00	
Michael Flynn	50 00	
Samuel Phister	35 00	
B. F. Sloan, Secretary	5 10	
R. J. Saltsman	193 20	
Erie Lime & Cement Co	131 50	
Weekly pay roll, street work	50 22	
W. A. Crawford & Co	35 10	
E. Walker Tool Co	27 15	
The Erie Gas Co	23 25	
Edward Donnelly	15 00	
Saltsman & Austin	12 55	
Edison Electric Light Co	10 55	
Keystone Carriage Works	10 05	
Frederick Diehl	3 00	
E. J. Morton	72 00	
Weekly pay roll, street work	54 18	
Cornell Lead Co	33 98	
Hollands Manufacturing Co	22 63	
Jarecki Manufacturing Co., L't'd	18 91	

Noble & Hall	5 99
John Meyerhoeffer	3 00
Erie Machine Shop	45 36
Weekly pay roll, street work	41 63
George W. Starr	35 26
J. C. Hilton, P. M	41 00
F. R. Simmons	4 76
George L. Siegel	8 80
M. R. Barr	6 12
Weekly pay roll, street work	89 25
Pennsylvania Railroad Co	38 68
Holly Manufacturing Co	14 40
Herald Printing & Pub. Co, L't'd	9 75
Erie Soap Co	5 00
J. C. Hilton, P. M	10 99
	$2,063 52

April, 1891—

B. F. Sloan, Secretary	125 00
Geo. C. Gensheimer, Asst. Sec'y	100 00
William O'Lone	100 00
A. F. Caane	70 00
F. W. Koehler	55 00
John D. Spafford	55 00
John Kolb	32 67
David W. Harper	34 58
F. A. Roth	100 00
George R. Miller	75 00
John Kelly	75 00
R. W. Simons	50 00
Joseph Burns	50 00
Jacob Mullen	50 00
Michael Flynn	50 00
Samuel Phister	25 00
R. J. Saltsman	356 80
The Sims Co., Limited	225 00
Weekly pay roll, street work	135 65
L. S. & M. S. R'y Co	87 06
E Walker Tool Co	19 10
Edward Donnelly	15 00
The Erie Gas Co	12 79
B. F. Sloan, Secretary	6 78
J. C. Quintus	5 00
R. D. Wood & Co	398 72
Union Iron Works	750 00
Weekly pay roll, street work	210 31
Erie Machine Shop	117 39
Eclipse Lubricating Oil Co	33 15
C. J. Brown	100 00
Hays Manufacturing Co	383 85
Weekly pay roll, street work	363 00
Noble & Hall	91 93
Hardwick & Himrod	45 51
John O. Baker	21 75
Ashby & Vincent	16 55
P. T Donnelly	2 25
Downing & Flickinger	12 00
E. A Steubgen	12 00
C. Swailey	12 00
Frank A. Sawdey	12 50
Shannon & Reitzell	12 00
Frank Schlaudecker	12 00
Elias Sturgeon	12 00
Scott & Arbuckle	12 00
Thomas M. Hemphill	12 00
L. J. VanAnden & Co	12 00
Lake Shore Foundry	1,580 15
Weekly pay roll, street work	439 76
W. A. Crawford & Co	36 25
Mehl & Sapper	28 84
P. T. Donnelly	21 37
Pennsylvania Railroad Co	8 73
	$6,689 14

May, 1891—

B. F. Sloan, Secretary	125 00
Geo. C Gensheimer, Asst. Sec'y	100 00

William O'Lone	
A. F. Crane	
John Kolb	
F. W. Koehler	
John D. Spafford	
D W. Harper	
F. A. Roth	
George R. Miller	
John Kelly	
R. W. Simons	
Joseph Burns	
Jacob Mullen	
Michael Flynn	
Samuel Phister	
C. Kessler	
Weekly pay roll, street work	
Globe Iron Foundry	
E Walker Tool Co	
Eclipse Lubricating Oil Co	
R. J. Saltsman	
Lyman Felheim	
George W. Starr	
Union Iron Works	
Cornell Lead Co	
National Tube Works	
Weekly pay roll, street work	
R. J. Saltsman	
L. S & M. S. R'y Co	
Noble & Hall	
Edward Donnelly	
F. W. Miller & Son	
B. F. Sloan, Secretary	
Hollands Manufacturing Co	
J. C. Hilton, P. M	
William Heidt	
The Erie Gas Co	
C. J. Brown	
Weekly pay roll, street work	
Dispatch Publishing Co., Limited	
E S. Greeley & Co	
N.Y & Pa. Telephone & Telegraph	
Thomas Tidman	
Pennsylvania Railroad Co	
J. C. Hilton, P. M	
J. E. Baker	
Erie Rubber Co	
George W. Starr	
Davenport & Griffith (acc't of 7 yes	
R. D. Wood & Co	
Weekly pay roll, street work	
A. Brugger	
Wissler & Hubbe	
Hays Manufacturing Co	
A. S. Pinney	
Erie Machine Shop	
Herald Printing & Pub. Co., L't'd	
Erie Soap Co	
Hardwick & Himrod	
Erie Paving Co	
O. C. Thayer & Son	
Constable Brothers	
Mehl & Sapper	
John J O'Brien	
Weekly pay roll, street work	
Geo. C. Gensheimer, Asst. Sec'y	

June, 1891—

B. F. Sloan, Secretary	
Geo. C. Gensheimer, Asst. Sec'y	
John Kolb	
David W. Harper	
A. F. Crane	
F. W. Koehler	
John D. Spafford	
William O'Lone	

F. A. Roth	100	00
George R. Miller	75	00
John Kelly	75	00
R. W. Simons	50	00
Joseph Burns	50	00
Jacob Mullen	50	00
Michael Flynn	50	00
Samuel Phister	35	00
Edward Donnelly	15	00
Geo. C. Gensheimer, Asst. Sec'y	13	08
B. F. Sloan	28	00
Weekly pay roll, street work	210	51
Globe Iron Foundry Co	301	40
National Tube Works	257	19
Noble & Hall	18	64
Eclipse Lubricating Oil Co	30	42
George L. Siegel	34	00
Geo. C. Gensheimer, Asst. Sec'y	96	14
National Meter Co	83	51
R. D. Wood & Co	167	40
Moore, Winschel & Co	58	48
R. T. Williams & Co	1	50
W. A. Crawford & Co	34	13
Erie Machine Shop	77	45
E. Walker Tool Co	58	90
Jarecki Manufacturing Co., L't'd	17	07
Hardwick & Himrod	12	00
Momeyer & Graf	430	92
Lake Shore Foundry	2,208	92
The Erie Gas Co	17	94
Geo. C. Gensheimer, Asst. Sec'y	18	85
Weekly pay roll, street work	430	94
O. C. Thayer & Son	7	00
John M. Glazier	3	50
R. D. Wood & Co	167	40
National Meter Co	16	75
Davenport & Griffith (acc't of 7 years)	460	00
Herald Printing & Pub. Co., L't'd	6	20
C. J. Brown	50	00
J. C. Hilton, P. M	22	00
J. C. Hilton, P. M	37	50
Weekly pay roll, street work	401	53
C. J. Brown, expenses	200	00
Weekly pay roll, street work	884	94
William Krueger	8	90
	$7,577	**83**

July, 1881—

William Himrod, Secretary	125	00
B. F. Sloan	125	00
Geo C. Gensheimer, Asst. Sec'y	100	00
John Kolb	70	00
David W. Harper	40	00
A. F. Crane	53	84
F. W. Koehler	55	00
John D. Spafford	55	00
William O'Lone	100	00
F. A. Roth	100	00
George R. Miller	75	00
John Kelly	75	00
R. W. Simons	50	00
Joseph Burns	50	00
Jacob Mullen	50	00
George Coverdale	7	00
Abraham Louch	6	12
Michael Flynn	50	00
John Meyerhoefer	5	00
Samuel Phister	35	00
Edward Donnelly	15	00
Geo. C. Gensheimer, Asst. Sec'y	7	63
B. F. Sloan	38	08
Weekly pay roll, street work	411	28
Globe Iron Foundry Co	144	10
Jarecki Manufacturing Co., L't'd	4	98
National Meter Co	151	50
William F. Nick	27	71
Detroit Lead Pipe & Sheet Lead W'k's	56	82

Erie Rubber Co	16	20
Erie Gun Store	10	78
Hardwick & Himrod	18	90
Saltsman & Austin	20	65
Martin Quigley	15	60
Geo. C. Gensheimer, Asst. Sec'y	58	66
Robert Dill	198	00
Momeyer & Graf	387	01
E. Walker Tool Co	28	60
Lake Shore Foundry	2,055	81
Eclipse Lubricating Oil Co	65	98
Erie Machine Shop	185	61
C. J. Brown	150	00
Geo. C. Gensheimer, Asst. Sec'y	38	04
The Erie Gas Co	13	44
Weekly pay roll, street work	311	06
R. J. Saltsman	24	50
George L. Siegel	6	63
F. E. Franz	11	60
R. D. Wood & Co	167	40
Hays Manufacturing Co	898	55
A. J. Schuster	22	11
R. J. Saltsman	81	87
C. Kessler	100	00
Weekly pay roll, street work	381	55
William Hardwick	150	00
Detroit Lead Pipe & Sheet Lead W'k's	1,780	23
Anchor Line	40	00
Weekly pay roll, street work	387	72
Weekly pay roll, street work	419	88
Lake Shore Foundry	2,826	88
Geo. C. Gensheimer, Asst. Sec'y	11	80
C. J. Brown	50	00
Ashby & Vincent	12	70
Hardwick & Himrod	16	65
Eclipse Lubricating Oil Co	33	60
A. S. Pinney	1	95
Murphy Bros	9	54
	$12,471	**52**

August, 1891—

L. S. & M. S. R'y Co	283	29
Monthly pay roll, accounting dep't	569	38
Monthly pay roll, operating dep't	485	00
Weekly pay roll, street work	453	12
National Meter Co	227	50
F. Dudenhoeffer	36	40
National Tube Works	245	56
Dispatch Publishing Co., Limited	55	35
A. P. Durlin & Son	96	00
Globe Iron Foundry Co	40	96
Keystone Carriage Works	19	05
Murphy Bros	14	95
Herald Printing & Pub. Co., L't'd	12	35
Constable Bros	27	25
Hardwick & Himrod	43	56
Eclipse Lubricating Oil Co	28	80
N.Y. & Pa. Telephone & Telegraph Co	21	00
Jarecki Manufacturing Co., L't'd	10	24
E. Walker Tool Co	15	00
Hays Manufacturing Co	219	18
Erie Machine Shop	25	66
Thomas Pickering	2	00
Moore, Winschel & Co	31	64
N. Lenschen	6	32
Momeyer & Graf	425	32
Weekly pay roll, street work	402	77
P. C. Thayer	20	00
Keystone Electric Co	693	25
The Erie Gas Co	4	14
Geo. C. Gensheimer, Asst. Sec'y	17	15
George L. Siegel	10	70
A. Brugger	17	90
W. H. Keeler	7	94
Edward Donnelly	15	00
William O'Lone	40	00
Lake Shore Foundry	1,698	63

Weekly pay roll, street work	451 79
Geo. C. Gensheimer	6 04
Weekly pay roll, street work	495 06
George Coverdale	5 26
C. J. Brown	50 00
Weekly pay roll, street work	593 14
Monthly pay roll, accounting dep't	495 00
Monthly pay roll, operating dep't	485 00
Globe Iron Foundry Co	10 56
Boston Woven Hose Co	10 92
Hardwick & Himrod	12 20
R. D. Wood & Co	100 08
A. S. Pinney	8 79
Eclipse Lubricating Oil Co	35 36
Noble & Hall	2 62
Herald Printing & Pub. Co., L't'd	17 15
George Schlindwein	8 50
L. S. & M. S. R'y Co	34 48
Geo. C. Gensheimer	4 10
Union Water Meter Co	9 00
National Meter Co	163 50
Saltsman & Austin	27 04
Edward Donnelly	15 00
Momeyer & Graf	294 70
Mehl & Sapper	9 81
Lake Shore Foundry	2,150 76
C. Kessler	100 00
	$11,926 24

September, 1891—

Weekly pay roll, street work	630 26
Geo. C. Gensheimer, Asst. Sec'y	7 50
Erie Machine Shop	18 69
Hays Manufacturing Co	125 86
E. Walker Tool Co	87 70
Henry Beckman & Son	52 40
A. P. Durlin & Son	16 25
R. H. Chinnock	13 50
O. C. Thayer & Son	35 58
Fred L. Cleveland	15 50
George Coverdale	2 50
C. J. Brown	175 00
Weekly pay roll, street work	430 43
William Krueger	5 75
Weekly pay roll, street work	545 90
Geo. C. Gensheimer, Asst. Sec'y	8 25
John C. Hilton, P. M	20 00
Conrad Brown estate	55 05
C. Kessler, expenses	200 00
Weekly pay roll, street work	585 38
	$2,982 50

October, 1891—

Monthly pay roll, accounting dep't	515 77
Monthly pay roll, operating dep't	485 00
Weekly pay roll, street work	552 43
Momeyer & Graf	391 36
Mrs. Bridget Donnelly	15 00
F. R. Simmons	4 26
N.Y. & Pa. Telephone & Telegraph Co	21 00
Robert J. Saltsman	33 25
Mehl & Sapper	36 85
A. S. Pinney	15 37
R. H. Chinnock	2 50
Globe Iron Foundry Co	6 82
Hardwick & Himrod	19 70
George Schlindwein	3 00
William Krueger	17 00
Solomon Levi	4 00
Keystone Electric Motor Co	8 80
Hollands Manufacturing Co	4 65
Ashby & Vincent	21 60
John J. O'Brien	9 30
Boston Woven Hose Co	33 06
South Erie Iron Works	68 07
Eclipse Lubricating Oil Co	65 40
A. J. Schuster	70 20
David Schlosser	30 23

E. Walker Tool Co	
L. S. & M. S. R'y Co	
Geo. C. Gensheimer, Asst. Sec'y	
Erie Machine Shop	
A. P. Durlin & Son	
Geo. C. Gensheimer, Asst. Sec'y	
Weekly pay roll, street work	
Frank Thayer	
John C. Hilton, P. M	
William Krueger	
Weekly pay roll, street work	
Geo. C. Gensheimer, Asst. Sec'y	
Lake Shore Foundry	
Fred Koehler & Co	
Weekly pay roll, street work	
C. J. Brown	
Pennsylvania Co	
Cleveland Supply Co	
Eclipse Lubricating Oil Co	
Boston Woven Hose Co	
David Schlosser	
Globe Iron Foundry Co	
Detroit Lead Pipe & Sheet Lead W'ks	110 11
Miller Bros	
Herald Printing & Pub. Co., L't'd	
Lyman Felheim	
Erie Steam Bending Works	
Paradine & McCarty	
George W. Bell	
A. S. Pinney	
Henry Beckman & Son	7 70
Mrs. Bridget Donnelly	
L. S. & M. S. R'y Co	
Ashby & Vincent	2 57
Geo. C. Gensheimer, Asst. Sec'y	5 00
Monthly pay roll, accounting dep't	505 00
Monthly pay roll, operating dep't	485 00
The Hurley Manufacturing Co	62 37
Buckeye Car Seal & M'f'g Co	2 00
Hays Manufacturing Co	221 39
Jarecki Manufacturing Co., L't'd	222 15
Weekly pay roll, street work	515 75
Lake Shore Foundry	3,233 56
James Gaffney	8 10
	$14,913 84

November, 1891—

Momeyer & Graf	296 36
Geo. C. Gensheimer, Asst. Sec'y	18 07
Globe Iron Foundry Co	68 20
C. Flickinger	2 66
Erie Machine shop	32 68
E. Walker Tool Co	41 96
R. D. Wood & Co	117 02
People's Ice Co	6 00
Union Ice Co	18 00
D. C. Weller, agent	7 68
The Erie Gas Co	1 27
Hardwick & Himrod	34 50
Eclipse Lubricating Oil Co	31 30
A. Brugger	10 35
Henry Beckman & Son	21 51
A. J. Black	6 00
Weekly pay roll, street work	500 57
Mehl & Sapper	5 66
P. T. Donnelly	31 75
C. Kessler	100 00
G. C. Gensheimer, Asst. Sec'y	15 61
Lake Shore Foundry	3,186 67
Weekly pay roll, street work	506 54
D. K. Dean & Son	10 00
Weekly pay roll, street work	460 34
William Hardwick	180 00
Weekly pay roll, street work	494 34
Jacob Zaun	3 25
	$6,107 91

December, 1891—

The Hurley Manufacturing Co	25	38
Herald Printing & Pub. Co., L't'd	5	25
F. Dudenhoeffer	10	50
Globe Foundry Co	22	66
Robert J. Saltsman	17	00
L. S. & M. S. R'y Co	70	65
Holly Manufacturing Co	7	67
Hardwick & Himrod	21	16
Henry Shenk	1	68
J. E. Baker	1	40
Keystone Electric Co	4	55
Ashby & Vincent	69	55
Dispatch Publishing Co., Limited	8	00
Mrs. Bridget Donnelly	15	00
Monthly pay roll, accounting dep't	469	80
Monthly pay roll, operating dep't	485	00
Geo. C. Gensheimer, Asst. Sec'y	10	35
Constable Bros	1	61
George Schlindwein	7	35
O. C. Thayer & Son	11	99
Lyman Felhelm		78
Eclipse Lubricating Oil Co	33	90
A. S. Pinney	4	27
J. W. Swalley	3	60
Herald Printing & Pub. Co., L't'd	4	75
R. D. Wood & Co	217	90
David Schlosser		40
Jarecki Manufacturing Co., L't'd	42	81
Hays Manufacturing Co	243	01
E. Walker Tool Co	50	35
Momeyer & Graf	367	68
Erie Machine Shop	123	33
Henry Beckman & Son	17	01
Weekly pay roll, street work	491	89

Weekly pay roll, street work	407	39
William Hardwick	100	00
William Krueger	10	00
Geo. C. Gensheimer, Asst. Sec'y	11	25
Weekly pay roll, street work	291	67
C. Kessler	200	00
Weekly pay roll, street work	195	45
Jarecki Manufacturing Co., L't'd	60	62
E. J. Riblet	286	95
Paradine & McCarty	12	00
Ashby & Vincent	63	20
Union Carriage Works	3	60
William F. Pfeffer	7	00
Saltsman & Austin	11	35
Robert J. Saltsman	30	50
Jarecki Manufacturing Co., L't'd	4	91
A. Brugger	12	35
David Schlosser	3	42
A. S. Pinney	1	35
Globe Iron Foundry Co	47	14
Geo. C. Gensheimer, Asst. Sec'y	4	45
Constable Bros	5	78
Eclipse Lubricating Oil Co	32	70
Mehl & Sapper	15	07
South Erie Iron Works	8	55
A. M. Carter	92	98
D. B. Meehan	4	80
Monthly pay roll, operating dep't	485	00
Monthly pay roll, accounting dep't	526	53
William Hardwick	100	00
	$5,904	24
Total	$96,368	51

Dis. Ledger Folio.	Department.	ACCOUNT.	From Beginning of Works to Dec. 31, '90.	In 1
1	Construction.	Advertising Books S. & P.	....	
2		Buildings and Grounds,	85,181 41	
4		Boilers,		8,:
7		Civil Engineering,	7,122 85	
8		Connections,	73,651,18	11,
26		Engines and Boilers,	98,296 61	
27		Engines,		
32		Engine Room Furniture & Fixtures	1,263 07	
34		Expense.	....	
36		Electric Light Plant,	....	:
37		Fire Hydrants,	19,316 71	£
45		Fuel.	....	
47		Gas Well,	8,148 59,	
48		Horse, Wagon and Cartage,	2,571 99,	1
53		Inlet Pipe,	45,032 59	
55		Interest and Discount,	99,065 41	
56		Light, Oil, Lamps, Wicks, &c.,	....	
59		Lowering Mains,	305 45	1
60		Mains and Branches,	406,089 96	
85		Mains, 30-inch,	60,937 64	
86		Meters,	7,254 89	
100		Office Furniture and Fixtures,	....	
109		Park Fountains,	3,244 68	
110		R. R. Switch and Scales,	2,918 99	
111		Reservoir,	123,150 83	
112		Stop Valves,	23,483 55	2,2
117		Superintendent's Stores,	215 11	
119		Superintendent's Expense,	....	
121		Shop Rent,	....	
123		Tools and Repairs,	2,712 39	4
130		Telephone and Telegraph,	....	
136	Maintenance.	Advertising, Books, S. and P.	....	
138		Buildings and Grounds,	....	2
142		Boilers,	17,481 04	4
151		Connections,	1,818 95	2
173		Engines,	12,035 07	£
208		Engine Room, Furniture and Fix.	....	
210		Expenses,	....	
214		Fire Hydrants,	....	5
225		Fuel,	....	
228		Horse, Wagon and Cartage,	2,571 92	2
233		Inlet Pipe,	....	
239		Light, Oil, Lamps, Wicks, &c.,	....	
243		Mains and Branches,	14,644 06	2
258		Main, 30-inch.	....	
259		Meters,	2,766 22	4
275		Office Furniture and Fixtures,	....	
279		Paving and Street Repairs,	389 54	
285		R. R. Switch and Scales,	....	
286		Reservoir,	11,388 06	1,4
318		Stop Valves,	2,899 69	2
323		Superintendent's Stores,	390 43	
325		Superintendent's Expenses,	....	
327		Shop Rent,	....	
329		Tools and Repairs,	2,712 38	6

WATER WORKS DISBURSEMENTS—Continued.

Dr. Ledger Fols.	Department.	ACCOUNT.	From Beginning of Works to Dec. 31, '90.	In 1891.	From Beginning of Works to Dec. 31, '91.
351	Operating....	Advertising, Books S. and P.	....	36 34	36 34
355		Engineers and Firemen,	89,759 95	5,405 95	95,165 20
370		Engineers' Stores,	2,281 49	61 40	2,342 89
378		Expense,	....	32 48	32 48
382		Fuel,	129,671 88	4,008 13	133,680 01
410		Insurance,	562 33	125 91	688 24
415		Light, Oil, Lamps, Wicks, &c.,	....	169 65	169 65
435		Oil and Tallow,	7,960 03	683 83	8,648 86
458		Tools and Repairs,	....	38 92	38 92
463		Taxes, State, County and School,	1,100 83	....	1,100 83
465		Telephone and Telegraph,	....	89 22	89 22
470		Waste and Packing,	3,474 25	276 55	3,750 80
475		Water Rents returned,	62 62	....	62 62
501	Accounting..	Advertising, Books, S. and P.	6,458 68	559 27	7,017 95
517		Expenses,	14,528 25	114 87	14,643 12
530		Postage,	3,539 99	561,08	4,101 07
550		Salaries,	133,430 99	6,840 68	140,271 66
626	Sundries.....	City of Erie Sinking Fund Com'rs,	76,500 00	5,000 00	81,500 00
703	Legal	Court Costs,	9 60	....	9 60
708		Counsel Fees,	1,805 38	760 00	2,565 38
715		Expense,	....	35 25	35 25
		Totals......................	1,605,385 28	96,368 51	1,701,753 79

WATER WORKS DISBURSEMENTS. .

DEPARTMENT.	From Beginning of Works to Dec. 31, '90.	In 1891.	Total to Dec. 31, '91.
Construction..	1,064,901 76	65,943 99	1,130,845 75
Maintenance..	69,037 26	5,925 79	74,963 05
Operating..	234,873 38	10,927 58	245,800 96
Accounting..	158,287 90	7,775 90	166,033 80
Sundries......	76,500 00	5,000 00	81,500 00
Legal..	1,814 98	795 25	2,610 23
Totals...	1,605,385 28	96,368 51	1,701,753 79

WATER WORKS BONDS.

Series	Date.		Amount.	Interest.	Water Bonds Exchanged for Consolidated Bonds. Interest 7 per cent.	Balance Water Bo
1	July	1, 1867	$ 250.000	7 %	$ 13 500	
2	July	1, 1868	50,000	7 %	8,000	$ 236,,
						42,
3	March	1, 1869	50,000	7 %		50 (
4	Sept	1, 1869	50,000	7 %		50 (
5	July	1, 1870	75.000	7 %	11 000	
						64,
6	Sept.	1, 1872	125,000	7 %	64,000	
						61 (
7	Sept.	1, 1873	75.000	7 %	67,000	
						8,

Total Amount issued. $ 675 000 $163,500 $ 511,
    "   "   paid,   132,000

Balance, $543.000 00
To which is to be added   214 62 Bills paid by the City di
                                   ending May 1, 1868.
           955 10 Warrant No 361, Septem
        5,000 00   "   " 198, July
                            Mrs Rebecca Thay
           30 00 Warrant No 292, Septer
                            to McConnell & Do
          140 00 November 11th, 1878, ma
           60 00 Warrant No. 526, Novem
                            to McConnell & Do
          131 00 Warrant No 585. Decem
                            to J J. Mc onnell.
          119 00 Warrant No. 587, Decem
                            to Wm Donald.
       3,327 86 Warrant No 576, Septen
                            to Mrs Rebecca Th
           35 00 December 28th, 1880.

      $553,012 58 Balance in the Controlle
                        tober 31st, 1891.

WATER WORKS BONDS.

When.	Amount Paid by the City.	When.	Balance of Outstandi'g Original Water Bonds.	Remarks.	Approximate Amount Paid for Interest by the City to December 31, 1891, inclusive.
				Converted into 4 per cent. Refunding Bonds, dated Jan. 1, '87	$ 381,599 00
July 1, 1888	$ 19,000	July 1, 1888		Converted into 4 per cent. Refunding Bonds, dated Mar. 1, '89	71 960 00
1889. Sept. Nov.	16,500	Sept. 1, 1889			75,667 00
					70,065 91
July, '90 Feb., '91	15,000	July 1, 1890	$24,000		108 100 83
			61,000		169,166 67
			8,000		96,250 00
	$ 50,000		$93,000		$ 972,809 41

RECAPITULATION

Total amount of Water Bonds issued.............	$675,000 00	
Converted into 7% Consolidated Bonds.........		$ 163,500 00
Converted into 4% Refunding Bonds...........		286,500 00
Amount of Water Bonds redeemed.............		132,000 00
Amount of Original Water Bonds outstanding...		93 000 00
	$ 675,000 00	$ 675,000 00

Statement of Cost of Fire Hydrants from Commencement of Works to December 31st, 1891.

YEAR.	NO. OF HY- DRANTS.	ANNUAL RENTAL.	INTEREST TO DECEM- BER 31, 1891.	TOTAL.
1870	97	● 9,700 00	30,463 48	40.163 48
1871	99	9 900 00	28 407 92	38.307 92
1872	103	10,300 00	27 034 28	37.334 28
1873	107	10.700 00	● 25.465 26	36,165 26
1874	107	10 700 00	23,099 30	33 799 30
1875	110	11,000 00	21 473 80	32,473 80
1876	112	11 200 00	19,702 20	30 902 20
1877	114	11,400 00	17 989 06	29.389 06
1878	115	11.500 00	16.241 74	27 741 74
1879	121	12,100 00	15 102 78	27 202 78
1880	126	12,600 00	13,921 12	26,521 12
1881	161	16,100 00	15.571 14	31.671 14
1882	171	17,100 00	14 337 64	31 437 64
1883	197	19.700 00	14.148 26	33 848 26
1884	248	24,800 00	15 023 38	39 823 38
1885	270	27.000 00	12 969 70	39,969 70
1886	280	28.000 00	11,271 44	39,271 44
1887	318	31.800 00	9 883 32	41,683 32
1888	333	33 300 00	7.488 92	40.788 92
1889	346	34,600 00	5.013 54	39 613 54
1890	372	37 200 00	2 604 00	39 804 00
1891	393	39 300 00	....	39,300 00
		430 000 00	347,212 28	777 212 28

Statement of Accounts with City of Erie, Pa.

CITY OF ERIE, PA.   DR.

CASH—Paid Sinking Fund Commission'rs $ 81,500 00
WATER—Fire Hydrants from Jan. 1, 1870,
    to Dec. 31. 1891, @ $100 each
    per year....................$430,000 00
    Fountains from Jan. 1, 1869, to
    Dec. 31, 1891, @ $1,251 05
    per year.................... 28,774 15
Engine Houses to Dec. 31, 1891......... 1,484 14
City Hall to Dec. 31, 1891.............. 519 75
                  ————— 460,778 04
INTEREST—On Water Furnished Fire
    Hydrants $347,212 28
    On Water Furnished Fountains. 38,075 60
    On Fountains................. 11,893 03
                  ————— 397,183 91
CONSTRUCTION—Amount Paid for Foun-
    tains in City Parks......... 3,237 98
    Balance...................... 718,322 06
                  ————$1,661,021 99

CR.

CASH—Different times................. $ 10,012 58
BONDS —...........................   675,000 00
INTEREST—Paid on Bonds..............   972,809 41
RENT—Of Offices.....................   3,200 00
                   ————— 1 661,021 99

December 31, 1891, by balance.......... $ 718 322 06

Statement of Resources and Liabilities, Dec

RESOURCES.

CONSTRUCTION ACCOUNT—Buildings and
        Grounds $104,302 57
        Boilers—From Jan. 1st, 1891....   3,409 15
        Connections 93,890 35
        Engines—From Jan. 1st, 1891...   15 25
        Engines and Boilers—From com-
        mencement of Works to Dec.
        31st, 1890.................. 104,309 95
        Engine Room Furniture and
        Fixtures   1,505,82
        Electric Light Plant............   725 27
        Fire Hydrants.................. 22,462 88
        Inlet Pipe...................... 50,326 95
        Mains and Branches............ 485,711 75
        Main 30 inch.................. 81,834 22
        Meters.......................   9,343 39
        Office Furniture and Fixtures...   384 48
        Railroad Switch and Scales.....   3,262 09
        Reservoir...................... 137,629 35
        Stop Valves.................... 28,487 60
                          —1,127,
CASH—In Office........................$ 175 00
        In Hands of Treasurer of City of
        Erie, Pa...................   2,261 83
                            2,
ACCOUNTS—Individual..................$ 2,970 34
        Meter 6,595 13
        Plumbing......................   625 15
                            10,

LIABILITIES.

ACCOUNTS—City of Erie, Pa............$718,322 06
        Individual 359 68
                       —$718,6
        Balance....................   421,5

Main Pipe Laid in 1891.

LOCATION AND SIZE.

STREET.	½ INCH.	1 INCH.	4 INCH.	6 INCH.	12 INCH.	20 INCH.	30 INCH
Short...............			551				
Second...............			799.4				
Third...............			768				
Fifth...............				818			
Sixth...............				60			
Eighth..........H B.			18	920 6			
Ninth...............				416			
Tenth...........H. B.			10.7	1,338 9			
Eleventh...........				78			
Twelfth.............				376 9			
Thirteenth..........				563.2			
Fourteenth..........				582.5			
Fifteenth...........			21				
Seventeenth				48 4			
Buffalo Road........				725			
Nineteenth..........				324			
Twentieth......H. B.			9 6	925.7			
Brown Avenue..H. B.			10 11	196 4			
Twenty-first....:....					2,733		
Twenty-second..H B		185	9.8	835.4			
Twenty-third........				1,816			
Twenty-fourth				1,265			
Twenty-fifth.....H. B.			9 4	1,134 6			
Twenty-sixth........		908	1,551 3	1,492 4	311	31.6	748
Twenty-sixth....H B			10.5				
Twenty-seventh				1,229 2			
Twenty ninth....H. B.			8 6	396 6			
Warfel Avenue..H B			11 3	1,208			
East Avenue.....H B			9 3				
East Avenue.........			1,130	377.2			
Ross...............			210.6				
Willson.............			209 6				
Wayne.............				167.4			
Reed...............				621.4			
Ash			174 6	1 034 3			
Wallace.............				258			
Parade.............			250				
German.............				314.7			
Division.............				21 6			
Holland.............				592.7			
French.............				772.10			
State ....H. B			8.6	605			
Waterford Ave..H. B			11	1,277.3			
Edinboro Road......			179.2				
Myrtle.............	68			403.2			
Chestnut............			317				1,524
Cherry..... ....H B			37 5				

STREET.	½ INCH.	1 INCH.	4 INCH.	6 INCH.	12 IN
Cherry...............			229.6	3,748.5	
Poplar...............				357 3	
Liberty..............			523 4	1,004 4	
Liberty.........H B.			12 4		
Plum				1,332.2	
Cascade..............		179			
Maple................			2,985.8		
Hazel................				75	
Waterford Plank Road				99.8	
Hess Avenue.........				968	
Pennsylvania Avenue.				604.6	
Moorhead............				102.6	
Kellogg..............				188 6	
Wood...........H.B			{ 9.6 161		
Cochran.......·..H. B.			8.8	644.8	
Total	68	1,272	10,255.7	32,320.8	3,(

RECAPITULATION.

DESCRIPTION.	FEET.	IN.
All sizes reported to December 31st, 1890....		
Laid during the year 1891, ¼ inch...........	68	
" " 1 "	1,272	
" " 4 "	10,255	7
6 "	32,320	8
12 "	3 044	
20 "	31	6
30 "	2,272	
	49,263	9

LESS.

Pipe taken up during the year 1891.		
¼ inch on Short Street west from		
Chestnut..................... 159 10		
6 inch on East Twenty first between		
Ash and East Avenue.......... 2,714 00		
	2,873	10
Balance in feet..............................	46,389	11
Total Miles increase in 1891................		
Total number of Miles of Mains and Branches		
to December 31st, 1891.................		

STREETS.	Number of Connections	FEET.	IN.	STREETS.	Number of Connections	FEET.	IN.
Front and Dock	3	15	6	McCarter's Avenue	1	9	....
Short	5	99	4	Warfel Avenue	10	216	....
Second	14	201	9	East Avenue	16	362	2
Third	13	242	3	Ross	3	43	....
Fourth	12	229	10	Newman	4	56	9
Fifth	25	348	5	Wilson	3	52	....
North Park	1	12	7	Wayne	2	25	....
Sixth	13	576	5	Reed	12	110	6
Seventh	23	374	11	Ash	1	8	....
Eighth	25	480	10	Wallace	3	76	6
Ninth	17	280	....	Vine	2	24	2
Tenth	14	558	1	Parade	11	430	....
Eleventh	16	185	10	German	10	191	2
Twelfth	16	404	3	Holland	9	99	2
Thirteenth	17	247	6	French	10	223	8
Fourteenth	8	148	5	State	14	348	....
Fifteenth	3	40	1	Peach	12	126	....
Sixteenth	9	170	8	Waterford Avenue	16	373	1
Seventeenth	20	320	8	Sassafras	2	51	8
Eighteenth	16	247	3	Myrtle	19	420	10
Buffalo Road	3	51	....	Hickory	1	7	6
Nineteenth	8	96	4	Chestnut	3	52	2
Twentieth	13	206	9	Walnut	10	120	10
Brown's Avenue	3	30	6	Cherry	29	559	4
Twenty-first	14	302	6	Maple	22	314	11
Twenty Second	14	201	9	Hazel	5	68	....
Twenty-third	36	561	2	Poplar	9	105	3
Twenty fourth	27	434	2	Liberty	11	248	9
Twenty fifth	27	420	11	Plum	17	338	....
Twenty Sixth	27	547	8	Cascade	3	78	6
Twenty-Seventh	18	330	9	Kellogg	2	53	2
Twenty Eighth	1	8	9	Cochran	8	155	9
Twenty-Ninth	1	27	8		742	13.753	4

LENGTH OF CONNECTIONS IN MILES.

	MILES	FEET.	IN.
Connections made in 1891	2	3,193	4
Previously made	25	34	......
Total to December 31st, 1891	27	3,227	4

Location, Size and Kind of Stop Valves Set I

STREET.	WHERE LOCATED.
Front	97 ft East of French ....
Second	West Line of Peach Street ....
Third	" " " " ....
"	" " " State " ....
Fourth	East " "Chestnut" ....
"	" " " Walnut " ....
"	" " " Liberty " ....
Fifth	West " " Parade " ....
"	East " " Liberty " ....
Sixth	" " " Walnut " ....
Seventh	" " " " " ....
"	" " " Cherry " ....
Eighth	West " " Perry " ....
"	" " " Ash " ....
"	" " " Cherry " ....
"	" " " Liberty " ....
Ninth	" " " Cherry " ....
"	East " " " " ....
Tenth	634 ft. East of East Line of Hess Ave..
"	East Line of City Limits ....
"	" " " Reed Street ....
"	" " " State " ....
"	West " " Cherry " ....
"	" " " Plum " ....
Eleventh	" " " East Avenue ....
Thirteenth	East " " Reed Street ....
"	" " " French " ....
Fourteenth	" " " Division " ....
"	" " " State " ....
"	West " " " " ....
Seventeenth	East " " " " ....
Eighteenth	" " " German " ....
"	West " " French " ....
Twentieth	" " " Cascade " ....
Twenty First	East " " Chestnut" ....
"	" " " Ash " ....
"	" " " Reed " ....
"	" " " Wayne " ....
"	" " " Perry " ....
Twenty-Second	West " " Liberty " ....
Twenty-Third	" " " Cherry " ....
"	East " " Reed " ....
"	West " " Wayne " ....
"	East " " Holland " ....
Twenty-Fourth	West " " German " ....
Twenty-Fifth	" " " Parade " ....
Twenty-Sixth	East " " Penn'a Ave. ....
"	West " " " " ....
"	" " " Wallace " ....
....	In Front of Reservoir ....
....	" " " . ...
"	East Line of Chestnut St ....
Twenty-Seventh	" " " Wallace St ....
"	West " " " St ....

STREET.	WHERE LOCATED.	KIND.	SIZE In Inches
Twenty-Ninth.......	West Line of Myrtle Street...............	Eddy	6
Hess Avenue........	South " " Tenth "	"	6
" "	North " " Twelfth "	"	6
Warfel Avenue......	South " " Buffalo Road...............	"	6
" "	North Line of Twenty-Second Street....	"	6
Pennsylvania Avenue	South " " Twenty Fifth "	"	6
Railroad............	" " " buffalo Road...............	'	4
Buffalo Road........	East " " East Avenue...............	"	6
East Avenue........	North " " Third Street............	"	6
Ross	" " " Fifth "	"	4
Reed	South " " Seventh "	"	6
"	North " " Tenth "	"	6
Ash...............	South " " Twenty-First Street.......	"	6
"	North " " Twenty-Seventh "	"	6
German	" " " Eighteenth "	"	6
Holland	South " " Tenth "	"	6
"	" " " Twenty Sixth "	"	6
French............	" " " Fourteenth "	"	6
"	North " " Sixteenth "	"	6
State.............	" " " Fourteenth "	"	6
"	South " " Sixteenth "	"	6
Moorhead..........	East " " Waterford Avenue.........	"	6
Waterford Avenue...	North " " Twenty-Ninth Street......	"	6
" " ...	" " " Myrtle "	"	6
Cochran..........	South " " Twenty-Sixth "	"	6
Myrtle............	88 ft. South of South Line of Scott Street	"	6
Chestnut	North Line of Eighth Street...............	"	4
"	South " " Twenty-First Street.	"	20
"	North " " " " "	"	12
"	" " " Twenty-Sixth "	"	6
Cherry	" " " Sixth "	"	6
"	South " " " "	"	6
"	North " " Tenth "	"	6
"	South " " Nineteenth '	"	6
"	" " " Twenty-Fourth "	"	6
"	" " " Twenty-Sixth "	"	6
"	North " " Twenty Ninth "	"	6
Maple	South " " Twenty Sixth "	"	4
"	" " " Thirtieth "	"	4
"	North " " Thirty Second "	"	4
"	" " " Edinboro Road "	"	4
Wood	137 ft. South of South Line Edinboro Rd	"	4
Brown Avenue......	East Line of Plum Street...............	"	6
Liberty............	North Line of Second Street...............	"	4
"	" " " Third "	"	4
Plum..............	South " " Tenth "	"	6
"	North " " Sixteenth "	"	6
"	South " " Twenty-Second Street....	"	6
"	" " " Twentieth Street..........		6
			113
	Stop Valves removed...............		17
	Total balance...............		96

Total number of Stop Valves set in 1891.......... 96
Previously reported.............. 606

Total............... 702

Number and Kind of Tees Placed in 1892.

SIZE.

4x 4	13
6x 4	43
6x 6	12
12x 6	5
12x12	1
20x 6	1
30x20	1
Total	76

Number and Kind of Crosses Placed in 1892.

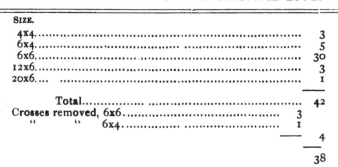

SIZE.

4x4	3
6x4	5
6x6	30
12x6	3
20x6	1
Total	42
Crosses removed, 6x6	3
" " 6x4	1
	4
	38

Cart Sprinkler Hydrant Placed During 1891.

| 1 | 1¼ inch | Set on Fourteenth Street, between State and French Street. |

Location and Style of Hydrants Placed and Hydrants Re-Placed in 1891.

STREET.	WHERE LOCATED.	NAME.
Eighth	Northwest corner of Liberty........................	Matthews
"	" " " Perry.	"
Tenth	" " " Payne Avenue	"
"	" " " Myrtle.......................	
Twelfth	Between Sassafras and Myrtle, for E & P. R. R	"
Twentieth	Northwest corner of Plum.......................	
"	Northeast corner of Raspberry...................	
Brown Avenue......	" " " Plum................	
Twenty-Second	265 feet East of Warfel Avenue	
Twenty-Fifth........	Northwest corner of Brandes.	
Twenty-Sixth	Northeast corner of Cascade....................	"
Twenty-Seventh....	" " " Wallace	Pittsburg
Twenty-Ninth.......	" " " Myrtle	Matthews
Warfel Avenue......	At City Line................	"
East Avenue.........	118 feet South of Twenty Sixth.............	Pittsburg
State	Southeast corner of Fourteenth...................	Matthews
Waterf'd Turnpike	197 feet South of Elliot	"
Cherry	Southeast corner of Twenty-Fourth.	"
"	" " " Twenty-Second	..
"	Northeast corner of Twentieth...	
"	Southeast corner of Twenty-Ninth..............	
Liberty, ...	Northeast corner of Twenty-Second............	
Maple	Southeast corner of Thirty-First............. ...	
Wood	135 feet South of Edinboro Road.................	
Cochran...............	603 " " " Twenty-Sixth.....	

RECAPITULATION.

HYDRANTS SET IN 1891.

Matthews	23
Pittsburg	2
	25

HYDRANTS REMOVED.

Bay State	1
Pittsburg	2
Matthews	1
	4

Net Gains in 1891 21

New Style Matthews	261	Morris, Tasker & Co	2
Old " "	11	Union	1
Bay State	26		
West Jersey	30		360
Pittsburg	23	Private Hadrants	33
Home made	2		
Ludlow	4		393

Statement of Water Meters Owned by the Water Works, January 1, 1892.

GOOD / POOR / TOTAL

Kind	GOOD ⅜	½	¾	1	1½	2	3	4	Total	POOR ⅜	½	¾	1	1½	2	3	4	Total	TOTAL ⅜	½	¾	1	1½	2	3	4	Total
Worthington			4	8	5	3			20			10	2	2	4			18			14	10	7	7			38
Crown			7	4	2	7	1	2	23												7	4	2	7	1	2	23
Union					2	6	4	7	19			1						1			1		2	6	4	7	20
National	1								1										1								1
Thomson		3	3	3	2	2	1	1	15											3	3	3	2	2	1	1	15
Empire					1	2	1		4														1	2	1		4
Total	1	3	14	15	12	20	7	10	82			11	2	2	4			19	1	3	25	17	14	24	7	10	101

IN USE / NOT IN USE / TOTAL

Kind	IN USE ⅜	½	¾	1	1½	2	3	4	Total	NOT IN USE ⅜	½	¾	1	1½	2	3	4	Total	TOTAL ⅜	½	¾	1	1½	2	3	4	Total
Worthington			4	7	5	4			20			10	3	2	3			18			14	10	7	7			38
Crown			6	3	2	5	1	2	19			1	1		2			4			7	4	2	7	1	2	23
Union						6	4	7	17			1		2				3			1		2	6	4	7	20
National	1								1									0	1								1
Thomson				3	2	2	1	1	9		3	3						6		3	3	3	2	2	1	1	15
Empire					1	1	1		3						1			1					1	2	1		4
Total	1		10	13	10	18	7	10	69		3	15	4	4	6			32	1	3	25	17	14	24	7	10	101

ERRATA —"Thenson" on this page should read "Thomson."

Pumping Engine Statistics for 1891.

The Pumps are three in number. Two are known as the Cornish Bull Pumps. The diameter of each plunger is 20¾ inches, and each has a stroke of 10 feet. The capacity of each pump is estimated to be 165 gallons to each stroke. The third pump is a Gaskill Horizontal Pumping Engine, of a guaranteed capacity of 5,000,000 gallons daily at a piston speed of 120 feet per minute against a head of 237 feet The Stand Pipe is 251 feet high. The Reservoir is nearly two miles from the Pumping Works, the bottom of which is 210 feet above the surface of the Bay, and the Water has been maintained during the year at an average depth in the Reservoir of about 25½ feet.

MONTHS.	DAYS ENGINES RUN — CORNISH NO. 28	NO. 89	TO-TAL	GAS-KILL.	GRAND TOTAL.	SERVICE — STROKES OF CORNISH PUMP.	REVOLUTIONS OF GASKILL PUMP.	GALLONS PUMPED — EACH MONTH AND YEAR.	DAILY AVERAGE.	AVERAGE LIFT IN FEET.	COAL — POUNDS USED.	COST.
January	.....	.....	.....	30	30	......	790,335	143,840,970	4,640,031	237.50	471,000	$282 60
February	15	14	29	28	28	......	712,800	129,729,600	4,633,200	237.00	396,750	338 05
March	.....	.....	.....	16	45	388,945	406,034	138,074,113	4,454,003	237.00	536,450	321 87
April	.....	.....	.....	30	30	......	736,761	134,090,502	4,469,683	237.00	407,400	280 44
May	7	5	12	27	39	125,582	716,280	151,083,990	4,873,677	237.00	516,350	333 04
June	6	16	22	26	48	250,094	649,450	159,465,410	5,315,513	236.9	567,600	366 10
July	.....	4	4	31	35	36,642	915,330	172,635,990	5,568,902	237	572,100	369 00
August	.....	5	5	31	36	46,424	881,820	168,151,200	5,424,232	237.79	528,100	340 66
September	4	11	15	25	40	206,429	694,770	160,508,925	5,350,297	237.14	597,750	385 54
October	.....	.....	.....	31	31	......	881,880	160,502,160	5,177,489	238.66	516,475	333 12
November	11	10	21	21	42	228,088	559,670	139,494,460	4,649,815	238	570,050	367 68
December	1	.....	1	31	32	10,634	811,575	149,461,260	4,821,330	238.16	504,450	343 43
Total	44	65	109	327	436	1,292,838	8,756,705	1,807,038,580	4,948,181	237.37	6,241,475	$3,941 53

The regular employes at the Pumping Works are one mechanical engineer, two assistant engineer, three firemen and one watchman The mechanical engineer stands a watch of five hours, from 7 to 12 every forenoon; the assistants divide the remainder of each day equally between them; each one of the firemen stands a watch of eight hours. Besides firing, the firemen unload the coal from the cars, except when both pumps are run, in which case they are assisted by the watchman or a laborer The mechanical engineer gives ten hours daily to the service of the Department, the hours when he is not on watch being employed in repairs, supervision, etc. In addition to standing their regular watch, the assistant engineers aid their superior officer in keeping the machinery in order. The watchman takes care of the buildings and grounds, besides doing such other work as may be required of him.

Amount of Coal consumed in Pumping, Gallons of Water Pumped, Average Height Pumped, Cost per Million Gallons, &c., from the First Year the Works were operated to Dec. 31, 1891.

YEAR	Tons of Coal consumed.	Price of Coal per ton from May 1st of each year.	Cost of Coal from Jan. 1st to Dec. 31st.	Grades of Bituminous Coal.	Gallons of Water Pumped.	Increase or Decrease.	Number of places supplied.	Number of Fire Hydrants.	Average height of Water in Reservoir above surface of Bay.	Cost of Coal per million gallons raised to Reservoir.	Gallons raised to Reservoir by 1 pound of Coal.
1868	59 1	5 05	$ 302 61	Lump.	......	......	......	......	......	......	......
1869	544 4	5 05	4,818 48	"	......	......	......	......	......	......	......
1870	1,064 5	5 05	5,159 10	"	246,648 960	......	1,218	97	232 0	......	......
1871	1,422 7	5 05	7,117 00	"	179,368,495	132,719 535 i.	1,727	99	232 0	$18 76	98 5
1872	1,308 5	5 05	6,528 50	"	39 676 00	115,708,505 i.	2,140	103	232.0	16 52	150 9
1873	1,672 5	5 05	8,412 65	"	38 462,415	11,013 585 d.	2,475	107	232 0	21 90	114 8
1874	1,759 0	4 85	7,709 54	"	444 817,395	60 759 80 i.	2,663	107	233 0	17 33	126 4
1875	1,836 4	4 85	8,657 61	"	531,005,475	86,181,080 i.	2,700	110	232 0	16 30	145 5
1876	1,105 1	4 00	8,925 22	"	670,726,650	139 721,175 i.	2,763	112	232 0	13 30	159 3
1877	2,456 6	3 70	8,509 33	"	660,981,810	9 744 840 d.	2,854	114	232 0	12 75	135 7
1878	2,463 3	3 35	7,945 37	"	682,399,315	21,390,505 i.	2,915	115	232 0	11 64	136 4
1879	2,628 1	3 09	7,428 92	Slack.	807,800,400	125 408,085 i.	3,011	121	232 0	9 19	153 6
1880	3,076 1	1 99	6,978 41	"	775,805,250	31,995,150 i.	3,568	126	232 0	8 99	126 0
1881	2,968 2	1 90	6,517 58	"	975,640,634	200,335,684 i.	4,110	161	234 0	6 68	142 2
1882	2,398 2	1 75	5,355 93	"	829,759,260	145,881,674 d.	4,687	171	234 7	6 45	139 7
1883	3,010 8	1 55	3,908 59	"	815,939,685	13,819,575 i.	5,077	197	234 3	4 66	152 4
1884	3,143 8	1 45	4,502 61	"	917,781,350	105,841,665 i.	5,395	248	232 9	4 99	170 0
1885	3,369 0	1 30	4,575 79	"	1,036,496,665	118,715 315 i.	5,658	270	233 3	4 40	159 7
1886	2,820 1	1 25	4,318 64	"	1,117,389,075	80,892,410 i.	6,140	280	233 3	3 86	165 8
1887	3,393 3	1 15	3,589 31	"	1,218,213,688	106 824 583 i.	6,368	318	234 1	2 95	216 0
1888	3,446 0	1 09	2,545 46	"	1,341,708,002	123 494,314 i.	6,600	333	234 6	1 89	292 1
1889	2,583 6	1 08	2,661 12	"	1,475,358,220	133,650,218 i.	7,086	346	235 2	1 80	301 5
1890	3,120 7	1 20	3,052 89	"	1,659,625,551	184 267,331 i.	7,728	372	236 9	1 81	322 4
1891		1 29	3,941 53	"	1,807,038,580	147,413 029 i.	8,255	393	237 3	2 18	291 42

Number of Families, Stores, Offices, Manufacto
Supplied with City Water During the Year

Asphalt Paving Plant	1	Internal Revenue Offic	
Breweries	4	Jail	
Board of Trade.	1	Laundries	
Boat Houses	4	Libraries	
Bakeries	19	Lumber Yards	
Butcher Shops	65	Livery Stables.	
Brick Yards	2	Manufacturers .	
Banks	6	Malt Houses	
Barber Shops	49	Orphan Asylums	
Billiard Rooms	5	Opera Houses	
Bottling Works	9	Oil Works	
City Hall	1	Offices	
Coffee and Spice Mill	1	Old Folks Home	
Churches	19	Photograph Galleries	
Cemeteries	1	Police Station	
Coal and Iron Docks	1	Public Halls	
Club Houses	5	Packing Houses	
Custom House	1	Printing Offices	
Court House	1	Passenger Depots	
Convent	1	Railroads	
Driving Park	1	Railroad Shops	
Dyeing Works	2	Soldiers' Home	
Engine Houses	7	Schools	
Express Offices	2	Stores	
Electric Light Plant	1	Saloons and Eating Ho	
Fish Hatchery	1	Slaughter Houses	
Families	6,887	Street Railway	
Fish Houses	4	Transfer Company	
Freight Houses	5	United States Signal S	
Fountains, Private	5	Work Shops	
" Public	2	Watering Troughs	
" Drinking	2	U. S Steamer Michiga	
Flouring Mills	5	U. S. Court House	
Gas Works	1	U. S. Post Office	
Grain Elevators	3		
Green Houses	4	Total	
Hospitals	2	Last Enumeration	
Hotels and Boarding Houses	82		
Ice Houses	3	Increase	

RATES FOR CITY WATER.

All are Annual, Except as Otherwise Indicated.

Bath Tub, private...$	2 00
" " additional....................................	1 50
" " public..	5 00
Bakery, per barrel of flour used (but no charge less than $5)....	01
Barber Shop, including Hand Basin, first chair............	4 00
" " " " " each additional chair...........	2 00
Blacksmith Shop, one fire............................	5 00
" " each additional fire.................	2 50
Boarding House (in addition to family rates), per room......	1 00
Brewery, per barrel brewed................................	03
Building purposes, per bushel lime........................	02
Butcher stalls...................................... 3 00 to 18 00
Charitable institutions, one-third annual rates...........	
Cow	75
Condensing Boiler for steam heating (per season of six months), per horse power	50
Eating Houses................................... 5 00 to 25 00
Family...	5 00
Hand Basin, for Dwellings, Hotels and Schools, first basin.....	1 00
" " " " " " each additional............	50
" " in Offices, Stores and Blocks, each........	1 00
Hotels (in addition to family rates), per room.	1 00
Livery Stable, per horse.............................	2 00
Maltster, per 1,000 bushels of malt....................	1 75
Offices................................... 3 00 to 10 00
Private Stable, one or two horses	2 00
" " each additional horse................	1 00
Printing Offices............................. 5 00 to 30 00
Public Halls................................ 5 00 to 25 00
Saloons.................................... 5 00 to 25 00
Stores.................................... 3 00 to 15 00
Schools, per pupil.....................................	10
Steam Engine, ten hours per day, each horse power....	2 50
Slaughter Houses........................... 5 00 to 50 00
Sleeping Rooms....................................	1 00
Sprinkling Streets or Lawns with hose, per season...... 3 00 and up.
Urinal, private, self-closing........................	2 00
" public, "	3 00
"   not self-closing........................ 3 00 to 10 00
"   continuous flow...................... 10 00 to 30 00
Wash Tub (permanent, with waste)..................	2 00
" " " " " each additional.............	1 00
Watering Trough, public................................	10 00
Water Closet (pan), in private houses................	3 00
" " " " " each additional............	1 50
" " " public...................	5 00
" " (hopper), private....................	6 00
" " " public...................	10 00
Work Shop (ordinary use).................... 3 00 to 5 00

All other uses, when not metered, to be assessed by the Department.

METER RATES (Per Quarter.)

Daily Average, 15,000 gallons or less........................	10 cents.
" 15,000 to 20,000 gallons	9¾ "
" 20,000 to 25,000 "	9 "
" 25,000 to 30,000 "	8½ "
" 30,000 to 35,000 "	8 "
" 35,000 to 40,000 "	7¾ "
" 40,000 to 45,000 "	7 "
" 45,000 to 50,000 "	6½ "
" More than 50,000 gallons,	6 "

Cost of Water to the Average Householder in Twenty-four Cities. Compiled from Official Reports to this Office.

CITIES.	Family Charge.	Pan Water Closet.	Self-closing Urinal.	Bath Tubs.	Self-closing Wash stand.	Permanent Wash Tub.	Two Horses.	Cow.	Street Sprinkler.	Total.
Allegheny	$8 75	$	$2 00	$3 00	$1 00	$1 50	$1 50	$	$3 00	$24 50
Boston	7 00	5 00	2 50	5 00	5 00	5 00	2 00	75	5 00	37 25
Buffalo	7 20	3 50	3 00	3 00	1 00	2 00	2 40	90	2 50	25 50
Chicago	6 00	3 00	1 00	3 00	1 00	2 00	2 00	75	3 00	21 75
Columbus, Ohio	6 00	3 00	3 00	4 00		5 00	4 00	2 00	5 80	32 80
Dayton, Ohio	6 00	2 50	4 00	2 00	2 00	2 00	2 50	1 00	3 30	45 30
Detroit	7 00	4 00	4 00	2 00	1 25	2 00	4 00	1 00	4 00	28 25
ERIE	**5 00**	**3 00**	**2 00**	**2 00**	**1 00**	**2 00**	**2 00**	**75**	**3 00**	**21 75**
East Saginaw, Mich	7 00	2 50	3 00	3 00	1 00	2 00	4 00	1 00	3 00	26 50
Fall River, Mass	5 00	5 00	2 00	5 00	1 00	2 00	4 00	1 00	6 00	31 00
Grand Rapids, Mich	8 00	4 00	2 00	3 50	2 50	4 50	2 50	1 00	6 00	33 00
Indianapolis	5 00	3 00	3 00	3 00	1 00	2 00	5 00		10 00	32 00
Lawrence, Mass	5 00	4 00	3 00	3 00	2 00	1 00	3 00	50	3 30	25 80
Milwaukee	6 00	2 00	2 00	3 00	1 00		2 00	1 00	5 00	22 00
Minneapolis	4 00	3 00	7 50	2 50	1 50	1 50	2 00	1 00	5 00	26 00
New York	6 00	10 00	2 00	3 00	1 00	2 00	6 00		3 00	32 75
Omaha, Neb	6 75	2 50	3 50	3 00		2 00	5 00	75	5 00	30 00
Philadelphia	5 00	5 00	5 00	3 00	1 00	2 00	2 00	75	5 00	28 75
Pittsburg	9 00	3 00	1 50	4 00	1 00	1 00	2 50	1 50	3 00	23 50
Sandusky, Ohio	6 00	2 50	2 50	3 00	1 00	2 00	4 50	1 50	3 50	25 50
St Paul	8 00	4 00	2 40	3 20			4 80		2 40	24 70
Syracuse	8 00	5 00	2 00	4 00	1 00	2 00	3 00	75	6 00	31 75
Toledo	5 50	2 50	2 50	3 50	1 00	2 00	5 00	1 50	5 00	28 50
Utica	7 00	6 00	3 00	5 00	1 00		6 00	1 50	8 00	31 50

Table Showing the Water Rates Per 1,000 Gallons in 164 Cities Where Meters are Used.

CENTS.	CENTS.	CENTS.
New Bedford,Mass 2¼to 15	Minneapolis, Minn.10 to 20	Clinton, Mass......15 to 50
Buffalo, N. Y...... 3	Lincoln, Neb......10 to 20	Quincy. Ill........15 to 50
Detroit. Mich...... 3½	Willmington, N. C.10 to 20	Yonkers, N. Y....16 to 40
Milwaukee, Wis... 4½to 20	Meridan, Conn....10 to 25	Easton, Pa.....16½to 40
McKeesport, Pa... 4½to 30	Owensboro, Ky...10 to 25	Atlanta, Ga....... 17
Bay City, Mich.... 5 to 10	St. Albans, Vt.....10 to 30	Lynn, Mass......17½to 20
Rochester, N. Y.. 5 to 13	Waterbury, R. I...10 to 30	Lexington, Ky ...17½to 25
Lebanon, Pa...... 5 to 15	Corning, N. Y ...10 to 30	Bridgeton, N. J... 20
Waterford, N. Y.. 5 to 20	Mt. Morris, N. Y..10 to 30	Manchester, N. H. 20
Pittsburg, Pa...... 5 to 20	Ottumwa,Iowa....10 to 30	Boston, Mass.....
Port Huron. Mich. 5 to 20	Knoxville, Tenn..10 to 30	Peabody, Mass...
Albany, N. Y...... 5 to 40	New Haven, Conn.10 to 35	Waverly, N. Y....
ERIE, PA......... 6 to 10	Bloomsburg, Pa..10 to 35	Atchison, Kan.... 20
East Saginaw,Mich 6 to 12	Kansas City, Mo..10 to 35	Lawrence, Mass..20 to 90
Sandusky, Ohio... 6 to 20	Springfield, Ohio..10 to 40	Bridgeport, Conn.20 to 30
Whitehall, N. Y... 6 to 20	Davenport, Iowa..10 to 40	New London, " .20 to 30
Binghampton, N.Y 6 to 25	Brooklyn, N. Y... 10½	London, Can.... 20 to 33½
Syracuse, N. Y... 6 to 25	Reading, Pa......10½to 21½	Portland, Me......20 to 40
Amsterdam, N. Y. 6 to 30	Terre Haute, Ind.. 11	Norfolk, Va......20 to 40
Flint, Mich........ 6 to 30	Brantford, Can....12 to 20	Fort Worth, Tex..20 to 45
Pawtucket, R. I... 6 to 30	Catskill, N. Y.....12 to 25	Cortland, N. Y... 20 to 50
Chattanooga,Tenn 6 to 33	Indianapolis, Ind..12 to 40	Homer, N. Y......20 to 50
Louisville, Ky..... 6 to 35	Burlington, Vt. ..12 to 50	Oneonta, N. Y....20 to 50
Birmingham, Ala.. 6 to 40	Hamilton, Can ... 12½	Oneida, N. Y....20 to 50
Cleveland, Ohio.. 6½to 13½	Taunton. Mass....12½to 25	Madison, Wis.... 20 to 50
Nashville, Tenn... 7 to 15	Quincy, Mass.....12½to 30	Hannibal, Mo....20 to 50
Columbus, Ohio... 7 to 20	St. Louis, Mo......12½to 30	Flushing, N. Y....20 to 60
Hartford, Conn.... 7½to 30	N'w Br'nsw'ck,N J.12½to 50	Jersey City, N. J..21 to 27
Philadelphia, Pa.. 8	Hackensack, N.J.13 to 23	San Francisco, Cal.23½to 46
Baltimore, Md.... 8	Sioux City, Iowa..13 to 40	Higham, Mass..... 25
Winona, Minn..... 8	Jacksonville, Ill...13 to 40	Johnstown, N. Y.. 25
Chicago, Ill....... 8 to 10	Salem, Mass.....13½to 20	Springfie'd. Mo.... 25
Toledo, Ohio...... 8 to 20	New York, N. Y... 13½	Montgomery, Ala. 25
Meadville, Pa..... 8 to 30	St. Catherine, Can. 14	Waltham, Mass...25 to 30
Dayton, Ohio...... 8 to 40	Allegheny City, Pa 15	San Antonio, Tex.25 to 50
Hagerstown. Md.. 8 to 60	Lowell, Mass..... 15	Charleston, S. C..25 to 60
Cincinnati, Ohio... 9	Saratoga, N. Y.... 15	Los Angeles, Cal.. 30
E'mira, N. Y...... 9 to 45	Conshohocken, Pa 15	Denver, Colorado. 30
Gr'nd Rapids,Mich 9½to 30	Richmond, Va..... 15	Bangor, Me...... 30
Pittsfield, Mass.... 10	Newark, N. J..... 15	Fall River, Mass.. 30
Norwalk, Ohio.... 10	Wooster, Ohio..... 15	Woonsocket, R. I. 30
New Britain, Conn 10	Haverhill, Mass...15 to 20	Kingston, N. Y.... 30
Gunnison, Col..... 10	Des Moines, Ia....15 to 20	Owego, N. Y...... 30
Wilmington, Del.. 10	Trenton, N. J.....15 to 20	Halifax, Can...... 30
Newport, Ky..... 10	Worcester, Mass..15 to 25	Abilene, Kan......30 to 50
Kalamazoo, Mich.. 10	Nashua, N. H.....15 to 30	Charlotte, N. C...30 to 50
N. Adams, Mass..10 to 15	Norwich, Conn....15 to 30	Amesbury, Mass..30 to 50
Hazleton, Pa......10 to 15	Providence, R. I..15 to 30	Oakland Cal......30 to 55
Bloomington, Ill..10 to 15	Utica, N. Y........15 to 30	Dubuque, Iowa.. 30 to 60
Kenosha, Wis.....10 to 15	Joliet, Ill........15 to 30	Morristown, N. J.. 33
Cambridge, Mass.10 to 20	New Orleans, La..15 to 30	Muscatine, Iowa..35 to 60
Northampton, " .10 to 20	Maysville, Ky.....15 to 30	Vallejo, Cal......40 to $1
Springfield, " .10 to 20	Council Bluffs, Ia 15 to 35	Westboro, Mass... 50
Stonington, Conn 10 to 20	Cedar Rapids, Ia..15 to 40	Franklin, Pa...... 60
Troy, N. Y........10 to 20	St. Paul, Minn....15 to 40	

ANNUAL REPORT

—OF THE—

COMMISSIONERS

—OF—

WATER ✳ WORKS,

—IN THE—

CITY OF ERIE,

—TO THE—

MAYOR AND COUNCILS,

—FOR THE—

YEAR ENDING DECEMBER 31, 1892.

ERIE, PA.:

HERALD PRINTING AND PUBLISHING COMPANY, LIMITED
1893.

COMMISSIONERS OF WATER WORKS.

The Commissioners of Water Works in the City of Erie are appointed by the Court of Common Pleas of Erie County, Pa., for a term of three years, one member being named annually, in May.

SERVED IN THE YEAR.	COMMISSIONERS FROM ORGANIZATION TO DECEMBER 31, 1892.		
1867	*Wm. L. Scott,	Henry Rawle,	Wm. W. Reed,
1868	*John C. Selden,	Henry Rawle,	Wm. W. Reed,
1869	*John C. Selden,	Henry Rawle,	Wm. W. Reed,
1870	*John C. Selden,	Henry Rawle,	Wm. W. Reed,
1871	*†John C. Selden,	Henry Rawle,	Wm. W. Reed,
1872	Matthew R. Barr,	John Gensheimer,	Wm. W. Reed.
1873	Matthew R. Barr,	John Gensheimer,	Wm. W. Reed,
1874	Matthew R. Barr,	John Gensheimer,	Wm. W. Reed,
1875	Matthew R. Barr,	John Gensheimer,	Wm. W. Reed,
1876	Matthew R. Barr,	John Gensheimer,	Wm. W. Reed,
1877	M. Liebel,	John Gensheimer,	Wm. W. Reed,
1878	M. Liebel,	*J. M. Bryant,	Wm. W. Reed
1879	M. Liebel,	*J. M. Bryant,	*G. W. F. Sherwin,
1880	M. Liebel,	*J. M. Bryant,	*G. W. F. Sherwin,
1881	M. Liebel,	Benjamin Whitman,	*G. W. F. Sherwin,
1882	M. Liebel,	Benjamin Whitman,	*G. W. F. Sherwin,
1883	M. Liebel,	Benjamin Whitman,	*G. W. F. Sherwin,
1884	M. Liebel,	Benjamin Whitman,	*G. W. F. Sherwin,
1885	M. Liebel,	Benjamin Whitman,	George W. Starr,
1886	C. Kessler,	Benjamin Whitman,	George W. Starr,
1887	C. Kessler,	C. J Brown,	George W. Starr,
1888	C. Kessler,	C. J. Brown,	George W. Starr,
1889	C. Kessler,	C. J. Brown,	George W. Starr,
1890	C. Kessler,	C. J. Brown,	George W. Starr,
1891	C. Kessler,	C. J. Brown,	Wm. Hardwick,
1892	T. W. Shacklett,	C. J. Brown,	Wm. Hardwick,

†Mr. Selden resigned before the expiration of his second term; Mr. Barr was substituted by the other Commissioners, and afterwards appointed by the Court.

*Dead.

THE PRESENT COMMISSIONERS.

C. J. BROWN, President.

WM. HARDWICK,   T. W. SHACKLETT.

OFFICE—City Hall.

OFFICE HOURS—From 7:30 A M. to 5:45 P. M.; Monday evenings from 7:30 to 9:00.

REGULAR MEETINGS OF THE COMMISSIONERS—Every Saturday at 3:00 P. M., and the first day of each month at 11:00 A. M., except when it occurs on Sunday ; then they meet the following day.

OFFICERS AND SALARIES PAID THEM IN 1892.

Commissioners—C. J. Brown	$ 900 00
Wm. Hardwick	850 00
C. Kessler	400 00
T. W. Shacklett	500 00
Secretary and Treasurer—Wm. Himrod	1,800 00
Assistant Secretary - Geo. C. Gensheimer	1,320 00
Book Keepers—John Kolb	960 00
R. H. Bear	840 00
Clerk—M. L. Whitley	600 00
Inspectors—John D. Spafford	720 00
Wm. McCleery	720 00
P. F. Weinheimer	720 00
Superintendent of Street Work—R. T. Walker	1,200 00
Foremen of Street Work—Fred Simons, per day	2 50
Fred D. Gross, per day	2 50
Chief Engineer—F. A. Roth	1,200 00
Assistant Engineers—Geo. R. Miller	900 00
John Kelly	900 00
Firemen—R. W. Simons	600 00
Joseph Burns	600 00
Jacob Mullen	600 00
Watchman at Pumping Station—Michael Flynn	600 00
Keeper of Reservoir—Samuel Phister	420 00
Janitress—Mrs. Matilda Sager	144 00

ANNUAL REPORT.

*To the Honorable Mayor and Members of the Select and Common
Councils of the City of Erie, Pa.:*

GENTLEMEN:—Another year having passed into history, we
beg to contribute our proportion by presenting you with a statement
of our official acts for the year ending December 31, 1892.

The business of the Water Works for the past year has shown
a marked increase over that of any similar period since its organization and clearly indicates, with no uncertain sound, that our beautiful City is having a natural and healthy growth. We hope this
prosperity will continue.

We are not insensible to the fact that much of our City's wel-
fare depends upon the purity and abundance of the supply of water.
These questions have been constantly before us, and how to produce
the greatest amount of good for the greatest number has been
uppermost in our thoughts and actions.

RECEIPTS.

The receipts from all sources for the use of water were
$11,635.48 greater than that of the previous year of 1891, and
$2,734.70 greater increase than that of any other year in the history
of the existence of the Water Works. The amounts were as follows :

From Assessments	$ 80,824 63	
" Meters	23,640 93	
" Building Permits	871 64	
" Special Permits	189 83	$105,527.03

Total receipts for water from the organization of the Water
Works to and including December 31, 1892, is $1,104.851.54.

DISBURSEMENTS.

During the year 1892 there was expended on account of

Construction...........................	$ 49,557 65	
Maintenance............................	11,633 15	
Operating	13,500 08	
Accounting.............................	9,281 30	
Sundries (City of Erie, $24,006 41.).................	24,134 93	
Legal (Court costs, etc.)...........	556 60	$108,663.71

CONSTRUCTION.

This Department did not have the same demands made upon it that it did the preceding year, the calls for *Mains* being almost one-half less — the amount of increase only being 4 miles 4,602$\frac{5}{12}$ feet, making the total length of mains at this time of 81 miles 4,438$\frac{7}{12}$ feet.

When petitioners for extension of mains guaranteed an annual revenue of 7 per cent., their request was granted. This rule proves to be a wise one, and enables the Water Works to assist in a substantial manner in the growth of our City, and also increase its own revenue.

Connections from the mains to the curb line is the next largest item of expenditure in this department, the number added this year being 709, making the total number of connections of all sizes, 8,018, the length of the same being 31 miles 976$\frac{1}{12}$ feet.

The next largest expenditure being on the present Inlet Pipe; but the greater proportion of this was in payment of the judgment obtained against us in the suit begun in the year 1885 by J. Lewis Linn and John Dunlap. The Commissioners at that time disputed the claim, were sued, and after carrying the case through the Supreme Court of the State of Pennsylvania, we paid the plaintiffs, this year, the sum of $3,998.95, which covered judgment, interest and costs.

A *Suspension Bridge* connecting the Inlet Pipe Pier and Cribs was constructed in the early part of the year, affording a safe communication at all times to the north end of the Inlet Pipe, thus giving the employes at the Pumping Station an opportunity to keep the mouth of the Inlet Pipe free from slush ice and other foreign substances.

Meters have been increased in number, and where the location demanded and permanent use permitted, brick pits have been constructed to contain them. In connecting them up, provision has been made, in some instances, to introduce a test meter without removing the one in use.

Stop Valves form a large item of expense in this department, but it is deemed necessary to place them at regular intervals in all mains, at such distances apart as to enable the repairs of breaks without turning the water off from too much territory and thus causing inconvenience to a great number of consumers.

Fire Hydrants have been increased in number during the past year, same being located at points where the growth of the City demanded, having now 415 in use.

This department is also charged with work done this year on foundations of new *Engine House* and the cost of surveys made the past summer for a route of an *Inlet Pipe* to the Open water of Lake Erie, for the purpose of obtaining purer water for our citizens than that now furnished from the Harbor.

MAINTENANCE.

Expenses of this department are large, the principal item being the repairs on the *Reservoir*. During the past summer portions of the banks sloughed off, caused by leaks. These places were repaired, tile being placed at such an angle in the banks that the water would be conducted to the surface and thence disposed of. This arrangement will, we think, obviate this difficulty in the future. October 3, 1892, we commenced drawing the water off from the Reservoir, and for a period of fifty days it was not used in supplying the city with water. It was found that the action of the water had worn the cement entirely off from the bricks that the Reservoir is lined with; also that a portion of the centre wall had fallen in. This wall was restored, new brick inserted in the lining where required, and the entire interior covered with cement, making the Reservoir, both outside and in, so far as we are able to judge, '' as good as new.'' This is the first general repairing done upon it since its erection. We will state that we did not find anything injurious to health, nor repulsive in any way, in the Reservoir after the water was removed, which statement we trust will set at rest all startling

rumors to the contrary. The other items of expense in this department are principally embraced in repairs of Engines, Connections,
Mains and Branches, Tools and Repairs, Meters, etc.

OPERATING.

The cost of this department is larger this year than that of the
previous one. It has been called upon to furnish 241,000,000 gallons more water than it did in the year 1891, which is a greater
increase than that of any previous year in the history of the Water
Works by 40,000,000 gallons. In July, 1891, we had put in place
at the Pumping Station, by the Keystone Electric Co., of this city,
an electric light plant with 40 lights of 16 candle power each and
one light of 50 candle power, at a cost of a little over $700.00.
During its first year, ending July 31, 1892, it furnished more and
better light than was ever had at the Pumping Station at $150.00 less
cost. We are very much pleased with the result, and in a few years
it will have saved enough over the use of gas for illuminating to
pay for the electric light plant.

ACCOUNTING.

The work in this department is growing in magnitude each
year, the records of Mains, Branches and Connections being entered
in books and atlases prepared for that purpose, house to house inspection made; also a record of all the fixtures, giving kind, location and rates on or about all pieces of property where water is furnished by assessment. The books are so arranged and kept that an
exhibit is made of the daily receipts, expenditures, balances of cash
in office and with City Treasurer, and the personal resources of the
Water Works, thus giving at a glance its financial condition at all
times.

GENERAL.

Under this head has been charged to the City of Erie the
amount paid to the Sinking Fund Commissioners for the purpose of
liquidating Water Works Bonds that matured July 1, 1892. The
amount paid this year was $24,000.00, making the total amount
paid for the purpose of retiring Water Works Bonds from July 2,
1888, to date, $105,500.00.

LEGAL.

The largest item in this department is in payment of the costs in the Linn and Dunlap case, details of which we have given in another part of this Report.

OUR NEEDS.

That we are called upon to furnish more water to meet the daily requirements of the City, we will state that in 1888 we furnished 1,341,708,002 gallons of water, that in 1892 we furnished 2,047,993,505 gallons, a daily average increase of almost 2,000,000 gallons. The following tabulated statement of the pumpage in the month of July in the following years will show more clearly the rapid growth of our City:

	1888.	1889.	1890.	1891.	1892.
Daily Average	3,643,687	4,945,873	5,357,974	5,568,903	6,476,842
Lowest	428,428	975,520	4,708,522	4,768,400	3,220,590
Highest	4,496,674	5,525,156	6,621,575	7,274,580	8,218,875
Days Between—					
0 and 4 Million Gallons,	12	2			1
4 " 5 " "	19	7	3	1	3
5 " 6 " "		22	25	26	7
6 " 7 " "			3	3	4
7 " 8 " "				1	14
8 " 9 " "					2

When it is recalled that our present daily pumpage capacity is only guaranteed to be 9,000,000 gallons, we are treading on very dangerous ground, and it became an absolute necessity to increase our capacity by putting in a

NEW PUMPING ENGINE.

Accordingly, on August 1, 1892, we invited proposals for one each 10,000,000 gallon and 12,000,000 gallon daily capacity "Horizontal Compound Condensing Pumping Engine" to force water to an altitude in the Reservoir of 240 feet above the level of Presque Isle Bay. We received proposals from three firms, viz.: Holly Manufacturing Co., of Lockport, N. Y.; Henry R. Worthington, of New York, and Geo. F. Blake Manufacturing Co., of New York, and herewith submit a tabulated statement of their proposals:

TEN MILLION GALLON PUMPING ENGINE

NAME AND ADDRESS OF BIDDERS.	DESCRIPTION. KIND.	CYLINDERS. Steam Pressure.	Each, High and Low.	HIGH. Inch's Diam.	LOW. Inch's Diam.	Stroke.	Diameter of Pump in Inches.	CAPACITY. Piston Speed for Millions Pumped. 6	7	8	9	10	12	DUTY. Million Foot Pounds. 6	7	8	9	10	12	COST.
Holly Mfg. Co., Lockport, New York.	Crank & Fly Wh'l Horizontal, Compound,	90	2	28	50	38	27	72	84	96		120		90	95	100		110		$30,000
H. R. Worthington, New York, New York.	Horizontal, Compound, Condensing.	90	2	30	60	48	26	90	93	107		134		90	90	100		110		43,500

TWELVE MILLION GALLON.

NAME AND ADDRESS OF BIDDERS.	DESCRIPTION. KIND.	CYLINDERS. Steam Pressure.	Each, High and Low.	HIGH. Inch's Diam.	LOW. Inch's Diam.	Stroke.	Diameter of Pump in Inches.	CAPACITY. Piston Speed for Millions Pumped. 6	7	8	9	10	12	DUTY. Million Foot Pounds. 6	7	8	9	10	12	COST.
Holly Mfg. Co.	Crank & Fly Wheel Horizontal, Compound.	90	2	30	54	40	29½	70		80			120		90	95	100		110	$49,500

After carefully investigating the propositions made, we arrived at the conclusion that the best interests of the city would be served by purchasing a twelve-million-gallon engine from Henry R. Worthington, of New York. Consequently a contract was made with this corporation to furnish us with this sized steam pumping engine, all complete in place, ready for use, on foundations prepared by them, for the sum of forty-six thousand three hundred dollars. As a guarantee that they will furnish us a pump that will do all they promised, they gave us a bond in the sum of forty-seven thousand ($47,000) dollars, with Messrs. Geo. Selden and John H. Bliss, of this city, as sureties.

Owing to the fact that the water in the bay is steadily lowering, it was deemed advisable to place this pump 6 feet 4 inches lower than the Gaskill engine. This, together with its size, made it impossible to place it in the present east Engine House. Arrangements have been made to erect, at once, on the east side of and adjoining the present Engine House a building suitable in size and to correspond with the other in exterior finish. The contract for the erection of the superstructure of the building was awarded to Messrs. Constable Brothers, of this city, (they being the lowest bidders) for the sum of seven thousand six hundred dollars.

The low stage of water, and the probability of its going still lower, admonished us to place the bottom of the new well much lower than the present ones, and the pipes to connect the new well with the present conduit to be placed correspondingly low. During the past year the water has been so low that the top of the north end of the present conduit was exposed; and, as the conduit ascends as it approaches the Pumping Station, fully one-third, if not more, of the capacity of the conduit has been lost. Knowing this, all work to be done will be placed low enough and of such material and dimensions as to form a part of a

NEW CONDUIT,

that should be put in place very soon. That portion of the present conduit enclosed in the pier is made of wood and as the upper parts of it are not submerged, at all times, decay will soon render it useless. The present plan for this new conduit contemplates it being the south terminal of the much-talked-of Inlet Pipe to cross the

Harbor, through the Peninsula, and out into the open waters of Lake Erie. Our reasons for planning this we fully presented to your honorable bodies October 10, 1892, when we asked you to approve a new schedule of rates that would yield us a greater revenue, and would soon enable us to give our citizens what chemists say is purer water than it is possible to obtain from the present source of supply.

To carry this proposed Inlet Pipe out into the open waters of Lake Erie it was necessary to have the consent of the National Government. Hon. Matthew Griswold, Member of Congress from this district, has, by his skill and ability, had a bill passed granting us this privilege.

All that is now wanting to enable us to make this much-needed improvement is funds.

We are in hopes that in the near future we will be able to commence this work, and prosecute it year by year, paying the cost of the same out of the earnings.

Appended to this report are the full reports of the three chemists who analyzed the waters in the City, Harbor and Lake. A careful perusal of these will, we think, satisfy the most skeptical that something must soon be' done to improve the quality of the water. Either the Inlet Pipe must be carried out into the open waters of the Lake, or, what is better yet, the Intercepting Sewer built and the Harbor thoroughly cleansed of sewer solids. We cannot refrain from saying that in our opinion much valuable time has been lost in dealing with this matter, and now some prompt and effective measures should be enacted by your honorable bodies to have the Intercepting Sewer constructed at the earliest possible moment.

All of which is respectfully submitted.

C. J. BROWN,
WM. HARDWICK,
T. W. SHACKLETT,
Commissioners of Water Works in the City of Erie.

Monthly Receipts from all Sources During the Year Ending December 31, 1892.

MONTH.	ASSESSMENT.	METER.	SPECIAL.	PLUMBING.	BUILDING.	TOTAL.
January..	$ 9.897 65	$ 3,555 89	$ 17 32	$ 15 38	$ 93 91	$ 13,580 15
February.	5,734 62	2,492 36	4 59	165 22	66 61	8,463 40
March ...	2,225 31	398 30	15 67	96 65	17 11	2,753 04
April	11,817 61	4,023 64	22 82	8 56	130 82	16,003 45
May....	5,227 01	1,323 19	8 34	37 57	90 67	6,686 78
June	2,020 95	..... .	14 01	35 90	113 97	2,184 83
July	12,198 28	3,735 18	15 42	174 00	65 68	16,188 56
August...	9,452 56	1,669 33	22 91	100 14	89 26	11,334 20
Sept.....	693 60	53	28 00	437 19	42 05	1,201 37
Oct......	11,404 58	3,337 69	25 09	10 23	97 32	14 874 91
Nov.....	5,200 65	900 29	9 59	....	29 08	6,139 61
Dec	4,951 81	2,204 53	6 07	9 99	35 16	7,207 56
Total..	$ 80,824 63	$ 23,640 93	$ 189 83	$ 1.090 83	$ 871 64	$ 106,617 86

Receipts from Each Ward During the Year Ending December 31, 1892.

WARD.	ASSESSMENT.	METER.	SPECIAL.	PLUMBING.	BUILDING.	TOTAL.
1st......	$ 11,848 02	$ 2,680 96	$ 46 84	$ 52 11	$ 67 04	$ 14,694 97
2nd......	17,572 93	14,116 48	37 08	586 76	176 52	32,489 77
3rd......	20,308 66	3,116 45	10 17	217 71	270 03	23,923 02
4th......	15,28 79	1,721 29	33 32	141 98	197 02	17.374 40
5th......	7,654 57	1,089 39	29 50	20 03	75 25	8,868 74
6th......	7,643 56	901 09	22 67	24 65	82 28	8,674 25
7th......	516 10	15 27	10 25	47 59	3 50	592 71
Total..	$ 80,824 63	$ 23,640 93	$ 189 83	$ 1.090 83	$ 871 64	$ 106,617 86

Cash Account of Treasurer of Commissioners of Water Works in the City of Erie for the Year Ending December 31, 1892.

DR.

To amount on hand January 1, 1892..................$ 175 00
To receipts for the year 1892 .... 106,617 86
                                                    ——————— $106,792 86

CR.

By amount paid Treasurer City of Erie...............$106,688 44
By balance on hand....... ....   104 42
                                                    ——————— $106,792 86

Statement of Account with the Treasurer of the City of Erie, Pa., for the Year Ending December 31, 1892.

DR.

To balance January 1, 1892............		$2,261 83
To deposits—		
January.........................$ 12,581 76		
February 9,514 91		
March............................ 2,679 40		
April.,............................ 15,661 81		
May........... .... 7,161 91		
June........................... ... 2,138 50		
July... .... 16,259 54		
August........................... 11,288 84		
September 1,246 50		
October... .... 14,403 52		
November....................... 6,563 50		
December 7,188 25		
	$ 106,688 44	
		$ 108,950 27

CR.

By Warrants for—		
Construction Department...........$ 49,557 65		
Maintenance '' 11,633 15		
Operating '' 13,500 08		
Accounting '' 9,281 30		
Erie, Pa.......................... 24,000 00		
Sundries 134 93		
Legal........................... 556 60		
	$ 108,663 71	
Balance	286 56	
		$ 108,950 27

Amount of Water Rents Collected Each Year, with the Increase and Decrease since the Commencement of the Works.

	AM'T REC'D.	INCREASE.	DECREASE.
From Jan. 1, 1869, to Dec. 31, 1869......	$ 4,264 47	....	....
" " 1870, " 1870......	9,237 30	$ 4,972 83	....
" " 1871, " 1871......	18,138 08	8,900 78	....
" " 1872, " 1872......	21,652 68	3,514 60	....
" " 1873, " 1873......	25,560 40	3,907 72	....
" " 1874, " 1874......	27,938 90	2,378 50	....
" " 1875, " 1875......	29,639 38	1,700 48	....
" " 1876, " 1876......	31,048 76	1,409 38	....
" " 1877, " 1877......	32,276 57	1,227 81	....
" " 1878, " 1878......	29,636 01	....	$ 2 640 56
" " 1879, " 1879......	33,343 20	3,707 19	....
" " 1880, " 1880......	37,385 00	4,041 80	....
" " 1881, " 1881......	40,385 87	3,000 87	....
" " 1882, " 1882......	43,818 73	3,432 86	....
" " 1883, " 1883......	48,269 89	4,451 16	....
" " 1884, " 1884......	51,852 78	3,582 89	....
" " 1885, " 1885......	53,550 35	1,697 57	....
" " 1886, " 1886......	58,725 00	5,174 65	....
" " 1887, " 1887......	67,121 92	8,396 92	....
" " 1888, " 1888......	73,197 03	6,075 11	....
" " 1889, " 1889......	81,110 68	7,913 65	....
" " 1890, " 1890......	87,279 96	6,169 28	....
" " 1891, " 1891......	93,891 55	6,611 59	....
" " 1892, " 1892......	105,527 03	11 635 48	....
Total...........................	$1,104,851 54	....	....

DISBURSEMENTS.

Department.	Account.	For the Year 1891.		
		Labor.	Material.	T(...)
Construction.	Ad. Books, Sta. and Prtg............	$ 1 33	$ 26 18	$
	Buildings and Grounds................	2 69	55 11	
	Boilers			
	Civil Engineering......................	1,389 50	49 45	
	Connections	4,118 54	3,553 60	7,
	Engines and Boilers................			
	Engines............................			
	Engine No. 4	49	10 00	
	Engine Room Fur. and Fix.......			
	Expense........................	89	11 67	
	Electric Light Plant...............	34	6 95	
	Fire Hydrants......................	293 71	1,044 10	1,
	Fuel........................	2 98	61 13	
	Gas Well			
	Horse, Wagon and Cartage..........	8 31	170 98	
	Inlet Pipe No. 1......................	206 74	4,235 05	4,
	Inlet Pipe No. 2......................	130 08	50	
	Interest and Discount.............	16 55	838 99	
	Light—Lamps, Wicks, Oil, &c.....	58	11 84	
	Lowering Mains..................	104 50		
	Mains and Branches..................	9,869 03	16,101 31	25,
	Main. 30-inch......................	204 08		
	Meters	661 96	3,132 25	3,
	Office Furniture and Fixtures......	20 56	421 09	
	Oil and Tallow	10	2 14	
	Paving and Street Repairs..........	4 67		
	Park Fountains			
	Railroad Switch and Scales........			
	Reservoir			
	Stop Valves	149 04	1,271 56	1,
	Superintendent's Stores...........			
	Superintendent's Expenses	96	19 72	
	Shop Rent........................	4 97	101 88	
	Tools and Repairs.................	40 27	318 25	
	Telephone and Telegraph	27	5 52	
	Engine House No. 3................	1,208 20	184 88	1,
Maintenance	Ad. Books, Sta. and Prtg............	45	9 28	
	Buildings and Grounds................	53 00	89 21	
	Boilers	91 85	380 27	
	Connections	762 75	29 79	
	Engines	54 59	717 98	
	Engineers' Stores	05	1 00	
	Engine Room Fur. and Fix	1 29	26 54	
	Expense........................	5 97	1 88	
	Electric Light Plant..............	1 30	26 56	
	Fire Hydrants......................	289 25	53 72	
	Fuel	85	17 41	
	Horse, Wagon and Cartage	8 37	171 51	
	Inlet Pipe No. 1.................	60 27	44 22	
	Light, Oil, Lamps, Wicks, &c	67	13 69	
	Mains and Branches..................	570 73	90 81	
	Main, 30-inch....................	28 97		
	Meters....................	240 40	86 86	
	Office Furniture and Fixtures......	47	4 50	
	Oil and Tallow.............	10	2 14	
	Paving and Street Repairs.........	4 07		
	Railroad Switch and Scales........	83 28	125 74	
	Reservoir	4,937 47	1,743 54	6,
	Stop Valves	196 70	24 28	
	Superintendent's Stores.............			

DISBURSEMENTS.—Continued.

Department.	Account.	For the Year 1892.			From beginning of Works to Dec. 31st, 1892.
		Labor.	Material.	Total.	
Maintenance	Superintendent's Expenses	* $ 95	$ 19 46	$ 20 41	$ 38 77
	Shop Rent	* 4 97	101 89	106 86	200 25
	Tools and Repairs......................	53 37	377 10	430 47	3,743 33
	Waste and Packing	1 03	21 15	22 18	22 18
Operating......	Ad. Books, Sta. and Prtg............	1 07	21 89	22 96	59 20
	Buildings and Grounds...............	* 629 29		629 29	629 29
	Engineers and Firemen...............	5,275 95		5,275 95	100,441 15
	Engineers' Stores	11	2 28	2 39	2,345 28
	Expenses	* 37 18	60 13	97 31	129 79
	Electric Light Plant....................	47	9 75	10 22	10 22
	Fire Hydrants............................	20		20	20
	Fuel	255 77	5,239 55	5,495 32	139,175 33
	Insurance	7 35	150 66	158 01	846 25
	Light, Oil, Lamps, Wicks, &c	* 1 76	36 14	37 90	207 55
	Meters.....................................	35 91	05	35 96	35 96
	Oil and Tallow...........................	26 82	549 51	576 33	9,220 19
	Reservoir..................................	* 440 50		440 50	440 50
	Rent of Office...........	16 52	338 38	354 90	354 90
	Tools and Repairs.......................	78	16 00	16 78	55 70
	Taxes—State, County and School·				1,100 83
	Telephone and Telegraph	* 4 49	92 02	96 51	185 73
	Waste and Packing	11 03	225 91	236 94	3,987 74
	Water Rents Returned.................	59	12 02	12 61	75 23
Accounting...	Ad. Books, Sta. and Prtg.	33 57	687 80	721 37	7,739 32
	Expense..................................	12 64	34 13	46 77	14,689 89
	Horse, Wagon and Cartage........	* 80	16 50	17 30	17 30
	Postage...................................	20 69	423 83	444 52	4,545 59
	Salaries...................................	8,051 34		8,051 34	148,323 00
Sundries	City of Erie Sinking Fund Commissioners....................		24,000 00	24,000 00	105,500 00
	City of Erie	* 6 41		6 41	6 41
	Engine House No. 3....................	*	128 52	128 52	128 52
Legal............	Court Costs...............................	* 5 50	426 10	431 60	441 20
	Counsel Fees	125 00		125 00	2,690 38
	Expense...................................	*			35 25
	Totals	40,885 70	67,778 01	108,663 71	1,810,417 50

* These accounts were not kept previous to 1891.

RECAPITULATION.

Department.	For the Year 1892.				From beginning of Works to Dec. 31st, 1892.
	Pro Rata.	Labor.	Material.	Total.	
Construction	.456 64402	$ 18,430 79	$ 31,126 86	$ 49,557 65	$1,180,403 40
Maintenance	.107056440 +	7,453 17	4,179 98	11,633 15	86,596 20
Operating	.124237245 +	6,745 79	6,754 29	13,500 08	259,301 04
Accounting....	.085413060 +	8,119 04	1,162 26	9,281 30	175,315 10
Sundries	.222106626 +	6 41	24,128 52	24,134 93	105,634 93
Legal.	.005122225 +	130 50	426 10	556 60	3,166 83
Totals	.999999998 +	$ 40,885 70	$ 67,778 01	$ 108,663 71	$1,810,417 50

Statement of Accounts with City of Erie, Pa..

CITY OF ERIE, PA.			DR.	
CASH—Paid Sinking Fund Commissioners..			$ 24,000 00	
WATER—Fire Hydrants..................	$41,300	00		
Park Fountains................	1,251	05		
Engine Houses...............	134	80		
City Hall....................	185	67		
Flushing Sewers..............	230	00		
			$ 43,101 52	
PLUMBING ACCOUNTS...................			36 98	
INTEREST—On $14,000 00 April 26 to December 31, 1892...........$	596	72		
On $5,000 00 June 27 to December 31, 1892...........	154	10		
On $5,000 00 July 11 to December 31, 1892..........	142	62		
			893 44	
Balance....................			694 589 44	
				$ 762,621 38
CR.				
BALANCE—December 31, 1891...........			$ 718.322 06	
INTEREST—On same to December 31, 1892.			43,099 32	
RENT—Of Offices.....................			1.200 00	
			762,621 38	
Balance............................			$ 694,589 44	

Statement of Resources and Liabilities December 31, 1892.

RESOURCES.

CONSTRUCTION ACCOUNT—Buildings and

Grounds.....................$ 104,361	40	
Boilers from January 1, 1891..... 3,409	15	
Connections.................... 101,697	91	
Engines from January 1, 1891.... 15	25	
Engine No. 4 from January 1, 1892........................ 36	12	
Engines and Boilers to December 31, 1890.................... 104,309	95	
Engine House No. 3 from Jan. 1, 1892...................... 1,417	85	
Engine Room Furniture and Fixtures........................ 1 505	82	
Electric Light Plant............ 732	69	
Fire Hydrants................. 23,814	30	
Inlet Pipe No. 1................ 55,568	44	
Inlet Pipe No. 2 from Jan. 1, 1892 1,590	31	
Mains and Branches............ 512,250	25	
Main, 30 inch................. 82,041	93	
Meters 13,205	07	
Office Furniture and Fixtures..... 833	98	
Railroad Switch and Scales...... 3,262	09	
Reservoir..................... 137,629	35	
Stop Valves.................. 29,933	46	

$1,177,615 32

CASH—In Office..................... 104 42
In hands of Treasurer of City of
Erie, Pa. 286 56

390 98

ACCOUNTS —Individual.............. 1,514 46
Meter. 6,107 67
Plumbing.............. 321 39

$ 7,943 52

$1,185,949 82

LIABILITIES.

ACCOUNTS —City of Erie............. $ 694,589 44
Individual 156 76

$ 694,746 20
Balance 491,203 62

$1,185,949 82

Pumping Engine Statistics for 1892.

The Pumps are three in number. Nos. 1 and 2 are known as the Cornish Bull Pumps. The diameter of each plunger is 20¾ inches, and each has a stroke of 10 feet. The capacity of each pump is estimated to be 165 gallons to each stroke. Pump No. 3 is a Gaskill Horizontal Compound Pumping Engine, having two H. P. cylinders 21 in. diameter, two L. P. cylinders 42 in. diameter, and two pumps 19½ in. diameter, and all 36 in. stroke, of a guaranteed capacity of 5,000,000 gallons daily at a piston speed of 120 feet per minute against a head of 237 feet. The Stand Pipe is 251 feet high. The Reservoir is nearly two miles from the Pumping Works, the bottom of which is 210 feet above the surface of the Bay, and the Water has been maintained during the year at an average depth in the Reservoir of about 25½ feet.

Months.	No. 1 Days Run.	No. 1 Gallons.	No. 2 Days Run.	No. 2 Gallons.	No. 3 Days Run.	No. 3 Gallons.	Totals Days Run.	Totals Gallons.	Daily Average.	Average Lift in Feet.
January.	1	1,253,670			31	157,556,490	31	157,556,490	5,082,467	237·92
February.	10	14,297,250	1	1,283,535	29	148,286,320	31	150,823,525	5,200,811	238·68
March.			14	19,048,590	27	120,848,000	51	154,193,840	4,973,995	237·69
April.	5	6,571,620	6	7,789,320	27	134,933,890	38	149,294,830	4,976,494	238·42
May.					31	160,109,950	31	160,109,950	5,164,837	237·53
June.	4	6,104,340	13	20,199,465	28	145,900,300	45	172,204,105	5,740,137	236·76
July.	2	1,322,145	21	38,675,710	31	160,784,260	54	200,782,115	6,476,842	236·63
August.	2	1,725,900	19	31,259,250	31	156,467,220	52	189,452,370	6,111,367	236·58
September.			10	11,360,250	30	164,757,320	40	176,117,570	5,870,585	236·83
October.	8	9,575,280	20	27,467,550	27	119,993,510	55	157,036,340	5,065,688	237·06
November.	5	6,757,740	28	54,425,250	30	137,727,590	63	198,910,580	6,639,353	237·06
December.	3	5,767,080	7	10,792,650	31	164,952,060	41	181,511,790	5,855,219	237·11
Total.	40	53,375,025	139	222,301,570	353	1,772,316,910	532	2,047,993,505	5,595,611	237·36

The regular employes at the Pumping Works are one chief engineer, two assistant engineers, three firemen and one watchman. The chief engineer stands a watch of five hours, from 7 to 12 every forenoon; the assistants divide the remainder of each day equally between them; each one of the firemen stands a watch of eight hours. Besides firing, the firemen unload the coal from the cars, except when two pumps are run, in which case they are assisted by the watchman or a laborer. The chief engineer gives ten hours daily to the service of the Commissioners of Water Works in the City of Erie, the hours when he is not on watch being employed in repairs, supervision, etc. In addition to standing their regular watch, the assistant engineers aid their superior officer in keeping the machinery in order. The watchman takes care of the buildings and grounds, besides doing such other work as may be required of him.

Amount of Coal Consumed in Pumping, Gallons of Water Pumped, Average Height Pumped, Cost per Million Gallons, &c., from the First Year the Works were Operated to Dec. 31, 1892.

Year	Tons of Coal Consumed.	Price of Coal per ton from May 1 of each year.	Cost of Coal from January 1 to December 31.	Grades of Bituminous Coal.	Gallons of Water Pumped.	Increase or Decrease.	Number of places supplied.	Number of Fire hydrants.	Average height of Water in Reservoir above surface of Bay.	Cost of Coal per million gallons raised to Reservoir.	Gallons raised to Reservoir by one pound of Coal.
1868	59 4	5 05	309 61	Lump.	...	...	...	...	...	...	...
1869	544 4	5 05	4,818 48	"	...	...	...	...	...	...	...
1870	1,064 5	5 05	5,159 10	"	246,648,960	...	1,218	97	232 0	...	...
1871	1,422 7	5 05	7,117 00	"	279,368,495	32,719,535 i	1,727	99	232 0	$18 76	98 5
1872	1,308 5	5 05	6,528 50	"	395,076,90	115,707,505 i	2,140	103	232 0	16 52	150 9
1873	1,672 5	5 05	8,412 65	"	384,062,415	11,013,585 d	2,475	107	232 0	21 90	114 8
1874	1,759 0	4 85	7,709 54	"	444,817,395	60,754,980 i	2,663	107	232 0	17 33	126 4
1875	1 836 1	4 85	8,657 61	"	531,005,475	86,188,080 i	2,700	110	232 0	16 30	145 5
1876	1,105 6	4 00	8,925 22	"	670,726,650	139,721,175 i	2,763	112	232 0	13 30	159 3
1877	2 456 3	3 70	8,509 33	"	660,981,810	9,744,840 d	2,854	114	232 0	12 75	135 7
1878	2,463 3	3 35	7,945 37	"	682,392,315	21,410,505 i	2,915	115	232 0	11 64	136 4
1879	2,628 1	3 09	7,428 92	Slack.	807,800,400	125,408,085 i	3,011	121	232 0	9 19	153 6
1880	3,076 1	1 99	6,978 41	"	775,805,250	31,995,150 d	3,568	126	232 0	8 99	126 0
1881	3,430 3	1 90	6,517 58	"	975,640,934	219,835,684 i	4,110	161	234 7	6 68	142 2
1882	2,968 2	1 75	5,355 93	"	829,759,260	145,881,674 d	4,687	171	234 3	6 45	139 7
1883	2,398 2	1 55	3,908 59	"	815,939,685	13,875 d	5,077	197	234 9	4 66	170 0
1884	3,010 8	1 45	4 502 61	"	917,781,350	101,841,665 i	5,395	248	232 0	4 99	152 4
1885	3 243 8	1 30	4,575 79	"	1,036,496,665	118,715,315 i	5,658	270	233 1	4 40	159 7
1886	3 369 0	1 25	4,318 64	"	1,117,389,075	80,892,410 i	6,140	280	234 6	3 86	165 8
1887	2,820 4	1 15	3,589 31	"	1 218, 21 388	100,824,613 i	6,368	318	234 2	2 95	216 0
1888	2,392 3	1 09	2,545 46	"	1 341,708,002	123,494,314 i	6,600	333	235 9	1 89	292 1
1889	2,446 6	1 08	2,661 12	"	1,475,358,220	133,050,218 i	7,086	346	236 3	1 80	301 5
1890	2,583 6	1 20	3,052 89	"	1,659,625,551	184,267,331 i	7,728	372	237 3	1 81	322 4
1891	3,120 7	1 29	3,941 53	"	1,807,038,580	147,413,029 i	8,255	393	237 3	2 18	291 42
1892	3,658 0	1 32½	4,807 11	"	2,047,993,505	240,954,925 i	8,998	415	237 4	2 35	279 43

Statement of Assessments in Effect December 31, 1892.

COMBINATION OF FIXTURE AND USE.	
Chemical Works	1
Court House	1
City Hall	1
Carpet Cleaning Establishment.	1
Chapel and Vault	1
Club House	1
Drill Room	1
Elevators	1
Fish Hatchery	1
Government Building	1
Green House	1
Horse Shed	1
Ice Cream Parlor	1
Jail	1
Lime Kiln	1
Marble Works	1
Opera House	1
Pond	1
Synagogue	1
Steam Yacht	1
U. S. S Michigan	1
Warehouse	1
Book Bindery	2
Brick Yard	2
Fish House	2
Hospital	2
Museum	2
Boat House	2
Glass Washers	2
Fountains	3
Milk Depot	3
Hotel	4
Engine House	6
Banks	6
Laundry	7
Slaughter Houses	7
Bottling Works	8
Motors	8
Printing Offices	11
Bakery	13
Photograph Gallery	13
Watering Trough	14
Eating House	17

Church	18
Club Room	26
Public Hall	26
Blacksmith Fires	29
Billiard Table	44
Beer Pump	48
Meat Market	70
Saloons	96
Workshop	114
Barber Chairs	125
Cows	128
Offices	323
Stores	483
Lodging Room	1138
Horses	1595
Scholars	7222
Family	7613

FIXTURES FOR FAMILY USE.

Goose Necks	94
Hydrants	1039
Draw-cock in House	7403
Urinals	271
Hand Basins	1786
Closing Hopper Closet	96
Non-closing Hopper Closet	280
Pan or Tank Closet	3088
Wash Tubs	532
Bath Tubs	1258

MEANS OF SPRINKLING—FROM

Adjoining Lot	98
Fixture in House	367
Hydrants	381
Lawn Sprinklers	452
Curb	503
Sill Cocks	1285

STEAM AND HOT WATER.
(HORSE POWER.)

Heating	1594
Manufacturing	776
Engine	1517

RATES FOR CITY WATER.

ALL ARE ANNUAL, EXCEPT AS OTHERWISE INDICATED.

Bath Tub, private..$	3 00
Bath Tub, additional..	1 50
Bath Tub, public..	5 60
Bakery, per barrel of flour used (but no charge less than $5)............	01
Barber Shop, including hand basin, first chair............................	4 00
Barber Shop, including hand basin, each additional chair..............	2 00
Blacksmith Shop, one fire...	5 00
Blacksmith Shop, each additional fire	2 50
Boarding House (in addition to family rates), per room..................	1 00
Brewery, per barrel brewed...	03
Building purposes, per bushel lime	02
Butcher Stalls..	3 00 to 15 00
Charitable institutions, one-third annual rates...........................	
Cow...	75
Condensing Boiler for steam heating (per season of months), per horse power..	50
Eating Houses	5 00 to 25 00
Family..	5 00
Hand Basin, for dwellings, hotels and schools, first basin............	1 00
Hand Basin, for dwellings, hotels and schools, each additional........	50
Hand Basin, in offices, stores and blocks, each.........................	1 00
Hotels (in addition to family rates), per room	1 00
Livery Stable, per horse..	2 00
Maltster, per 1,000 bushels of malt...	1 75
Offices..	3 00 to 10 00
Private Stable, one or two horses	2 00
Private Stable, each additional horse.......................................	1 00
Printing Offices	5 00 to 30 00
Public Halls	5 00 to 25 00
Saloons	5 00 to 25 00
Stores	3 00 to 15 00
Schools, per pupil..	10
Steam Engine, ten hours per day, each horse power...................	2 50
Slaughter Houses..	5 00 to 50 00
Sleeping Rooms..	1 00
Sprinkling Streets or lawns with hose, per season......................	3 00 and up
Urinal, private, self closing...	2 00
Urinal, public, self-closing...	8 00
Urinal, not self-closing..	3 00 to 10 00
Urinal, continuous flow	10 00 to 30 00
Wash Tub (permanent, with waste)..	2 00
Wash Tub (permanent, with waste), each additional.....................	1 00
Watering Trough, public...	10 00
Water Closet (pan) in private houses.......................................	3 00
Water Closet (pan) in private houses, each additional.................	1 50
Water Closet (pan), public...	5 00
Water Closet (hopper), private..	6 00
Water Closet (hopper), public...	10 00
Work-shop (ordinary use)	3 00 to 5 00

All other uses, when not metered, to be assessed by the Commissioners.

METER RATES (Per Quarter). Per 1000 Gallons.

Daily average, 15,000 gallons or less		10 cents
"	15,000 to 20,000 gallons	9¼ "
"	20,000 to 25,000 gallons	9 "
"	25,000 to 30,000 gallons	8½ "
"	30,000 to 35,000 gallons	8 "
"	35,000 to 40,000 gallons	7½ "
"	40,000 to 45,000 gallons	7 "
"	45,000 to 50,000 gallons	6½ "
"	more than 50,000 gallons	6 "

Cost of Water to the Average Householder in Twenty-four Cities. Compiled from Official Reports to this Office.

CITIES.	Family Charge.	Pan Water Closet.	Self-closing Urinal.	Bath Tubs.	Self-closing Wash stand.	Permanent Wash Tub.	Two Horses.	Cow.	Street Sprinkler.	Total.
Allegheny	$8 75	$3 00	$2 00	$3 00	$1 00	$1 50	$1 50	$ 75	$3 00	$24 50
Boston	7 00	5 00	2 50	5 00	5 00	5 00	2 00	75	5 00	37 25
Buffalo	7 20	3 50	3 00	3 00	1 00	2 00	2 40	90	1 50	25 50
Chicago	6 00	3 00	1 00	3 00	1 00	2 00	2 00	75	3 00	21 75
Columbus, Ohio	6 00	3 00	3 00	4 00		5 00	4 00	2 00	5 80	32 80
Dayton, Ohio	6 00	2 50	4 00	2 00	2 00	2 00	2 50	1 00	3 30	45 30
Detroit	7 00	4 00	3 00	2 00	1 25	2 00	4 00	1 00	4 00	28 25
ERIE	**5 00**	**3 00**	**2 00**	**2 00**	**1 00**	**2 00**	**2 00**	**75**	**3 00**	**21 75**
East Saginaw, Mich	7 00	2 50	3 00	3 00	1 00	2 00	4 00	1 00	3 00	26 50
Fall River, Mass	5 00	5 00	2 00	5 00	1 00	2 00	4 00	1 00	6 00	31 00
Grand Rapids, Mich	8 00	4 00	2 00	3 50	2 50	4 50	2 50	1 00	6 00	33 00
Indianapolis	5 00	3 00	3 00	3 00	1 00	2 00	5 00		10 00	32 00
Lawrence, Mass	5 00	4 00	2 00	3 00	2 00	1 00	3 00	1 50	3 30	25 80
Milwaukee	6 00	2 00	2 00	3 00	1 00		2 00	1 00	5 00	22 00
Minneapolis	4 00	3 00	7 50	2 50	50	50	2 00	1 00	3 00	26 00
New York	6 00	10 00	2 00	3 00	1 00	2 00	6 00	75		32 75
Omaha, Neb	6 75	2 50	3 50	3 00	1 00	2 00	5 00	75	5 00	30 00
Phila-delphia										

Table Showing the Water Rates Per 1,000 Gallons in 164 Cities Where Meters are Used.

City	Cents	City	Cents	City	Cents
New Bedford, Mass	2½ to 15	Minneapolis, Minn.	10 to 20	Clinton, Mass......	15 to 50
Buffalo, N. Y......	3	Lincoln, Neb......	10 to 20	Quincy, Ill........	15 to 50
Detroit, Mich......	3½	Wilmington, N. C.	10 to 20	Yonkers, N. Y.....	16 to 40
Milwaukee, Wis...	4½ to 20	Meridan, Conn....	10 to 25	Easton, Pa......	16½ to 40
McKeesport, Pa...	4½ to 30	Owensboro, Ky...	10 to 25	Atlanta, Ga........	17
Bay City, Mich....	5 to 10	St. Albans, Vt.....	10 to 30	Lynn, Mass......	17½ to 20
Rochester, N. Y...	5 to 18	Waterbury, R. I..	10 to 30	Lexington, Ky ...	17½ to 25
Lebanon, Pa......	5 to 15	Corning, N. Y ...	10 to 30	Bridgeton, N. J...	20
Waterford, N. Y..	5 to 20	Mt. Morris, N. Y..	10 to 30	Manchester, N. H.	20
Pittsburg, Pa......	5 to 20	Ottumwa, Iowa....	10 to 30	Boston, Mass.....	20
Port Huron, Mich.	5 to 20	Knoxville, Tenn..	10 to 30	Peabody, Mass....	20
Albany, N. Y......	5 to 40	New Haven, Conn.	10 to 35	Waverly, N. Y....	20
ERIE, PA.........	6 to 10	Bloomsburg, Pa...	10 to 35	Atchison, Kan....	20
East Saginaw, Mich	6 to 12	Kansas City, Mo...	10 to 35	Lawrence, Mass..	20 to 25
Sandusky, Ohio...	6 to 20	Springfield, Ohio..	10 to 40	Bridgeport, Conn.	20 to 30
Whitehall, N. Y...	6 to 20	Davenport, Iowa...	10 to 40	New London, "	20 to 30
Binghampton, N.Y	6 to 25	Brooklyn, N. Y...	10½	London, Can.....	20 to 33½
Syracuse, N. Y...	6 to 25	Reading, Pa.......	10½ to 21½	Portland, Me......	20 to 40
Amsterdam, N. Y.	6 to 30	Terre Haute, Ind..	11	Norfolk, Va.......	20 to 40
Flint, Mich.......	6 to 30	Brantford, Can....	12 to 20	Fort Worth, Tex..	20 to 45
Pawtucket, R. I..	6 to 30	Catskill, N. Y.....	12 to 25	Cortland, N. Y...	20 to 50
Chattanooga, Tenn	6 to 33	Indianapolis, Ind..	12 to 40	Homer, N. Y......	20 to 50
Louisville, Ky....	6 to 35	Burlington, Vt. ..	12 to 50	Oneonta, N. Y....	20 to 50
Birmingham, Ala.	6 to 40	Hamilton, Can....	12½	Oneida, N. Y......	20 to 50
Cleveland, Ohio..	6½ to 13⅔	Taunton, Mass....	12½ to 25	Madison, Wis....	20 to 50
Nashville, Tenn..	7 to 30	Quincy, Mass.....	12½ to 30	Hannibal, Mo.....	20 to 50
Columbus, Ohio..	7 to 20	St. Louis, Mo......	12½ to 30	Flushing, N. Y....	20 to 60
Hartford, Conn....	7½ to 30	N'w Br'nsw'ck,N.J.	12½ to 50	Jersey City, N. J..	21 to 27
Philadelphia, Pa..	8	Hackensack, N. J.	13 to 23	San Francisco, Cal.	23½ to 46
Baltimore, Md....	8	Sioux City, Iowa..	13 to 40	Higham, Mass.....	25
Winona, Minn.....	8	Jacksonville, Ill...	13 to 40	Johnstown, N. Y..	25
Chicago, Ill......	8 to 10	Salem, Mass......	13½ to 20	Springfie'd, Mo....	25
Toledo, Ohio......	8 to 20	New York, N. Y...	13⅗	Montgomery, Ala.	25
Meadville, Pa.....	8 to 30	St Catherine, Can.	14	Waltham, Mass...	25 to 30
Dayton, Ohio.....	8 to 40	Allegheny City, Pa	15	San Antonio, Tex.	25 to 50
Hagerstown, Md..	8 to 60	Lowell, Mass.....	15	Charleston, S. C..	25 to 60
Cincinnati, Ohio....	9	Saratoga, N. Y....	15	Los Angeles, Cal..	30
E'mira, N. Y......	9 to 45	Conshohocken, Pa	15	Denver, Colorado.	30
Gr'nd Rapids,Mich	9½ to 30	Richmond, Va.....	15	Bangor, Me.......	30
Pittsfield, Mass....	10	Newark, N. J.....	15	Fall River, Mass..	30
Norwalk, Ohio....	10	Wooster, Ohio.....	15	Woonsocket, R. I.	30
New Britain, Conn	10	Haverhill, Mass...	15 to 20	Kingston, N. Y....	30
Gunnison, Col....	10	Des Moines, Ia....	15 to 20	Owego, N. Y......	30
Wilmington, Del..	10	Trenton, N. J.....	15 to 20	Halifax, Can......	30
Newport, Ky.....	10	Worcester, Mass..	15 to 25	Abilene, Kan......	30 to 50
Kalamazoo, Mich..	10	Nashua, N. H.....	15	Charlotte, N. C...	30 to 50
N. Adams, Mass..	10 to 15	Norwich, Conn....	15	Amesbury, Mass..	30 to 50
Hazleton, Pa......	10 to 15	Providence, R. I..	15	Oakland Cal......	30 to 55
Bloomington, Ill..	10 to 15	Utica, N. Y........	15	Dubuque, Iowa..	30 to 60
Kenosha, Wis.....	10 to 15	Joliet, Ill.........	15 to 30	Morristown, N. J..	33
Cambridge, Mass.	10 to 20	New Orleans, La..	15 to 30	Muscatine, Iowa..	35 to 60
Northampton, "	10 to 20	Maysville, Ky.....	15 to 30	Vallego, Cal......	40 to 51
Springfield, "	10 to 20	Council Bluffs, Ia	15 to 35	Westboro, Mass...	50
Stonington, Conn	10 to 20	Cedar Rapids, Ia..	15 to 40	Franklin, Pa......	60
Troy, N. Y........	10 to 20	St. Paul, Minn....	15 to 40		

ANALYSIS NO. 7893—NO. 2.

Examination made June 9th-15th, by C. M. Cresson, M. D.   Amount of sample, one gallon ; reaction, alkaline ; condition, slightly turbid, with sediment.

Contains.	Parts in 1,000,000 Parts.
Solid matter to dryness	136.
Solid matter to redness	96.
Chlorine	5.0
Sulphuric acid	13.7
Free ammonia	0.324
Albuminoid ammonia	0.675
Nitrogen as nitrates	0.05

Microscopical examination of this water shows the presence of zocglea, ciliata and diatoms of various sorts in great numbers.   I do not find any germs of disease.

Chemical examination indicates this water to be largely polluted with decaying organic matter, and it is therefore unfit for household use.

ANALYSIS NO. 7984—NO. 3.

Examination made June 9th-15th, by C. M. Cresson, M. D.   Amount of sample, one gallon ; reaction, alkaline ; condition, clear, with slight sediment

Contains.	Parts in 1,000,000 Parts.
Solid matter to dryness	140.
Solid matter to redness	106.
Chlorine	5.2
Sulphuric acid	9.3
Free ammonia	0.216
Albuminoid ammonia	0.810
Nitrogen as nitrates	0.05

Microscopical examination of this water shows the presence of zooglea, diatoms and plant spores.   I do not find any germs of disease.

Chemical examination indicates this water to be largely polluted with decaying organic matter, and it is therefore unfit for household use.

ANALYSIS NO. 7985—NO. 4.

Examination made June 9th-15th, by C. M. Cresson, M. D.   Amount of sample, one gallon ; reaction, alkaline ; condition, very slightly opalescent, with sediment.

Contains.	Parts in 1,000,000 Parts.
Solid matter to dryness	132.
Solid matter to redness	92.
Chlorine	5.3
Sulphuric acid	10.3
Free ammonia	0.243
Albuminoid ammonia	0.540
Nitrogen as nitrates	0.09

Microscopical examination of this water shows the presence of zooglea, ciliata, diatoms and vegetable wash ; it also contains suspicious bacilli, but not in such' condition as to enable identification.

Chemical examination indicates this water to be largely polluted with decaying organic matter, and is unfit for household use.

ANNUAL REPORT

—OF THE—

COMMISSIONERS

—OF—

WATER ✳ WORKS,

—IN THE—

CITY OF ERIE,

—TO THE—

MAYOR AND COUNCILS,

—FOR THE—

YEAR ENDING DECEMBER 31, 1892.

ERIE, PA.:
HERALD PRINTING AND PUBLISHING COMPANY, LIMITED
1893.

COMMISSIONERS OF WATER WORKS.

The Commissioners of Water Works in the City of Erie are appointed by the Court of Common Pleas of Erie County, Pa., for a term of three years, one member being named annually, in May.

SERVED IN THE YEAR.	COMMISSIONERS FROM ORGANIZATION TO DECEMBER 31, 1892.		
1867	*Wm. L. Scott,	Henry Rawle,	Wm. W. Reed,
1868	*John C. Selden,	Henry Rawle,	Wm. W. Reed,
1869	*John C. Selden,	Henry Rawle,	Wm. W. Reed,
1870	*John C. Selden,	Henry Rawle,	Wm. W. Reed,
1871	*†John C. Selden,	Henry Rawle,	Wm. W. Reed,
1872	Matthew R. Barr,	John Gensheimer,	Wm. W. Reed.
1873	Matthew R. Barr,	John Gensheimer,	Wm. W. Reed,
1874	Matthew R. Barr,	John Gensheimer,	Wm. W. Reed,
1875	Matthew R. Barr,	John Gensheimer,	Wm. W. Reed,
1876	Matthew R. Barr,	John Gensheimer,	Wm. W. Reed,
1877	M. Liebel,	John Gensheimer,	Wm. W. Reed,
1878	M. Liebel,	*J. M. Bryant,	Wm. W. Reed
1879	M. Liebel,	*J. M. Bryant,	*G. W. F. Sherwin,
1880	M. Liebel,	*J. M. Bryant,	*G. W. F. Sherwin,
1881	M. Liebel,	Benjamin Whitman,	*G. W. F. Sherwin,
1882	M. Liebel,	Benjamin Whitman,	*G. W. F. Sherwin,
1883	M. Liebel,	Benjamin Whitman,	*G. W. F. Sherwin,
1884	M. Liebel,	Benjamin Whitman,	*G. W. F. Sherwin,
1885	M. Liebel,	Benjamin Whitman,	George W. Starr,
1886	C. Kessler,	Benjamin Whitman,	George W. Starr,
1887	C. Kessler,	C. J Brown,	George W. Starr,
1888	C. Kessler,	C. J. Brown,	George W. Starr,
1889	C. Kessler,	C. J. Brown,	George W. Starr,
1890	C. Kessler,	C. J. Brown,	George W. Starr,
1891	C. Kessler,	C. J. Brown,	Wm. Hardwick,
1892	T. W. Shacklett,	C. J. Brown,	Wm. Hardwick,

†Mr. Selden resigned before the expiration of his second term; Mr. Barr was substituted by the other Commissioners, and afterwards appointed by the Court.
*Dead.

THE PRESENT COMMISSIONERS.

C. J. BROWN, President.

WM. HARDWICK,   T. W. SHACKLETT.

bacteria in the zoogloea or gelatinous condition. Thus, microscopically, it is not unlike No. 2, and the comparative value of these two specimens must be estimated by chemical analysis, and by a careful examination of the proximity of sources of impurity.

No. 5, if fairly collected, not from the sediment, but from near the surface of a water supply, is under the microscope the worst of the specimens, being remarkable for the great abundance and offensive character of its sediment. Besides the same vegetation as in No. 3, it showed in the portion examined by me a vigorous naidiform worm with his sets of dorsal spines in 4's, also small anguillula worms and a crustacean carcase crowded by infusorian animalcules which were vigorously dancing round and enjoying their feast. This is not the kind of water that people desire to drink.

GEORGE MACLOSKIE, Professor of Biology.

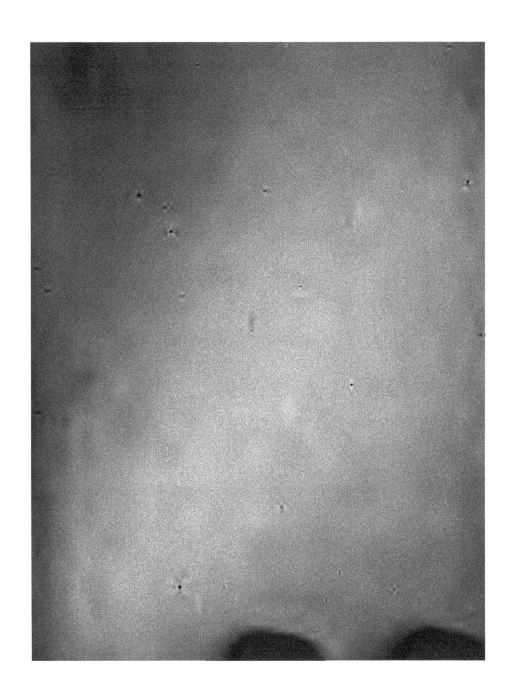

Lightning Source UK Ltd.
Milton Keynes UK
UKHW010017120119
335297UK00010B/885/P